Okfuskee

A Creek Indian Town in Colonial America

———

Joshua Piker

HARVARD UNIVERSITY PRESS

Cambridge, Massachusetts

London, England

2004

Copyright © 2004 by the President and Fellows of Harvard College
All rights reserved
Printed in the United States of America

Library of Congress Cataloging-in-Publication Data

Piker, Joshua Aaron.
    Okfuskee : a Creek Indian town in colonial America / Joshua Piker.
      p. cm.
    Includes bibliographical references and index.
    ISBN 0-674-01335-2 (alk. paper)
    1. Creek Indians—Alabama—Oakfuskee—History—18th century.
  2. Creek Indians—Alabama—Oakfuskee—Government relations.
  3. Oakfuskee (Ala.)—History—18th century.   4. Southern States—History—
Colonial period, ca. 1600–1775. 5. Great Britain—Colonies—America—
History—18th century. 1. Title.
E99.C9P55   2004
976.1′64—dc22   2003067735

For Francesca

Contents

Acknowledgments

I always read the acknowledgments first, partly to ease into the book and partly out of nosiness, but mostly because this section provides me with my first sense of how the author fits into the broader scholarly universe. Now that it is time to write my own acknowledgments, however, I can't help but feel that my earlier confidence in the revelatory powers of such sections was misplaced. I am only too aware that what follows can never adequately convey the degree to which I have benefited from the kindness and generosity of a host of people and institutions. If these acknowledgments reveal anything about this book, then, I hope that they show that its author has been very fortunate.

I have, to begin with, been lucky in my scholarly homes. The University of Oklahoma is a fine place for a young assistant professor to learn the ropes, not least because of the administration's generous support of the junior faculty's research. I am grateful to my colleagues in the Department of History, who have helped me get my feet on the ground professionally. I would especially like to thank Robert Griswold (chairman extraordinaire), Paul Gilje (advisor and motivator), and Cathy Kelly (confidant and sounding board). The Huntington Library has provided me with three fellowships; the most recent, a Barbara Thom postdoctoral fellowship, allowed me to finish the book manuscript. I am grateful to the Library's director of research, Robert Ritchie, for his continued support; to the Library's entire staff—especially Susi Krasnoo and Mona Shulman—for their mix of professionalism and hospitality; and to the Huntington's community of scholars—especially Peter Mancall—for their free-flowing collegiality. Cornell University's Department of History provided this refugee from anthropology with four years of generous support, thereby enabling me to figure out what becoming a historian entailed. Mary Beth Norton helped the process along in many ways, but no one could have done more in this regard than Dan Usner. I am profoundly grateful for his advice, support, and friendship, none of which show any signs of abating.

It is also a pleasure to have an opportunity to acknowledge the archives and archivists whose collections and knowledge provide the backbone of this book. I am grateful to Rachel Onuf, Brian Dunnigan, and Arlene Shy at the University of Michigan's Clements Library; Kimberly Ball and Frank Wheeler at the Georgia Historical Society; Melissa Bush at the University of Georgia's Hargrett Rare Book and Manuscript Library; Robert Mackintosh Jr., and Charles Lesser at the South Carolina Department of Archives and History; Dale Couch at the Georgia Department of Archives and History; and James Page at the University of Georgia's Laboratory of Archaeology. I have also benefited from time spent at the South Caroliniana Library, the South Carolina Historical Society, and the American Philosophical Society.

The field of early Creek history is a small but friendly one. I am grateful to Michael Green and Kathryn Braund for their continued willingness to listen to my ideas and suggest refinements. I am, likewise, grateful to Andrew Frank, Steve Hahn, Joe Hall, and Claudio Saunt—people to whom I have turned time and again for advice and collegiality. Other scholars have read parts of this book in various forms. Each has improved it, and so I am pleased to be able to thank Ned Blackhawk, José Brandão, James Carson, Jason Jackson, John Juricek, Cathy Kelly, Gary Kornblith, Michael McDonnell, James Merrell, Matthew Mulcahy, Jon Parmenter, Wendy St. Jean, and Gregory Waselkov.

And, of course, I am happy to acknowledge the fine work of the people at Harvard University Press, especially my editor, Kathleen McDermott, and her exceptional editorial assistant, Kathi Drummy. Their patience and support has been most appreciated. Not the least of Kathleen's contributions came in the rounding up of two fine anonymous readers. I am indebted to them for their generous, thoughtful, and cogent critiques. I am also grateful to Geoff Mauss for his skill as a mapmaker.

As I worked on this book, I met two extraordinary groups of people. In Norman, Ari and Lesley Kelman, Julie Gozan, Tom Keck, Julie and Adam Cohen, Cathy Kelly, Sandie Holguin, Jason and Amy Jackson, Randy Lewis, and Circe Sturm proved that small towns can provide a valued social and intellectual community. In Pasadena, John Herron, Jennifer Frost, Cheryl Koos, Charles Romney, Susanah Shaw, Carla Bittel, Mark Wild, and Greg Jackson showed that close friends can be found in big cities too. Those who know the Pasadena folks will recognize that one name is missing: Clark Davis, whose energy, charm, and good nature brought this group together and who died on the steps of the Huntington at the age of 36. Words fail, but, as Clark's life showed, friends don't.

Neither, fortunately for me, does family. My greatest debts are to these people: to my uncle, Jeff Piker; to the Massachusetts Pikers, my brother Tobin, his wife Jill, and daughter Tessa; to my aunt, Dottie Nathan; to my in-laws, Fares Sawaya, Ann Rosa, and Marie Rosa Sawaya; to the Egans, my step-father John and his children, Heather, Deirdre, and Sean; to my cousin, Michael Israel; and, finally, to the three people whose influence on me has been so profound that I no longer know how to measure it—my father, Steven Piker, whose example I have emulated in my career choice as in so much else; my mother, Eleanor Ryan, whose enthusiasm and intelligence enrich my life; and my wife, Francesca Sawaya, whose life I am privileged to share and whose love I return in kind.

Okfuskee

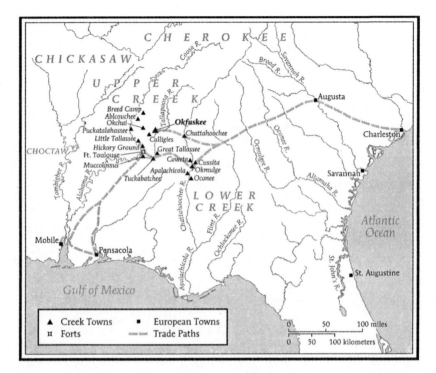

The Creeks and their neighbors, circa 1763. Geoff Maas.

Introduction:
Peculiar Connections

In November 1757, Governor Henry Ellis of Georgia wrote to the Board of Trade back in London. Ellis had just bid farewell to 150 of the "principal" men from Okfuskee and 20 other Creek towns. These visitors, whom Ellis himself invited to Savannah, had stayed "near" three weeks. In his letter, Ellis labored to make his superiors understand "what consequence it is to keep well with the Creek Indians," a people who were not only numerous and nearby but also "peculiarly connected with this Province."[1] This book is indebted to Ellis's turn of phrase and his guest list. It focuses on the town of Okfuskee and on its ties—its peculiar connections—to colonial British America. *Okfuskee* is, in other words, a community-centered Indian history with an explicitly comparativist structure and agenda. It looks to reframe our narratives of both Native and American experiences, to provide a new model for studying colonial-era Indians while simultaneously revitalizing the link between Native and Euro-American histories.

To date, American Indian history has not been a history of communities, and the history of American communities has not included American Indians. Historians have, to begin with, been slow to appreciate—and even slower to investigate—the local level of Native life. Scholarly tardiness notwithstanding, Natives were profoundly influenced by events and processes that centered on their towns and villages. Okfuskee's history must thus be understood in its own right, both for the window it opens onto a curiously neglected aspect of the Native past and as an object lesson in the value of a community-based Indian history. At the same time, historians have all too frequently elided or ignored the connections linking the developmental trajectories of colonial America's Indian and European peoples. Okfuskees,

1

in fact, took part in processes recognizable to any student of British America. Following Ellis, I label these cross-cultural connections "peculiar," but they are so only because they are unfamiliar, not because they are intrinsically odd. Demystifying these ties—familiarizing ourselves, that is, with processes that crossed cultural and political frontiers—will allow for histories that are at once Native and American. This book is such a project. In the final analysis, it traces the history of a Native community that was also, in many ways, an American town.

The efficacy of, and the need for, such an approach is perhaps best grasped by imagining that time has a spatial component. In Henry Glassie's words, "Think of the past as space expanding infinitely beyond our vision . . . Then we choose a prospect. The higher it is, the wider and hazier our view. Now we map what we see, marking some features, ignoring others, altering an unknown territory . . . into a finite collection of boundaries made meaningful through their connections." If nothing else, such a perspective reminds us that our narratives of the past are themselves historical documents, creations of a particular mapmaker situated at a chosen vantage point and possessing an eye for certain details. "History," as Glassie puts it, "is not the past, but a map of the past drawn from a particular point of view to be useful to the modern traveler."[2] And, of course, such maps are fluid, shifting as new points of view emerge and new observers appear.

The map of American history, for example, has changed a great deal since the late 1960s. In the intervening years, historians have marked features which, for one reason or another, failed to interest past travelers. Among the features now mapped are a new people, American Indians, and a new level of social organization, the community. Unfortunately, they rarely appear together. Our maps show communities without Indians and Indians without communities.[3] From the point of view of Glassie's traveler, we have marked out new points of interest, but they cannot be seen on the same trip. There are a number of reasons why this is the case—reasons that run the gamut from processes of national development to patterns of disciplinary maturation—but intertwined with these is the simple act Glassie describes as "marking some features, ignoring others." Much of mainstream American history, in fact, takes its structure from this process of sorting and categorization; our narratives, after all, frequently depend on sociopolitical categories such as town, colony, state, and nation. Euro-Americans, we know, lived in such units; American Indians, it is often assumed, did not. The implication for the historical map is clear. To include

Indians on our map is apparently to dabble in exotica, to seek out new symbols—tribe, hunting ground, band, confederacy—which are ephemeral to the map's narrative.

This clarity is, however, an artifact of our map of the past, not of the past itself. And, in fact, our maps are beginning to change—our certainty that Natives cannot appear on American maps has faded; our categories for mapping Indian history are being rethought. Scholars have, for example, become increasingly wary of referring to the Indians of early America as tribal peoples.[4] To be sure, monographs and articles continue to focus on the familiar tribal names—Iroquois and Cherokee, Choctaw and Shawnee—but they increasingly do so in a way that acknowledges the polyvocality and diversity beneath each tribal aegis. In fact, it is becoming clear that seventeenth- and eighteenth-century Indian life did not center on the tribe or confederacy after all. Many Native Americans, certainly most of those who figure in colonial American history, lived in sedentary or semisedentary communities. Indian towns were linked together into associations—nations or confederacies—that had meaning for Native peoples, but these were rarely the primary foci of allegiance, much less the monolithic and homogeneous units depicted in earlier histories. Rather, multitown associations were, for much of the colonial period, both fluid and ephemeral. Increased contact with colonial powers forged them into entities that gradually took on predictable structures and a greater role in the lives of their members; but the process took generations, and in many places the consolidation of Native nations continued into the nineteenth century. During this era, then, communities remained the focus of Native life.[5] Our tardiness in taking seriously this basic fact of Native life has undermined the accuracy of the stories we tell about their past.

In keeping with our newfound appreciation for the local in colonial-era Indian society, leading scholars have, since the late 1980s, proclaimed its importance. Thus, James Merrell suggests that we "consider Indian people in colonial times [as] communities," while Richard White notes that the "meaningful political unit in this study is the village." Likewise, Gerald Sider advocates investigating "the underlying town and clan matrix of social relations"; "[t]o ask . . . for a history or an anthropology of '*the* Cherokee,' or '*the* Creek' . . . is to miss, from the outset, some of the most fundamental features of native social life and historical process." In the same vein, Colin Calloway warns against approaches that "obscure and distort local diversity"; he urges historians to investigate "the range of experiences of groups and communities." Frederick Hoxie goes even further, cautioning against investigations that "collapse community histories for interpretive ends" and proposing that we "describe community lives in their own terms." Daniel Usner, for his part, advocates paying "greater attention to change and continuity at the village level."[6] We are, then, ready to redraw our maps, to privilege town over confederacy, the local over the tribal. We are ready to move beyond categories that, in the case of Indians' place in American history, are frequently inaccurate and consistently, and needlessly, exclusionary. We are ready, in other words, to create new maps of both Native and American history.

Or, rather, we should be ready to do so. The emerging consensus about the importance of Indian communities in early America has not, unfortunately, led to a significant body of work focused on Indian villages. Mission towns have received some attention, as have those Native communities that retained a presence near Euro-American towns.[7] Moreover, a number of works consider community process in Native societies without focusing on a particular community.[8] What we lack, however, are in-depth, monograph-length studies of Indian towns in Indian country, of communities that retained complete control over their land base, social structure, and cultural patterns.[9] We are missing, in other words, the intensive investigations that would allow us to redraw our maps of Native and American history. To remedy this problem, this book reconfigures our map of Indian country in such a way that it both more accurately represents Indian life and more persuasively locates Native peoples on the broader map of early American experience.

I will argue that colonial-era communities, Euro-American and Native American alike, are broadly comparable and that each people's experiences have relevance for our understanding of the other. Our maps must reflect the peculiar connections Ellis invoked when the Okfuskees and their fellow Creeks arrived in Savannah; we should trace out the ties binding Native and newcomer, Indian towns and "the little communities" of Euro-America.[10] Having said that, however, we ought not lose sight of a fact that Ellis and the Creeks knew well: Savannah's Native visitors were not colonists. Comparisons between Native and Euro-Americans cannot become attempts to obscure or elide the significant differences between the two peoples. A history that neglects such distinctions misses a key part of the American story. Difference, though, does not equal incommensurability, just as similarity does not entail homogeneity.[11] Early American history is much more complicated than that. In many cases, in fact, Euro-Americans and Native Americans were brought together by their differences and divided by their similarities. A history of an Indian town must trace the points in their histories where Native and Euro-American communities overlapped, just as it must mark the separate paths that each people took to their very different places in modern America. Ellis's peculiar connections thus call on us to acknowledge the relationship between "peculiar" and "connection," to demonstrate how—in an Indian people's relations with their Euro-American neighbors—the former came to override the latter, producing Native difference out of broadly American experiences.

This book is structured with these imperatives in mind. Each chapter focuses on one aspect of the Okfuskees' eighteenth-century experience, and each chapter ends with a discussion of the manner in which the issue at hand played out in colonial British America more generally. Such a framework allows for a nuanced examination of Okfuskee while, at the same time, calling attention to the ways its developmental trajectory intersected with, and diverged from, that of colonial British America. Or, to put it another way, the book's chapters center on Okfuskee while at the same time placing the Okfuskees within the processes central to early American history. In opting for such an approach, I ask that two frequently distinct groups of historians consider two broadly overlapping claims. To my colleagues in Native history, I argue that we can write histories of Indian communities in Indian country, and that doing so allows us to reconsider Native history's form and content. To my colleagues in American history, I argue that we can examine the manner in which processes central to early American experience crossed cultural frontiers, and that doing so allows us to uncover broader connective systems.

Okfuskee might seem an odd place in which to anchor such arguments. During the eighteenth century, its people lived in what is now Alabama, hundreds of miles from the colonies of Britain, France, and Spain. Worse still for the modern investigator, the Okfuskees were nonliterate. Moreover, no missionary set up shop in the town; no army marched through it; no proto-ethnographer or tourist thought it worthy of more than a cursory mention. And yet, as one of the leading Creek towns, Okfuskee was deeply involved in Creek–British diplomatic relations. As a result, its people frequently visited colonial capitals and, when travel was impractical, their speeches and concerns were commonly relayed to British officials. Okfuskee was also the place where the upper trading path from the British colonies entered Upper Creek country. As a result, British traders frequently mentioned Okfuskee, even if they did not trade there, and British diplomats habitually passed through the town, even if they had business elsewhere. For an Indian town in Indian country, then, Okfuskee is well represented in the documentary record. It therefore offers us the chance to consider at length the history of one such community, to chart the complexities of colonial-era Native life, and to reconsider Native history's shape and subject matter. Okfuskee's history brings into focus the peculiar—again, in the sense of unfamiliar—aspects of both Native and American history.

Of course, Okfuskee's connections to the British and its status as one of the largest of eighteenth-century Creek towns—in 1763, about 1,500 people lived in Okfuskee—raise the issue of typicality. Okfuskee was not a Creek every-town; neither were Coweta, Okchai, Muccolossus, nor any of the approximately fifty-five other Creek towns. Each had its own history, and each had a unique combination of attributes—for example, location, size, relationships with other Creek towns, ability of leaders, and character of traders—that helped to determine its course during the eighteenth century. Okfuskee and its Creek neighbors did, however, share certain traits and participate jointly in a number of processes. Their common attributes and experiences allow historians to discuss a shared Creek history without slighting the diverse experiences of individual towns and their people. Like American history, the map of Creek history is a patchwork of peculiar connections.

My book is based on the twin facts of Creek unity and diversity. Okfuskee serves as the baseline for my discussion, and I focus, where possible, on the Okfuskees' experiences with particular events and trends. But throughout this book, I supplement my treatment of Okfuskee's history with material from other Creek towns. The spotty nature of the documentary, archaeological, and ethnographic record makes such a tactic necessary; the commonalities in the histories of the various Creek towns make it possible; and the chance to shed light on a shared Creek community history makes it desirable. Narrating Okfuskee's history requires placing what we know regarding the town into dialogue with our knowledge of Creek communities more generally. Throughout, I will mark the provenance of my information. Where the data do not permit specific conclusions about Okfuskee, I will discuss the ways in which the issue at hand played out in the other segments of Creek society that encompassed

Okfuskee. For example, the Creeks were divided into two geographic units; Okfuskee was an Upper—as opposed to a Lower—Creek town. The Upper Creeks themselves included three ethnic and geographic divisions; Okfuskee was an Abeika—as opposed to a Tallapoosa or Alabama—town. Okfuskees, then, were Creeks, Upper Creeks, and Abeikas, and my discussion will invoke each of these identities. Inevitably, Okfuskee's history emerges within the context of other, better-known but more general histories.[12]

An imperfect historical record must not, however, deter us from focusing on Indian towns such as Okfuskee. Communities of this sort were at the center of Native American experiences with the trends and processes that dominated the eighteenth century. They played a critical role in structuring intercultural relationships between Indian peoples and their neighbors, Native and non-Native alike. Without histories of Indian communities, scholars will have a stunted understanding of American history and cannot hope to understand Indian history. Creek history is especially dependent on community-level events and developments. Towns were at the heart of eighteenth-century Creek life[13] and, although their configuration and function changed over time, they retained this position into the twentieth century.[14]

Eighteenth-century records attest to the centrality of Creek towns in a number of ways, most notably in the context of diplomatic and political conferences. Again and again, Creeks and Euro-Americans mentioned that "headmen from every town" attended these events. In 1759, for example, the Okfuskee Captain told a British agent, "the Headmen from every Town in the Upper Crick Country are met"; four years later, Handsome Fellow of Okfuskee reminded Georgia's governor, James Wright, that "there are two head Men from every Town in the upper Creeks at this Meeting." The British soon recognized that each town was a reasonably independent variable, and they adapted to the reality of Creek politics. Thus, in 1722, South Carolina's officials recommended that an agent to the Creeks "go from town to town, and firmly imprint on their minds our resolutions." A year before, Governor Francis Nicolson informed a Lower Creek headman that "severall of your Head Men has been at several times down [to Charleston], to whom the Talk has been given, but . . . when they went home . . . only the people of their Towns took notice of the Talk that they brought up with them. Therefore . . . I have sent up once more for the Cheif of every Town to have the Great Talk once more for all." Georgia's officials learned a similar lesson, as their 1749 request "to send for a Head Man out of every Town in the Lower Creeks" attests.[15]

Likewise, the heavily ritualized gift-giving that took place at conferences was often structured around individual Creek towns. The Creeks themselves frequently offered presents to colonial officials, as in 1733 when "the Chief Men of each Town, brought up a Bundle of Buck-Skins, and laid 8 Bundles, from the 8 Towns, at Mr. [James] Oglethorpe's Feet." The gifts that the Creeks received in return were often presented in such a way that the centrality and independence of the individual towns was reaffirmed. The Creeks could request such treatment, as they did in 1769 when one asked that "a good many Keggs of Rum [be] sent to each Town"; six years before, the Lower Creeks requested that traders bring supplies "to every Town" and that Georgia give "each Town" a "Bag of Powder and two of Balls." Again, the British quickly picked up on the proper protocol. By 1734, for example, two South Carolina merchants knew enough to send a Georgia official "Eighteen Colours [flags]," rather than the fifteen he planned to use as "presents for the Creek Towns." Eighteen, they said, was the "Number of Chief Towns." Calculations of this sort soon became second nature for Georgians as well.[16]

The Creeks' reliance on towns was so strong that they assumed Euro-Americans organized their lives in similar ways. As late as 1769, South Carolina's lieutenant governor twice reminded a visiting Creek party "that he could not make a formal Treaty with one particular Town." Creek intercultural diplomacy was structured around towns to such a degree that the relationship between Okfuskee and Charleston became something of a pole star, a fixed point to which the Upper Creeks could refer in times of trouble. Moreover, Creek rhetoric occasionally equated British colonies with towns, as when a headman called Georgia "the neighbouring Town" in 1753. In their speeches, Creeks referred to South Carolina's leader as the "Governor of Charleston"; Savannah and Saint Augustine also had "Governors," and West Florida was home to "the King of Pensacola."[17] The Creeks, of course, recognized that these officials controlled more expansive sociopolitical entities, but for Creeks, towns were the basis of larger polities, not vice versa.

Numerous other aspects of Creek life and culture suggest the importance Creeks placed on towns. Examples range from the seemingly inconsequential—such as towns owning the throwing stones used in the game of chunkey—to evidence pointing to the ways that language privileged the town as an organizing concept, including a trader's effort to translate the Lord's Prayer, an effort which produced "Our Father which art atop . . . Thy Great Town come."[18] Even the Creeks' origin story depended upon the actions of specific towns.[19] It is, however, only when we turn to the daily life of the Creek people that we can truly understand the centrality of towns in the eighteenth-century Creek world.

For all of their connections to Native networks stretching across large swaths of North America and to Euro-American networks linking North America with Asia, Africa, and Europe, the Creeks inhabited a world focused on the town square and the life such a communal space made possible. In fact, Creek notions of social organization privileged the town square and its sacred fire over mere contiguity. To the Creeks, a collection of people who happened to live near each other were a *talofa,* or village. By contrast, a Creek town, a *talwa,* consisted of people who shared a square ground and a fire, whether those people lived near each other or not. A *talwa,* in fact, could encompass several *talofas,* even if they were located many miles from the principal town. Thus, for much of the eighteenth century, the *talwa* of Okfuskee included a number of *talofas,* including Elkhatchie and Sugatspoges—located four and nine miles, respectively, from Okfuskee proper—as well as several villages on the Chattahoochee River, over seventy miles from Okfuskee's town square. This square, and the fire that was at its center both spatially and symbolically, tied the townspeople together despite the distances between them. The whole was "institutionally complete"; as a colonist writing from Okfuskee put it, "[e]ach town . . . is a sort of petty republick."[20] It contained the full Creek complement of civil, military, and religious specialists; it controlled the productive resources necessary for its own reproduction and that of its people; and it was linked to the other-than-human beings upon which all life depended. Despite ties to other towns, an individual's home town was at the center of his or her social, economic, political, and spiritual life. The Creek world was a world of towns.

For all of its importance, the town was, of course, not the only level of social organization relevant to eighteenth-century Creeks. Simply in terms of the number of individuals included within a specific designation, family was beneath town, and clan, regional, moiety (red/war versus white/peace towns), and national affiliations were above it. Of these designations, clan was certainly the most important, with one scholar suggesting that "clan loyalty was greater than town or tribal loyalty." There is some support for this conclusion in the historical record. Incidents of clan-based revenge abounded; headmen referred to clan connections and clan history to explain their position relative to other headmen; and Creeks without clan connections were extraordinarily vulnerable. In a 1735 version of the Creeks' origin story, for example, the Creeks twice sacrificed motherless children to save the group as a whole. Creek clans were matrilineal. A motherless child lacked a link to the Creeks' clan system, and thus, in theory, could be sacrificed without fear of clan retribution.[21]

When we examine the logic and practice of Creek life, however, the clan's importance diminishes, although it does not disappear, and towns return to center stage.[22] Without the town, in fact, Creek society would not have existed. At the town level, the factions and centripetal forces unleashed by individual and clan interests were harnessed to whatever degree possible. Town-based networks, events, and rituals called on townspeople to transcend—although not forsake—personal and familial agendas and loyalties. In doing so, towns became not only the building blocks of regional and national associations, but also the loci of the discussion, mediation, and reconciliation which made interclan relations, and thus Creek life, possible.[23] Not surprisingly, then, the people of Okfuskee, like their neighbors throughout Creek country, were first and foremost members of a particular town. To the extent that we neglect their identity as Okfuskees, we misrepresent their history.

This book consists of two parts, the first of which, "The Town and Its Neighbors," focuses on the Okfuskees' actions outside of their community; Part II, "The Town and Its People," turns to life within Okfuskee. Within the first section, Chapters 1 and 2 trace the diplomatic ties that developed between the Okfuskees and their British neighbors, focusing especially on the townspeople's relations with Charleston. What emerges is a picture not just of cross-cultural negotiations but also of the Okfuskees' geopolitical worldview—their understandings of the options available in a particular present, their stories about the past, and their visions of the future. Chapter 3 examines the implications of the Okfuskees' shifting worldview (as outlined in the preceding chapters) for the townspeople's extracommunity economic system. Part II begins with a chapter devoted to the Okfuskees' agricultural activities (Chapter 4) and especially to the impact that European animals had on the social and spatial systems at the center of the town's production of food and reproduction of community. Chapter 5 refines our understanding of Okfuskee's developmental trajectory by discussing how British traders were integrated into the town, their role in the food and deerskin trades, and the manner in which both sorts of exchange evolved over time. Finally, Chapter 6 examines the implications that the Okfuskees' involvement in market relations and international diplomacy had for relations between townsmen and townswomen, on the one hand, and the town's young men and older men, on the other. This book, in other words, takes a "from the outside in" approach to Okfuskee's history, working from the Okfuskees' relations with their Euro-American neighbors toward the Okfuskees' ties to their fellow townspeople. And even as we move progressively deeper into the town, each chapter's concluding section reminds us that the Okfuskees were intimately—if peculiarly—connected to American experiences more generally.

Just over a decade before Governor Ellis remarked on the peculiar connections linking the Creeks and Georgia, Governor James Glen of South Carolina commented on a similar phenomenon in his own colony. During a 1746 speech, Glen argued that "The fate of this Country is so interwoven and inseparably connected with Indian affairs that we must always be attentive to every thing that concerns them." This conviction was no passing fancy. Less than three years later, Glen made a knowledge of Indian affairs the basis for being judged a competent governor, writing that "The Concerns of this Country are so closely connected and Interwoven with Indian affairs so great a Branch of our Trade and the safety of this Province depends so much upon preserving their Friendship that it would be unaccountable Indolence and supiness in any Gentleman that had been here near Six Years in the station of Governor if he could not readily answer any Query that could be put to him relating to Indians."[24] Judged by his chosen criteria (and not, say, by his syntax), Glen was a competent governor, although not as competent as he believed. And judged by the same criteria, past generations of American historians have been, if not indolent and supine, then at least neglectful. The situation in the discipline, however, is changing. Scholars have begun to address the peculiar connections alluded to by Ellis and the closely connected and interwoven affairs described by Glen. My book was inspired by their work. I hope, above all else, to demonstrate that the study of Indian communities—and of the Native American

past more generally—can transform our understanding of American experiences. The peculiar connections binding Okfuskee and British America
offer us a new model for thinking and writing about our shared history.
Refocusing colonial-era Indian history so as to include towns like Okfuskee
will encourage narratives that are at once Native and American.

I

The Town and
Its Neighbors

Okfuskee and the British, 1708–1745: Formation, Assertion, Indecision

Diplomatic history and community history make strange bedfellows. Macro and micro, the impersonal and the intimate, the broad narrative and the narrow discussion—bringing these attributes together can be like trying to look through a telescope and a microscope at the same time. And yet this is exactly what must be done to write the history of a colonial-era Indian community in Indian country. Historians interested in reconstructing the stories and lifeways of early America's nonliterate Native peoples should begin their investigations of particular Indian communities by focusing on those towns' dealings with Europeans. For scholars interested in the history and structure of Indian communities, this suggestion apparently puts the cart before the horse, privileging European–Indian relations over Native community life. The shortcomings of the historical record, however, require us to take a circuitous route to our destination.[1]

Europeans had a keen interest in Native Americans' relations with other imperial powers, and this aspect of Indian life figures prominently in colonial-era documents. As a result, although it is often difficult to observe how Indians of a particular town organized their local world, we can reconstruct their efforts to form, maintain, and adjust relations with outsiders. In doing so—in focusing on the regional, the continental, and the international—we set the stage for a return to the local because intercultural diplomatic relations can provide a framework for a community-focused narrative. After all, by chronicling the townspeople's words and actions in the diplomatic sphere, we uncover aspects of life that go well beyond cross-cultural negotiations. We see, in addition, their perspective in a particular present, their stories about the past, and their visions of the future. What emerges, in fact, is a portion of the townspeople's evolving worldview. This package—the actions, histories, and visions—does not represent their conceptual apparatus *in toto,* and yet it would be short-sighted to deny a link between the outside world and the shifting pattern of town life. We can, then, begin to trace a town's developmental trajectory by outlining the course of its relations with neighbors; we can enhance our understanding of how an Indian community's inhabitants related to each other by watching them interact with outsiders. The local and geopolitical are, in other words, compatible and mutually reinforcing.

A reconstruction of Indian–European diplomatic networks thus starts us along the path toward a more complete social history of a Native community. Okfuskees dealt on occasion with the French and Spanish, but such ties were never at the center of the townspeople's diplomatic world. Relations with the British, by contrast, were critically important. The three events at the center of Chapter 1 thus focus on the townspeople's evolving diplomatic ties to the British. Each event—a 1708 ceremony, a 1732 treaty signing, and the mid-1730s and early 1740s construction of two forts—either took place in Okfuskee or involved Okfuskees in key roles. Each represents a particular stage in the development of the Okfuskee–British bond: formation, assertion, indecision. From a historian's perspective, in fact, the ever-changing nature of this relationship lends it much of its interest. As we watch the Okfuskees adjust the terms of their alliance with the British—as we begin to understand their facility at manipulating both social metaphor and tangible fact; as we come to appreciate their ability to seize opportunities and deflect dangers; as we become conversant with their goals and fears—we take a first step toward a fuller, more nuanced understanding of Okfuskee and its people. In this way, following the diplomatic trail laid out by the Okfuskees brings us back into the center of Okfuskee. We arrive in possession of a framework that allows us to understand much of what we see there.

Formation

Thomas Nairne, a British agent, traveled from Carolina to the Mississippi River in 1708, all the while writing letters to the commissioners of the Indian trade in Charleston. Nairne was in Okfuskee on January 18, 1708, when he had "the opportunity of seing a Coronation or what's answerable to it among the Tallapoosies. The Governor having sent a Commission for

Cossitee (commonly called the Ogfaskee Capt. because Chief of that Village) to be head of all the Tallapoosies setlement, with a Blank Comission for a Deputy." Nairne noted that Cossitee "would not so much as touch the Comissions" until "a generall meeting" was convened, at which point he was "installed in his dignity, with these formalities always heretofore used by his nation in investing their Chiefs with the Authority." This ceremony apparently was held in Okfuskee's square. First Cossitee and then his deputy were carried around the central fire four times by "the head warriors," who were followed by "most of the Company . . . in manner of a procession." Cossitee was "saluted" by Nairne and his men, and then by "his own subjects present." His townsmen next "washed his head and face with cold watter," after which both men remained awake and without food until the next day.[2]

Nairne was not particularly interested in what this ceremony signified to the Okfuskees and their Creek neighbors. For him, the meaning was obvious: a branch of the Creeks accepted Cossitee as their leader, as the British directed. The Okfuskees would have been shocked to hear such an interpretation. In the first place, Cossitee was already an important headman. Nairne himself noted that Cossitee was "commonly called the Ogfaskee Capt.," and, in 1705, he presented himself as the "Great Captain of the Ocphuscas" when he signed an agreement of alliance between the Creeks and Carolina. To the Okfuskees, therefore, the British merely bestowed recognition where it was due. Second, no outsider had the power to select a leader for a Creek town, much less for "all the Tallapoosies setlement." In the Creek world at this time, centralized power above the level of an individual town was practically nonexistent; even within a town, the consensual nature of Creek society meant that a headman's authority depended on the support of his clan and townspeople. Nairne's interpretation of this ceremony thus says more about British needs and desires than it does about the Okfuskees' beliefs and actions.[3]

Yet the Okfuskees were not simply humoring Nairne. They knew the ceremony that Cossitee underwent was an important one. Cossitee's insistence that "these formalities" be enacted, the large number of townspeople who took part, and the procession four times—a sacred number for the Creeks—around the town's holy fire all suggest that the Okfuskees took the ritual seriously. Instead of signifying their submission to the directives of outsiders, however, the Okfuskees saw the ritual as solidifying their relationship with the British through the person of Cossitee. Any contemporary Creek town would have seized such an opportunity, and the Okfuskees made the most of their chance.

By the time of Cossitee's "Coronation," the British were the dominant European power in the Southeast, although they had achieved preeminence only recently. In fact, both Nairne's trip and the Okfuskees' willingness to welcome him with open arms depended upon the profound shift in the regional balance of power that followed the British-led destruction of Spain's Florida missions. The extent of Okfuskee involvement in these raids is unclear, but many of their allies joined the Carolinians in a series of attacks, culminating in a 1704 expedition that destroyed numerous missions, enslaved over a thousand Indians, and saw thousands more abandon the Spanish to move either inland or west. What is now the Florida panhandle was almost completely depopulated, and Spanish influence in the region declined dramatically.[4]

The Spanish would never again regain the upper hand in the region, but their years as the region's dominant European power cast a large shadow over the eighteenth-century Southeast. That was especially true in the case of the Creeks, whose strength in the eighteenth century owed a great deal to their experiences with the Spanish in the preceding century and a half. In fact, when considered within the more general context of Native American–European interaction, the Creeks benefited from the Spanish presence in a very real way. To be sure, their good fortune did not mean being spared the epidemics, military forays, and missionization that disrupted other Native societies. The Creeks experienced all of these things to one degree or another. Indeed, their society underwent a dramatic restructuring in the generations following Hernando de Soto's sixteenth-century *entrada;* the Creek towns of 1700 were very different from the communities that had been there in 1500.[5] But the upheavals that characterized sixteenth- and seventeenth-century Native society in what became Creek country also, ironically, permitted the eighteenth-century Creeks to prosper.

The intensive Spanish presence in Creek country during the sixteenth century meant that the Creeks experienced the worst consequences of European contact early in their relationship with Europeans. A century of adjustment followed, during which the Spanish in Florida and the English in Virginia remained, to a large extent, on the margins of the Creek world. The Spanish mission system, although extensive, did not stretch directly into Creek country; and the effects of the English trade in skins, slaves, and firearms—although threatening—could be kept at arm's length. At times, the ancestors of the eighteenth-century Creeks must have wished that arm was longer and stronger, but, for the most part, these people could deal with European influences in their own time and in their own way. The Creeks' good fortune, then, was not that they avoided catastrophe and disruption, but that circumstances permitted them to orchestrate and fine-tune their adaptation to their new world. By the time Europeans returned to the interior Southeast in the mid-1680s, the Creeks had survived the worst the foreign epidemics had to offer; they had become familiar with European material culture; and they had experienced the beginnings of a new trading ethic. Compared to Indians in New England and the mid-Atlantic, the Creeks were in good shape when it came time to engage more directly with the Europeans' colonial systems.[6]

The founding of Carolina in 1670 heralded a new era in the region's geopolitical struggles. Competing European powers were now separated by only a few hundred miles, and the area's Native inhabitants were thrust into the midst of long-standing imperial conflicts. The Creeks were suddenly confronted with both real possibilities for profit and the equally real potential for disaster; the founding of the French colony of Louisiana in 1699 only raised the stakes.[7] Many Creeks, recognizing the benefits of a close association with the English and fearing Spanish aggression, moved east to be closer to Carolina. Some Okfuskees may have been part of this movement. A 1700 journal places Okfuskee in the approximate area—the Alabama River watershed—it would inhabit for the rest of the century, but a 1708 map produced by an enslaved Towasa shows "Oufusky" on the Flint or Oconee Rivers, over 150 miles to the east of the Alabama and its tributaries. Most likely, however, the Towasa's map refers not to Okfuskee proper but rather to one of its villages. Two other contemporary maps support this conclusion. Both place the "Chatahuches" or "Chattahuces" at the spot where the path linking Okfuskee and Charleston crossed the Chattahoochee River; later in the century, the Okfuskees had a village of the same name at this important ford.[8]

The people living at "Chatahuches" in the early eighteenth century, then, were probably Okfuskees who had moved east. Both these migrants and the Okfuskees who remained at home involved themselves in the trading and slaving that accompanied alliance with the English. By the late 1690s, the main English trading path to the West passed through Okfuskee. Nairne himself followed this trail when he visited Okfuskee in 1708, and that same year Carolina's governor and council noted that the Chattahoochee village was "settled for Conveyniency of Carrying on Trade." Its inhabitants seem to have found their location convenient for slaving, as well; thus, in 1714, a trader "bought a Slave Girl of a Chatachooche Indian." Seven years before, a pro-French war party reported seeing 100 English and French Protestants at Okfuskee. These Europeans were to join 2,000 Indians in attacking Pensacola; the French letter reporting the Okfuskee gathering noted that England's Indian "allies . . . often come to take prisoners from our Tohome and Choctaw neighbors." Lamhatty, the Towasa mapmaker, may have been captured in the 1707 raid. His map shows that Okfuskee was the last Creek town through which he passed before being sold to the Shawnees.[9]

The ceremony Nairne witnessed in January 1708, then, was performed by townspeople who were quite familiar with the role of Europeans in the Southeast's political, military, social, and economic equation. The Okfuskees knew what disease could do to their families and friends, and the antisocial behavior of some English traders would have been equally familiar. Moreover, the Okfuskees were aware of the real military and economic advantages that came from having access to both European firearms and the English market for slaves and furs; the fate of Native peoples denied these favors served as an object lesson in the dangers of alienating the Europeans. Finally, the Okfuskees would have suspected that the power brought by the Europeans went beyond that bestowed by guns and knives. European goods held out the promise of personal and societal access to important sources of other-than-human power, while also hinting at the dangers of allowing Europeans to wander around unfettered.

The ceremony Cossitee underwent takes on a different meaning when seen in this context. Both Nairne and Cossitee recognized that the Okfuskee ritual revolved around power, but where Nairne saw Indians bowing to Carolina's will, Cossitee saw townspeople taking steps to defuse and profit from the forces the newcomers brought with them. From an Okfuskee perspective, domestication, not submission, was the order of the day. In emphasizing incorporation, the Okfuskees ensured that the ties solemnized on January 18, 1708, would grow more important with time. Nairne's commission and Cossitee's ceremony opened up new possibilities for the Okfuskees, possibilities which they would investigate thoroughly over the next three generations.

Assertion

In June 1732, almost twenty-five years after Nairne left Okfuskee, "Fannemiche King of the Oakfuskeys" accompanied a Creek delegation to Charleston and made his mark on the "Articles of Friendship and Commerce" between South Carolina and the Creeks.[10] The document marked the culmination of fifteen years of concerted effort by the Okfuskees to reestablish relations with the British in the aftermath of the Yamasee War (1715–1717). The origins of this wide-ranging war remain murky, but we do know that a number of Creeks joined their Yamasee friends and kinsmen in attacking and almost overwhelming South Carolina. Early successes lured more Creeks into battle, although the Lower Creeks seem to have predominated. A decade later, a headman of the Abeikas—an Upper Creek division that included Okfuskee—told the British that "tho we Latly had a Difference yet it was never our seeking . . . But we were Brought into it By the Tallopoops Coweetaws and other of the Lower people." Exaggeration or no, all Creeks soon had cause to regret the war. Initial triumphs gave way to discouraging news from war parties, to the cessation of Creek–British trade, and to a devastating Cherokee attack on a Creek diplomatic party. By 1717, the Creeks and the British were ready for peace.[11]

The war's impact was felt by the inhabitants of the Southeast for generations. No event until the departure of the French in 1763 had such a lasting effect on the region. For the British colonists, the specter of a potentially apocalyptic Indian war never receded from view; their fears led to fitful efforts to reform the Indian trade and cultivate Native leaders. For the French and the Spanish, by contrast, the war was a boon. The French seized upon the Creeks' need for European goods and their dissatisfaction with the British to negotiate the placement of a French garrison in Upper Creek country; Fort Toulouse ensured the French a foothold in Creek affections into the 1760s. The Spanish, too, sought to use the opening provided by the Yamasee War to improve their position in the region. Spain could not match France's gains, but Spanish envoys did reestablish contact with the Creeks. Such initiatives, combined with the presence of a large number of ex-mission Indians among the Creeks, ensured that a significant minority of Creeks would listen to future Spanish requests.[12]

For the Creeks, the Yamasee War highlighted both the pros and cons of their relationship with the British. The Creeks who lived near South Carolina learned the dangers of being too close to the colonists; their descendants moved west, back to the Tallapoosa, Coosa, and Chattahoochee river valleys. The village of Chattahoochee was not abandoned, however, perhaps because it served as a marker of the Okfuskees' connections to the British, perhaps because it was already over 150 miles from South Carolina's westernmost outpost. In either case, Creeks immediately found that the western river valleys were no refuge from attacks by the Cherokees, who sided with the British. The resulting war continued on and off for decades; Okfuskee itself became a target for Cherokee war parties.[13] Even Creeks who had resisted the temptation to move east and who had not lost relatives to Cherokee war parties could not help but be struck by the changes in their lives when the war halted trade with the British. The French and Spanish failed to fill the void left by the departure of the British traders, and the Creeks had to wonder if their ties to the British might be more important than they had originally suspected. As the Creeks reevaluated that relationship, the Okfuskees began to search out ways to recapture the potential that Cossitee's "Coronation" had once offered. The arrival of "Fannemiche King of the Oakfuskeys" in Charleston tells us a great deal about the town's approach to the postwar world.

The appearance of the title Fannemiche on the 1732 "Articles" represented a tribute to Thomas Nairne, who died in the Yamasee War. The war that took his life, however, ended with the Okfuskees calling upon the relationship that he helped solemnify in their town square. Nairne certainly had not understood what he set in motion in January 1708, but by the early 1720s the Okfuskees were using the bond that Nairne and Cossitee had cemented to bridge the gap between the Creeks and the British and to assert their own special place in this alliance. The Fanni Mico[14] of Okfuskee would play an important role in the Creeks' relationship with the British into the 1750s. And even when Creeks no longer invoked his title, echoes of it would be heard in Creek country into at least the 1780s.

Fannemiche's mark on the 1732 "Articles" reflected Creek understandings of the ways kinship ties structured diplomatic relations. The Creeks and their Native neighbors believed that a corporate group could adopt an individual who would serve as a mediator between his natal polity and his adopted one. These polities would then, as a Creek origin story put it, "have a chief in common." As someone with friends and relatives in both towns, this man united social worlds; he represented a creative melding of the familial and the political. And, as Nairne's letters makes clear, a Fanni Mico was such a person. Writing from Chickasaw country, Nairne noted that the "people of these parts have one prety rationable Esteablishment": "Two nations at peace, each chuse . . . protectors in the other, usually send them presents. His bussiness is to make up all Breaches between the 2 nations, to keep the pipes of peace by which at first they contracted Freindship, to devert the Warriors from any designe against the people they protect, and Pacifie them by carrying the Eagle pipe to smoak out of, and if after all, ar unable to oppose the stream, are to send the people private intellegence to provide for their own safty . . . The Chicasaws call thes protectors Fane Mingo." Patricia Galloway, in her discussion of Fanni Mingo, argues that Nairne's letter points to a Fanni Mingo functioning "as a clan uncle for the adopting group in the councils of his own people." In Creek society, Galloway notes, the senior man of a matrilineal clan served as clan uncle; he "represented the clan in council and enjoyed great authority in the lineage itself." In a Creek context, then, a Fanni Mico was a fictive relative who functioned as a spokesman for his adopted family or nation in the councils of his original family or nation. He was, as Nairne put it, supposed "to protect" his new "Fameily and take care of it's concerns equally with those of his own." A Fanni Mico acted, in other words, as a go-between, a person whose kinship ties allowed him to bring two peoples together in peace and harmony.[15]

Nairne follows his description of a Fanni Mingo's duties with a detailed account of the way in which "they are made" by the Chickasaws. It may be possible to link the ceremony Nairne observed in Chickasaw country with the one he participated in while at Okfuskee. There are certain similarities: both culminated in the home square of the headman being honored; both featured prominent roles for the town's warriors; both involved a procession four times around the square or fire; both included the carrying of the headman; and, in both ceremonies, one of the closing acts involved washing the headmen. Galloway, however, argues that the Chickasaw ritual Nairne described was a version of the calumet ceremony,[16] and the Okfuskee event lacked key elements of this rite. Most notably, the Okfuskee ceremony took place without the "Eagle pipe" (the calumet) that played such an important role in the Chickasaws' ritual; moreover, the Okfuskees did not begin with four days of fasting and singing, and they never invoked the Sun. Nairne himself did not equate the ceremonies.

These missing elements notwithstanding, the Okfuskee and Chickasaw ceremonies were most likely similar rituals aimed at producing a Fanni Mico/Mingo.[17] In addition to the parallels in content noted above, two points from Nairne's letters support such a conclusion. In the first place, the differences between the rituals, while significant, suggest that the Okfuskee ceremony suffered from errors of omission, not commission. That is, many discrepancies can be explained by the fact that the adopting group had certain roles to play, and the British, whom the Okfuskees cast in this role, failed to fulfill them. In terms of the differences between the rites, the adopting group was to bring the calumet and conduct the dancing and fasting. I suspect that British failure to follow accepted protocol led the Okfuskees to improvise. Cossitee's insistence that a ceremony be held, juxtaposed with the British combination of willingness and ignorance, resulted in the creation of a ritual hybrid.

The second hint that the Okfuskee and Chickasaw ceremonies were functionally similar surfaces in the reaction of the Okfuskee headmen to the ritual. Nairne says, "I observed both Cossitee and his Deputy shake and seem concerned. Enquiring the reason, was informed 'twas for fear of being bewitched, for the generall opinion of the Indians is, that men of power and authority are generally the objects of the Vizards mallice, who frequently bewitch them into lingering distempers. After this Inauguration the Chiefs neither Eate nor slept during the remaining part of the Day nor the night following for this watching and fasting, they affirme, breaks all manner of spells, and enchantments that may be formed against them." The anxiety shown by the headmen, as well as the care they took to ward off danger, suggests they were aware of the ceremony's shortcomings. Even if Nairne is correct and the headmen dreaded "Vizards malice,"[18] it might be argued that "lingering distempers" were more likely to appear in the context of hitching one's star to kinsmen who could not conduct a ceremony properly. Relatives who failed to live up to their responsibilities represented liabilities. The British were a good catch, so the Okfuskees overlooked their *faux pas;* but, for Cossitee and his fellow Okfuskees, a little judicious worrying was certainly in order.

In the final analysis, of course, these two points represent circumstantial evidence. The strongest argument for an Okfuskee becoming a Fanni Mico for the British remains the mark of Fannemiche of Okfuskee on the 1732 "Articles." Whether or not this was Cossitee is impossible to know. It is certain, however, that the appearance of the title "Fannemiche" in connection with Okfuskee was no accident. Beginning with the "Articles" of 1732 and ending with the mark of Fanni Mico, "head King of the Oakfusskees," on a 1751 deed, there are four examples of Okfuskees (and, among the Creeks, *only* Okfuskees) claiming the title of Fanni Mico.[19]

Whether one Okfuskee or several bore the title of Fanni Mico, the towns-people's actions in the 1720s make it clear that the honorific had impli-cations for the community as a whole. As the Creeks struggled to restore intercultural trust and civility in the aftermath of the Yamasee War, the Okfuskees based their own efforts on understandings that predated the conflict. Again and again during this decade, the Okfuskees acted to re-inforce and foreground their town's connections to the British. In doing so, they drew on Creek beliefs regarding the centrality of both family and town. The kinship ties embodied by Fanni Mico allowed him to present the proper symbols and talks to each party, and he was uniquely qualified to represent the concerns of each side to the other. From an Okfuskee perspective, however, fulfilling this role implied both responsibilities and rights. Being Fanni Mico, or the hometown of Fanni Mico, conferred certain privileges; the Okfuskees expected not only respectful treatment but also the material and social rewards that accompanied kinship. As Nairne put it, "they who chuse [Fanni Mico] . . . for the head or Chief of their Fameily, pay him severall little devoirs as visiting him with a present." Perhaps in keeping with this tradition, an alternate title for Okfuskee's Fanni Mico—Red Coat King—made reference to a garment that British diplomats re-served for leading headmen; likewise, the 1751 appearance of Fanni Mico coincided with Georgia's decision to present "2 Suits Colours [flags], One to the Okfuskees," the only Upper Creek town so honored.[20]

As the Creeks and British gradually knit together their relationship in the 1720s, Okfuskees repeatedly strove to fulfill their obligations toward their kinsmen, to maintain their position in the relationship, and to achieve recognition for their role. So, for example, in the immediate aftermath of the Yamasee War, the Okfuskees allowed a British trading factory in their community, thereby adding a physical dimension to the social fiction of Okfuskee–British kinship.[21] British traders operating out of Okfuskee made forays into Choctaw country looking for customers, and many Choctaws came to Okfuskee to trade. In addition, the factory made Okfuskee a magnet for British traders; thus, in 1727, traders were ordered "to the Tocobatcheys or Oakfuskey Town with their Effects" because South Car-olina officials sought to halt trade with the Lower Creeks. Incidents of this sort validated the Okfuskees' understanding of their ties with the British, while simultaneously raising Okfuskee's profile in the Native world. More-over, the Okfuskees benefitted materially. As early as 1725, South Caro-lina's governor worried that "the affairs of the Great Number of Indian traders . . . causes a Larger Quantity of goods to be carried among the Indians than their necessity requires Especially among the Creeks."[22] Okfuskee's position relative to the British traders meant that its people were perfectly positioned to profit from this situation.

The Okfuskees also supported their British kinsmen in matters that went beyond trade relations. Thus, the British agent Tobias Fitch wrote that he arrived in Okfuskee on November 1, 1725, "which was the Time and place appointed [for the Creeks] to make payment" for goods and slaves seized from a trader in Cherokee country. The next month, after hearing of a Choctaw attack on British traders, "Dogg king of the Oakefuskeys" said that he awaited Fitch's command to lead 100 warriors against the Choctaws. In February 1728, "Hobohadgee [of Abicouchee] & the Dog King sent very severe Messages down [from Okfuskee] . . . to the [Lower Creek towns of] Cowetaws and Pallachocolas threatening them that if they did not comply with their Promises to the English that they would oblige them to do it"; the headmen in Okfuskee "sat up a whole night drinking of black drink Exhorting them to stir their Warriours to comply with what they had promised." Several weeks later, Dog King returned from the Lower Creeks, having carried a British message to their headmen.[23]

The British certainly did not recognize that Okfuskee support was rooted in a relationship embodied by Fanni Mico, but they nonetheless came to depend on his town. Thus, in 1726, South Carolina's council instructed Fitch that he should "with all dispatch proceed to the Oakefuskee Towne . . . & make knowne to ye Head men of the said Towne that you are sent from the government with a Great talk"; the Okfuskee leaders were to summon "all ye Towns of the Abeca & lower Tallapooses" to a meeting. The agent should then visit the Lower Creeks—accompanied by a party that included "the old King of the Oake-fuskee" and "Dogg King of the Oake Fuskee"—and learn if they intended to fulfill their vows. The high regard shown Okfuskee could hardly have taken Fitch by surprise. A year earlier, he had requested "a Flagg for the Oakfuskey Town who . . . is some of our best friends."[24]

In keeping with the importance they attached to their newly won role in regional diplomacy, the Okfuskees were willing to assert and protect their privileged place in the Creek–British relationship. More often than not, they were successful. Thus, in 1723, the Okfuskees rejected efforts by Lower Creek headmen from Coweta to encourage anti-British sentiment and to come between them and the British. Dog King of Okfuskee was among those who refused to "hear the Talk" regarding a proposed meeting in Coweta with a British agent. Etchachawee of Okfuskee and several other headmen reported to South Carolina's officials that the Cowetas said that there was "no hope of any more friendship with [the British], upon which [Etchachawee and the other headmen] answered . . . they would come down [to Charleston] and know the truth themselves." Later that year, an Upper Creek party arrived in Charleston. One of the two men named in the letter announcing their imminent arrival was "Dog King of the Oakfuskees," whom the colonial officials recognized as "a hearty friend to the English."[25] By 1727, as South Carolina grew increasingly worried about Lower Creek participation in Yamasee raids on British settlements, the Upper Creeks—if not the Lower—seem to have accepted Okfuskee's place at the center of negotiations to resolve the crisis. Thus Oboyhatchey, "King of the Abecoes," sent a letter to the president of South Carolina's council saying, "I have heard of some Disturbance amongst the Lower Creeks, which caused me to come to the Oakfuskeys to hear the certainty *they being your friends as well as mine.*" And, given their status as "friends" of all concerned, Oboyhatchey expected the Okfuskees to pass along any news; as he put it, "I am in the Oakfuskey King's House with him & his head Men who will inform me of all matters that may happen."[26]

Representing their Creek neighbors' concerns to the British, in fact, allowed the Okfuskees to assert their importance while simultaneously fulfilling Fanni Mico's responsibilities. Thus, in 1725, when the Creeks gathered in Okfuskee to make reparations for goods that had been stolen in Cherokee country, the "King of the Oakfuskys" represented the assembled headmen, telling Fitch that they made these payments even though "We are no[t] the people that was Concerned in the Plundering the White Man." They did so, the Okfuskee said, "to let your king see that we doe Designe to see him paid." He then assured Fitch that they had already paid for the stolen slaves, and he concluded by laying out the conditions under which the Creeks would make peace with the Cherokees. Three years later, shortly after Oboyhatchey labeled the Okfuskees "your [British] friends as well as mine," the Abeika "King" rebutted a British accusation that he had failed to communicate with the British, claiming "I went to the Okefuskeys and told them I was not as good as my word in not acquainting your King."[27] Oboyhatchey had, in other words, alerted the Okfuskees, an act equivalent, in his eyes, to speaking directly to the British.

Fanni Mico's 1732 arrival in Charleston, then, represented the public acknowledgment of a status already achieved. Certainly his townspeople had long since begun to act the part implied by his title. They saw themselves—and were recognized by others—as people intimately connected with the British. The title "Fanni Mico" does not, however, appear in the documents from the 1720s. Perhaps the Okfuskees used it only on certain occasions; perhaps the Europeans failed to record an unfamiliar term. Whatever the reason, two trends are clear: the Okfuskees became increasingly invested in their ties to the British, and Okfuskee itself became the pivot around which many events moved. Whether they explicitly invoked Fanni Mico or not, the Okfuskees asserted their place at the center of the British–Creek relationship. "Fannemiche King of the Oakfuskeys" involved himself in the effort, and his townsmen worked toward Creek–British peace throughout the 1720s. As their Creek neighbors knew, this was as it should be. After all, what were kinsmen for?

Indecision

The ships carrying British colonists to a bluff overlooking the Savannah River in 1733 also brought a new variable to the Okfuskees' world. The town of Savannah, which James Oglethorpe marked out on this site, became the capital of Georgia. Savannah and Augusta—founded in 1735, 200 miles upriver from the capital—emerged as important players in the British relationship with the Creeks. Georgia's presence changed the southeastern geopolitical picture drastically. For the Creeks in general, not only did Georgia's existence mean that their relationship with the British would be fundamentally different, but it also signaled a real shift in their dealings with other European imperial powers. For the Okfuskees in particular, the founding of Georgia was directly linked to the construction of two British forts in their town in the next decade.[28] These forts, and the events surrounding their construction, marked the growing importance of the Okfuskee–British bond, while also underscoring the increasingly complex nature of that relationship.

As early as 1727, a committee of South Carolina's councilmen recommended that their government build a fort in Okfuskee, but the plan never left the drawing board. The founding of Georgia, however, aggravated British–Spanish relations, leading British colonists to think once again about an Okfuskee fort. In a geopolitical sense, Georgia served as a buffer colony, a shield interposed between an established province and the forces that threatened it. Given its place in the region, the new colony engendered predictable reactions from the Europeans living on the Atlantic Coast: South Carolinians, whom Georgia was to protect, eagerly did what they could to help their new neighbors; the Spanish in Florida, whom Georgia was to guard against, regarded the newcomers with alarm, and worked to destroy the fledgling colony. South Carolina grew significantly less enchanted with Georgia when it attempted to regulate the Indian trade in the mid- to late 1730s. The Spanish, on the other hand, remained implacable enemies of the new colony, which they rightly viewed as a threat to their own imperial ambitions. Relations between Georgia and Florida were tense through the 1730s, with occasional flare-ups, usually involving raids on one side's out-plantations by another side's Indian allies. By 1739, Spain and Great Britain were openly at war, an imperial conflict that had its counterpart in the Southeast. Florida and Georgia each invaded the other; neither expedition met with great success.[29]

For the Creeks, the founding of Georgia offered, at the very least, the possibility of enhanced economic options. The Lower Creeks were especially eager to cultivate these possibilities; their headmen took the lead in establishing ties to the new colony. Savannah, however, never eclipsed Charleston as the center of the Indian trade, and Augusta, while becoming the gateway to the Creeks and points west, remained dependent on the merchants of Charleston. The Creeks also saw advantages in the Spanish–British hostilities. Young men eager for war-honors had an outlet for their energies, and European wars meant an increase in European gifts and services. Again, the Lower Creeks involved themselves most heavily in the conflicts. Their participation, though, was sporadic at best.

In terms of the Creeks' economic and military relations with Europeans, then, Georgia's founding did not represent an earth-shattering event. The presence of a new British colony did, however, have serious implications for the Creeks' political and diplomatic relationships. The Creeks suddenly confronted the possibilities, both positive and negative, offered by an entity without an established place in the region's diplomatic structure. Individual Creek towns and divisions responded in different ways. The Lower Creek community of Coweta, for example, forged strong ties with Georgia by combining its prominent place in Creek politics with its connections to Coosaponokeesa, a woman of Creek-British descent married to a British trader based near Savannah. The Coweta–Georgia relationship frequently became a source of frustration for both peoples, but, even in bad times, much of their respective energies were focused on each other. For Upper

Creek towns, on the other hand, the effect of Georgia's arrival on the scene was muted by both distance and the Lower Creeks' intermediary role. Upper Creeks were less likely to take part in Savannah-based conferences and military adventures.[30] But Georgia's forays into regulating trade did reach into Upper Creek towns, perhaps none more so than Okfuskee. Like their Upper Creek neighbors, then, the Okfuskees had to decide what to make of the new colony. They had, in other words, to recalibrate their geopolitical worldview, reassess their connections to the world around them, and redefine the identity or identities they both internalized and projected.

As the Introduction to this book noted, Creek political science privileged towns over other sociopolitical entities. When it came time to deal with Georgia, the Creeks confronted the task of figuring out how the new polity related to the *status quo ante*. Was it a "daughter town" of Charleston? Should it be treated as an independent town? Some evidence pointed to a Georgia–Charleston connection. During the early months of colonization, for example, South Carolina provided Georgia with supplies, labor, expertise, and connections to the area's Native inhabitants. Moreover, the Creeks could not have missed the hostility between Charleston and Savannah, on the one hand, and the Spanish, on the other. That antipathy, in fact, led South Carolina to agree to pay Georgia for maintaining a fort among the Upper Creeks. As late as 1736, South Carolina's lieutenant governor passed up a chance to encourage the Creeks to distinguish between South Carolina and Georgia, while also telling them that both colonies favored a fort in Upper Creek country.[31]

The Creeks knew, of course, that Georgia and South Carolina disagreed over a number of issues. For the Upper Creeks, the most notable arguments surfaced in the context of Georgia's efforts to regulate South Carolina's traders. The resulting disputes often played out in Creek communities, with Georgia's officials seizing goods from South Carolina's traders and evicting them from certain towns. The most dramatic conflict occurred in Okfuskee's square in mid-May 1735, when Captain Patrick McKay, Georgia's Indian agent, attempted to whip William Edwards, an Okfuskee-based South Carolina trader. The incident placed the Okfuskees in the uncomfortable position of choosing between several competing interests. Not only were the European powers—as usual—pulling the Creeks in different directions, but the British themselves had begun to make conflicting, and confusing, demands.

The McKay–Edwards incident, by itself, would have dramatized the choices confronting the Okfuskees. But, because it occurred within the context of a British effort to build a fort in Upper Creek country, the dilemma facing the Okfuskees became especially clear. During the spring of 1735, McKay divided his energies between policing the Indian trade and persuading the Upper Creeks to permit the construction of a British fort on their land. The latter endeavor culminated in a meeting McKay called in Okfuskee, a meeting that probably coincided with his run-in with Edwards.[32] The South Carolina–Georgia trade dispute and the British push for a fort thus shared ties of time, space, and personnel. A review of the events involved in both the trade dispute and the fort's construction will show how the Okfuskees responded to the challenges that followed Georgia's founding.

McKay spent the early months of 1735 reorganizing the Indian trade, a process that meant, to him, limiting the number of traders in Creek country and ensuring that those who remained abided by Georgia's laws. In the process, McKay and Edwards ran afoul of each other. Edwards claimed that he was manacled, tied to a pole in Okfuskee's square, and then "came Capt. Mackey and all the Master Traders that were in Town to see the Whipping performed; then the One Handed King and an Indian (called the Lieutenant) caught hold of the said Deponent [Edwards], and said he should not be whipped; and Capt. McKey said he would not be spared, and the little Lieutenant took the Switches and threw them away, and Captain McKey asked what that was for, and he, i.e., the little Lieutenant, say'd that the Deponent was his Friend and he should not be whipped, and so they let the Deponent go." William Williams, who witnessed the shackling of Edwards but not the attempted whipping, gave a slightly different account of the incident, which Edwards apparently related to him several days later. Williams's deposition attributed a greater role to the One Handed King and did not mention the Lieutenant.[33] In their essentials, however, the two accounts agree: a Georgia official would have beaten a South Carolina trader if not for the intercession of the Creeks; and the confrontation took place in Okfuskee's square.

The One Handed King was an Okfuskee headman. He had made his mark, immediately following that of Fannemiche, on the 1732 "Articles," and he played a minor role in the British diplomacy aimed at cutting Creek–Yamasee relations in the winter of 1727–1728.[34] His involvement in the McKay–Edwards incident once again thrust him, and his town, into the center of a delicate situation. In this case, the issue was not only how the British should treat each other while in Creek towns but also how the Creeks, and especially the Okfuskees, ought to be linked to the feuding colonies to their east. As part of the fallout from the founding of Georgia, then, the Okfuskees found themselves reevaluating the nature and implications of their ties to old allies in Charleston and new neighbors in Savannah. Competition between South Carolina and Georgia threatened the Okfuskees' established frameworks, a fact that they could no longer ignore by May 1735.

While McKay attempted to impose his brand of order on the Creek trade, he simultaneously pressured the Upper Creeks for permission to build a fort in their country. In late April 1735, "there was," according to Williams, "Orders given by . . . Patrick McKey for a general Meeting of both Indians and white People, and accordingly they met at Oakfuskees," probably "some time about the middle of May." Only vague descriptions of the ensuing conference survive, but McKay demanded—one Upper Creek characterized his message as "a strong talk"—that the Upper Creeks either tear down the French fort in Upper Creek country or allow the British to construct a fort of their own; he threatened to withdraw the traders if the Creeks did not comply with his ultimatum. The headmen debated for a week, finally telling McKay, in Williams's words, that "he might build a Fort." Georgia's garrison—"an Officer & some Soldiers"—was in Okfuskee by summer, although the fort's construction date remains unclear.[35]

Historians have concluded that McKay picked Okfuskee as the site of the fort, but the evidence suggests that the process was not that simple. On the one hand, the British mentioned Okfuskee as a possible location for a fort as early as 1727. Williams, the trader who provides our only account of the 1735 Okfuskee conference, said McKay demanded that the Creeks "let him build a fort wherever he should think convenient." McKay himself wrote that the "Indians have agreed to build a Fort in their Nation, in any part I should chuse."[36] On the other hand, though, the Upper Creeks' deliberations and their general approach to the British imply that the Okfuskees suggested, perhaps reluctantly, that the fort should be in their town, despite firm opposition from other Upper Creek towns. In doing so, the Okfuskees no doubt responded to the desires of their British kinsmen, but their willingness (not to mention their ability) to champion the fort originated in their own understanding of Creek sociocultural forms and imperatives. Okfuskee's support, not British policy, determined whether and where the fort was built. The British proposed; the Okfuskees disposed.

Several pieces of evidence point in this direction, the first of which is the length of time the Upper Creeks took to reach a decision. Creek conferences generally followed a standard pattern: the presentation of a proposal by one side; a night for the other side to consider that proposal; and a response on the following day. A week-long deliberative session was unheard of; when consensus could not be reached, a spokesman would declare an impasse within a day or so. In other words, something happened during the 1735 conference to disrupt the pattern. A serious dispute must have emerged, one that may have centered on the Okfuskees in two ways. To begin with, Okfuskee's support for a British fort would have split the conference; moreover, the Okfuskees, one of whose headmen may (as host) have served as spokesman, might simply have refused to declare a deadlock.

The other piece of evidence suggesting that the Okfuskees helped select the site of the fort is, in fact, the site of the fort. Okfuskee seemed, from the Creek perspective, to be the right place for a British fort. The Okfuskees were linked to the British by bonds of kinship; if anyone had to deal with a garrison of these bumptious outsiders, it was the Okfuskees. Moreover, it is impossible to conceive of a sequence of events that would have resulted in a fort being built in Okfuskee without the townspeople's permission. Logistical realities militated against building and provisioning a fort without local support; but, even beyond that, Creek society lacked a mechanism that would enable outsiders (be they Europeans or other Creeks) to intrude on an unwilling town. The later attempts by Wolf, headman of Muccolossus, to have a British fort built in his community—despite the vocal opposition of other Upper Creek headmen—demonstrate very clearly that a critical element in a fort's placement was the support of the affected town.[37] In the Creek world, all politics was local.

The sequence of events in May 1735 probably went something like this. McKay asked the Okfuskees to call a meeting; they agreed, feeling obligated to give a kinsman the opportunity to present his case to their people. At the conference, McKay's demands met strong opposition from the Upper Creeks. The Okfuskees, having the most to lose and unwilling to risk the breach in relations that McKay threatened, emerged as reluctant champions of the British fort. They refused to grant their fellow Creeks the luxury of declaring an impasse, and the other towns refused to support the Okfuskees' position. In the end, the McKay–Edwards spat broke the deadlock. The actions of the Okfuskee headmen during the incident reminded their fellow Creeks of the Okfuskees' obligation to support their kinsmen, and the incident itself offered an object lesson in the disruptions other towns could expect if Georgia's agents wandered around free and unfettered. The Upper Creeks who opposed the fort capitulated, perhaps agreeing to disagree. The assembled headmen told McKay that "he might build a Fort," but they did not endorse the second half of his original demand: that he might do so "wherever he should think convenient." McKay's assertion that he could choose where to locate the garrison represented either self-promotion or self-delusion. The fort that the Upper Creeks approved would be an Okfuskee fort. In agreeing to this, however, the Okfuskees' reluctant neighbors no doubt consoled themselves with two thoughts: that if the fort should incite violence between the British and French, then that would be, most emphatically, Okfuskee's problem; and that the British soldiers would be under the watchful eye of their kinsmen, who could be expected, perhaps, to keep them out of trouble.

As the May 1735 conference demonstrates, then, the Okfuskees found themselves pulled in different directions. Their British relatives' demands for a fort conflicted with the desires of their Upper Creek neighbors, and the British themselves were divided over trade policy, leaving the Okfuskees to contemplate the perils of alienating either Georgia or South Carolina. The path the Okfuskees eventually charted through these diplomatic pitfalls suggests that they initially sought to cement their ties to the British without siding explicitly with either colony. Thus, Georgia's agent won the right to build a fort, and he left a contingent of Georgia rangers in Okfuskee to begin construction. Georgia supplied a small garrison until the post was abandoned in 1743, and the colony's officials recognized early on that the garrison furthered Georgia's interests. The rangers stationed there enforced the colony's trading regulations, while being able "to observe the Motions of the Indians, and to give Intelligence &c." Fort Okfuskee's commanding officer, Anthony Willey, not only received a salary from Oglethorpe for "Pay as Lieutenant of the garrison in the Creek Nation" but was also compensated for "Disbursements to ye Creek Indians." Willey's generosity—he disbursed more than 75 percent of his salary—no doubt helped endear him to his Okfuskee hosts. By 1740, he could write from Okfuskee that, although the French had called a general meeting of the Creeks, "I had taken care that none went out of this Town; but the Red Coat King who I could trust."[38]

If, as seems clear, Georgia's representative was right to trust that Red Coat King—a man who, by 1749, bore the title Fanni Mico—would ignore

French entreaties, it did not follow that the headman or his townspeople would be equally dismissive of South Carolina. In fact, while the Okfuskees permitted a Georgia garrison in their town, they seem to have moved steadily toward closer relations with Charleston. Thus they continued trading with Alexander Wood through the early 1740s, even as Wood further cemented his status as a leading South Carolina trader and even as Georgia's officials occasionally sought to discipline him. Wood, in fact, served as a semiofficial agent of South Carolina's government, something the Okfuskees surely noticed. In 1740 alone, his duties ranged from mediating a Creek–Chickasaw conflict and passing out "Sundries . . . to the Creek Indians" to providing colonial officials with information and presenting "a Talk . . . to the Creek Indians at the Oak Fuske Town." Many years after the South Carolina trader's death, James Adair attested to his ties to Fanni Mico's people when he wrote of meeting "Captain W—d, an old trader of the Okwhuske."[39] Okfuskees also began making frequent trips to Charleston, sometimes escorted by Wood; for example, in 1739, "the King of the Okfuskees" and the town's "Head Warrior" visited South Carolina's capital, where Wood served as interpreter during their meeting with the lieutenant governor. In contrast, after Georgia garrisoned the fort, Okfuskees avoided Savannah for decades. All of this may explain why, after receiving a 1742 talk from a group of Creeks headed by Okfuskee's Red Coat King, South Carolina's Commons House noted "that the Indians make Distinctions between his Majesty's Subjects of Georgia and this Province." The Commons House thought that such developments "ought not in any Manner to be countenanced," but colonial officials could do little about the Okfuskees' increasing willingness to privilege Charleston over "his Majesty's Subjects of Georgia."[40]

Perhaps the most significant sign of the Okfuskees' growing attachment to South Carolina, however, surfaced after the 1743 departure of Georgia's garrison, when South Carolina won permission to construct a second fort in Okfuskee. As with its predecessor, the proposal to build this fort led to controversy among the Upper Creeks, but a party of their headmen seeking British help in ending a Cherokee–Creek war "Consented to" the plan during an October 1743 visit to Charleston. Lieutenant Governor William Bull reported that his visitors "have promised also to assist in building the Same, and . . . I directed Capt. Wood to take the Care and trouble of laying out the Fort, in the most proper Situation which he was of the opinion, was near the Oakfuskee Town." Although the town affiliations of the Creek diplomats went unrecorded, the placement of the new fort, the Okfuskees' frequent involvement in Creek–Cherokee diplomacy, and the prominent role played by the Okfuskee trader all suggest that Okfuskees were both part of the 1743 party and supportive of South Carolina's plans. That Wood's "opinion" regarding the fort's placement accorded with Okfuskee desires is further supported by Edmond Atkin's 1755 report. According to Atkin, "The Cheifs of the Tallipoosie and Abeka Towns the most in our Interest"—a group that certainly included the Okfuskees—gave their "Consent" to the fort; it "was begun by the Traders, according to the advice of those Chiefs, opposite to Ockfuskee Town . . . that place being Judged by them to be the most Convenient & Secure."[41] As Atkin mentioned, however, South Carolina's Fort Okfuskee was completed but never garrisoned. By October 1745, Louisiana's governor noted, "As for the so-called fort of the Great Akfaske . . . [it] has totally fallen into ruins . . . It was only a house surrounded by a stockade, which was occupied by the English traders which they seem to have abandoned."[42] The Okfuskees' reaction to this abandonment was not recorded, but South Carolina's failure in fort-building apparently did nothing to discourage the Okfuskees from further focusing their diplomatic efforts on Charleston. The late 1740s saw an ever-increasing number of contacts between the two towns, most of which addressed the continuing quest for a stable Creek–Cherokee peace.

The forts built in Okfuskee thus serve as windows onto Creek decision-making processes. An increasingly tense situation involving competition between European imperial powers meant that the Creeks had to choose their path with care. The Okfuskees sided with the British, building upon the relationship established a generation before. Many Creeks disagreed, opting either for neutrality or for a pro-French or pro-Spanish stance. Okfuskee's choice could not be gainsaid, however, in part because of the autonomy enjoyed by Creek towns and in part because the Okfuskees so obviously benefitted from their decision. The town, in fact, emerged as a diplomatic and economic entrepôt, a gateway through which merchandise and proposals entered and left Creek country. Two maps attest to Okfuskee's rising status. The first, a 1723 Chickasaw production, shows a circle for the English and one for the Chickasaws; a circle for the Creeks lies in between (Figure 1). A path linking the English and the Chickasaws passes through the northern part of the Creek circle; Okfuskee was located on that path, but does not appear on the map. The second map is from 1737, and is also the work of a Chickasaw; unlike the 1723 map, however, the 1737 effort is fairly detailed, showing several Creek towns, rather than just "Creeks" (Figure 2). For my purposes, the crucial aspect of the 1737 map is the prominent place given to Okfuskee. The map shows a path leading from the British (A) through Coweta (B) to Okfuskee (G), and then from Okfuskee directly to the Chickasaws (L). Since the map centers on the Chickasaws, Okfuskee's location denotes a position of considerable importance. Moreover, Okfuskee was on the eastern border of Upper Creek country; thus the path between Okfuskee and the Chickasaws passed through other Creek towns on the way west. In choosing not to depict this geographic reality, the Chickasaw mapmaker shows us a more interesting social reality. By 1737, the Chickasaws thought it necessary to be more precise about their relations with the Creeks than they had been in 1723. One aspect of this precision involved emphasizing the place of Okfuskee, a town that not only sat on the Chickasaw–British trading path but that also housed both a British fort and Fanni Mico.[43] In choosing the British, the maps suggest, the Okfuskees selected wisely.

But Okfuskees of the mid-1740s still confronted the question of what "choosing the British" meant. Could they be connected by kinship to both British colonies to their east? Or should they phrase the relationship so that one was privileged over the other? The events surrounding the construction of the forts suggest that these questions perplexed the Okfuskees into the mid-1740s; no clear pattern emerges from their actions. From the mid-1730s to the mid-1740s—as the Okfuskees sorted out the implications of Georgia's arrival on the scene—the townspeople apparently settled for solidifying both their pro-British credentials and their position at the center of the British–Creek relationship. They drew upon a 40-year-old relationship—one personified by Fanni Mico and buttressed by Fort Okfuskee—to address pressing concerns at home and to maintain their pivotal role in regional diplomacy. In doing so, they helped to refine and articulate a narrative of Okfuskee's history that influenced the townspeople's actions for another forty years. Their inability to choose between Georgia and South Carolina—or perhaps their unwillingness to choose unnecessarily—should not surprise us. Recall the fear of "Vizards malice" that Cossitee exhibited in 1708. For the Okfuskees, decisions that combined alliance and kinship were neither made quickly nor taken lightly.

I began this chapter by comparing the process of simultaneously writing community and diplomatic history to the act of trying to look through both

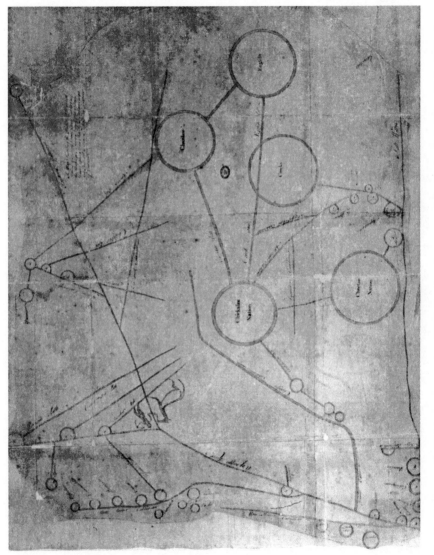

1. English copy of a Chickasaw map, circa 1723. Reprinted courtesy of the National Archives, United Kingdom.

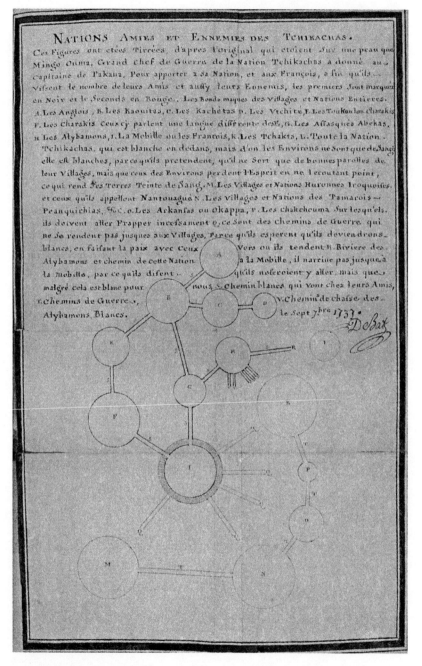

2. French copy of a Chickasaw map, 1737. Reprinted courtesy of the Centre des Archives d'Outre-Mer. Aix-en-Provence (A.N. France). 8 Fi 112/67. All rights reserved.

a microscope and a telescope. The same analogy could be applied to the effort to discern connections between a Native American town and a European empire. The results are bound to be peculiar, to put it mildly. That said, however, eighteenth-century Okfuskees were not entirely mistaken in believing that their town-centered model of diplomatic relations could be successfully deployed when dealing with the British. Naturally, the need to enact such a framework—to choose, for example, between Charleston and Savannah—came primarily from the logic of Creek culture, not from the empirical reality of British life; but Okfuskees who looked to the East could be pardoned for thinking that their traditions would serve them well in negotiating with the British. There were real reasons why such an approach was eventually ineffective, but for a time Okfuskees succeeded by treating the empire as a recognizable variation on a familiar theme. The peculiar connections binding Okfuskean and early American history, then, begin here, with the Okfuskees' efforts to engage a premodern empire on a community-to-community basis. Both their early success and their eventual failure are indicative of the process by which Native peculiarity came to outweigh American connections.

The Okfuskees' ability to forge connections with units of the British Empire stemmed from the fact that this empire was not the ordered, coherent, and centralized polity that "empire" usually connotes. As late as the mid-eighteenth century, the British Empire was characterized more by colonial autonomy and localized agency than by imperial hegemony and metropolitan mastery. In most cases, the word from on high was not the final word; London's "make it so" did not, in fact, make it so. Rather, decrees filtered through layer after layer of administrative bodies, a process conducive to carefully qualified obedience and subtly phrased resistance. The contingent and negotiated nature of this system owed something to the vicissitudes of governing a far-flung empire, but it was not simply a creation of transatlantic distance. Great Britain's experience with a composite monarchy that united distinct peoples, territories, and institutions argued for a certain fluidity in both national and imperial affairs; domestic British political culture helped produce an imperial system in which "effective administrative power remained diffuse, flexible, and limited." As a result, for the inhabitants of Britain's American colonies, empire was a structure that encompassed and shaped, rather than determined or defined. More than a shallow veneer but less than an all-pervasive essence, empire fit loosely around, into, and over most colonists' daily lives, producing a geographically extensive entity at once deeply fragmented and routinely unified. Of course, the British Empire was not the Creek Confederacy writ large, but the British penchant for indirect rule and negotiated authority created an opportunity for Okfuskees to forge diplomatic ties with the always fragmented and often fractious components of Britain's empire.[44]

In such an empire, after all, local autonomy was qualified and circumscribed but still effective. Founded and administered by an ad hoc collection of entities and personalities, Britain's colonies were places where power was a local creation and authority emerged through negotiations between a colony's newly powerful elite and the imperial center. During the late seventeenth and early eighteenth centuries, crown rule impinged more directly on colonial life, but colonists still managed to preserve "most of the institutions of semi-autonomous and highly localized government . . . developed in their founding years." Individual colonies, in other words, retained individualized agendas, ambitions which were not entirely divorced from imperial affairs but which also were shaped to a large extent by a colony's local context. "Local" could, however, refer to units significantly smaller than a colony. Even in England, the eighteenth century was characterized by a tradition of politically and culturally vibrant "provincial towns," and the realities of transatlantic governance meant that the political centrality of small-scale administrative units—towns, counties, parishes— was even more pronounced in America. Here, relations between colonial centers and the outlying communities paralleled those between the colonial centers and London. In each case, order flowed less from centrally organized coercion than locally given consent, a consent dependent upon the perception that local concerns were being addressed. Such a situation has led Jack Greene to suggest that "[t]o a not insignificant degree . . . effective government in the empire resided not in London, and not even in the colonial capitals, but in local communities."[45]

Because imperial government relied so heavily on colony and community, and because these subimperial polities necessarily had fewer coercive resources at their disposal, the Okfuskees and their Native contemporaries often dealt with the British Empire from a position of strength. For example, Britain's relative weakness on the imperial periphery encouraged its agents to adopt—albeit often in modified form—Native diplomatic tropes in order to win allies and concessions. The Okfuskees' efforts to forge enduring town-to-town bonds drew on the same impulse that saw other Indians pressure colonial officials to honor kinsmen, present wampum belts, and cover the dead. By the same token, the empire's fragmented political structure offered Natives the opportunity to play one British colony off against another. Just as the Okfuskees found themselves wooed by Georgia and South Carolina, the Catawbas benefitted from their position between Virginia and South Carolina, and the Iroquois profited from the conflicting ambitions of New York and Pennsylvania. A similar process manifested itself on a more local and personal level. The Okfuskees' relationship with Alexander Wood enhanced their access to both South Carolina's largesse and Charleston's decision makers; by midcentury, Okfuskees—as I discuss in Chapter 2—decided that their interests were best served by privileging this town and its governor over Savannah and its leaders. Other Native groups made comparable decisions, appealing, for example, to local officials and colonial capitals to ward off threats from their Euro-American neighbors, or forming relationships with those neighbors to thwart the plans of a colony's officials.[46] Oddly enough, then, local ambitions, personal ties, and Native forms frequently undergirded relationships that appear on the surface to have sprung from imperial plans, political machinations, and British traditions. Connections peculiar to us today—connections that intertwined the diplomatic histories of Native communities and European empires—were a fact of life in early America.

That said, however, connections of this sort were provisional and temporary, a condition rooted in fundamental differences between Native and British political theory and exacerbated by Britain's trajectory of imperial development and its ideology of empire. To begin with, Okfuskees, unlike their contemporaries in colonial British America, lived in a culture that explicitly granted small-scale sociopolitical entities a central role in the creation, maintenance, and re-creation of diplomatic frameworks. The British system implicitly allowed locally based alliances, but such ties were always at best necessary evils. Euro-American communities—such as Albany—that claimed a privilege similar to that embraced by Okfuskee operated on the fringe of legality and risked sanctions; African-American communities—such as Gracia Real de Santa Teresa de Mose—that made similar claims were even more vulnerable.[47] As a result, Okfuskees discovered real limits to the efficacy of community-based relationships with their colonial neighbors.

To make matters worse, in the middle decades of the eighteenth century, Britain's leaders sought "to substitute a new *directive* mode of imperial governance for the traditional *consensual* one." Gone were the days when American colonies could count on a great deal of de facto autonomy; suddenly, relations with the mother country were "decidedly more 'imperial' in the modern sense of the word: hierarchical and bureaucratic and dominated by a distant authority." And thus, to take only one example, the empire's policy toward Native Americans grew increasingly centralized; Okfuskees who once dealt with Georgia's Patrick McKay or Carolina's Thomas Nairne found themselves, after midcentury, negotiating with Edmond Atkin or John Stuart, men bearing the title of Great Britain's Superintendent of Indian Affairs in the Southern District of North America.[48] Britain's empire still had its inefficiencies and fissures, but the trend away from local autonomy was marked. A parallel development characterized political relations within the American colonies. Even prior to the mid-eighteenth century and even at their most fragmented and divisive, the colonists found that their commitment to community and colony rarely clashed with their loyalty to the empire. This mental melding of allegiances became easier and more commonplace during the eighteenth century as the various colonies' politics took on a more uniform character and as colonial legislatures gained more power vis-à-vis towns and counties.[49] Like the empire itself, America's colonies were centralizing, leaving less and less room for the fluid, locally based relationships the Okfuskees envisioned. Localized geopolitical agency—once merely a Creek variation on a broadly shared theme—continued to facilitate Okfuskee's integration into transoceanic networks, but now it did so in a peculiarly Native way.

British views of Indian peoples further inscribed their peculiarity. Cossitee's coronation, Fanni Mico's embassy, and Fort Okfuskee's construction notwithstanding, Okfuskees never succeeded in transcending their status as—from a British perspective—people who lived on the imperial margin's margin. If, as John Brewer asserts, the "heavy-handedness of British rule increased the further it extended beyond the metropolis," then the Okfuskees were in a vulnerable position. Their marginal status—and the vulnerability it entailed—was a function, however, not simply of location, but also of the complex intersection between geography, ethnicity, and ideology. For the British public, Indian country was analogous to the ocean, "a zone where the government did not need to worry about the finer points of international law." Expediency might demand a conditional adherence to cross-cultural agreements, but, in the end, Britain's people "acknowledged almost no constraints" in their nation's dealings with Indians. Okfuskee's relations with the British thus foundered on incompatible invented traditions, one positing that the creative deployment of ritual, diplomacy, and influence had transformed strangers into friends and kinsmen, and the other that Native peoples were literally and figuratively beyond the pale. That the former's emphasis on connections seems impractical and outlandish while the latter's emphasis on peculiarities appears only distasteful suggests the degree to which the British succeeded in making their invention real.[50]

2

Okfuskee and the British, 1749–1774: Decision, Correction, Reassertion

Throughout the eighteenth century, the Okfuskees' military initiatives exposed them to danger and death. Warfare had its risks. Even the town's leaders were not safe, as the death of "Oakfuskee King" in a 1767 engagement demonstrated. The peaceful end of the diplomatic spectrum, however, was also dangerous. One of Red Coat King's sons, for example, was "shot, and his Scalp with part of his Scull was carried away," reportedly by "Northern or French Indians." The attack occurred near Charleston as the son returned from a 1753 conference that was supposed to produce a Creek–Cherokee peace treaty. In revenge, his father said, "we met with two of the Northerns at Augusta . . . which we killed for Satisfaction." A witness noted that the avenging Creeks returned carrying "the Scalp, with Part of the Scull of one they kill'd," and went on to explain "that to take Part of the Scull (with the Scalp) is the greatest Indignity that can be offered to Indians, and that they seldom forgive it." Perhaps because Red Coat King's son had been visited with just this "Indignity," the war party "brought one fellow [back] alive, whom they had beaten very much . . . they carried him to Mr. Rae's, there beat him again, and stuck their Knives into his Body, and at last with a Hatchet chopt of[f] his Head." A trip that began in peace, therefore, ended with Red Coat King invoking the tradition of "Blood for Blood." Even those seeking a white path could find themselves walking a red one instead.[1]

In fact, Okfuskee's status as Fanni Mico's hometown and its people's frequent efforts at peacemaking may have exposed them to more than their share of violence. For example, the townspeople's role in mediating an Upper Creek–Cherokee peace made them tempting targets for the Cherokees whenever relations between the two peoples broke down. Because of the Okfuskees' intimate involvement with the peace process, an attack on the townspeople was a powerful symbolic statement.[2] Cherokees angry with the Creeks struck Okfuskee as a way either to provoke the Creeks into a more general war or to head off a new truce; pro-peace Cherokees, by contrast, used violence to punish the Okfuskees for the misbehavior of their fellow Creeks. Whatever the motive, the Okfuskees suffered from Cherokee attacks. Between 1751 and 1753, Cherokees killed thirteen Okfuskees in three separate raids; a fourth saw the Cherokees kill "some Oakfuskee Men." The attacks led the Okfuskee Captain to tell a Charleston conference that "since the peace with the Cherokees was proposed, I have kept my Warriours at Home, notwithstanding we lost many of our Friends." Three days after this speech, Red Coat King's son was killed while leaving the same meeting, a meeting which the Cherokees avoided despite an Okfuskee headman's "Hopes of seeing" them. It was likely no coincidence, then, that the "Northern" tortured to death at Rae's house spoke Cherokee and was thought by one observer to have belonged to that nation. Later that summer, Red Coat King told James Glen, South Carolina's governor, that his people would make peace "providing the Cherokees will bring to us two Slaves of the Northern French Indians, one to be sent to the Cowetas and the other to the Oakfuskees"; an Okfuskee trader explained that if "the Creeks might have the burning of the said Slaves . . . then . . . they will think it is all streight."[3] The Okfuskees, that is, wished the Cherokees to provide captives whose deaths would comfort grieving townspeople, reaffirm Creek–Cherokee relations, and sever Cherokee–"Northerns" ties. The townspeople were willing to deploy deadly symbols.

For Okfuskees, then, peace and kinship were never far removed from war and death. Townspeople invoked the white to ward off the red, while showing a willingness to use the red to restore the white. As Okfuskees charted a course through the uncertain geopolitical terrain of the mid- to late eighteenth century, they increasingly found themselves presenting a Janus-like visage to the world. Warfare became an ever-larger part of their lives, and they both used violence and struggled to overcome its effects. Still, the white path remained attractive, and Okfuskees continued to place themselves at the center of the Creeks' peaceful relations with their British neighbors. In these difficult years, however, even the whitest of bonds— including those undergirded by kinship and friendship—were periodically bloodied. The Okfuskees paid a high price for their privileged role in regional and international diplomacy; the price they exacted from others to protect their influence could be just as steep. Their willingness to sustain and inflict grievous injuries suggests just how important these relations were to the townspeople. International maneuvers and personal security, diplomatic relations and family safety, cross-cultural bonds and community well-being—each had implications for the other. Living comfortably in Okfuskee required an active engagement with the world at large. Three events demonstrate the Okfuskees' efforts to define, protect, and revitalize their place in regional and international diplomacy from mid-century to the American Revolution. Each event represents a new stage in the Okfuskees' relationship with the British: the decision to privilege Charleston over Savannah that led to the 1749 arrival of Fanni Mico in South Carolina's capital; the effort at correction which produced the 1760 Okfuskee attack on British traders; and the reassertion of a long-standing relationship that led to the 1774 Okfuskee visit to Augusta. Each incident thus allows us access to the townspeople's understanding of their past, present, and future; each offers us the chance to understand their evolving worldview.

Decision

The late summer of 1749 was a busy time for Indian diplomacy in Georgia and South Carolina. In early August, a large party of Lower Creeks, led by Coweta's headmen, arrived in Savannah; they had, Governor Glen complained, been "sent for to Charles town," but "declined coming, alledging that they were going to Georgia." Once there, the combination of Georgia's political situation, the lure of an unprecedented amount of presents, and the plans of Coosaponokessa, her husband, Thomas Bosomworth, and her kinsman, Malatchi of Coweta, led to a potentially explosive confrontation. This incident has intrigued historians, who have been both fascinated by the personalities involved and gratified by the extensive paper trail. Less than two weeks after the Lower Creeks left Savannah, a large party of Upper Creeks arrived in Charleston. Nine Okfuskees traveled to South Carolina's capital, where they, along with a subset of their fellow travelers, were recognized as people "who value themselves upon being more particularly attached to the English Interest than the other parts of the Nation." Once in town, the Upper Creeks concluded a peace treaty with the Cherokees and Catawbas, renewed their ties to the British, saw the curiosities of Charleston, received their presents, and departed.[4] In contrast to the Lower

Creeks' diplomatic shenanigans, historians have found little of interest in the sequence of events in Charleston. One historian, in fact, devotes an entire chapter to the goings on in Savannah but deals with the Upper Creeks' visit in a long paragraph, assigning leadership of the party to two Creek headmen whose participation cannot be confirmed. The tendency to overlook the Upper Creeks' mission and to misidentify their leaders is unfortunate. Their embassy to Charleston allows us to identify several patterns that would be at the center of southeastern geopolitics, and Okfuskee's history, for the next generation. The visit's significance comes into focus when we realize that the Upper Creeks were led by "Old Fannee Mico alias Red Coat King" of Okfuskee.[5]

Fanni Mico arrived in Charleston at an interesting moment. The end of King George's War (1744–1748) left the Southeast in a familiar situation. Britain, Spain, and France still maintained colonies in the area, which continued to squabble with each other and to seek the support of Native peoples. Spain's importance, however, continued to decline. Britain and France, after agreeing to an inconclusive and unsatisfactory 1748 peace treaty, increasingly focused their energies on each other.[6] Much of the diplomatic intrigue centered on the Ohio Valley, and the Seven Years' War began there in 1754. The Southeast played little role in these maneuvers. The region's position on the sidelines did not mean, however, that its people were unaffected by the tumult. Both the British and the French sought to secure Indian allies and to woo the other's supporters, while Georgia and South Carolina continued to bicker over trade, defense, and diplomacy. The Indians, in turn, sought advantageous positions within the increasingly heated imperial conflict, a process that resulted in both disagreements over the proper course of action and a marked rise in international diplomacy. For the Creeks, these developments meant that they had to juggle their bellicose Euro-American neighbors, to stabilize their relations with the Cherokees, and to decide how to phrase their interactions with Georgia and South Carolina. The 1749 appearance of Fanni Mico in Charleston suggests that the Okfuskees were intimately involved in all three of these efforts.

Fanni Mico's ability to bring two peoples together, combined with his duty to act on behalf of his kinsmen's interests, meant that he could play a central role in creating and maintaining harmony across ethnic and political boundaries. Red Coat King attempted to do just that when he presented himself as Fanni Mico in 1749, and his actions were recognized by other Creeks as both legitimate and necessary.[7] In performing as Fanni Mico, then, Red Coat King, at one level, only followed through on the commitment Okfuskee had made to the British in 1708. On another level, though, the presence of Fanni Mico reveals a great deal about the decisions Okfuskees made at midcentury, decisions regarding their relations with both the Cherokees and the colonies of Georgia and South Carolina. The impact of these decisions influenced Native and Euro-Americans into the post-Revolutionary era. Two generations of Okfuskees flattered and argued, gave and stole, hosted and visited, killed and died, all in the name of asserting and protecting their understandings of Fanni Mico's visit to Charleston.

By the late 1740s, the Creek–Cherokee war that began in 1716 had become a liability for some members of the warring parties and for the British, who had previously used the conflict to their advantage. Okfuskees participated in British efforts to mediate a Creek–Cherokee peace in 1745, but the pace of negotiations accelerated in the winter of 1748–1749 as the British truly threw themselves into the peace process. Okfuskee's part in the British initiative was in keeping with its role as a Creek–British go-between. In negotiations with the Cherokees, Okfuskee worked with the Upper Creek town of Okchai; several years later, a Cherokee headman noted that, in the question of "War against the Cherockees . . . thirty Towns are to be ruled and governed by the Oakefuskeys and Oakchoys." The two towns' partnership built on Okfuskee–British and Okchai/Okfuskee–Cherokee connections. The British channeled their messages to the Creeks through Okfuskee, with Creek concerns and suggestions going the other way through the same channels. Many key decisions, however, were made at Okchai, which also controlled much of the Creek–Cherokee contact.[8]

The 1749 negotiations allow us to witness this process in action; they also call attention to the importance of both Okfuskee and its relations with its neighbors. On January 31, 1749, Governor Glen sent letters to the Cherokees and Creeks, informing them that each sought peace. Two traders read Glen's letter "to the Head Men at the Oakfuskee Town, whereupon they Sent notice to all the other Towns to meet at said Town." Creek–Cherokee diplomacy was already underway. Three Creek "Ambassadors" arrived with five Cherokees in time for a "Meeting of all the Headmen of the Upper Creek Nation" on May 1 "at the Oakfuskees." The traders again interpreted Glen's letter, and the headmen sent him thanks for his "Fatherly Care & tenderness," passed along the conditions under which they would make peace with the Cherokees, and requested that Glen invite both parties down to seal the agreement. On May 7, a letter was sent from Okfuskee to the Cherokees, who sent Glen word of their agreement on July 5.[9]

A few days later, a Cherokee headman, Tasata of Hiwassee, dictated a letter to the Creeks, saying that he had "received your Talk per the Messenger the King that you made at the Oakfuskees and give you thanks for the present of the Conch shell that you sent him and as for the Corn & water million seed that you sent to the Town they have planted and Expects that you'll be as good as your word to come and eat part of them with us as also anything that we have." Tasata followed up his reference to "the King that you made [adopted/appointed] at the Oakfuskees" by saying that his own people hoped to see "our beloved Man Alletuny whom we made a beloved Man of Little Tellico" and whose son resided with the Cherokees. Tasata also informed the Creeks that "The beloved Women of our beloved Town little Tellico has sent some White Beads to the King of the Oakfuskees," and that "the Women of his Town [Hiwassee] sends you the King of the Oakfuskees a White Flag that when you and your People take hold of it you may think of him that his heart is streight towards you all and Expects that your is the same." Even before Tasata's letter arrived, the Creeks received another message from Glen. It was "Interpreted to the Headmen of the Oakfuskees and they readily agreed to it and said that it was very good and the aforesaid Headmen referred it all to the Gun Merchant" of Okchai, who called the Upper Creek headmen to a meeting at Okchai. They again thanked Glen for his "Fatherly Love," and agreed to set out for Charleston. Their decision was reinforced by Tasata's letter, with its references to adoptive kinsmen, future visits, and powerful tokens of peace and goodwill, all of which centered on Okfuskee.[10]

These exchanges set the stage for Fanni Mico's September 1 arrival in Charleston. The title that he invoked, combined with the large delegation of Okfuskees (and the absence of Okchais), testified to his and his town's leadership in the peace process. When six Creek headmen were invited into the council's chambers on September 5 "to know their Sentiments on the proposed Peace," "Red Coat of Oakfuskee" was the first man listed, and only Okfuskee had more than one representative present. Six days later, when Glen brought all the visitors together to cement the peace with a round of smoking, the governor stated "that he would begin with the Old Red Coat King as he . . . had the greatest hand in bringing about the Peace."[11] Okfuskee, then, had succeeded in using both its place within the

Native world and its ties to the British to command center stage during an important episode in the region's diplomatic history. This central position left its people vulnerable to attacks by disaffected parties, but it also ensured their continued relevance. The Upper Creeks' relations with the Cherokees and British would, to some extent, pivot on the Okfuskees' actions throughout the 1750s and into the 1760s.

Of equal importance, however, was that Okfuskee's involvement in the Creek–Cherokee negotiations both signaled and reinforced the town's attachment to Charleston. The 1749 parleys were conducted under Charleston's aegis, and the Creeks and Cherokees acknowledged the part Glen played in bringing them together. Okfuskee's prominent role in the give-and-take leading to the meeting and the recognition Glen accorded its headman both during the conference and afterwards contributed to the Creeks' belief that Okfuskee and Charleston were closely connected. Glen's continuing efforts to achieve a lasting Creek–Cherokee peace only furthered this impression. By 1753, in the aftermath of Red Coat King's son's death, Glen publicly told the Okfuskee Fanni Mico, as the headman remembered it, "that when my Son was killed it was the same as if he had been your own Son." Later that year, a trader wrote to Glen that the Gun Merchant of Okchai believed that the peace "was intirely owing to your Excellency's Goodness in taking so much Trouble and Care . . . and the old Red Coat King says the same and he returns your Excellency many Thanks for your great Friendship and Care of them all." Okfuskee's headman concluded by promising "that all your Commands shall be always observed by him, and Nothing in his Power shall be wanting to the great King of the English as long as he lives in the Ockfuskees." Even before this exchange, Okfuskee's connection to Charleston had become such an accepted part of Creek life that the Upper Creeks twice expressed surprise when Red Coat King declined to represent them during a Charleston conference.[12]

The 1749 arrival of Okfuskee's Fanni Mico in Charleston, then, marked the end of Okfuskee's indecision about its relationship with the British— for the next three decades, Okfuskee would be linked to Charleston. Okfuskees did stay in contact with Savannah; Fanni Mico, "head King of the Oakfuskees," even made his mark on a 1751 deed between Georgia and the Upper Creeks, an action that may have been in response to a Georgia agent's symbolically resonant presentation of a flag "to the Oakfuskees." The ties suggested by the flag, however, were of secondary importance to those the Okfuskees maintained with South Carolina's capital. Savannah, the townspeople had decided, was a daughter town of Charleston, and the Okfuskees were content to let other Creek towns take the lead in dealings with Georgia's capital. Fanni Mico's people would focus on Charleston.[13] This decision did not mean that the Okfuskee–Charleston relationship was trouble free; in fact, the 1750s witnessed moments of significant tension between the towns. Strains in the relationship should not, however, obscure the important position the Okfuskees had staked out.

Okfuskee's ties to Charleston were built upon fundamental Creek assumptions about the nature of politics (the centrality of towns) and kinship (the reality of familial obligations and prerogatives). These ties were, from the Creek perspective, profoundly legitimate. As such, they could help to structure Creek relations not only with the British but also with the allies of the British, such as the Cherokees; they could also be used by Okfuskees to assert and protect their place in regional and international diplomacy. Legitimacy did not, of course, mean immunity from challenge or negotiation. It did mean, however, that the Okfuskee–British relationship had as solid a base as possible given the vagaries of both Creek politics and intercultural diplomacy. French–British conflict in the 1750s and 1760s tested the strength of the ties embodied by Fanni Mico and enacted by his townspeople. Both imperial powers were eager for Creek support; unlike their Cherokee neighbors, though, the Creeks remained largely neutral during the Seven Years' War. Creek neutrality cannot, of course, be attributed only to the Okfuskee Fanni Mico, but neither can his (or his town's) contribution be ignored. To do so is to misunderstand the nature of Creek diplomacy and the role it played in the Southeast at midcentury. In 1760, the British would learn how dangerous such a misunderstanding could be.

Correction

On May 16, 1760, Okfuskee was at the center of a surprise attack on British traders and their servants. The violence began at Sugatspoges, an Okfuskee village. Led by Handsome Fellow, an Okfuskee headman and the son of Red Coat King, parties of Creeks looted trading houses in Sugatspoges and Okfuskee; the attack then spread to other towns. When the dust settled, two British traders and three servants residing in Okfuskee and its villages were dead, as were three traders and three servants in other Upper Creek towns. That night, Okfuskee's square hosted what one trader described as a well-attended "War Dance." As the attack unfolded, some Okfuskees labored to save the traders in their midst and to warn the British on the coast. Their efforts, however, did not offset the enormities of the day—the violence was widely viewed as the Okfuskees' fault. Tomathla-Hago, "Head Man of Oakfuskee," admitted as much, saying that his town bore responsibility for "the Mischief"; the Okfuskee Captain also noted the threat "this mad Affair" posed for Okfuskee's relationship with the British.[14] All knew, as well, that the attack came at a crucial moment. By 1760, the Seven Years' War had finally come to the Southeast; in fact, the spring and summer of that year marked the low point in South Carolina's war with the Cherokees. A Cherokee–Creek alliance would have been disastrous for South Carolina, and the prospect of a Creek war inspired panic in Georgia.[15] The attack of May 16, 1760, hinted to the British that such calamities were within the realm of possibility.

Historians have placed the events of May 16, 1760, in a variety of contexts. John Alden and David Corkran portray the violence as part of a French conspiracy to foment a Creek–British war. Both believe that the attack was organized by Mortar, an Okchai headman in league with the French and the Cherokees; both put the Okfuskees solidly in the pro-French camp. In contrast, Kathryn Braund uses the attack to illustrate the dangers faced by colonists who traded with the Creeks; she argues that "the affair had a more personal beginning," developing from a dispute between the Sugatspoges headman's son and a trader's slave. Edward Cashin, for his part, treats the violence as an example of both Georgia Governor Henry Ellis's prudent administration and the Augusta traders' knowledge of, and influence over, the Creeks.[16]

All of these treatments of the 1760 attack are incomplete. Cashin, for example, does not address Creek motivations, thereby transforming the attack from a moment fraught with meaning into a problem requiring a solution; he emphasizes the British role in defusing the situation but does not explain why Okfuskees lit the fuse in the first place. Braund properly returns to Creek country, reminding us of the important role interpersonal relations of the most basic sort played in the colonial-era Southeast. That said, however, her explanation has two weaknesses. In the first place, it rests on one citation—a letter in a Charleston newspaper passing on a report "to which," the publisher noted in a depreciative aside, "the writer seems to give some credit." The report did not resurface in later discussions of the events, and the same edition of the paper contains a contradictory account by a trader, just returned from Creek country, who was "not of this opinion."[17] Second, Braund fails to place the attack in the context of Okfuskee's history with the British. For Braund, the town where the violence occurred hardly matters; for reasons that will become clear below, I disagree.

The claims made by Alden and Corkran are more sweeping, and thus more difficult to address. They are, however, riddled with problems. To begin with, far from linking Mortar to the incident, the evidence suggests both that he was not in Creek country at the time and that the Creeks did not associate him with the attack. Instead, the Creeks placed blame squarely on the Okfuskees, who consistently affirmed their responsibility.[18] In addition, the dead traders' backgrounds show that they had strong ties to Okfuskee. Despite reports that the attackers had killed "all the white people in their Nation," the killings were not random acts of violence aimed at any British man. The Okfuskee–British relationship helped determine the identities of both the assailants and the victims.[19] Finally, Corkran and Alden's placement of Okfuskee within the "French conspiracy" and "the long-continued intrigues" of Louisiana's governor—to say nothing of Corkran's reference to "the English-baiting Red Coat King"—reflects a misunderstanding of Okfuskee's role in imperial politics and of the legacy conferred by Cossitee's "Coronation," Fort Okfuskee's construction, and Fanni Mico's missions.[20]

The townspeople, by contrast, understood that, as an Okfuskee put it two months after the attack, "the Oakfuskee and Charles Town was always reckoned as one." Okfuskee's Fanni Mico no longer appears in the documents after 1751, but the Okfuskee–Charleston bond did not disintegrate. In 1755, Governor Glen—even while worried that the Creeks' "Affections are to a great degree alienated from us" by French schemes—trusted an Okfuskee headman to persuade his fellow Creeks to visit Charleston: "the Circumstance of the Handsom Fellows being sent in lately to enforce my Invitation puts their coming out of dispute." The feeling was apparently mutual, for Handsome Fellow told Georgia's governor that "the King in Charles Town . . . is very much the Indians Friend." When this same headman visited Charleston two years later, he informed a different governor "That for his own part, he had always lived in Friendship with the English and was determined so to do, For the Forefathers of the Creek Nation who were dead loved the English and recommended to their Children to do so likewise, That at the Creation of the World, it was Ordered that the white and Red People should live together upon the same Land

and in Friendship with one another." And although Fanni Mico no longer appeared as the embodiment of this relationship—perhaps because of Red Coat King's "Old" age—a new symbol linking Charleston and Okfuskee emerged at about this time. By 1760, the townspeople characterized their bond to the British as one based at least in part on a shared fire. Creek town squares centered on a sacred fire; by invoking a shared fire, Creeks recalled a time when Okfuskee and Charleston were one town. Their shared past, and the continuing power of the still-burning fire, tied the Okfuskees and the British together in the present.[21]

The Okfuskees asserted their fire-based connection to the British in a number of situations during the 1760s and 1770s. Some references to a shared fire involved efforts by their headmen to make explicit an old tie and thus smooth the way for the achievement of specific goals. For example, when the Okfuskee Captain tried to repair the damage done by the 1760 attack, he noted that "the Oakfuskee People were always reckoned one People and one Fire with the English"; the "mad Affair" threatened to "put the Fire out," but he hoped it would burn "as long as the Sun shines and the Rivers empty themselves into the Sea." Okfuskee's most influential leaders were not, however, the only ones to cite the shared fire. It had broad enough currency that a young Okfuskee head warrior with a Euro-American father referred to it while visiting the British; and the formulation was sufficiently ingrained that it was even mentioned by a party of Okfuskee common warriors intent on severing relations with the British. Moreover, headmen of other Creek towns invoked the symbol, noting in 1770 that "many years ago the Oakfuskies made friends with Charles Town & has always called themselves one Fire." The Okfuskees' relationship with the British, as their Creek neighbors knew, was embodied by this fire, "their Old Promise."[22]

The work of modern scholars leaves little doubt that the metaphor of a shared fire was deeply meaningful for the Creeks, implying the ability to participate in the town-based rituals that sustained life and society. According to one historian, the town-square fire "represented the entire community and the people's connection to their ancestors and the Maker of Breath." The Creeks believed that their towns descended from four "Mother Towns." A new town took embers from its Mother Town's fire, and all communities that descended from a particular Mother Town "use the same fire." The Okfuskees' claim—validated by their fellow Creeks—that they shared a fire with the British suggests that the ties embodied by Fanni Mico in the early to mid-1700s continued to have meaning for the townspeople and their neighbors until at least the American Revolution. As White Lieutenant of Okfuskee said in 1777, the relationship between Charleston and Okfuskee "is not a new Friendship"; it was rather an ancestral bond—"from [the] Time [that] Charles Town was settled on the Edge of the Marsh"—between two towns that shared the same fire and were "one people."[23]

The notion, then, that the 1760 attack can be traced to a French-inspired plot seems far-fetched, requiring not only a repudiation of Okfuskee's past but also a break with its future. Given this, I suggest that we seek a motive for the attack in the history and logic of Okfuskee's relationship with the British. Recall Patricia Galloway's insight that a fanni mico functioned "as a clan uncle for the adopting group in the councils of his own people." If a fanni mico fulfilled this role for his adoptive kinsmen, and if the Okfuskee–British relationship enjoined Okfuskees to act as fanni micos for the British, then the 1760 attack was not a political or personal clash (although, of course, political and personal factors played a role) but rather a manifestation of the Creek clan system in action. More specifically, the events of May 16, 1760, exemplified the punishment meted out by a clan uncle to an offending member of his clan.

Why Okfuskees felt their British clan-mates merited punishment remains unclear, although there are several possibilities. To begin with, by the late 1750s, the Okfuskees feared that a changing diplomatic milieu threatened their control over an important axis of British–Creek relations. Okfuskee's role in southeastern geopolitics depended, to a large extent, on its ties to Charleston. As South Carolina's frontier situation deteriorated in the late 1750s, however, Charleston's attention increasingly focused on the Cherokees. After the 1760 attack, South Carolina's governor belatedly recognized that his province's ties to the Creeks had eroded; thus he told an Upper Creek that "many of your Countrymen, used frequently to come to Charles Town till lately . . . What is the reason they have not come so often of late?"[24] By the time he thought to ask, however, Creek diplomacy had begun to center on Savannah, a result that likely left the Okfuskees feeling marginalized. In the fall of 1757, for example, the Creeks refused South Carolina's invitation to visit Charleston in favor of Georgia's counteroffer. Okfuskees were not represented in the large Creek party that arrived in Savannah, perhaps reflecting Okfuskee uneasiness over the Creeks' decision to renege on "their promises" to visit Charleston. A second group—consisting of "some of the headmen of the Cheehaws, Oakfuschees, Uchees, & Tuckabachees"—did show up in Savannah four days after the treaty signing, but, even in this party, Okfuskees played such minor roles that the official "Proceedings" failed to note their presence. In addition, other Upper Creek headmen, most notably Wolf of Muccolossus, seemed to supplant the Okfuskees in British affections. The fact that Wolf spoke for the Upper Creeks during the 1757 Savannah conference only highlighted the growing influence of a man whom Red Coat King believed "is mad after makeing such large Promises to the English King."[25]

Within Creek country, the diplomatic situation was no more favorable for the Okfuskees. British ambassadors increasingly set up shop in other Creek towns and undermined Okfuskee's place in Creek–British relations. Indian Superintendent Edmond Atkin, for example, began his 1759 trip to Upper Creek country by visiting Tuckabatchee, responding rudely to the Okfuskee Captain, and snubbing Gun Merchant of Okchai in favor of Wolf. He then argued that "[i]t was in this Town [Tuckabatchee] the Peace was first made" with the British, a suggestion a Tuckabatchee had already put forward: "it was this Town that made the Peace . . . *whatever others pretend to*." As time went on, Atkin's trade policies angered many Creeks, as did his fawning treatment of the Choctaws; in fact, his designation of Wolf's town as the base for the Choctaw trade—the "Store must be in that Town"—threatened to erase Okfuskee's long-standing role in that exchange network. Moreover, as the Okfuskees surely noticed, Atkin spent a fair amount of time in Tuckabatchee and Muccolossus, and made much of Wolf, telling the Creeks, "I rely upon him, & I shall not believe any to be a Friend to the English that he does not." Atkin's actions led a Lower Creek to complain "Nor did [Atkin] show more Regard to our Head Towns than to particular People"; an Upper Creek likewise noted that "the Indians had chalked down near forty Talks delivered by the Agent at different Times in their Nation of which they could make no Sense, except that the same contained provoking Words and much Abuse." Perhaps in response to Atkin's behavior, Handsome Fellow left a Tuckabatchee conference—Atkin wrote he "went away . . . sick"—where the Superintendent was attacked by a Lower Creek who, Atkin noted, had been "sitting next to" Tahaulky, "a head Warriour of Ockfusky." Atkin's attribution of guilt by association notwithstanding, there is no evidence that Okfuskees sought his death. Still, the Okfuskees would not have welcomed the diplomatic developments his trip produced, and, when taken in conjunction with Savannah's rising influence, the Okfuskees might justifiably have felt alarmed at their new role in Creek–British affairs.[26]

Many Creeks also were angered over British efforts to push them into a war with the Cherokees. In the spring of 1760, Britain's war against the Creeks' northern neighbors was going badly. The colonists needed Creek aid, but plans such as Ellis's "to embroil [the Creek] Nation insensibly, and as it were against their inclination" led to widespread Creek dissatisfaction. Okfuskees—leaders in earlier, British-inspired peace initiatives—may have felt particularly aggrieved. They had, after all, remained heavily involved throughout the 1750s in efforts to solidify Creek–Cherokee relations. Red Coat King, in particular, may have felt bound by the Cherokee peace tokens he accepted in 1749. If so, he would not have welcomed war. His son, Handsome Fellow, led the 1760 attack, and Wolf of Muccolossus claimed that "one Man of our Nation, Red Coat King . . . was the Cause of all the mischief." Some Okfuskees felt a continuing attachment to the Cherokees into the 1760s, with a few of the town's young warriors actively supporting them. Thus, a party of Okfuskees and Cherokees looted British stores in 1761; at the same time, Okfuskees were thought to be "amongst the Cherokees."[27]

Finally, the Okfuskees had grown increasingly irritated with the British traders. During the 1750s, Okfuskees took the lead on several occasions in asking for price reductions. In 1753, for example, Handsome Fellow twice requested lower prices during a meeting with Glen; when he was refused, the Okfuskee Captain resigned his commission and left the council room. In 1755, Red Coat King and the Okfuskee Captain attended an Okchai meeting at which Gun Merchant demanded lower prices. When he was rebuffed, the Okfuskees aided in tying up the traders present, after which the Okfuskee Captain spoke "in great Wrath," advising the Creeks not to visit Charleston. During this confrontation, the "Traders at the Oakfuskees" were accused of promising lower prices while in the governor's presence but then "them Traders rose their Trade to the Old Standard." The town's traders, for their part, did not require being tied up to recognize the declining regard their Okfuskee hosts had for them. Rumors spread in both 1754 and 1755 that the Okfuskees, in trader John Ross's words, "concluded to cutt of[f] the English in that Town." By September 1759, Ross was worried enough to write in his will that "I am in a short time to depart . . . for the Upper Creek Country . . . [C]onsidering the dangers I am daily exposed to," he left his whole estate to "the only friend I have got in this part of the world." Two weeks earlier, William Rae reported from Okfuskee that "there were very bad talks," to which Lachlan McIntosh responded that he had been told that "it would not be long before a Blow would be given to the white People." McIntosh also reported being threatened by "one of the Warriours of Ockfuskey," an incident which led him to conclude that "three parts of the People of that Town are become Frenchmen." Rae, McIntosh, and Ross all died on May 16, 1760. Ross, in fact, was "chopped to pieces" at the Okfuskee village of Sugatspoges, perhaps because he was, as his shortage of friends suggests and a fellow trader confirmed, "surly and ill-natured," even "vicious."[28]

Most likely, Ross's character flaws were simply one small factor in a cascade of incidents and injuries that led some Okfuskees to decide that an object lesson in clan responsibility, and clan power, was needed. Discussions of the Creek system of justice and punishment do not generally leave room for actions of the sort represented by the 1760 attack. A Creek belonged to his or her mother's clan; clan-mates had the responsibility to protect each other and to avenge injuries. Scholars emphasize the protective aspect of the clan system, detailing the clan's role in exacting justice for a wrong done to one of its members by punishing either the offender, who is assumed to belong to another clan, or one of the offender's clan-mates. Once the injured clan meted out punishment, the cycle of revenge stopped. In terms of the Okfuskees' 1760 attack, the points to note are that clans had the right to punish offenders, and that, if done properly, no one could complain. The corollary was that if the clan chose not to seek revenge, that was the end of the matter. And the further corollary was that if a clan chose to punish one of its own people, no one could challenge its right to do so. The logic of the Creek clan system accordingly meant that clan-mates looked to each other for punishment as well as protection.[29]

Intraclan capital punishment occurred infrequently, but one incident of note occurred in 1752, when an Okfuskee's kinsman was killed at the behest of the British. That year, Acorn Whistler, headman of Little Okfuskee, attacked a Cherokee party then under British protection. He was eventually put to death, but only after the British brought extraordinary pressure to bear on the Creeks. The incident's significance arises from the Creeks' belief that British demands for Acorn Whistler's death put them in an extremely awkward position, one that they could escape only if his relatives would kill him themselves. As Chigelley of Coweta told two of Acorn Whistler's kinsmen, "You are his own Flesh and Blood. Either of you or any of his own Relations may kill him and who has any Thing to say to it?" Later, upon hearing that Acorn Whistler had been killed by his nephew, an assembly of Creek headmen "shook Hands, and returned

Thanks to those three Men, the Acorn Whistler's Relations (who were the only persons that had any Thing to say in the Affair) for the great Regard they had shown to their Nation by giving this Satisfaction to the English." One of those thanked, the Okfuskee Captain, told the conference that "his own Relations and a very great Man had suffered Death for Satisfaction to the English," but that "he was very well contented" because the execution prevented "a Breach of Friendship with the English which he hoped would never happen."[30]

And yet, of course, such a breach did happen. That it happened in the Okfuskee Captain's own town is ironic but not surprising. The Okfuskees had the option, as kinsmen, to correct their British kin, and the British insistence, during the Acorn Whistler affair, that relatives could punish each other with impunity only served to underline the validity of intraclan justice. Significantly, however, the Okfuskees' decision to kill the British traders was not a unanimous one. In the months leading up to the assault, some Okfuskees insisted—apparently in good faith—on their firm attachment to the British. On March 18, for example, one young war leader told an Augusta audience that "he always looked upon his Town as a Coal of the same Fire that burns in Carolina and Georgia"; given that he had earlier warned Lachlan McIntosh of his townspeople's unhappiness with the British, and given that his father was a longtime trader in Okfuskee, there is no reason to doubt his word. The Okfuskee Captain, for his part, stated that "we have not a small hold of the English, but will hold them fast. The day will never come that we'll through them away." If his actions during the attack are any guide, he too was telling the truth: although out of town when the violence began, he worked to save the trader who fell into his hands; his success at this "gave him a great deal of Pleasure." Other Okfuskees were likewise willing to oppose their townspeople's violent course of action. Even some of the men involved in the attack itself sought to lessen its effects. Robert French, an Okfuskee packhorseman, thus testified that he survived because he "was taken hold of by three or four Indian fellows who told him that they were sent to take his Goods away and to kill him but that they would not do the latter"; his robbers/rescuers "immediately hurried him forceably away to a Place of Safety."[31]

The Okfuskees who committed to the assault, however, believed they were well within their rights to behave as they did. They knew, all the same, that their actions must be limited in scope—strong enough to send a message; restrained enough to permit reconciliation. They were punishing and correcting kinsmen, not declaring war. To some extent, in fact, the attack can be read as an effort to head off a more permanent separation. The Okfuskees' actions, oddly enough, staked out a middle ground, a position which offered disaffected Creeks the opportunity to express their anger without either committing the nation to an all-out war or watching it dissolve in a welter of competing agendas. Both were possibilities at the time. Writing only two days before the attack, a South Carolina official neatly summarized the moment's contingent nature: "The Upper Creeks and lower are in the utmost confusion, being divided into Parties, one for the French and Cherokees, the other for us, which are carried to such a height, that in the Upper Towns they are like to come to blows among themselves; And upon the whole it is thought there, that our Interest among the Creeks is in a very tottering condition." Less than a year before, Handsome Fellow counseled the leader of the Upper Creeks' anti-British faction, "Don't be rash, or in a hurry. Have Patience; Let the War break out first else where. Consider what you are about."[32] By mid-May, however, the time for patience had passed; hesitation might lead to catastrophe. And yet rashness was equally unacceptable; it too could produce a conflagration. "Consider[ing] what you are about," in Handsome Fellow's case, led to an attack that mixed destruction and correction, kin-based punishment and cross-cultural education. The events of May 16, 1760, were a family affair.

Failure to understand the Okfuskees' motivations led one historian to comment that, "[s]trangely, the conspiracy did not get off the ground." Far from trying to get it off the ground, the Okfuskees quickly took steps to show that the violence did not signal, in Ellis's words, "a Rupture between those Indians and Us." The town's headmen sent assurances of their goodwill, a message reinforced by a gift of tobacco, a powerful symbol of peace. Ellis responded in kind in a talk delivered at Okfuskee, after which, a newspaper reported, "the Bones of our murdered People [were] collected and decently interred in white Skins." At the same time, the Okfuskees demonstrated that they were not in the Cherokees' camp. In August, after the townspeople received a Cherokee war talk "accompanied with a bloody stick and two Englishmen's Scalps," they publicly terminated diplomatic contact: "the Oakfuskees took and threw them into the river, declaring that they were tired of the Cherokee talks, and would hear no more of them." To underline the point, later that month, "two of the Oakfuskees met with two Cherokees of Noucassih, at Chotih old-town, exchanged cloaths and arms, and pretended the utmost friendship, but in the night killed and scalped one of the Cherokees, and let the other escape (it was thought) purposely to tell his countrymen the news."[33] The Okfuskees, of course, also made sure that the British heard "the news."

Perhaps most significantly, while all this was going on, Handsome Fellow himself arrived in Augusta bearing a Cherokee scalp, thereby using a Cherokee's body to send a message of loyalty to the British. Once there, he was joined by "Tomathli-hacho, Italali Mico, and other Creeks of the Oakfuskees" in saying that the Creeks had "unanimously resolved to maintain peace and good understanding with the English; that as a token of their sincerity, they had sent down a Cherokee scalp lately taken at Hywassee to wipe away a few of the tears for the murder of the traders in their nation." In taking this bloody step back to the white path, Handsome Fellow hoped to accomplish much more than simply, as Ellis put it, "to vindicate himself." Wiping the tears of a grieving person provided comfort and, of equal importance, brought that person back to equanimity, back to a state of mind where he or she could reenter old relationships and resume old responsibilities. That Handsome Fellow did this with a Cherokee scalp represented, in the context of a continuing British–Cherokee war, an important statement of mutuality. That the scalp came from the Cherokee town of Hiwassee, however, was especially revealing. Hiwassee, after all, was the town that the Okfuskees had dealt with so closely during the 1749 peace negotiations, the town that had received shells and seeds from the Okfuskees and responded with a white flag and an invitation to eat the crops that grew from those seeds.[34] The scalp Handsome Fellow brought to Augusta did not mean that Okfuskees intended to fight the Cherokees. Rather, it signified—along with the Okfuskees' other actions in the months following the attack—the great value the Okfuskees placed on their relationship with the British.

Over the next two decades, Handsome Fellow became Okfuskee's leader in its dealings with first the British, then the Americans. He died on the path from Augusta to Okfuskee while carrying a talk from the United States. Handsome Fellow's townsmen obviously did not believe that participation in the events of May 16, 1760, disqualified him from playing a critical role in Okfuskee's relationship with its eastern neighbors. To the contrary, in accepting Handsome Fellow's leadership, first in the attack on the British traders and then in subsequent relations with the British and their American successors, Okfuskees demanded that their Euro-American contemporaries acknowledge the relevance of a Native history and logic. The sociohistorical model that served as the foundation for Handsome Fellow's attack—the constellation of customs and understandings upon which the Okfuskees based their worldview—had to be taken into account. By violently reminding the British that failing to meet their obligations to their Native neighbors had consequences, the Okfuskees drove home a point that would be made again and again over the next fifteen years: Euro-Americans could not act without considering Native Americans' views and interests. In the words of an observer writing just as the Seven Years' War was ending, "the *Indian* Nations will not allow themselves to be Subjects of *Britain,* but the Friends and Brethren of the *English* . . . they have the Power of Life and Death, Peace and War, in their own Councils, without being accountable to us."[35] The attack of May 16, 1760, reasserted Okfuskee's place in the events that determined the shape of the continent's history; it corrected British views on the nature of the geopolitical situation in the Southeast.

Okfuskees might disagree over the proper approach to their straying "Friends and Brethren," but all Okfuskees—both those who participated in, and those who dissented from, the 1760 attack—could agree on the fundamental truth of Okfuskee's long-standing, deeply rooted, profoundly important connections to the British. The Okfuskee Captain could work to save a packhorseman and later refer to his townspeople being "one Fire with the English"; Handsome Fellow could lead the attack that killed that packhorseman's employer and later successfully play a role very similar to that of his father, Fanni Mico. Their seemingly incompatible actions reflected a disagreement over means, not ends. And, in the attack's aftermath, even those differences fell away, allowing the two headmen to make four trips together to the British colonies between March 1761 and August 1764. The talks they delivered on those occasions worked "to explain and clear up the late rumors" and renew "their professions of friendship"; to reassure the British that "We have been for some time past, doing every thing in our Power, to get things made straight again"; to remind their listeners that "we hold fast by the Old talk and intend to hold the English always fast by the hand." Their speeches worked, in other words, to attest to the enduring relevance of the Okfuskees' worldview, to assert that the bonds linking the town to its British neighbors remained strong.[36]

Reassertion

On August 23, 1774, David Taitt, a British agent to the Creeks, was alarmed to discover that nine Okfuskees had suddenly appeared within 100 yards of Robert Mackay's Augusta house. They had crossed the Oconee River and made their way through Georgia's backcountry unobserved, marching up to the house with guns in their hands; Taitt noted that they could easily have killed every person in the house. In fact, he was surprised they had not done so since "there is not a worse Sett of Villians in the Nation than these Men are." Instead, they presented a peace talk and departed the next day. Taitt's letter shows that he was unsure what to make of the party's behavior, and, even after the Okfuskees left, he did not believe that they intended merely to deliver a talk. "[I]ndeed," Taitt said, "I wish they may not turn desperate and do Some mischief"; he was certain "that these men came down . . . to see the Situation of the Country or to try to get a Clandestine Trade." He noted that, several miles from Augusta, the homeward-bound Okfuskee party encountered a trader. They responded by throwing down their "Bundles," keeping their guns in hand; they treated the trader courteously after he spoke to them, but they "were all naked and painted" (an attribute of a war party), and they had scouts out "in the same Manner as they go to War." Yet, strangely enough, nothing untoward occurred, leading Taitt to write soon after that "nothing very material has happened here."[37]

As I discuss below, Taitt had reason to wonder about the motives of Creeks who arrived unannounced and unobserved. However, several characteristics of the Okfuskees and their talk might have set his mind at ease. In the first place, while the Okfuskees marched up to Mackay's house with guns in hand, the first two men "had White Wings," which Taitt knew were signs of peace and goodwill. Second, the Creeks and the British had been caught in a tense standoff since December 1773; the Okfuskees recognized that their lives were in danger while in the colonies, and Taitt should not have been surprised at their caution. Finally, the talk delivered on behalf of five Upper Creek towns by the party's leader, Cujesse Mico, confirmed the Okfuskees' goodwill. The headman began by presenting the white wings and some tobacco; he then said that "formerly the Oakfuskies and Charleston were one Fire, and we hope they will always continue as one, although at present there seems to be some Difference between us but we want Peace. Trees may fall across the Path but I have taken them all out from Oakfuskie to this white House, and have the Path straight and white. We hold this Wing fast by the Root, and hope that Capt. Stuart at Charleston will hold fast by the middle, and the Governor of Savannah by the Point." Cujesse Mico closed by stating that the "Upper Towns were for Peace," and asking that their trade be restored.[38]

The party that Cujesse Mico led, then, followed in the footsteps of generations of Okfuskee mediators and peacemakers. They did so, however,
in a difficult and dangerous situation. Much had changed since Red Coat
King led his party to Charleston in 1749. The Okfuskees' position in the
region was increasingly insecure, and so the violent, aggressive solution to
a strained British–Creek relationship adopted by Handsome Fellow in 1760
was no longer practical. Cujesse Mico's 1774 mission to Augusta allows us
to understand the nature of the shifts in the southeastern geopolitical
system, and it points us toward future patterns in the region's development.
Or, more simply, the 1774 visit shows us where the Southeast—and
Okfuskee itself—had been and where it was going.

The 1774 crisis began with a series of Creek attacks on backcountry
colonists in December 1773 and January 1774; it escalated when the
British, in response, embargoed the Creeks' trade. This standoff, however,
followed a decade's worth of tension and accommodation within Creek
society and the Creek–British relationship. The 1763 Peace of Paris ended
both the Seven Years' War and the delicate balance of power that had
characterized southeastern geopolitics since the Yamasee War. France, after
ceding its claims on mainland North America, was no longer a factor; and
Spain, which lost Florida but gained Louisiana, saw its already diminished
role in the Southeast decline even further. Great Britain, by contrast,
emerged as the acknowledged power in eastern North America, having
extinguished its European rivals' claims to both Canada and Florida. The
peace treaty altered the official maps; what this meant on the ground would
take years to discover. Britain's efforts to administer its enlarged empire,
combined with the inhabitants' reactions and innovations, produced a half-
century of dramatic transformation.

For the Creeks, the Peace of Paris ended their position at the center of
competing European imperial powers. The days when Creek headmen
played the British off against the Spanish or French were over; they could
no longer count on receiving presents from Euro-American suitors, and
their traders now came exclusively from British trading centers. In addition,
the Creeks no longer controlled Britain's trade routes to the Chickasaws
and Choctaws, making them more vulnerable to attacks from those quar-
ters. The Creeks, moreover, faced encroachment on their land as British
subjects swarmed into Georgia and the Florida colonies. Developments of
this sort were particularly alarming for the Okfuskees. As Georgia expanded, Charleston's role in Creek affairs receded, with the result that

Okfuskees conditioned to relying on eastern connections for support and influence now found that the eastern colonies all too often ignored their concerns and usurped their resources. Moreover, with the British ensconced in the Gulf Coast ports, paths to the South became important avenues for diplomatic influence and economic prosperity. Creeks towns like Little Tallassee that were located on these paths now threatened to eclipse towns like Okfuskee whose path to the East suddenly looked less desirable. The Okfuskees and their Creek neighbors spent years adjusting to these new realities.

Historians have been unanimous in recognizing the 1760s and 1770s as a period of intense adjustment in Creek society. There has, however, been significantly less unanimity when discussing the efficacy of Creek efforts to come to grips with their new world. One school of thought suggests that Creeks were largely helpless in the face of economic imbalances, social pathologies, and military inequalities,[39] while other scholars discuss both the problems and the possibilities confronting the Creeks.[40] My research supports the latter position. The departure of the French and the distancing of the Spanish did not mean that the Creeks were suddenly helpless. The outlines of such a condition were visible; they would become increasingly obvious by the 1790s, and the defeat of the Red Stick movement in 1814 would carve them into stone. In the period between 1763 and the American Revolution, however, the Creeks still had some cards to play.

The Creeks owed their options to a number of factors. In the first place, the Creeks remained a significant military presence in the region, and the British continued to be wary of the costs associated with an Indian war. Second, imperial reform notwithstanding, the British system was riven with tensions within and between colonies and departments; these fault lines created numerous opportunities for colonists and Indians who wished to evade official mandates. Finally, the imperial crisis that led to the American Revolution increased the room to maneuver for those who sought alternative avenues of trade and alliance. The departure of European counterweights to Great Britain meant, then, that the Creeks had fewer options in times of crisis, but it also meant that the British had to deal with the contradictions and conflicts within their own system. Of course, the Creeks confronted their own crises during these years, crises that set the stage for the deterioration of Indian power in the region; the Okfuskees' struggles to retain and assert influence were localized manifestations of more generalized problems. The Creeks, however, did not view such decline as in-

evitable. They recognized the problems they faced; they also saw possibilities and a future worth working toward, even if they could not always
agree in which direction it lay. The Okfuskees' 1774 arrival in Augusta
attests to the Creeks' continued belief in their own influence and power.
For the Okfuskees themselves, however, the embassy also testified to the
continuity of something that was at once farther reaching and deeper
rooted, more specific and more localized. Cujesse Mico's mission—in its
timing and function, in the words used and the symbols deployed, in the
attachments called upon and the history invoked—demonstrated the enduring power of Okfuskee's relationship with the British living to the east.
The solution to the townspeople's current problems lay in the assertion of
old connections.

The Okfuskees' mission had its origins in the assaults made by rogue
Creek warriors on the Georgia backcountry in the winter of 1773–1774.
On January 22, a trader from the Okfuskee village of "Chattahugee" arrived
in Augusta, accompanied by Mad Turkey, an Okfuskee headman. On their
way down, the two men had encountered Skutchiby, the Young Lieutenant
of Coweta, who had taken part in the attacks. He gave Mad Turkey a talk
to take to George Galphin (Coweta's trader) in Augusta, explaining why
his people had behaved as they had and promising that all would now be
peaceful. The Okfuskee could not deliver the message to Galphin, however,
because of threats against the headman's life by incensed colonists. Instead,
he presented the talk in Fort Augusta, remaining there until he could be
escorted "safe out of the settlement." Whether Mad Turkey set out to mediate the crisis or not, both he and the Coweta headman quickly recognized
the part an Okfuskee could play in defusing the situation. Mad Turkey
apparently took his role as go-between seriously. After leaving Augusta, he
went to Coweta, returning to Augusta by late March. Once there, a colonist
"invited the Indian to drink with him, and, whilst the fellow had the bottle
at his mouth, he gave him a stroke with the bar of iron he had in his
hands."[41]

The murder of a townsman who was "remarkably attached" to the British
and who had thrown himself into mediating the crisis alarmed the Okfuskees. Such a turn of events called for some clarification. "Some days" before
May 3, the trader Michael Myers arrived in Augusta from Mad Turkey's
town. He reported that the dead man's relatives "have burned his house
and effects on account of his being killed," a traditional part of the
mourning complex, "but [they] were not acquainted with how it [the

killing] was done." Four "Indians" accompanied Myers, but it was too dangerous for them to come into Augusta. They "expressed great dislike at being turned back, and it is said even used some threatenings in case Myers should not fulfill his agreement with them and let them have the presents he had promised." The newspaper account of the Indians' visit portrays the goods they demanded as payment for escorting Myers, but the items may have been viewed by the Okfuskees as gifts for Mad Turkey's grieving relatives; such presents allowed offenders "to wipe away" the tears of the bereaved. Some Okfuskees obviously needed such appeasement. They were "well disposed" and "kind to the white people amongst them" in late winter, but, in late April or early May, an Okfuskee assaulted the trader Thomas Graham, declaring "that as his uncle the Mad Turkey who was a beloved man, had been killed by the white people, and as he (Mr. Graham) was a beloved man among these, it was fit that his life should pay for the other's." Graham fled the town, "pursued by several Indians of Ockfusky" who came "very nigh [to] doing his Business." As in the 1760 attack, Graham was not chosen at random. He was the Okfuskee trader Robert Rae's partner, and was thus closely connected not only to Okfuskee but also to Augusta's elite traders. And, as an Augusta merchant noted, the Upper Creeks "say that unless they get the Right Man they will not take a Mean white Man as Satisfaction, but some Beloved Man out of this Place."[42]

The appearance in Augusta of Cujesse Mico and eight other Okfuskees in August 1774 did not, therefore, mark the first Okfuskee attempt to resolve the crisis. Mad Turkey's efforts had only drawn the town into the fray, and the four men who came to Augusta that spring had not even been allowed to enter town. The anger Graham witnessed in Okfuskee was therefore understandable. Given the realities of post-1763 regional politics, however, the Okfuskees decided that outrage was counterproductive; thus, they acquiesced in the execution of an Okfuskee who helped lead the attack on Georgia.[43] The actions of Cujesse Mico's party demonstrate the lessons that the Okfuskees had learned. They knew the colonists were dangerous, so they emphasized both stealth and, once they revealed themselves, the prominent display of peace symbols. More importantly, the town's young men and Mad Turkey's relatives recognized the necessity of maintaining old ties. In Augusta, the Okfuskees who offered the traditional symbols and words that had secured the town's relationship with the British so often before were the very men the British thought were their most inveterate enemies. Cujesse Mico himself "is a nephew of the Mad Turkey and has as is said often threatened to take Satisfaction for the murder of his Uncle." But, in his speech, the Okfuskee noted that "I am not come with a bad Talk for my near Relation that fell at this Place some time ago."[44] Unlike the situation in 1760, the 1774 crisis could not be resolved with violence.

The composition of Cujesse Mico's party, combined with their actions and words, attest to the challenges and opportunities confronting Okfuskee. On the debit side of the equation, the British trade embargo alarmed the Creeks. Okfuskee's connections to traders willing to overlook legal niceties may have buffered its impact to some extent, but Cujesse Mico still asked to bring "our Trader & Pack horses back with us into the nation as we are now very poor for Goods."[45] Not only did Okfuskees experience shortages, but some of their Creek neighbors stepped up long-standing efforts to devalue the trading path linking Okfuskee to Augusta and Charleston. Thus Mico Hlucko stated in February 1774 that the Creek trade should focus on "the Safe Path" from Pensacola, rather than on the Augusta path, and that "the Hillabie, Oakfuskie & Chatahootchie people may think otherwise, but these two Rivers [the other Upper Creeks] here would be glad of a Supply from thence." In addition, Okfuskee's young men were often out of control, especially those who accompanied Cujesse Mico. Most shockingly, Okfuskees robbed a Euro-American caravan in 1773, stating that "they were once of the Same Fire with Charleston but now they will be by themselves";[46] the 1774 attack on Graham represented more of the same.

In the face of these problems, the Okfuskees turned to the rituals and symbols that had worked so well in the past. Cujesse Mico hoped, of course, that his talk, the white wings, and tobacco would lead to the traders' return. Of equal importance, however, he meant the talk to remind the British of the proper path and old friends. He spoke, therefore, of clearing trees from the path linking "Oakfuskie to this white House" in Augusta, and of making the path "straight and white"; he used a white wing to demonstrate the unmediated relationship between his town ("the Root") and Charleston ("the middle") rather than Savannah ("the Point"); and he speculated that "perhaps our Friends may have thought long to hear from us . . . as Old Friends are always glad to hear from, and to See one another." In addition, the composition of his party, with so many real and potential troublemakers in it, suggests that the Okfuskees were turning to traditional forms and narratives to heal divisions within the town itself. Significantly, none of the leading Okfuskee headmen—those who had been in the forefront of Creek–British relations for the past decade and who would lead the town through the American Revolution—came to Augusta. Instead, they remained at home while the town's past leaders in chaos and disruption committed themselves, in a public forum, to peace. As Cujesse Mico noted, "Our Headmen in the Upper Towns thought long to hear from Our Friends and have therefore made a Talk and Sent us with it." A shared fire and a white wing could, apparently, heal a number of different wounds.

The Okfuskees, then, saw that old ties and traditional symbols offered them a way out of the crisis. Their efforts must be taken seriously, despite our knowledge that they would finally become dead ends, because the belief in their efficacy produced actions that are both worthy of understanding in their own right and important for our narratives of Okfuskee and American history. The solutions that the Okfuskees worked toward in August 1774 would, for example, figure prominently in the course of the American Revolution. Rebel forces controlled Charleston until 1780 and Augusta until 1779, and Robert Rae, a prominent Okfuskee trader, participated in American efforts to woo the Creeks. Okfuskee's history of relations with Charleston, Augusta, and Rae, combined with the town's rivalry with those Creeks who sought to reorient the axis of trade and diplomacy, led many of its people to support the Americans. Okfuskees turned back Creek raiding parties heading for the American backcountry in 1777 and 1778, thereby preventing the outbreak of a more general Indian war and freeing up American resources for other purposes. In the words of an American envoy writing to his supervisors from Okfuskee, "while you send Good Talks I can make this Town Keep the rest at Peace." Okfuskees also led a 1777 attack on British representatives in the Upper Creek country, and Cujesse Mico was himself involved in efforts to secure Creek support for the Americans.[47]

Okfuskee's leaders opted for a cautious neutrality when British forces took control of the Southeast in the latter stages of the Revolution, but they eagerly welcomed signs of a United States' resurgence. Thus, an American agent noted that a 1782 party of Creeks—his list begins with "handson Fellows Nephew & ten warriors from the Oackfreskeys"—told Georgia's governor that "it is a long time since they saw thire olde friend in possession of thire country"; the Creek party intended "to Renue the chean of friendship, that thire olde men have ever adheared to and hope they and you will smock the pipe of friendship." Okfuskee headmen quickly resumed their tradition of facilitating the Creeks' relations with their eastern neighbors. In 1786, for example, Daniel McMurphy, frustrated that a conference had not attracted enough headmen, complained to two Okfuskees, White Lieutenant and Will's Friend. In response, White Lieutenant "said he would call a meeting at his Town and see if they would not come." Both his uncle (Handsome Fellow) and grandfather (Red Coat King) would have responded in the same way.[48]

The ties that Cossitee and Thomas Nairne solemnized in 1708, then, continued to have meaning into the 1780s. The twists and turns that characterized this relationship's development were linked to the changing fortunes of the parties involved; they highlight processes central to the contest for local, regional, and international influence. Of equal importance, however, is the fact that the relationship's evolving form and meaning points us toward the habits and outlooks that conditioned the Okfuskees' world. At any point in time from the early eighteenth century through the mid-1780s, the Okfuskees believed that their past, present, and future—their histories, circumstances, and expectations—were wrapped up with their ties to the British colonies to the east. As we uncover the meanings and values underlying this relationship, we move toward a more complete understanding of the Okfuskees themselves. As we watch the Okfuskees work to maintain their bond with the British, we open up new windows onto the town's history. And as we come to appreciate the complex reality of life in a colonial-era Native American community, we take yet another step toward a more complete—and more compelling—narrative of both Native and American history.

The Okfuskees' long-running efforts to assert the relevance of their social constructs and cultural values are striking. Their beliefs and practices were distinctive and revealing, as were the processes by which those meanings and patterns were communicated, challenged, and revised. Like their Euro-American neighbors, Okfuskees were political actors, publicly deploying power in order to assign significance, establish categories, and produce results.[49] To take an obvious example, the traders who died on May 16, 1760, fell victim to the Okfuskees' worldview as well as to their weapons. In this case, violence was the end result of a particular sociopolitical vision enacted in town squares, communicated in talks, and—when necessary—inscribed on bodies. That this process necessitated the killing of eleven men, however, suggests the instability of early American systems of meaning and practice. For the Okfuskees and their contemporaries, the creating, testing, and re-creating of cultural norms was a continuous process. Early Americans called on coercion and destruction, friendship and kinship, stories about the past and views of the future, all to facilitate the emergence of a world that more closely conformed to their interests and ideals. They did so privately, of course, but also while publicly engaged with outsiders, with people whose own identities were dependent upon systems of thought and patterns of behavior that were more or less foreign or recognizable. Early America, then, was characterized by a politics of insecurity, a politics in which unsettled social conditions and divergent cultural traditions combined to create a seemingly endless series of challenges to established systems and cherished identities.

Relations between Native peoples and their Euro-American neighbors demonstrate this instability quite clearly. These two peoples could neither avoid each other nor ignore their very real differences. Frequent contact with people conditioned to embrace different values and to accept unfamiliar assumptions led both Natives and newcomers to ponder a disturbing series of questions. How could Indians have a relationship with Europeans, a people who so profoundly misunderstood the ways of the world that they confused temporary possession with exclusive ownership, claimed dominion over nature, and believed in a tripartite monotheism? How could Europeans possibly deal with Indians, a people so ignorant of the basics of kinship that they believed that uncles were more powerful than fathers, that children belonged to their mother's family, and that marriage was not a fundamentally hierarchical relationship? How could a European hope to conduct diplomacy with Natives who were convinced that relationships needed to be renewed periodically, that gifts showed respect, and that leaders were persuasive? How should an Indian react to being told that treaties were permanent, that goods bought services, and that leaders were commanding? The process of answering these questions might, in the right situation, produce a middle ground, a temporary and expedient convergence of compatible misunderstandings. At the other extreme, though, the encounter with foreign systems of behavior and thought simply destabilized each people's own ground, producing a common sense of insecurity but no mutuality, a shared fear unleavened by empathy.[50] In either case, Natives and newcomers found that their mutual connections—both the actual interactions themselves and the shared process of confronting cultural difference—produced a peculiarly insecure world.

And yet, if a politics of insecurity characterized eighteenth-century

America as a whole, the politics' burden was not spread evenly across the social landscape. When it came to relations between Indians and colonists, the former found themselves in an increasingly untenable situation after midcentury. The Natives' peculiar connections to the British Empire ensured endemic insecurity in Indian country. In the years following Fanni Mico's 1749 trip to Charleston, the Okfuskees and their Native neighbors confronted an ever more centralized, expansive, numerous, and hostile colonial population. British efforts at imperial reform, combined with the resounding victory over France and Spain in 1763, endowed "Empire"—as both an intellectual construct and a sociopolitical reality—"with new significance," leading to an unparalleled commitment of British energy and resources to colonial issues. Expansion and rule over newly acquired lands were seen as crucial to maintaining Britain's economic, political, and military well-being; the ongoing growth of the colonies' population and the arrival in America of huge numbers of immigrants exacerbated these trends. And, to make matters more alarming for Native Americans, British territorial acquisition went hand-in-hand with social and political exclusion. Colonists had, for generations, claimed the status of civilized people, a narrative of self-identity and societal destiny that "required a continual labor of ejecting from oneself all that is wild or savage." Indians, it was widely assumed, lacked the essentials to be civilized British subjects. As colonial expansion took off after midcentury, beliefs of this sort became especially salient, with colonists and British officials sharing "in the conviction of British superiority and in the expectation that Indians would, before long, surrender their homelands to British subjects who were racially white." When combined with British military power and American population growth, then, rising levels of imperial optimism and colonial self-regard signaled that early America's Native inhabitants confronted an ever more insecure future. By the 1760s, Indians faced the prospect of a continual battle to assert their political independence and social worth.[51]

This struggle, however, became increasingly difficult over time. Diplomatically and militarily, the balance of power tipped away from Indian country. Thus Okfuskees who confidently claimed a relationship with Charleston in 1749 were, in 1760, worriedly correcting British sociodiplomatic faux pas; by 1774, the Okfuskees abandoned correction in favor of an anxious reassertion of past ties. The American Revolution, of course, offered Natives a chance to recoup their loses, but even the Crisis of Empire could only temporarily recalibrate the imbalanced politics of insecurity. In the 1780s, United States "conquerors" did, as Greg O'Brien puts it, "meet the unconquered" southeastern Indians, but the long-term trends were unsettling. Abutting an aggressively expansionist nation that continually dismissed their claims to independence; controlling lands fervently sought by a booming backcountry population; interacting with Euro-Americans who habitually viewed them as savages—Native Americans had many reasons to worry. In response, some turned to political and social reform, projects aimed, in part, at constructing coherent Native nations that could respond effectively to the threats posed by their Euro-American neighbors. Others sought supernatural solutions to chronic insecurity.[52]

At least where Natives and newcomers were concerned, therefore, the brunt of dealing with America's politics of insecurity had, by the United States' early national period, fallen on Indians. People of European descent no longer felt compelled to compromise in the face of Native traditions, and they no longer believed that their very survival was threatened by Indian initiatives. Confidence of this sort was a luxury, one that people of Native descent rarely enjoyed when dealing with Europeans. The colonial-era politics of insecurity had emerged out of three truths: Indians and Europeans would occasionally disagree; no one knew when those disagreements would explode into violence; cross-cultural warfare endangered Indians and Europeans alike. By the early decades of the nineteenth century, Indian–European disagreements, and even explosions, remained part of life, but they assumed world-altering significance only for Indians, a sure sign that the insecurity that had once connected early America's peoples was now a peculiarly Native characteristic.

3

Leaving Okfuskee: Economic Activities Outside of Town

Okfuskee was on the northeastern border of Upper Creek country, a geographic fact that opened certain doors for the townspeople, while closing others. When Handsome Fellow told Governor James Glen, "I live in a frontier Town," he did so in a context which emphasized that the Okfuskees were linked to the Cherokees to the north and the British to the east. Almost two decades later, as the Creeks tried to make peace with their southwestern neighbors, the Choctaws, an Upper Creek headman sent the Choctaws a talk saying that "The Long String of Barley Corn Beads is Sent by the Handsome man of the Oakfuskies from the farthest part of our Nation to be sent to the farthest Part of yours as the Beads are Long & White so may the Path to your Nation be the Same." Handsome Fellow's beads showed that, in terms of social distance, it was a long way from Okfuskee to the Choctaw nation. In contrast, the Creeks could have represented the distance—geographic and social—between Okfuskee and either the British or the Cherokees with a short string of beads. As a result, Okfuskees rarely participated in either Creek–Choctaw negotiations or Gulf Coast affairs, but frequently took the lead in dealing with the British and the Cherokees.[1] The Okfuskees' economic activities reflected this sociogeographic reality.

No Creek town or individual could survive without access to resources and services from outside of the community. Before sustained contact with Europeans, social reproduction in southeastern Native communities depended on exchanging the raw materials and finished products that facilitated town governance and religious observance. After Europeans became a regular part of the sociopolitical landscape, the importance of extracommunity economic activity increased dramatically. European goods, like their Indian-produced counterparts, buttressed social hierarchies and spiritual traditions, but European goods also conveyed unique material advantages. Native interest in foreign merchandise was most pronounced in the case of firearms, which quickly became the cornerstone for warfare and hunting, but Indians came to value European metal goods and cloth as well. The resulting "consumer revolution"[2] depended, to a large extent, on activities which brought Native Americans outside of their communities. Okfuskee, located on the eastern frontier and with a major trade path running through it, offered its people numerous opportunities to participate in the new economy.

The activities that brought the Okfuskees outside of their community on a consistent basis ranged from hunting to trading to the various levels of diplomacy, from renewing old friendships to attacking old enemies. Such a list, though, is misleading to the extent that it implies that each type of behavior occurred in isolation. In fact, the various activities the townspeople performed after leaving Okfuskee were intimately linked to each other. Where one hunted, and how, where, and with whom one traded, often depended upon the current diplomatic situation. Moreover, Okfuskees combined hunting, trading, and diplomacy, frequently engaging in two or more of these activities on any given trip. Such a list is also misleading to the extent that it obscures other economic tasks that Okfuskees pursued when away from town. In their dealings with Euro-Americans, for example, Okfuskees not only traded skins but also procured food, carried messages, escorted parties, provided information, and captured runaway laborers.

This chapter focuses on the varied economic activities the Okfuskees performed outside of their community. Deer hunting, for example, became the central method by which the Okfuskees assured themselves of a steady supply of European goods and services. I argue that, by the 1750s, changes in the timing and location of the Okfuskees' hunts led the townspeople into a more direct involvement with the British colonies to their east, a development which brought together economic opportunity and geopolitical worldview. For better or worse, however, other Creeks had already committed themselves to exploiting the economic possibilities offered by Georgia and South Carolina. A web of interlocking relations—a "frontier exchange economy"[3]—linking Native, African, and Euro-Americans emerged in the colonial backcountry during the early years of the eighteenth century. This network was not without problems for the people involved, but it did create a context in which Creek–colonist relationships exhibited a degree of interdependence and mutuality. I argue, however, that as Okfuskees came into sustained, face-to-face contact with Euro-American settlers after midcentury, relations of this sort were being undermined by colonial expansion, competition for resources, and mutual intolerance. By the 1760s, cross-cultural contacts tended to produce tension, anger, and violence, rather than mutually beneficial exchanges. Thus, as the townspeople's hunting and trading strategies evolved, leaving Okfuskee increasingly thrust them into the center of an unsettled situation.

The outcome endangered not only the Okfuskees' new hunting and trading patterns but also their geopolitical worldview. Leaving Okfuskee created a dialogue—a never-ending, always shifting conversation—between local and regional, Okfuskee and colonist, Indian country and backcountry, economy and ideology. As a result, leaving Okfuskee for the hunting grounds or the colonial backcountry inevitably brought the townspeople back to Okfuskee, back to the understandings and meanings, the norms and practices, that structured their world. In leaving Okfuskee, then, its people illuminated the peculiar connections at the heart of this book. Rooted in the local, enacted in the regional, and enmeshed in the cross-cultural, the Okfuskees' economic activities outside of their community transcend our narrow categories of town and colony, culture and frontier. Establishing peculiar connections by leaving their community did not always make the Okfuskees' lives easier or more pleasant. If we wish, however, to understand the role of Indians in early American history, then it must be acknowledged that connections cut both ways. The ties that bring one generation together in peace can trap the next in a cycle of recrimination and violence. Shared processes, common patterns, and joint experiences may produce mutuality in one context and friction in another.

Hunting

On April 3, 1754, the trader Lachlan McIntosh wrote, "About 20 Days ago the Handsome Fellow belonging to the Ockfuskees killed another Indian in the Woods belonging to the same Town coming up to some Game." Seventeen years later, Handsome Fellow's son arrived in Augusta to report that, on October 14, "while he and others were out a hunting Eleven white Men came to their Camp Over Ocone River where they found two of his people—that they killed one and whipped the other very Severely and left him tyed to a Tree—and took away their Skins and every other Article they found there." An investigation determined that the incident was precipitated by a bout of horse-stealing on the Okfuskees' part; a Lower Creek talk confirmed not only that "some of the Oakfuskee people went out a hunting on the Oconee River" but also that several members of the Okfuskee party had a history of bothering Georgia's colonists.[4]

The men in Handsome Fellow's family played many roles within Okfuskee over the course of their lives. In the incidents mentioned above, however, both Handsome Fellow and his son were hunters, a role that allowed Creek men to make a significant contribution to the economic life of their towns. Much of the Okfuskees' ability to purchase the European goods so important to the fabric of daily life depended on the men's hunting prowess. Hunting took able-bodied Okfuskee men, and many women, out of the community for months at a time. As such, it dominated their extra-community yearly calendar. Simply asserting the importance of hunting for Okfuskees, however, can only go so far in tracking Okfuskee's eighteenth-century development. Creek hunting practices changed dramatically over time, and the incidents involving Handsome Fellow and his son, although separated by only seventeen years, highlight the changes and continuities in this important aspect of Okfuskean life.

Creek hunting parties typically consisted of people who shared clan and town ties. Thus, Handsome Fellow and his son hunted with fellow townsmen, although both soon had cause to regret it. Such groups were not particularly large; Handsome Fellow's son's party consisted of three other men. Fire-drives or surrounds required more people. These techniques, however, disappeared over time, and there is little evidence to suggest that the Creeks engaged in frequent communal drives. Instead, stalking became the technique of choice, a development that favored small parties.[5]

Its size notwithstanding, Handsome Fellow's son's party was atypical because it included only men. Creek women frequently accompanied hunting parties, performing a variety of tasks ranging from collecting firewood and wild plants to butchering and cooking. Of equal importance, women used their months in the woods to begin dressing the hunters' deerskins. Thus, David Taitt's 1777 report that "some young men and women belonging to the Oakfuske . . . were Carried off this winter from the north side of the Cherokee River" refers to a group closer to the Creek norm. A 1736 drawing by Philip Georg Friedrich von Reck shows a fairly typical hunting camp scene (Figure 3). Von Reck depicts two men and two women under a bark-and-pole lean-to; one of the men rests, while the other talks to one of the women, who scrapes a deerskin; two other skins are hung up to dry; the second woman stands near a kettle suspended over a fire. Even this small party, then, succeeded in procuring and processing deerskins, and in providing its people with food and shelter. Moreover, the presence of several manufactured items (a gun and two kettles) suggests the success of past hunts. Given that the men who robbed the Okfuskee party took "away their Skins and every other Article," these Okfuskees were successful hunters as well. Handsome Fellow's son alone lost "all his Skins, blankets, &c," a loss which a British trader felt could be partially ameliorated by a gift worth between twenty and thirty pounds of deerskin.[6]

Finding prosperous Creek models would have been easy for von Reck since the Creeks were the most proficient procurers of deerskins in the eighteenth-century Southeast. It was likewise no surprise that Euro-Americans attacking an Okfuskee hunting camp stumbled upon a well-stocked party since Okfuskees held their own as hunters. One Okfuskee village took in over 3,000 pounds of deerskins during the winter of 1759–1760, and between November 1762 and May 1765, the Macartan & Campbell company credited its Okfuskee store with 12,394 pounds of "dressed" and 4,932 pounds of "raw" deerskins, in addition to 466 pounds of beaver pelts.[7] The Okfuskees and their Creek neighbors could not, however, afford to take the supply of deerskins for granted. Their constant efforts to maintain or expand production led to changes in hunting strategies, changes which had a significant impact on the Okfuskees' lives and relations with neighbors. The times of year that Handsome Fellow and his son were in the woods point to one such shift; the places where they hunted suggest another.

Handsome Fellow's son had, by mid-October 1771, traveled over 200 miles from Okfuskee and hunted long enough to acquire at least some deerskins. This itinerary suggests he left Okfuskee in September, significantly earlier than was common for previous generations of hunters. In 1736, a Lower Creek headman noted that the prior year's "Winter Hunt" began in November. By September 1749, however, a large party of Upper Creeks led by Red Coat King of Okfuskee was eager to leave Charleston so that they could begin hunting as "they commonly did in October." Throughout the 1750s, Creeks began their winter hunt in October; thus,

3. Philip von Reck, "An Indian Camp." Reprinted courtesy of the Royal Library, Denmark.

in 1756, a British agent suggested traders leave Creek country by October 25 since, by then, "the Indians will be all gone out to their Hunts." In fact, though, by the late 1750s and early 1760s, many Creeks left their towns well before late October. For example, on August 8, 1760, Gun Merchant of Okchai noted that "hunting Time draws near" and, in an accompanying talk, Tomathla-Hago of Okfuskee urged Georgia's governor to send the necessary supplies "as soon as possible." Their urgency suggests that when Cujesse Mico of Okfuskee remarked on August 23, 1774, that "the Hunting Season [is] near at Hand," it was not simply a rhetorical flourish.[8] As the experiences of Handsome Fellow's son demonstrate, the Okfuskees and their Creek neighbors now left very little time between the harvest and the winter hunt.

By the 1760s, in fact, the Creeks' winter hunt not only started earlier but ended later. Charlesworth Glover wrote from Okfuskee that, by mid-January 1728, "The Indians begins to Drop in from their hunts," although two Okfuskees were among the headmen who told him they could not assemble the Upper Creek leaders for a meeting until February 7. Few important meetings would ever again take place so early in the year, and, over the next four decades, the date of return from the winter hunt both fluctuated wildly and grew steadily later. The agent who suggested in 1756 that traders leave the nation after October 25 noted at the same time that they need not return before February 25; a year later, a trader began his summary of February by noting "Very few Indians come in from their Hunts." On February 22, 1764, Governor James Wright informed John Stuart that an embargo on the Creeks' trade was possible, "But the [Creek] People are not yet returned from their Hunt, they will not all be in 'till the Middle or End of next Month;" and in 1766, West Florida's governor suggested attacking the Creeks in March, in part because, at that time, "the Indians are dispersed a Hunting."[9] In fact, some Creeks continued hunting into April, as Governor Henry Ellis discovered when, during a spring 1757 tour of Georgia, he encountered "many parties of Indians that were hunting"; three years later, the Upper Creeks' "young men" had not returned from their hunts as of April 25. Handsome Fellow's hunting accident in mid-March 1754 represented, therefore, part of a trend toward a redefinition of the winter hunt. He himself noted on April 4, 1763, that "a great many of their People are now below," that is, hunting in or around the Georgia backcountry.[10]

In fact, the winter hunt expanded to such a degree that it merged with the summer hunt, traditionally both a shorter and a less important undertaking than its cold-weather counterpart. Late March and early April marked the beginning of planting season in Creek country, and in May the smaller cornfields needed weeding and the larger ones were planted. These agricultural chores involved the town's women and men, and Creeks expected hunters to return home in time to participate. Only upon finishing would some of the townspeople resume their hunting; Creek men rarely left town "till they have helped the women to plant a sufficient plenty of provisions," a trend that continued, to some extent, into the 1770s. For example, a Lower Creek told Taitt on May 25, 1772, "that they were now planting their corn and as soon as that was over they would go and hunt to pay their debts."[11] By the 1750s, however, Okfuskees and their neighbors might remain in the woods through April. Their activities merged with those of their kinsmen who left town after finishing their agricultural chores. The result was an extended hunting season, with some Okfuskees in the woods from late spring through mid-July, when the hunters returned to town for the Busk. It was not a surprise, therefore, that on August 20, 1759, an Okfuskee spoke of returning from hunting at "the beginning of the last Moon"; nor was it shocking to find "an Oakfusky Fellow" beginning a July 19, 1778, report on recent events with "I was a hunting." In fact, the violence visited on Handsome Fellow's son and his companions in 1771 quite possibly had its roots in a deadly August 1770 encounter between "some Hunting Indians" from Okfuskee and a group of backcountry colonists. And, in a sign that hunting was becoming a year-round occupation, the headmen who attempted to defuse the resulting dispute noted that nothing could be resolved "till they return from their Hunt, which may not be till March."[12]

As one would expect, the longer hunting seasons adopted by the Okfuskees and their Creek neighbors produced a steadily rising number of deerskins. One scholar's "very conservative estimate" places production per Creek hunter at 100 pounds of deerskin (approximately fifty deer) per year in the 1760s. This level of hunting outpaced the deer's ability to reproduce. By the late 1750s, Creeks commonly complained about the scarcity of deer; and Creek efforts to gain access to new and more productive hunting territory stretched back at least into the 1740s.[13] The incidents involving Handsome Fellow and his son demonstrate that the Okfuskees, like their Creek neighbors, sought to maintain or increase their production of deerskins through the expansion of their hunting grounds. In the Okfuskees' case, the townspeople looked both north and east for opportunities, an approach entirely in keeping with their position on the Upper Creeks' northeastern frontier.

When Handsome Fellow shot a townsman in March 1754, he probably did so in the area north of Okfuskee, between the Upper Creeks and the Cherokees. The headman spent part of that winter on a diplomatic mission to the Cherokees, and the Okfuskees and their immediate neighbors in Upper Creek country traditionally hunted in these northern forests. Okfuskees, in fact, "built a corn house"—which became a village—forty miles north of Okfuskee "for the convenience of their hunters," and the "pretty good and direct" path Handsome Fellow most likely followed to "Cherokee country . . . winds down the mountains to this" village.[14]

Handsome Fellow's errand, and the Okfuskees' continuing efforts to secure a Creek–Cherokee peace, were driven in part by the townspeople's desire for the increased access to northern hunting grounds that would accompany peace. Creek–Cherokee relations, in fact, were intertwined with hunting-related issues. During the 1749 peace effort, the Cherokees suggested, in response to letters from Okfuskee and Coosa, that the Creeks hunt in the southern part of the area, while they hunted in the north. At the same time, Cherokee "beloved women" from the town of Tellico sent "some White Beads to the King of the Oakfuskees," telling him that "they think of time to come they may be out in the Woods when they think they be in no more danger." Two years later, violence arising from the murder of some Okfuskees by the Cherokees led a trader to speculate that the Upper Creeks would be driven out of their hunting grounds; and in the early spring of 1752, the Cherokees sent "some of our Men on this [north] side [of] the Oakfuskees where they killed 3 Men." By the spring of 1753, Handsome Fellow was eager to meet the Cherokees in Charleston. When they failed to arrive, he told Glen that, as an inhabitant of a "frontier Town," he was "willing to go out to hunt for Skins, but we do not know how Matters are at Home"; he evidently feared either that his town would be attacked while he hunted or that he would be set upon in the woods if the situation at home had deteriorated. The summer and fall of 1753, though, saw a flurry of diplomatic activity centered on Okfuskee, and by the winter of 1753–1754, the Upper Creeks and Cherokees "met in the hunting Ground, eat, drank, and smoaked together."[15]

Both peoples responded eagerly to the opportunity to hunt in safety. In the same April 1754 letter in which he reported Handsome Fellow's hunting accident, McIntosh noted that "We have had good Hunts in the Upper Creek Nation"; and in July of that year, a Cherokee trader wrote that "Companies of the Creeks have been in this Nation this summer." By all accounts, Creeks and Cherokees hunted together amicably, with Creek hunters feeling secure enough to bring women and children along. The area to the north of Okfuskee remained an important hunting ground for the Upper Creeks. Reports from 1761 and 1777 show that Okfuskees themselves continued to hunt there. Moreover, the Okfuskee village of Toohtocaugee—the "corn house" located forty miles north of town—was home to enough people by the time of the American Revolution to merit, in the opinion of Okfuskee's White Lieutenant, its own shipment of trade goods. Twenty miles further north, the Okfuskee village of Auchenauulgau was, by the 1790s, "the farthest north of all the Creeks."[16]

Of course, since both the Cherokees and the Creeks frequented the northern woods, they placed great pressure on the deer herds. In the winter of 1754–1755, the Cherokees "made very poor Hunts," possibly due to the influx of Creeks following the peace settlement; by 1772, Stuart reported that the scarcity of deer was a serious problem in Cherokee country. The Creeks, too, worried about the northern deer herds. In 1766, a trader noted that "the Creeks . . . has made poor Hunts." The year before, Mortar of Okchai told the British that his people now hunted deep into the north: "We had formerly good Success in hunting but we are now obliged to Cross the Cherokee River for Game."[17] The 1777 Okfuskee party that crossed the same river had a great deal of company as they pushed the bounds of Creek hunting grounds farther and farther north.

Handsome Fellow's hunting accident, then, points us toward a sustained effort by the Okfuskees and their Creek neighbors to gain valuable hunting grounds to the north. At the same time, though, expansion in this direction meant that the Creeks and Cherokees competed for deerskins and that hunting success depended on a diplomatic relationship that occasionally broke down. In 1758, for example, a trader reported, "there happened to be some of the Upper Creeks of the Oakfuskee Town in the Cherokees who were beat and abused by the latter at a Rum frolick, the Creeks resented this treatment, next day took their departure, killd two Cherokees and scalpd them." The 1771 incident involving Handsome Fellow's son allows us to see how Okfuskees dealt with uncertainties in the north: they began hunting in the east, near the British settlements. In doing so, Okfuskees no doubt sought to take advantage of a 1754 peace treaty between the Lower Creeks and the Cherokees requiring the latter to relinquish claims to hunting grounds near Augusta.[18]

The Okfuskees, to be sure, were familiar with the British colonies from their diplomatic initiatives. The Lower Creeks, however, had been the dominant Native presence in the colonial backcountry for generations; as late as 1763, they refused to allow the Upper Creeks to "speak a word" at an Augusta conference. Despite Red Coat King's 1753 reference to meeting Indians "at Augusta on our own Ground," there is little evidence that Okfuskees considered exploiting the economic potential of the area near the British settlements.[19] They changed their minds in the 1750s. In the fall of 1756, Handsome Fellow took the lead, albeit reluctantly, in defusing a crisis that arose out of Creek anger over an illegal Euro-American settlement on the Ogeechee River, west of Augusta. That summer, a trader wrote from Okfuskee that "Indians all over the Nation are in great confusions," in part due to the Ogeechee settlement. Several Upper Creek headmen sent a talk warning of the dangers of encroaching on "our Hunting Ground," but, when violence did erupt, Handsome Fellow made it clear that anger about the Ogeechee situation was strongest among the Lower Creeks. He noted, however, that, on his way home, "I shall take time . . . in order that I may hunt and get Skins," and he asked for supplies.[20] The headman's plans represent the first unambiguous example of Okfuskees hunting in the area between Creek country and the British backcountry.

By the late 1750s and the early 1760s, references to Okfuskees hunting in the east became more frequent. When Superintendent Edmond Atkin left Upper Creek country and headed for Augusta in December 1759, he was accompanied by "the Ockfusky Captain & a few other Indians . . . under the Notion of hunting for me on the path." Several months later, the ministers of Georgia's Salzburger community noted, "We do not know what it means that so many Creek Indians, who have always been our friends up until now, have come down from their villages with their wives and children." Some of the Creeks in the area that winter were Okfuskees. On February 18, 1760, "a Half-Breed, who is a Leader and Head Warrior of three Squares of the Oakfuskees, with another Warrior, and their Attendants" arrived at Fort Augusta; Atkin noted that "he came with a hunting Party to trade," possibly from the Oconee River area, and that "several more, hunting Creek Parties [were] coming to Augusta." Okfuskees were also among the Creeks who, in early 1761, "continually" came "in from their hunts . . . to trade at the stores about Augusta"; and, in 1762, the Okfuskee

Captain and Handsome Fellow accompanied Gun Merchant of Okchai when he cautioned Georgia's governor against allowing their people to frequent the colonies. The value of their warning became clear in 1763 when, as hundreds of Creeks hunted near Augusta, a party of Upper and Lower Creek renegades, including one Okfuskee, killed fourteen South Carolina colonists. Seven years later, Okfuskees took part in "a Fray" near the Oconee River between some of their hunters "and a party of Back Settlers who were in Search of Horses which they supposed to have been stol'n, the later were the aggressors & having the superiority beat some Indians who they met belonging to the Town of Oakfuskee[;] some of their Companions coming to the assestance in Revenge killed two of the white people." The deaths, at a "hunting Camp of Oakfuskee Indians," may have contributed to the attack on Handsome Fellow's son's hunting party the next year. In any event, both confrontations owed something to the presence of Okfuskee hunters in an area where Okfuskees had not traditionally sought game.[21]

In fact, the region between Okfuskee and the eastern colonies became important enough to the Okfuskees that many relocated to new villages in the east. The trader James Adair noted this migration, writing that "since the year 1764" the Creeks "have settled several towns, seventy miles eastward from Okwhuske, on the Chatahooche river, near to the old trading path." Adair does not say that Okfuskees themselves moved, but Okfuskee already had a village where the path crossed the Chattahoochee. Moreover, the Creeks viewed the settlements as a part of Okfuskee, and Okfuskee's headmen were involved with the new villages. By 1775, William Bartram recorded the names of five Okfuskee settlements on the Chattahoochee. And, not surprisingly given their location, the people of these villages quickly proved to be committed hunters. The Okfuskee hunting party involved in the 1770 "Fray" on the Oconee most likely lived in these new villages. By 1767, four British deerskin traders had "settled" on the northern reaches of the Chattahoochee, and at least three of these men found it worth their while to frequent the Okfuskees' eastern villages into the 1770s.[22] Moving to the eastern hunting grounds obviously had its advantages.

As the hunting grounds near Georgia and South Carolina became more important for the Okfuskees, the town's headmen emerged as leaders in the Creek effort to resist British encroachment in the area. In 1756, Handsome Fellow's advocacy of Creek land claims had been lukewarm at best. In 1763, however, he stated that "his Talk is . . . that white People were to drink upon one Side of Savannah River, and red people on the other," but "he sees the Virginia People settled upon a great Part of their Lands which they never granted," and "he therefore desires all these stragling People may be ordered off." Handsome Fellow and Fog (from the Okfuskee village of Sugatspoges) were present in 1764 when Mortar warned the British against settling between Mobile and Creek country, "as they are determined to keep free possession of all that and other Lands they have enjoyed for many Years." The Okfuskees, however, were less concerned with Gulf Coast lands. Thus, when the "Oakfuskie King" spoke in 1767, he lamented losses in the East: "I remember Well to have heard my forefathers say that Savannah River was esteemed the Boundary between the White people and us, that however is forgot and new Boundaries are made."[23]

As British pressure for land cessions mounted in the late 1760s and early 1770s, Okfuskee resistance became more pronounced. One sign of the townspeople's discomfort with these threats to their new eastern hunting grounds surfaces in the declining frequency with which Okfuskees made diplomatic trips to Georgia and South Carolina. Between 1755 and 1764, there was only one year (1758) in which Okfuskees failed to visit the eastern colonies; from 1765 to 1774, however, Okfuskee diplomats came down only in 1767 and 1774.[24] Predictably, the period when Okfuskee headmen absented themselves from the colonies coincided with their efforts to prevent the loss of eastern lands. In 1772, for example, David Taitt called a meeting in Okchai to deliver a message about a proposed land cession. The assembled Upper Creek headmen were prevented from answering "by Stochlitca [White Lieutenant of Okfuskee] who was drunk . . . he spoke much against giving Lands on any Account"; Handsome Fellow was likewise accused by Taitt of exhibiting "Villanous Behavior towards us."[25]

A letter Taitt wrote prior to the Okchai meeting helps explain the headmen's anger. He noted that the Lower Creeks refused to cede lands on the Oconee River "as they say that it is the Only Hunting Ground which they have left . . . both the upper Creeks & they Hunt about that River & Complain very much of the Virginia People hunting there and destroying their deer." John Stuart agreed with his deputy, writing that the Creeks "lay claim to Said Lands . . . as their most valuable hunting Grounds" and "are beyond measure Jealous. [T]he most sensible amongst them, are the most Strenuous opposers of such a Cession." When the proposed cession went through in 1773, some Okfuskees turned their anger on the "Virginians."

The crisis of 1774, however, demonstrated the futility of violence, and Okfuskees responded by reemphasizing diplomatic visits, arriving in the colonies at least once a year between 1774 and 1778. No longer given to drunken threats, Stochlitca of Okfuskee settled for reminding the Americans "that Ogeechee [River] is the Line" between Georgia and Creek territory, that the Creeks "have been very good to the white People and have been giving them [many?] lands," and that the eastern territory was important to his people. They required, he said, a "quantity of Land to hunt on for the support of our Women and Children," a quantity that, for Okfuskees, had come to include the area between their town and the eastern colonies.[26]

Okfuskees and the Backcountry

The concerns expressed by Okfuskee headmen during the 1760s and 1770s were, of course, intimately linked to the changing geopolitical situation. The departure of the French and the emergence of a newly assertive British Empire contributed to the fears reflected in the rhetoric adopted by the Okfuskees and their Creek neighbors. Geopolitical shifts were not, however, solely responsible for the contentiousness that characterized Creek–British relations in the generation preceding the American Revolution. Many problems can be traced, instead, to the economic maturation of both the Creek nation and the southern British colonies. The changes in Okfuskee's hunting patterns—including a longer hunting season and a greater utilization of eastern hunting grounds—were matched by equally significant developments in the colonies—including a growth in commercial, slave-based agriculture, a steadily rising Euro-American backcountry population, and a deemphasis of the deerskin trade.[27] The new conditions were reflected in the Okfuskees' appearance in and around the British backcountry and in the reactions they encountered there.

By the late 1750s, Creeks and Euro-Americans had met each other in the backcountry for several generations, often with mutually satisfying results. The pattern of relations that developed resembles closely the one Daniel Usner attributes to the eighteenth-century Lower Mississippi Valley, a pattern he labels the "frontier exchange economy." For Usner, frontiers were not boundaries but rather regional "networks of cross-cultural interaction through which native and colonial groups circulated goods and services." The frontier exchange economy depended upon "face-to-face marketing" between people with small-scale surpluses. In this system, productive activities were rarely culturally specific, and attempts by colonial officials and merchants to regulate the area's inhabitants generally did not succeed.[28] A similar system existed for several generations in the frontier region to the east of Okfuskee, but while some Creeks participated regularly, the Okfuskees played only a minor role in the backcountry trade prior to the 1750s. During that decade, however, Okfuskee's eastern political orientation began to be matched by an eastern economic focus, and Okfuskees began to appear in the British backcountry with some frequency.

Georgia and South Carolina's developmental trajectory, however, differed from the one Usner describes in the Lower Mississippi Valley.[29] Within the southern British backcountry by the late 1750s and early 1760s, the social space necessary for informal, face-to-face exchange was increasingly being circumscribed from above and eroded from below. In other words, the Okfuskees arrived in the backcountry just as the system of intercultural exchange that had prevailed for several generations began to fall apart. Frontier exchange, it must be noted, did not suddenly disappear; it continued to be a part of backcountry life, even as the region's peoples dealt with the implications of the Seven Years' War and the crises that led to the American Revolution. Increasingly, however, there was less room (both socially and spatially) for cross-cultural encounters, and, even where there was space, tempers were often so frayed that the opportunity was not matched by the inclination. The old system of interaction could absorb peacefully neither the new people nor the new demands those people made upon the area. Okfuskee hunters who sought more deerskins did not pose a problem by themselves, but once combined with large numbers of Euro-Americans—either those whose livelihood resembled the Native mixture of agriculture and forest-based pursuits or others who depended on controlling an unfree African-American labor force—the situation became increasingly volatile. And, ironically, the continued incidence of frontier exchange exacerbated the situation. People intent on maintaining old patterns of interaction frequently encountered others with no such desire; Okfuskees could be found in both camps, some working to maintain and others to subvert frontier exchange. For the individuals involved, results ranged from the frustrating to the fatal; for the region as a whole—and certainly for the Okfuskees—tension became the order of the day. In order to understand this tension and its effects on Okfuskee, we must first examine the context from which it emerged—the Creek–British version of the frontier exchange economy.

Prior to circa 1750

By the time Okfuskee hunting parties began to appear in and around the British backcountry in the late 1750s, the Okfuskees were quite familiar with their eastern neighbors. Their headmen came to Charleston a number of times in the 1720s and 1730s, and the visits became frequent by the 1740s. The trips occasionally included a significant number of Okfuskees. As early as 1731, South Carolina's leaders expressed dismay at the size of Dog King's party, apparently to no effect since Fanni Mico brought a retinue of eight townsmen to Charleston in 1749; seventeen more arrived four years later. Okfuskee also appears on the 1732 list of Creek towns whose leaders promised "not to suffer any of the People of our said Towns to come into the Limits of the English Settlements, without Leave from the English Governor or his beloved Man," a promise which, judging by the number of times the British requested it be repeated over the years, the Creeks honored in the breach.[30] That said, however, Okfuskees were not intimately involved in the economic activities of the British colonies prior to the 1750s, except as producers of deerskins and consumers of manufactured goods. As Usner demonstrates, the large, relatively distant Indian nations tended to have relations of this sort with their Euro-American neighbors. Thus John Brownfield, a Savannah merchant, distinguished between the "considerable Nations," such as the Cherokees and Creeks, and "a near Nation called the Utchees."[31]

Brownfield's distinction can only take us so far, however. Lower Creeks frequently visited the British backcountry, especially after the founding of Georgia in 1733, and a number of Lower Creeks lived in small towns near the Savannah River. In fact, the Yuchis, mentioned by Brownfield as a "near nation" in 1736, had once been Lower Creeks, and would be again. Other Lower Creeks oscillated back and forth between nation and colony; these peripatetic people included those characterized by a South Carolina official as "the Stragling Creeks, that live in those lower Parts [of the colony] & Seldom go up to their Nation." Lower Creeks were not the only Indians in the area, of course. Several smaller Native groups lived in or near the British colonies, and enslaved Indians from a number of nations were a significant presence in the region. As late as 1761, a former South Carolina governor claimed that 66 percent of the colony's population consisted of "Indian subjects," a figure which encompassed the Native "Nations" living "on the western side of this Province."[32] Many of these Indian peoples—including a significant number of Lower Creeks—participated in day-to-day economic activities in the colonies.

The diverse nature of their activities seemingly defies categorization, and the complexities of cross-cultural interaction on a daily basis produced a number of contradictions. Creeks captured and sold Natives and Africans, pursued runaway slaves, and received rich rewards for both chores; they also facilitated the escape of enslaved African and Native Americans. Creeks rounded up stray livestock and returned them to their owners; Creeks also stole horses and shot cattle. Creeks sold food, especially venison; Creeks also appropriated produce, and frequently demanded (and received) provisions from public officials and private citizens. Creeks hosted colonists, easing their journeys and providing neighborly cheer; Creeks also expected to be treated with the appropriate degree of hospitality when they came to call. Creeks helped sick Euro-Americans, while materially hastening the deaths of others. Creeks carried messages, guided parties, and served as river pilots; Creeks also led parties into swamps. Creeks traded deerskins for dry goods and metalware; Creeks also demanded manufactured items as gifts, and stole them in need and in anger. Creeks aided the British against their enemies, thereby shielding the colonies and allowing for growth and diversification; Creeks also terrified the colonists and brought their routines to a crashing halt simply by showing up unexpectedly.

For those involved, the peculiar connections produced by the frontier exchange economy were a mixed blessing. Colonists who welcomed Creek contributions when a farmstead or community was being established lived near others who believed frontier exchange inhibited the creation of an orderly, prosperous society. Even after personal economic stability was assured, a number of colonists continued to embrace opportunities for cross-cultural trade, but many others—including some who had once participated in frontier exchange—became more and more convinced that a Creek presence retarded individual advancement and undermined social order. As one minister put it, "The more friendly we are the more we give in and trade with them . . . the more we will have them around our necks and suffer trouble." Colonial officials faced a similar dilemma. While never favoring Creek–colonist contact, they enacted laws that, for much of the early eighteenth century, permitted a wide array of interactions between the two peoples, and some government policies actually served to increase the importance of such relationships.[33] By the 1750s, however, strategies that encouraged Indians to remain in the colonies were being rethought. The Creeks' frequent visits became one of the officials' greatest worries, a development that meshed with their constituents' growing intolerance for both Natives and frontier exchange.

The Creeks themselves also struggled with the contradictions in their relationship with the colonists. On the one hand, Creeks living in the back-country welcomed the economic opportunities that associations with African Americans and Euro-Americans brought; and Creeks from the nation appreciated the chance to visit the colonies while hunting to pick up provisions and acquire manufactured goods at discount prices. Gifts that flowed from Creek–British diplomatic and military efforts were also most welcome, as were the sociopolitical benefits which accrued to those Creeks upon whom the British relied. On the other hand, Euro-Americans increasingly treated Creeks who lived in the settlements as trespassers, and traditional methods of production became difficult or impossible to sustain in the face of the colonists' own traditions. The clashing of systems reinforced Creek anger over the colonists' failure to treat Creeks, both neighbors and visitors, properly. As the Creek way of life became increasingly untenable in the backcountry, ties to their Euro-American neighbors frayed. By the 1750s, few Creeks lived amidst the British towns and farmsteads, and while many Creeks still visited, they expected less from (and offered less to) the colonists.[34]

Circa 1750–1775

Okfuskees who began hunting near the British settlements in the 1750s were thus moving into an area that was anything but settled. Their arrival did nothing to calm things down. A frontier exchange economy of sorts continued to exist into the Revolutionary era, bringing Creeks and colonists together in a variety of familiar ways. The Okfuskees, with their long history of peaceful and productive ties to the British, were ideally suited to participate in this cross-cultural network. The area's system of frontier exchange, however, reeled from crisis to crisis as Creek–colonist contact was increasingly characterized by a mix of aggression and accommodation, competition and cooperation. In following such a course, the region's peoples built on the experiences of the previous generation, while bringing their own concerns and interests into play. The Okfuskees who traveled to the back-country did the same. For people from this particular Creek community, however, the dictates of the past and the demands of the present were especially inharmonious. Fanni Mico's legacy could withstand only so many incidents of theft and murder; the ideal of a shared fire could not long coexist with the exchange of gunfire. The Okfuskees' backcountry activities after midcentury attest to the frontier exchange economy's en-during relevance and to its very real limits.

When Cujesse Mico led his party of Okfuskees to Augusta, Taitt was shocked that "They came within One hundred Yards of this House before they were observed by any Person and what is very extraordinary Travelled from Occonee to this Place without seeing or being seen by any White Person." Whatever else the ability to pass undetected through thirty-plus miles of settlements tells us, it demonstrates that the Okfuskees were, by 1774, familiar with the area. They knew where to go so colonists would not find them, suggesting, of course, that they knew where to find colonists if they wished to do so. Creeks had possessed such knowledge for years, and British officials had fretted about it for at least as long. The party that worried Taitt, however, came from a town that sent relatively few of its people to the colonies before the 1750s. Moreover, the Okfuskees traveled with ease through settlements of an extremely recent vintage. In other words, a new segment of Creek society had acquired an old level of fa-miliarity with the newly arrived Euro-Americans. And, as in the years be-fore midcentury, the familiarity depended upon a multifaceted system in which people from different social groups exchanged goods and services on an informal basis. Thus, Taitt believed that an ulterior motive lay behind the Okfuskees' trip—"to try to get a clandestine Trade, as they have some Skins at Occonee." His suspicions were certainly understandable. The Okfuskees, after all, elected to deliver the talk at a house where their townsmen had traded in the past, and they concluded by saying "we in the Upper Towns were for Peace and hope to have a Supply of Goods."[35]

Taitt's concerns notwithstanding, Cujesse Mico's mission was primarily diplomatic, but such an agenda did not rule out trading on the side. In fact, informal exchange had become, by this time, an accepted part of a trip to the colonies. Thus, a party of Creeks who visited Georgia's governor in 1758 "had some Skins and requested it as a favour that they might be

Permitted to dispose of them in Town." The only unusual thing about the incident was that they bothered to ask. A year earlier, a British agent, writing from one of Okfuskee's neighboring towns, noted that the "Creeks . . . frequently go down to trade at the Stores in Augusta"; five years before, a trader mentioned "12 Oakfusskees People going down to Georgia upon the Path." Certainly the "two Creek Indians [who] arrived at Mr. Trewin's [in Augusta] from the Oakfuskees, to trade" in 1761 expected, correctly as it turned out, that they could exchange their skins for British goods. A little more than a year earlier, another "Ockfusky Party" arrived, uninvited, "to trade" in Augusta. Okfuskees might disagree, as they did in 1767,[36] over whether such exchanges were beneficial, but they could not deny that their people traded in and around the colonies. Some transactions took place in licensed trading houses such as the one managed by Trevin, but unlicensed traders were common in the backcountry and Okfuskees certainly traded with them. Thus, Georgia's governor responded to the incident involving Handsome Fellow's son by writing of the need to find "some Means . . . to keep stragling Parties of them, from having so much Intercourse and traf-icking with the white People in the Settlements"; despite a "Law subjecting such Persons to a heavy Penalty," some "back Settlers traffick with these People and encourage them to come amongst them." Among these "back Settlers" were "Sanders and Whitefield," who, by 1769, operated a "Trading House" on the boundary line between Creek country and Georgia. George Whitefield was at the time also a partner of the Okfuskee trader Robert Rae, and he himself had enduring ties to the community, ties which most likely resulted in Okfuskees visiting his store. No wonder, therefore, that Handsome Fellow noted, "We have no Objection to the Settlement of Au-gusta Which is usefull for the Trade of our Nation."[37]

Okfuskees found trade in the backcountry, both legal and illegal, attrac-tive for a number of reasons. In the first place, they often received better prices—what a spokesman for a party that included Okfuskees referred to as "the Advantage of Trading upon Easy Terms"—there than in the nation, both because merchants avoided transportation costs and because the system of weighing skins in the colonies could work to the sellers' advan-tage. Moreover, Okfuskees hunting in the area appreciated the opportunity to trade some skins immediately, rather than hauling them back to town. Several of the Okfuskee hunting parties cited above appear in the records only because they sought to take advantage of Augusta's markets. Some of these hunters may have traded with Macartan & Campbell, a firm with stores in Okfuskee and Augusta; the latter "Bought" 1,696 pounds of deerskins "of the Indians" in 1763. In addition, Okfuskees, like other Creek hunters, recognized that British towns offered a chance to acquire provisions and to get equipment (especially guns) repaired. The Creeks' ability to resupply while in the colonies may, in fact, have contributed to their willingness to lengthen their hunting season. Finally, Creeks in debt to traders back home were often eager to deal with someone who would not demand all or part of their skins as payment for an outstanding loan. Except in the case of a few prominent headmen, Macartan & Campbell's Augusta employees would not know if the Okfuskee at their store already owed the company's Okfuskee outlet the skins he now offered to trade, and the area's illegal storekeepers had neither the incentive nor the ability to inquire into an Okfuskee's credit history.[38]

Trading and hunting were not, however, the only profitable activities which drew Okfuskees to the colonies. A number of men found employment as guards for packhorse trains from Creek country to Augusta. For example, eleven Okfuskees arrived in Augusta "as an escort to some packhorses laden with leather" in May 1760, and Mad Turkey "Escorted some Traders with their Loaded horses to Augusta" before he was killed in 1774. Escorts expected to be paid, as an Okchai made clear when he complained about Upper Creeks who "go [as] Guards to the Pack Horses that get nothing for their Trouble which makes the Young People indifferent of going down." Two Okfuskee headmen witnessed this talk, and in 1774 several Okfuskees "even used some threatenings in case" the trader they were escorting "should not fulfill his agreement with them and let them have the presents he had promised."[39] Other Okfuskee men carried messages to and from Creek country, an activity which they were performing by 1749 and which they continued to engage in through the American Revolution.[40] From September 1755 to December 1756, for example, Handsome Fellow: delivered Governor Glen's letter to the Creeks; brought an Upper Creek "Letter" to Glen; headed toward Creek country with Glen's response; picked up, in the headman's words, another "Letter from the beloved Men at Augusta to the Nation," while simultaneously accepting responsibility for escorting Thomas Ross, the "Old Man sent up with me"; arrived in Savannah with a new Creek talk; and returned to Creek country after promising that "he would represent [the position of Georgia's governor] to his Nation accordingly."[41] Other Okfuskees generally accompanied him on his journeys, and these trips were almost always paying propositions for all concerned.

The payments received were often described as "presents," a significant distinction (especially for the Natives involved), but one that should not obscure the role such items played in the Okfuskees' economic lives.[42] Presents were, in fact, very much a facet of the frontier exchange economy, and opportunities to obtain them—and the social, political, and economic advantages they conferred—frequently drew Okfuskees to the back-country. In 1764, for example, Handsome Fellow, referring to a party of over a dozen Okfuskees, said "that they were Inform'd lately by some of the Traders: that there were Presents left here [Augusta] to be Delivered them when they came down for them." Will's Friend, a member of this group, received another sort of gift while in Augusta: Macartan & Campbell's Augusta store "Trusted" him with almost £50 worth of "Sundrys."[43] Eight years before, at the end of Handsome Fellow's extended tour of duty as a messenger, the Okfuskee "made a pretty large demand of Presents" while in Savannah. These included "Rum and Wine to be given to some other Head Men in the Nation," but he also "named Sundry things that he and his People wanted." In the end, his party received sixty-nine yards of cloth, twelve looking glasses, almost a pound of vermillion, ten hatchets, two kettles, three pots, ten guns, fifty pounds of both gunpowder and bullets, and four saddles. In addition, Handsome Fellow received "a fine Suit of Clothes"—most likely including a coat of the "1st Sort," a "Laced" waistcoat, and a hat of the "2d Sort"—and the party's other headman was given a coat of the "2d Sort." All told, the twelve party members received goods worth approximately 600 pounds of dressed deerskins, a figure that does not include the headmen's apparel, which generally could not be purchased. Less than three months earlier, a party led by the Okfuskee Captain and Handsome Fellow received a similar assortment of goods from South Carolina's governor.[44]

Given this bounty, it was entirely understandable that Okfuskees were not shy about either asking for gifts or traveling to the colonies. British complaints about the expenses associated with feeding and giving gifts to the visitors rarely stopped them from coming down. Thus, a 1753 Creek party that included seventeen Okfuskees prompted South Carolina's governor to tell his council "that he had not Expected so great a Number in Town." A generation later, a 1778 party from Okfuskee intending "to settle matters with" John Stuart consisted of "upwards of two hundred men & women," far more than the British expected. As Taitt remarked, however, "it is impossible to Prevent these followers, when their Chiefs go they will accompany them." Colonial officials, for their part, frequently reinforced the Okfuskees' behavior, both by promising "a Supply" of "Provision" before being asked and by planning around presenting the townspeople with "large Presents." The 1753 party, for example, asked "that the following Addition of Presents may be made," leading the colony's council to order "that the Commissary General do furnish the said Creek Indians with the Goods they requested." All-in-all, then, Okfuskees were simply following standard practice when, in 1782, a party that included eleven men from the town sent word that "they expect that they will gett goods boath as presents and for them to have a treat." Their reluctant hosts, assuming their own accustomed role, began making plans to supply the visitors.[45]

The presence of large numbers of Okfuskees and their Creek neighbors in the Georgia and South Carolina backcountry, and the range of economic opportunities they found there, ought not, however, obscure the very real changes that had occurred in the area's frontier exchange economy. Even the Creeks' visits suggest that the economic system that predominated prior to 1750 was in trouble. In the first place, Creeks came to the colonies, but they no longer had towns there. Headmen such as Captain Aleck and St. Jago owned land "almost in the middle of our Settlements," but the Creek communities once based near the Savannah River had moved further west. In addition, more informal sorts of Creek–colonist exchange, such as the selling of small quantities of food, rarely appear in Georgia and South Carolina's records by the 1760s. True, the Telfairs of Georgia "Paid the Indian for a Turkey" in 1773, and Willaim Maine of South Carolina's "Indian Land" owned an "Indian pot" in 1760, but fewer and fewer of their neighbors dealt with Natives for such commonplace goods.[46]

Creek–colonist relationships were also more likely to be tinged with mistrust. Thus, the Creeks whom the British "handsomely rewarded" for "preserving the Lives of several people . . . who had fled & lost 'emselves in swamps" during a 1760 Cherokee scare were also suspected of looting abandoned houses. The next year, two Okfuskees arrived in Augusta to trade and then left "very early the next morning," a chain of events which an Augusta resident found ominous: "Their short stay, bringing no letters and purchasing so much cloth, occasions some suspicions." For their part, the Okfuskees found that too many of the colonists were simply, as Handsome Fellow's son put it, "bad white people." The most basic of transactions with them were problematic; even ostensibly friendly colonists were dangerous. After all, Mad Turkey was killed in 1774 when an Augusta resident "invited the Indian to drink with him"; that the murderer became a local hero and was rescued from jail by an armed mob certainly did nothing to improve the Okfuskees' image of their Euro-American neighbors. By 1777, in fact, Handsome Fellow believed it was necessary to remind these people of the basics of civility: "we expect you will use our people well among you."[47] Face-to-face interaction—the *sine qua non* of the frontier exchange economy—threatened to become a *casus belli*.

The changes in the frontier exchange economy can be traced to a number of factors. In the first place, competition between Creeks and colonists for resources increased markedly after the late 1750s. Georgia's African- and Euro-American population grew from 3,447 in 1753 to 33,000 in 1773. The Creeks' population also increased, although only from 12,000 in 1745 to 14,000 in 1775. Okfuskee, for its part, grew from 100 "Gun Men" in 1725 to 300 in 1764, making it the largest Upper Creek town. As the region's population swelled, its people were increasingly likely to be living in, or traveling to, the backcountry west of Augusta; Okfuskees—with their eastern villages and newfound interest in frontier exchange—contributed to the backcountry's population boom. This area itself was quickly being claimed by Georgia, which acquired over 5,500,000 acres of Indian land in three cessions between 1763 and 1773.[48] From the perspective of the Okfuskees and their Creek neighbors, more people were using less land, an explosive combination, not just for the Okfuskees but for all of the region's inhabitants.

The situation was exacerbated by the marked similarities in modes of production embraced by Creeks and backcountry colonists. Colonial officials, in fact, routinely lumped the two peoples together, as Georgia's governor did in 1761 when he referred to the colonists as "a kind of Vagrants who live like the Indians by Hunting, & Stealing." Stripped of their pejorative language, such statements suggest the type of overlap that bred problems when resources became scarce. In the first place, some colonists were skilled hunters. In 1759, the Lower Creeks complained about "a great many Virginia people settled . . . in our hunting Grounds, who have Guns that will kill Deer as far Distant as they can see them; those People live chiefly by Hunting, wandering all over the Woods destroying our Game, which is now become so scarce that we cannot kill sufficient to supply our Necessities." Creeks meeting colonists in the woods did not hesitate to seize their deerskins, and several parties of Euro-American hunters were killed. Moreover, colonists, like Creeks, often depended on forest products. So, for example, a merchant noted in 1751 that "Deer skins are paid to Merchants as Cash all seasons of the Year," while a colonist apologized to a merchant in 1768, writing that "I should have been down some Time ago but was disappointed I expected to have received some Beaver Fur for money is very hard to be got."[49]

The ownership of livestock represented another facet of the colonial economy with implications for both Creek–colonist relations and the continued productivity of the region. The Okfuskees and their Creek neighbors were quite familiar with European animals by the 1750s. Okfuskees going to the settlements frequently went mounted, as the documents relating to Handsome Fellow's travels in 1755 and 1756 attest. The settlers among whom they moved were, if anything, more dependent on livestock. A mutual reliance on domesticated animals did not, however, prove conducive to Creek–colonist mutuality. Creeks in the settlements frequently appropriated horses, with one headman noting that his people "make their Living by Stealing Horses from the White People." Settlers responded by stealing whatever Creek horses they could lay their hands on. As early as 1762, two Okfuskees attended a meeting of Upper Creek headmen at which a spokesman told the British that they "hope . . . that when our People go to your Countrey the white People will not trouble their Creatures." Continued theft bred frustration; continued frustration encouraged violence; continued violence justified more theft. This cycle ensnared several Okfuskee parties, including the one led by Handsome Fellow's son, which had the misfortune to steal horses from colonists already angry at "other Indians which had got some of their horses and had fired upon the white people sometime before."[50]

Creeks who stole horses also shot and, less frequently, stole cattle. They did so for a number of reasons. To begin with, Creeks felt entitled to provisions when on lands they had ceded to the British. Hunting livestock could also make a point, either of dissatisfaction with a particular colonist or policy, or of Creeks' continued rights to, and interest in, the ceded land. Moreover, Creeks saw cattle as a threat to their remaining hunting grounds. Stock straying over the boundary line posed a frequent problem, and Creeks killed cattle belonging to settlers who herded their animals onto Creek land. In doing so, Creeks felt they protected not only their rights but also their very survival. Mortar said as much in 1763 when, after discussing British encroachment, he linked grass, the food of the settlers' cattle, with his people's health and well-being: "we . . . love our Lands a great deal . . . the Wood is our Fire, and the Grass is our Bed, and our

Physic when we are sick." Eight years later, another Upper Creek headman again equated cattle with unwelcome environmental change, noting that the Creeks had received promises "that no more Cattle should be drove tho' our Nation but that the Path should be always kept Green and we hope it will remain so." The fact that several of Okfuskee's British traders were heavily involved in backcountry cattle ranching—and that at least one of them allowed his livestock to wander unsupervised—could not have made the townspeople happy. If, as the Okfuskee Captain asserted, "[t]he Earth we go upon is the same as our Bodies . . . the Woods is our covering & the Leaves serves us for Beds," then the herding practices of the traders and their ilk threatened to deprive Okfuskees of both health and comfort.[51]

The various forms of Creek–colonist competition—over land, deer, and livestock—should not obscure the competition that existed within both societies. These were not monolithic, homogeneous entities facing each other across an unbridgeable chasm. Instead, each society featured a variety of interests and loyalties, some of which led individuals and communities to look for opportunities in directions that were anathema to their neighbors. Moreover, in each system, traditional patterns of deference and leadership, and long-standing assumptions about the structure of society itself, were increasingly under assault.

The result, for Creeks and colonists, was a period characterized by disruption and discord, in which different visions and agendas were debated and enacted, challenged and reasserted. For the colonists, the problem surfaced most clearly in the mutual antipathy that existed between the backcountry settlers and the colonial elites on the coast and in government; but even within backcountry society significant divisions emerged over the proper socioeconomic model for the area.[52] In the case of the Okfuskees and their fellow Creeks, many young men distanced themselves from traditional avenues of trade and diplomacy, opting for associations and activities that were beyond the control of their towns' headmen.[53] And, frequently, those Okfuskees seeking freedom of one sort or another headed for the backcountry. As early as 1763, Handsome Fellow and the Okfuskee Captain were members of a party whose spokesman said "That he thought permitting their People to be in the Settlements amongst the white People was a great Evil, especially as those who come here are generally such as have left the Nation for Crimes, or at least to avoid Controul; that they themselves had tried means to prevent it but could not, and believed that if nobody was suffered to trade with them in the Settlements it might have a good Effect." A decade later, two Okfuskees blamed "White" traders in "the Woods" for encouraging "their Young People to Committ such Things as they do" and for making "them regardless of their Head men." By 1774, a Lower Creek headman compared one group of "Renegadoes" led by an Okfuskee to "the Virginians, who won't give Ear to Sense more than they."[54]

The fault lines in Euro-American and Creek society served both to make a continuation of a variant of the frontier exchange economy possible and to ensure that the system would never be far from collapse. On the one hand, the declining relevance of traditional forms and figures of authority, the absence of an effective institutional structure to enforce compliance, and the inability of either society to achieve consensus as to what "compliance" might mean—each of these factors guaranteed that, after midcentury, there would be colonists and Creeks willing to engage in a variety of mutually beneficial economic activities, no matter what their neighbors or leaders thought. Colonial officials found themselves reduced to scolding Creek headmen for allowing their people to venture into the colonies, while headmen resorted to reminding the officials of their promises to prevent Euro-Americans from trading with Creeks at illegal stores. On the other hand, the above factors, when combined with a rising level of Creek–colonist competition, meant not only that conflicts between the two peoples were inevitable but also that diplomacy would be ineffective and reconciliation would be, at best, temporary. For both Okfuskees and colonists, grievance piled on grievance, and one person's legitimate satisfaction became another's open wound. The result was a rising level of intolerance for the other. Animosity between settlers and Creeks reached alarming levels by the mid-1760s. The Okfuskees—whose leaders increasingly absented themselves from the colonies and whose fellow townsmen increasingly looked east for economic opportunity—found themselves in the thick of things, able neither to defuse the crisis nor to disengage from the backcountry.

For a time, in fact, Okfuskees must have felt overwhelmed as they faced wave after wave of bad news from the colonies. Again and again—August 1770, October 1771, December 1773, January 1774, March 1774, June 1774—Okfuskees killed or were killed in backcountry-related incidents.[55] The fallout triggered crises in Okfuskee itself. The "Uncle of the Man" killed in 1771 had to restrain the town's "Young People who at first Wanted to fall on the white people"; he succeeded only because he argued that his own family owed "the white people Satisfaction for two white Men killed" in the 1770 incident. Three years later, a trader passing through Okfuskee saved himself from an enraged nephew of the recently murdered Mad Turkey by striking the man and fleeing to the arms of some nearby Chickasaws. To make matters worse, the Okfuskees certainly knew that their Creek neighbors were equally unhappy with the backcountry situation, and that Creek anger was returned by the colonists in kind. Thus, in 1768, the Lower Creek headman Captain Aleck asserted that his people "learnt to be theives and rogues from these back Settlers, before these Virginia Men came to Settle in the Back Country, the White men and Red men lived like Brothers." Aleck was followed by Escotchaby of Coweta, who asked that "the Virginians, may be kept back from settling near us." That same year, a trader noted that colonists on the Ogeechee River "intends to Kill all the Indians that comes into that Settlement." By 1770, John Stuart would write, "I have had several accounts of mutual thefts & quarrels between the Frontier Inhabitants of the Province of Georgia & the Creeks, against which evil I know of no Remedy." Four years later, in the midst of the crisis that claimed Mad Turkey's life, an Okfuskee executed at the British behest died exhorting "his Relations to revenge his Death on the Virginians, and not give out untill every one of his Relations should fall," while a trader wrote that the "rascally Crackers want to Kill" two Creek emissaries to Augusta.[56] The Okfuskees who approached Augusta with a peace talk in August 1774 were cautious for a reason.

In a situation of this sort—where contact was both frequent and frequently unsatisfactory—it is not surprising to find such attitudes and actions. By the late 1760s and early 1770s, the frontier exchange economy involving Creeks and colonists was coming apart at the seams. Crosscultural relations were unavoidable, cooperation was all but impossible, and competition was increasingly unbearable. And yet, even the examples cited above suggest that the frontier exchange economy in and around the backcountry was not dead. The Okfuskees' 1774 mission, for instance, demonstrated a mix of suppressed hostility—concealment, guns, war paint, scouts—and latent mutuality. "Old Friends," their leader said to his Euro-American host, "are always glad to hear from, and to See one another," and this proved true even outside the ritually charged conference setting. Thus, on the Okfuskees' way home, when they suddenly encountered a colonist, "they stopt and threw down their Bundles and keept their guns in their Hands." Their fear, however, dissipated "after Mr. [Thomas] Grierson spoke to them," and "they took him by the hand" before parting peacefully. Other backcountry inhabitants were similarly conflicted. Escotchaby of Coweta, whose speech condemning Virginians appears above, simultaneously praised Georgia's Quakers as "good and Peaceable" people who should be encouraged to settle near the Creeks. For their part, the Ogeechee colonists, who planned to kill any Indians they could find, were angry because Creeks took "a good many things from" James Carter, "one of the Inhabitants." When the Creeks returned his possessions, they consisted of Indian "Trading Goods," not the household furniture Carter had reported stolen. Carter himself lived "close by the Trading Path" leading to Okfuskee, but lacked a trading license.[57] Despite their professed hatred of Indians, then, the Ogeechee settlers championed a man who epitomized the frontier exchange economy, a man who stocked goods meant for the Indian trade, lived near a well-traveled trading path, and concealed his activities from the authorities.

Similar actions persisted into the post-Revolutionary years. Creeks, for example, continued hunting in the backcountry, with one party "eating at the white peoples houses and bueying goods of them wich the white women had made up into Shirts and frocks for them." Similarly, in 1793, a Creek headman asserted that his people should be allowed to hunt "onmolested" in the east; "if in Wont," he said, they would "Gett provistion from the White People." For the most part, though, such activities were not enough to maintain the level of mutuality the frontier exchange economy required. Thus, "two white men very meanly dressed" attacked the Creek party that ate "at the white peoples houses"; they killed a Creek man, wounded another, and "entirely plundered" their camp. Likewise, the 1793 talk came in response to an attack on the Chatahootchee village of Okfuskenena, an attack which led to the deaths of six Okfuskee men and the capture of eight Okfuskee women. Their village was burned—despite the fact that they were "among the most friendly of the Creeks and no way concerned in stealing horses"—by Georgia militiamen searching for stolen horses; they left a note in the ruined village warning the Creeks against hunting in the east. By the end of the century, the inhabitants of Okfuskee's five eastern villages had abandoned their settlements and returned to the Tallapoosa River Valley. The breakdown of the frontier exchange economy suggested by their decision and the violent acts that precipitated it had its roots in the years preceding the Revolution when this economic system increasingly became a source of tension, rather than a middle ground upon which adjustments and understandings could be negotiated and renewed.[58]

Of course, previous generations of Creeks and colonists had never enjoyed uniformly congenial relations, nor had the compromises they reached gone unchallenged. In the years before midcentury, examples of stresses and strains surfaced frequently. By the late 1760s and 1770s, however, such incidents multiplied wildly and became increasingly deadly. Perhaps more significantly, in the years immediately prior to the Revolution, it becomes more and more difficult to locate references to other sorts of behavior, to actions that might have reinforced mutuality. In the Lower Mississippi Valley, the two decades that followed the Seven Years' War produced changes in the frontier exchange economy that "were more transitional than transformative."[59] In Georgia and South Carolina, by contrast, a new economic pattern emerged during these years, one that incorporated certain characteristics of its predecessor but that could not be mistaken for it. For the inhabitants of Okfuskee, the implications of the frontier exchange economy's deterioration were alarming. Rather than a mutually reinforcing system of economic and political relations, Okfuskees who left town and headed east increasingly helped to create a socioeconomic pattern that threatened to undo carefully constructed bonds of kinship and friendship. By the eve of the American Revolution, the connections that had once brought Okfuskees and colonists together peacefully were either broken or peculiarly twisted. The former no longer functioned, and the latter served only to bind people together in a cycle of recrimination and destruction. Leaving Okfuskee to pursue opportunities for hunting and trade led, then, to a series of conflicts that undermined the Okfuskees' place in, and understanding of, the region. Connections forged in one context shattered in another.

Leaving Okfuskee was an action that paralleled conduct characteristic of early American life more generally. Historians have long since abandoned the notion that colonial-era communities were "closed." Goods and services flowed into and out of towns on a regular basis and, beyond that, regularly leaving one's town for economic purposes was common in early America. In fact, Okfuskees traveling east frequently encountered colonists heading west for stays of several months in Native villages; these traders were living examples of Euro-American willingness to travel in the pursuit of personal gain. Many of the traders' contemporaries left home for good, either by intent or by accident, but others returned, sometimes forever and sometimes for a relatively brief stay before repeating the process. Indian traders and urban merchants, sailors and ship captains—these people made a habit of leaving their communities. However, they also represent only the most obvious of colonial America's economic travelers.

Young men in New England, for example, frequently sought their living as fishermen and whalers. For some, seagoing pursuits were at the center of their economic lives; others used the sea as a way to supplement land-based activities. Further south, Euro-Americans tended to look not east toward the ocean but rather west to places where hunting and open-range livestock ranching promised economic opportunity for men who were willing to leave their communities on a regular basis. Hunters and herders were joined in their efforts to exploit America's "vacant" territory by wealthy men willing to travel hundreds of miles to advance speculative schemes.[60] Especially after the Revolution, some land speculators were army veterans who had been promised land by one governmental body or another. In fact, recruiters for colonial militias had long used promises of financial rewards to encourage enlistment; military service, then, emerged as yet another economic reason for men to leave their communities.[61] Activities closer to home could also bring colonialists out of their towns on a regular basis. Farmers who lived within a day's ride of an urban area frequently hauled produce and drove livestock to city markets; those who lived farther away made similar journeys to market towns or nearby wholesalers. And, of course, colonists left their communities to pursue opportunities as wage laborers—women as school teachers, tailors, or domestics; men as agricultural field hands or craftsmen.[62]

Like the inhabitants of Okfuskee, then, residents of communities throughout British America were willing, even eager, to travel for economic purposes. Security, they recognized, often required mobility; a carefully planned itinerancy could produce a well-deserved competency. Economically motivated travel also reordered the worldview of the Okfuskees' colonial contemporaries. Thus, Massachusetts soldiers who served in the Seven Years' War found that their "personal experiences of the war" served "as a guide to understanding their world"; they returned to their communities "transformed." A dozen years later, soldiers in the Continental Army also found that military experience meant that their perspectives on the events of the day were at odds with those of other Americans. Hunting and herding—especially if such activities provoked conflict with Indians—could likewise produce a distinctive worldview. Racial ideology and genocidal rhetoric flourished in soil disturbed by the backcountry colonists' extensive and intrusive economic activities. Even marketing could have profound ideological consequences. Traveling to markets was part of a larger socioeconomic shift that increasingly "thrust people from British and colonial localities into an expansive world of shared experience," a world in which "private choice" and "individual assertiveness" were integral to one's sense of self.[63]

Far from being alone in leaving their community for economic reasons, then, and far from being alone in experiencing ideological fallout from this leave-taking, Okfuskees were part of a larger American tradition, one that both embraced economically motivated travel and struggled with its implications. Okfuskees moving to the Chattahoochee Valley or visiting the British backcountry; British merchants getting their start as factors in the colonies; South Carolina and Georgia farmers selling their produce in Camden or Augusta—all of these people sought economic opportunity; all of these people participated in a world where migration was "normative" and "[a]ll was movement, change, growth, dispersal." Early America was a world in motion, and few of its people sought to stand entirely outside its confusing, chaotic, and attractive orbit.[64]

Early America, though, was confusing without being entirely confused; this was a world that could be chaotic without falling into absolute chaos. Thus travelers moved within established social structures. Their ambitions were founded on time-tested mechanisms, networks, and patterns. Like the New Englanders whose model of "serial town settlement" saw them "moving away from familiar places accompanied by kin and arriving at their destination to find old acquaintances,"[65] eighteenth-century Okfuskees' eagerness to embrace mobility depended upon both the durability of the routine and the continuity between tradition and innovation. And there, from the Okfuskee perspective, was the problem: the connections between imperial, colonial, and Native life meant that their routines were particularly fragile and that continuity was peculiarly elusive. Americans of all backgrounds sought far-flung economic opportunities so as to become more secure, not less. Unlike their Euro-American contemporaries, Okfuskees and their Native neighbors rarely succeeded in achieving this goal.

The situation the Okfuskees encountered in the British backcountry attests to the difficulties Indian peoples faced. Okfuskees seeking economic opportunity after midcentury reasonably believed that they could build on both their town's long history of relations with Charleston and on their fellow Creeks' tradition of mutually beneficial frontier exchange with

British colonists. The Okfuskees were, in the end, wrong on both counts. To begin with, the ties to Charleston were a disappointment. As Georgia expanded and took on a larger role in Creek relations, as South Carolina's own focus shifted to the Cherokees, as Britain increasingly centralized the administration of Indian affairs—as each development unfolded, the Okfuskee–Charleston tie became increasingly ineffective and anachronistic. The Okfuskees learned that although Charleston was a colonial center, it remained, in imperial terms, very much a peripheral town. As such, its ambitions could be overshadowed by those of other peripheries; its agenda could shift rapidly; and its plans could be eclipsed by metropolitan policies. The Okfuskees must have grown ever more worried that the relationship that encouraged them to look east for economic opportunity was, finally, an insubstantial ideal, one with enough power to bring Okfuskees east but one that could neither protect them while there nor sustain itself in the face of mounting backcountry violence. The townspeople's efforts to use a traditional diplomatic relationship as the basis for an innovative economic strategy brought them, in the long run, neither geopolitical security nor material prosperity.

A similar outcome met the Okfuskees' efforts to participate in the frontier exchange economy. Okfuskees who sought economic opportunity in the backcountry after midcentury encountered newly arrived colonists who presented two sorts of problems. Most obviously, Virginians often had little interest in mutually beneficial relations with Indians, an approach to the world which necessarily endangered the Okfuskees' plans to profit from their own travel to the backcountry. Of equal importance, however, the colonists were at once hostile interlopers and British subjects; they were unfamiliar and unwelcome neighbors who enjoyed the support—often grudging but nonetheless real—of the very imperial and colonial officials whom the Okfuskees believed were their friends, kinsmen, and allies. The Virginians' arrival, in other words, drove home the point that the British Empire's scale—demographic and geographic, social and political—was fundamentally incompatible with Creek aims. The empire's interwoven patterns of emigration from Britain and migration within America; its growing focus on territorial expansion; its predisposition to ignore Indian claims and exclude Indian people; its inability (and often, unwillingness) to enforce its laws when backcountry colonists harmed Indians—each undermined the frontier exchange economy and contributed to the collapse of the Okfuskees' efforts to profit from travel to the backcountry.[66]

The end result of the Okfuskees' decision to seek opportunity outside of town, then, was the emergence of a new and disturbing connection with Euro-America, one based not on a common heritage of economically motivated travel and mutually beneficial exchange but rather on the peculiar bond that comes from the development of mutual disdain and shared anger.

II

The Town and
Its People

4

Agriculture and Livestock: Changing Patterns of Land Use in Okfuskee

To discuss the land-use patterns characteristic of eighteenth-century Okfuskee is to confront a peculiar problem: little is known about the layout of the town. We do know that Okfuskee was named for its location: "Ocfuskee, derived from Oc, in, and fuskee, a point. The name is expressive of the position of the old town . . . on the right [west] bank of the Tallapoosa River." By the early 1770s, at least some townspeople had moved across the Tallapoosa, constructing "houses and corn lofts" on the river's east bank. The river at Okfuskee was 300 yards wide but "fordable"; here the upper trading path from Charleston and Augusta entered Upper Creek country. Perhaps because of the ford, the river itself was occasionally referred to as the Okfuskee River. Around Okfuskee, the valley was "flat for half a mile on the river and fit for culture; back of this, there are sharp, stoney hills, pine and in the branches reeds." No descriptions of the town itself survive, and a reservoir now covers the site, effectively precluding archaeological reconstruction.[1]

The lack of knowledge about the specifics of Okfuskee's physical situation is unfortunate but not catastrophic. Eighteenth-century Creek communities shared a basic layout. Assuming the Okfuskees conformed to this town plan, it becomes possible to discuss the townspeople's agricultural practices and the ways in which such practices, because of their focus on community-centered production, brought the Okfuskees together. The widespread adoption of livestock raising, however, led to new patterns of land use and interpersonal relations. By the 1760s and 1770s, in fact, the Okfuskees' agricultural system showed signs of fracturing into two competing subsystems. The activity that traditionally worked to bind townspeople together—cultivating domesticated plants—was increasingly disrupted by novel behavior—herding domesticated animals—that encouraged social and spatial division. These divisions manifested themselves in the settlement pattern Okfuskees adopted in the years immediately prior to the American Revolution, a pattern suggesting that Okfuskee—as place and process—was being remade. As Okfuskees integrated livestock into their agricultural traditions, they created a new sort of town, one in which neighborhood society and community geography took on forms at once recognizable and unfamiliar. Inevitably, the meeting of flora and fauna, cultivating and herding, implicated norms and networks beyond the agricultural. With the arrival of livestock, the meaning of "Okfuskee"—as a community and an identity—was suddenly up in the air.

Creek Towns

Although the details of eighteenth-century Okfuskee's layout remain obscure, Creeks built their towns along broadly similar lines. They were "always near running water," placed "if possible on an isthmus betwixt two waters, or where the doubling of a river forms a peninsula." Intratown spatial arrangements were equally distinctive, as suggested by William Bartram's reference to "the most common plan or arrangement of the Chunkey Yards, Publick Square & Rotunda, of the Modern Crick Towns." Okfuskee—whose name alone suggests conformity to Creek preferences for riverside sites—was certainly laid out in keeping with Creek conventions for spatial organization, especially with regard to Bartram's "Publick" buildings.[2]

Eighteenth-century Creek towns centered on the complex of three public structures mentioned by Bartram: the square, rotunda or town house, and chunkey yard. Townspeople used the square during the warm months for town governance, ceremonies, and celebrations. It consisted of four three-sided buildings opening onto (and enclosing) a half-acre area, at the center of which was the town's sacred fire. The square's buildings were arranged in relation to the four cardinal directions, and seats within them were assigned according to a man's clan and status. The town house or rotunda served as the cold-weather equivalent of the square. It generally stood just outside the square's northwest corner, with its door facing the square. The rotunda, like the square, centered on the town's fire, and its seating pattern followed the rules used in the square. The chunkey ground was on the far side of the square from the rotunda. It consisted of a cleared rectangular space enclosed by low earthen banks and opening onto the square. Towns-people used the chunkey ground for dances and games, but also for tor-turing captives. As a *talwa,* Okfuskee had a "square" and sacred fire, and the community had a "town house" as late as 1799; several Okfuskee vil-lages likewise had rotundas, including Okfuskenena, where Okfuskees erected at least two (and possibly three) such structures. No direct evidence exists for an Okfuskee chunkey yard—Okfuskees, at one point, intended to burn "a Northward Slave," an activity that would have taken place there—but, given the consensus about Creek public architecture, it is in-conceivable that the town lacked one.[3]

The consensus about Creek public buildings breaks down slightly when the subject turns to the arrangement of homes within Creek towns. For example, David Taitt and Bartram left their readers with different impres-sions of the Creeks' 1770s settlement patterns. Taitt, for his part, stated that "their Villages are Generally built . . . without any Kind of Regularity, the houses being at the Distance of Sixty to one hundred yards a sunder." Bartram, by contrast, suggested that Creek towns were relatively ordered places, although he acknowledged variations on the basic model. In the book-length presentation of his travels, Bartram wrote that an Upper Creek town had "neat commodious buildings." "Every habitation," he stated, "consists of four oblong square houses, of one story . . . so situated as to form an exact square, encompassing an area or court yard of about a quarter of an acre of ground, leaving an entrance into it at each corner." In an earlier, less lyrical essay, however, Bartram qualified his claim about "every habitation": "Every family . . . have not four of these Houses-some 3, -some 2, -and some but one, according to their circumstances, of largeness of their family, &c." His map of an "Upper Creek Town" confirms the diversity of domestic arrangements; of the fifty-seven households depicted, only nine have the ideal four-building configuration (Figure 4). At the same time, though, Bartram's map demonstrates that Creek domestic units were ar-ranged in relatively orderly rows, which were themselves laid out in relation to the public complex; moreover, even those households lacking the ideal complement of structures "are situated so as to admit of four building[s] when conveniency or necessity require it."[4] With respect to the arrange-ment of homes, then, Creek towns were "regular," if regular means "or-derly," not "homogeneous."

Whatever their complement of buildings, each Creek household was

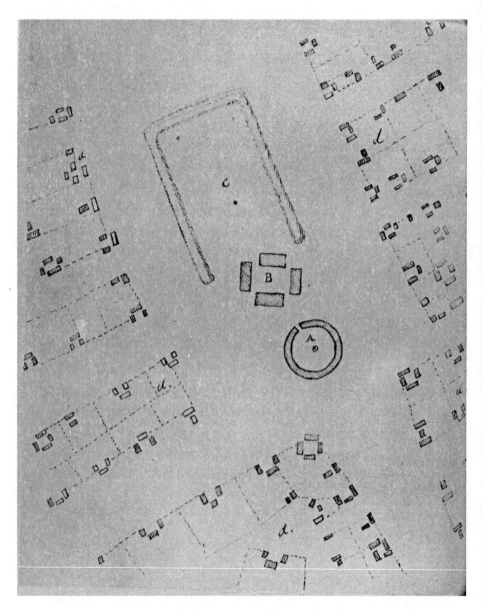

4. Edwin H. Davis's copy of William Bartram's "A Plan of the Muscogulge or Upper Creek Town." Reprinted courtesy of the National Anthropological Archives, Smithsonian Institution/MS. 173.683.

bordered by a small garden, which was, by the 1760s or 1770s, frequently fenced. Each town also had an unfenced "common plantation" located "some Distance off," where "the whole town plant[ed] in one vast field together." Trade was likewise town-based, and several generations of British traders had houses within Creek communities. These visitors followed the Creek "mode," erecting four structures enclosing a central square, although their buildings were "like towers in cities, beyond the common size of those of the Indians." By the late 1760s, however, the traders' houses were generally located outside of town, a trend that may have started in Okfuskee. A 1757 map shows three detached "store[s]," two of which were across the river from Okfuskee; the third was the property of an ex-Okfuskee trader. Three years later, "the traders storehouses lay opposite the town," as did William Rae's "dwelling house."[5]

Creek Agriculture

Creek agriculture was community agriculture. Other aspects of social organization—family and clan, gender and age-grade—were important, but agricultural production finally depended on the town. A trader attested to the Creek system's community-focused nature when he described an Okfuskee as the "Great beloved Man, owner of all the Lands." Six years later, four Okfuskees, including "the master of the Ground," arrived in Augusta. Other towns had Masters of the Ground. For example, Edmond Atkin met with the leaders of eight towns in mid-September 1759, four of whom bore the title "Okeelysa, or Master of the Ground." Less than two weeks later, four men, each an Okeelysa, attended Atkin's conference at Tuckabatchee, and his October 10 treaty with six towns was signed by five "Proprietor[s] of the Ground."[6] Altogether, Atkin met with Masters of the Ground from ten Upper Creek towns.

The Master of the Ground owed his position to his clan connections. Thus, Mortar of Okchai stated that "he and his Family are Masters of all the Land," and Atkin referred to "4 vile Brothers Owners of the [Coweta] Town Ground." In each case, the family in question was probably the town's founding clan since, as Thomas Nairne noted, "after the Town is setled the headship goes in a family out of respect to him who first kindled the fire."[7] Whatever his clan ties, however, the Master of the Ground belonged to his town's council, the body that advised the mico/headman. Some Masters of the Ground may have been *henihalgi,* the "Second Men" who handled the day-to-day administration of towns; some, though, held other positions. As Master of the Ground, Okeelysa participated in—possibly even led—the council's annual efforts to assign space within the town's communal agricultural field to individual clans. The clans, in turn, divided the allotments among their constituent households,[8] thereby linking household and clan to both the council and the Master of the Ground. The Creeks' system of landholding thus neatly intertwined clan and town. In doing so, the centrifugal forces created by conflicting clan loyalties were subsumed within a unifying framework in which land ownership was clan-based but town-centered.

Ownership of land by the Master of the Ground's clan did not mean, then, that the town's other clans were precluded from farming. In fact, by allowing more recently arrived clans to join their fire, the founding clan guaranteed them access to land. To do otherwise was to consign the newcomers to slavery since, for Creeks, landlessness and slavery were explicitly linked. Creek reactions to European efforts to acquire their land demonstrate the force of the connection. For example, a trader wrote from Okfuskee that the Creeks viewed British initiatives in Cherokee country as a plot "to ingross all their Land and make them all Slaves." The French, recognizing Creek fears, warned of British plans to "get all their [the Creeks'] Lands from them in order to make them Slaves"; the British could play the same card, as one did while in Okfuskee: "the French . . . [will]l have all your Land in time and make you slaves." Landlessness equaled slavery because slaves lacked clan ties, and clans provided individuals with town land.[9] For Creeks, then, land represented much more than simply a place to grow food. It served as a tangible marker of a person's connection to family and community.

The Creek practice of communal planting further established the link between clans and households, on the one hand, and the town and its Master of the Ground, on the other. "Each town," Adair notes, "usually works [at planting] together. Previous thereto, an old beloved man warns the inhabitants to be ready to plant on a prefixed day." Prior to entering the fields, townspeople were told "that he who expects to eat must work, and that he who will not work, must expect to pay the fine according to old custom, or leave the town, as they will not sweat themselves for an healthy idle waster." Once summoned by "the overseer," townspeople met "at the public square," and then went to the communal field, "where they begin to plant, not every one in his own little district, assigned and laid out, but the whole community united" working "from field to field, till their seed is sown." They were cheered on by songs and jokes from "one of their orators," who also beat time on a drum.[10] Most likely, the "orator," "old beloved man," and "overseer" was Okeelysa, the Master of the Ground.

The planting of household gardens provides an important contrast to the practices associated with the town's field. Garden work lacked the community-focused activities connected with the town "plantation." Householders planted their own plots. More specifically, townswomen— who shared in planting the town's field—were responsible for the gardens. No one was punished for failing to help with the household gardens, in contrast to the fines or ostracism visited on a nonparticipant in the community-wide planting party. Gardens were, moreover, planted before the town's field, with garden cultivation beginning "as soon as the spring of the year admits," while the "out-fields" were planted "in the beginning of May";[11] many young men, busy with the winter hunt, were not in town when the gardens were planted. Both socially and temporally, then, the planting of the town's common field was distinct from the Creeks' personal and familial agricultural tasks.

Harvest practices paralleled planting rituals in foregrounding communal production at the expense of private gardens. The corn planted in the household gardens at "the beginning of Aprile and the end of March" was of a different variety than that planted in the town's field. Garden corn usually ripened two months after planting. It thus afforded "an earlier supply than their distant plantations," an important consideration since Creek towns periodically experienced food shortages in the spring and early summer. As Taitt discovered in a visit to Okfuskee in late March 1772, Creeks sometimes "had but very little" at that time of year.[12] For all of its importance, however, the garden harvest was not marked by a ceremony that caught the eye of eighteenth-century Euro-American observers; nor were all the townspeople present for the occasion, since many young men would already have departed for the summer hunt. The low profile of garden supplies is perhaps best shown by contemporary assertions that Creeks ate no fresh produce before the Busk,[13] a ceremony generally held in late July or early August. The garden corn ripened (and began to be consumed) two months earlier.

Euro-Americans who mischaracterized the Busk made an understandable mistake. The Busk was far and away the most important Creek ceremony, and it focused, at least in part, on the sanctification and consump-

tion of previously forbidden agricultural products. The proscribed foods—
the produce that could not be eaten before the Busk—were not, however,
agricultural goods in general but only those foodstuffs produced by communal labor on town land. The Busk began with a general cleaning, in
which "all the remaining grain and other old provisions" were "cast together
into one common heap" and burned, effectively removing garden produce
from the subsistence equation; the ceremony then removed the prohibition
on eating town-field crops. At its heart, then, the Busk was a town-centered
ceremony which called on the townspeople to acknowledge their dependence on the town's spiritual and material resources. In using a communal
fire to destroy the remaining provisions (including the "new" garden corn),
in bringing the townsmen out of their households and into the square to
renew the town's fire, and in passing that fire back to the townswomen's
newly cleaned homes, the Busk implicated every individual and clan in a
community-wide project to ensure mutual health and prosperity. Their
efforts cleansed and united the town, allowing the townspeople, for the
first time, to partake of the fruits of their communal labor—the corn from
the town's field.[14]

Corn from the family gardens was eaten before the Busk. It was, to begin
with, necessary to stave off serious deprivation. More fundamentally, however, garden corn could be eaten because the attention lavished on the
Busk made it clear that communal production was at the heart of Creek
life. Town-field corn required special treatment precisely because of its
social and spiritual power; improper handling threatened the town's very
existence. Garden corn, despite its dietary importance, could never approach the significance of its town-field cousin. Both the agricultural cycle's
course and the Busk's structure, therefore, produced a simple set of
weighted comparisons: clan was subordinate to town; hearth fire was subordinate to town-square fire; household garden was subordinate to communal field. Society, spirituality, and prosperity were rooted in the town,
its fire, and its field.[15]

Livestock

In some respects, the Creek agricultural system changed very little between
1700 and 1775. Europeans brought new crops—most notably peaches and
potatoes—but these supplemented rather than replaced Native domesti-
cates. Thus, the only non-Native plant remains uncovered while excavating

the Okfuskee village of Nuyaka (inhabited from 1777 to 1813) were peach pits, possibly relatives of Okfuskee's own peach trees; Okfuskee's Chatta-hoochee villages apparently added plums to their orchards of "thriving peach trees."[16] Creek agricultural practices also remained remarkably stable. Euro-American observers cast aspersions on Creek customs—women working in the fields, intercropping, failing to weed—while trying to explain how "their laziness and unskilfulness in planting" could "commonly" lead to "pretty good crops" and "the greatest plenty imaginable." In the years prior to the American Revolution, Creeks did adopt fences, and they replaced stone hoes with metal ones. They were, however, not particularly interested in Euro-American agricultural techniques and equipment, and they remained aggressively uninterested in Euro-American critiques of their gender roles.[17]

The exception to the general continuity in Creek agricultural techniques was the adoption of livestock. American Indians were unprepared for the array of animals accompanying the European invasion, and while Native groups incorporated the unfamiliar fauna into their economic routines and ideological categories, the new animals frequently had a profound impact on Native societies. Moreover, the decisions made by one generation often had unanticipated consequences for their descendants. Pros and cons are difficult to weigh, after all, when one knows little about the subject under consideration.

In the Creeks' case, their ancestors had domesticated only the dog. By the early eighteenth century, however, Creeks had incorporated several of the new animals into both their worldview and their daily lives. Horses proved especially popular. Creek participants in the raids on Spanish missions brought back horses, and the Yamasee War offered Creeks more chances to seize Euro-American livestock. As the century went on, Creeks stole horses from Cherokee traders, captured them during their periodic raids on the Spanish, acquired them in various ways in the British colonies, and bred their own. Traders also brought horses into Creek country, a number of which wound up in Creek hands. Occasionally, the traders sold horses to their Creek customers, but mutually agreed-upon transactions were not the only option for Creeks in need of horses. In 1749, for example, traders complained of "The Indians making a common Practice . . . to Steal their Horses," which could only be ransomed at "an Extravagant rate," and "frequently" not even then. Likewise, among "the dayly Insults and Abuses" Upper Creek traders mentioned in 1752 was the Creeks' habit of "stealing their Horses," and in 1763 the Creeks were told that "great complaints have been made by the Traders, that some of you have stolen their Horses, and refuse to deliver them when found in your possession."[18]

Creek ownership of horses was common enough by 1732 that an agreement between the Creeks and South Carolina contained Governor Robert Johnson's promise to punish traders who in "any ways injured" the Creeks "in their . . . Horses." By the early 1770s, Adair claimed that "almost every" Creek "hath horses, from two to a dozen." A 1776 bill for "ferryage" of Indians suggests that Adair exaggerated, but horses were certainly an important part of Creek life by midcentury. Thus, Georgia's officials knew that their 1740 request for Creek help against the Spanish necessitated hiring someone for "looking after the Indian horses," while the Upper Creeks who came to Charleston in 1755 both demanded "large Presents . . . in particular, Sadles" and received "Corn for the People who were left behind for to take care of the Headmen's Horses." Twenty years before, a Savannah merchant claimed that he could trade six dozen saddles, bridles, and related hardware per year to the Creeks. In 1763, the 305 Creeks attending the Augusta Congress received as gifts 44 saddles, 228 bridles and girths, 80 pairs of stirrup leathers, and 170 cruppers; the 145 Creeks present at a 1771 Pensacola conference were given 100 bushels of corn "for 205 Horses during their Stay."[19]

Okfuskees shared in the Creek appreciation for horses. Two Okfuskee headmen approved the 1732 treaty that promised to protect Creek horses, and the 1755 party that demanded saddles included Handsome Fellow. A year later, the group he led received four saddles as gifts; earlier that year, he and the Okfuskee Captain were given fresh horses while carrying a message to the nation. During the May 1760 attack, the Okfuskee Captain returned the favor, giving Robert French "an Horse . . . to get him safe off." Like their Creek neighbors, Okfuskees acquired some horses by theft. In 1728, a British agent wrote from Okfuskee that the French made "several Complaints" against an Okfuskee trader "for setting the Indians to steal their Horses." Just over a decade later, however, the shoe was on the other foot as the traders discovered that Okfuskees viewed British horses as fair game. As a result, "the King of the Oakfuskees" and the town's "Head Warrior" received a lecture from South Carolina's lieutenant governor: "[Y]ou know my people can't carry their goods to your Towns without Horses which are their burdeners[,] notwithstanding which Some of your people catch and take them out with them when they go to make their

Hunts, and when they bring them back will not deliver them to the owners without their being pay'd near the Value of the Horses." The lieutenant governor's translator, the Okfuskee trader Alexander Wood, must have been gratified by the speech, but the town's headmen were apparently unmoved; as a result, Okfuskee's traders only became more worried about protecting their own herds in the years to come. Three of the traders who signed the 1749 complaint about horse-stealing either were or would be Okfuskee traders, and the Okfuskee Captain was among the men to whom the Upper Creek traders addressed their 1752 complaint.[20] Again, the results must have disappointed. Okfuskees were accused of horse-stealing in 1760, 1770, 1771, 1773, and, possibly, 1778. Small wonder that after the 1771 incident, an Okfuskee promised "that he would go home immediately and let his people know the Talk and represent to them the necessity of keeping their people from Stealing the white people's horses." Such a speech, if it was ever delivered, would have been a case of "Do as I say, not as I do" since "8 or 9 of [the colonists'] Horses" were "found at a small Distance from the . . . Camp" this Okfuskee shared with three townsmen.[21]

Okfuskees may, in fact, have had significantly more experience with horses than other Creeks because of the combination of Okfuskee's location, the official British presence in town, the travelers who visited Okfuskee, and the business strategies of the Euro-Americans who traded there. Beginning in the seventeenth century, the direct route for British traders and diplomats bound for either the northern Upper Creeks or the Chickasaws went through Okfuskee; the 1737 Chickasaw map mentioned above attests to the importance of Okfuskee's position on this path. The British trading factory and forts in Okfuskee also contributed to the traffic, both Native and foreign, passing through the town. As early as 1723, two deserters from Fort Toulouse testified that the French had "no Trade with the Indians who goes all to the Okfuskees to Trade with the English"; nine years later, the French worried that the British lured Choctaws to Okfuskee for presents and that the British "warehouse at the Affasquees" endangered France's Choctaw trade.[22]

The visitors to Okfuskee—Native and Euro-American, trader and diplomat—frequently came mounted. Envoys, for example, had entourages and equipment, all of which required horses, and envoys called meetings, which brought more mounted guests to Okfuskee. So, on Edmond Atkin's 1759 mission, twelve "Light Horse[men]" accompanied the agent; they, their horses, and the "Horses for carrying Provisions" spent from mid-

October to December 6 in Okfuskee. While there, Atkin met with a party of seventy-six Choctaws and several smaller Native groups; many would have arrived on horseback. A generation before, when Georgia's Patrick McKay sought to persuade the Upper Creeks to accept a British fort in their territory, the Okfuskee conference he called became "a general Meeting of both Indians and white People"; it was attended not just by McKay and his mounted escort but also by a number of "Master Traders" and "all" Upper Creek "Chiefs." The assembled multitudes, and their horses, stayed in Okfuskee "for about a Week."[23]

Even when not attending such meetings, traders who simply passed through town brought more horses into Okfuskee, horses that could then remain in town for a prolonged period of time. In late October 1752, for example, John Pettycrew was escorting 70 heavily loaded horses to the Chickasaws when he received news that led him to leave "my Horses and Things at the Oakfuskees"; he did not return for the pack train until December. Pettycrew's fellow Chickasaw trader, John Buckles, behaved in a similar manner. In 1753 and 1754, he escorted a total of 233 horses to Okfuskee on his way either to or from the Chickasaws. On one trip from Augusta, he arrived in Okfuskee with 30 packhorses on January 8, 1754. Worn out by the journey, Buckles "stayed at the Oakfuskees 7 Days to rest my Horses and provide Provitions" for his party, which included 17 Chickasaws, some of whom were certainly mounted; he then went on to Chickasaw country. In early May, Buckles again traveled through Upper Creek country, following the upper path back to Augusta with 53 horses loaded with deerskins. He continued dealing with Okfuskee's traders into the 1760s, a habit which led to a 1763 purchase of goods from the town's store, goods which he most likely hauled away on horses purchased in Okfuskee. That same year, Okfuskees took charge of "80 loaded horses going to the Chickesah and Chactah nations" to prevent the pack train from being plundered; the townspeople returned the "horses and goods" to John Brown once the danger passed. The activities of Brown, Buckles, and their fellow Chickasaw traders explain why the Creeks referred to the Okfuskee–Augusta path as "Chelucconene," the "Old Horse Trail."[24]

Even without the arrival of packtrains and mounted diplomats, Okfuskee's own traders brought an abnormally large number of horses into the town. A 1741 list of Creek traders shows that Okfuskee's Alexander Wood (and his partner, Patrick Brown) owned 60 horses; the other 11 men on the list owned an average of 23 horses, with no man having more than 30.

Two decades later, Macartan & Campbell used their Okfuskee store to collect and sell horses. They paid Henry Dalton "for Packing a Gang of Horses from the Okefuskees" in 1762. A year later, John Buckles & Co. paid them for "2 head of Oakfuskee Horses"; and a year after that, George Whitefield owed the Okfuskee store for "3 Horses Bought there." In 1765, Paine, Scott & Munro first bought £1,885 worth of "sundries" from the Okfuskee store and then, in the next account, purchased "15 Head of Horses & Tackling" from Macartan & Cambell's livestock account. Other Okfuskee traders were likewise heavily invested in horses. John Rae, for one, promised prospective Georgia colonists that "I can . . . furnish them with Horses and Mares, any number they may want."[25]

Horses, then, were common in Okfuskee, both because of the towns-people's own predilections and because of the actions of their Euro-American allies, traders, and guests. The Okfuskees and their Creek neighbors were, however, less enamored by (and had less experience with) cattle, which threatened the unfenced fields and competed with deer for food without providing the advantages in transportation and warfare offered by horses. Their opinion of the relative merits of cattle and horses surfaced in the Euro-American complaints about Creek assaults on their livestock: "Cattle killed and Horses stole." Dead cattle and missing horses, in fact, became a mantra in complaints to or about the Creeks, Okfuskees included.[26] The formula changed by the 1770s, when statements to the effect that Creeks "did drive & carry away several Horses & Cattle" became more frequent; but, even then, a colonist was still warned that Creeks "would kill his cattle and steal his horses etc." Creek cattle raising did not take off until the American Revolution.[27]

That said, however, some Creeks acquired cattle well before the 1770s. Although cattle raising may have been more popular among the Lower Creeks, several Upper Creeks owned herds. In 1737, Dog King of Eufalees "Complain'd" that a trader "frequently Kill'd his Cattle," including "a Cow big with Calf," which he insisted be replaced "because he Wants it for Increase of Stock." Gun Merchant of Okchai also raised cattle. In 1749, he purchased livestock from Fort Toulouse and then claimed that he could not go to Charleston because "he has building to do and his Catt[le to] look after." Two years later, he told an Upper Creek meeting that "as he had Cattle enough to kill if the Head Men would wait they should be welcome to the best entertainment his House could afford." South Carolina's 1756 gift of "6 Cows" augmented his herd, and in 1763 he was angered that "the Governor would not send him a Negro Boy to mind his Stock."[28]

Whether Okfuskees adopted cattle herding before the American Revolution remains unclear. Many Creeks did not. As late as 1764, Thomas Campbell noted that while Creeks had "a great many" horses, they "have not many [cattle] at present"; a decade later Adair wrote that "Some of the natives are grown fond of horned cattle, both in the Cheerake and Muskohge [Creek] countries, but most decline them." The only direct reference to cattle in Okfuskee prior to the Revolution comes from 1745, when a French officer referred to South Carolina's Okfuskee fort as having "diminished to a cow pen." Even this report may be less an accurate description of the fort's purpose than a derogatory comment on its size and condition. By the end of the century, however, the garbage from an Okfuskee village included cow bones, and Okfuskees had "cattle, hogs and horses, and the range for them is a good one. The shoals in the river afford a great supply of moss, called by the traders salt grass. The cows which frequent these shoals, are the largest and finest in the nation." Although it cannot be established that earlier generations of Okfuskees owned cattle, Creeks in the neighborhood did so, as did local traders. The 1737 complaint by Dog King came from a town less than five miles from Okfuskee, and Gun Merchant lived thirteen miles from the town. Okfuskees were thus familiar with cattle from an early date, and, given the herding techniques common among eighteenth-century Native and Euro-Americans, some cows probably wandered onto Okfuskee land. In fact, the man who "frequently Kill'd" Dog King's cattle was Alexander Wood, Okfuskee's trader.[29]

The presence of horses, cattle, and other livestock—most notably pigs and chickens—influenced Okfuskee town life in a variety of ways. Horses allowed hunters to travel farther afield and to bring back more skins and meat, and they became a valuable trade item in their own right. They also freed townspeople from carrying skins and goods between the nation and the colonies. Other sorts of livestock were traded or given to Euro-Americans, and provided a reliable source of food. In 1726, Hopeahachy, the headman of an isolated Upper Creek town, told Tobias Fitch, "When you are at home your Dyet is kept more under Command. Your Chatle are kept in large pens and Likewise your Sheep; your Turkeys and Ducks are at your Doores. Now with us its not so. We are forced to hunt and Take a Great deale of pains To get our provisiones befor we eat it." Even at this relatively early date, though, other Creek towns could draw on stocks of domesticated animals. Thus, prior to visiting Hopeahachy, Fitch received "Some fowls" from the Okfuskees, and in 1728 an Upper Creek town presented Charlesworth Glover with "three hogs"; a 1735 report claimed that Creeks "raise many hogs and fowls." Because of the Creeks' dietary beliefs, however, Euro-American traders and diplomats may have been the major consumers of domesticated animals, but, in times of scarcity, Creeks would eat livestock.[30]

Domesticated animals did not, however, have an entirely beneficial impact on Okfuskee town life. Neither the Okfuskees nor their traders kept livestock in pens. Thus, a "Linguist" suggested in 1757 that an Okfuskee head warrior, Beau, could leave town without arousing suspicion if he claimed to be "Hunting for Horses." Two years later, the Okfuskee trader William Rae—worried about "very bad talks"—said he would leave town if only he could find his horse; he suspected that two of his men, who had gone out to catch horses, had already decamped. The traders in the Okfuskee village of Sugatspoges had a "horsepen," but they apparently used it only when preparing for trips, a fact which allowed Moses Price "to be out horse-hunting" and thereby survive the May 1760 attack; another trader learned of the attack from a Chickasaw who returned from Sugatspoges "where he had been a horse hunting." Permitting livestock to wander freely eased the burdens of caring for the animals, but it also threatened the agricultural fields that served as the foundation of the town's economy. The 1732 treaty signed by two Okfuskee headmen contained South Carolina's promise to punish traders who "injured" the Creeks "in their Crops," and as early as the 1720s, Creek headmen explicitly linked these injuries to traders' horses that "come into their Corn, and destroy their Provision." The Okfuskee forts and trading factory meant that damage to the town's fields was that "much more" likely, and Creeks complained about livestock into the Revolutionary era.[31]

In the years before the Revolution, in fact, problems with livestock created tensions within Creek towns and forced the townspeople to change their land-use patterns. In 1773, Taitt noted that Creeks now fenced "all around their towns to Prevent their horses & Cattle from destroying their Cropes." The fences, however, protected only crops planted "between their houses," meaning that "Their large fields lie quite open with regard to fencing." The lack of fences around the towns' fields led townswomen to "tether the horses with tough young bark-ropes, and confine the swine in convenient pens" from early spring through the harvest. These precautions did not, however, prevent livestock from damaging the crops. Even household gardens were threatened because "many of the old horses will creep through these enclosures, almost as readily as swine, to the great regret of the women, who scold and give them ill names." Confrontations of this sort happened frequently, and, faced with equine recidivism, frustrated women "usually" responded "by striking a tomohawk into the horse."[32]

As several Upper Creek headmen noted, however, to "shoot or chop" a horse that "happens to eat a little of our Corn" inevitably "causes Disturbances among us." On the one hand, when the offending horse belonged to a Creek, townspeople quarreled with each other. More specifically, since horses frequently belonged to Creek men while women tended the crops, the death of a trespassing horse often pitted townswoman against townsman. If, on the other hand, a trader owned the dead horse, then Creeks and Euro-Americans had to reach an agreement regarding liability and compensation. In either case, livestock disrupted interpersonal relations within the community. The tendency for Creek complaints about traders' livestock to surface at even the highest levels of Creek–British diplomacy hint at the problems that livestock created in Creek towns. Given that there were "no fences around" Okfuskee as late as 1799, that the town's "range" for livestock "is a good one," and that both townspeople and visitors were committed to herding horses, Okfuskees could not hope to avoid these problems.[33] Hungry horses and ripening crops were a disruptive combination, and bad fences made for bad neighbors.

Putting some distance between your livestock and your neighbors' crops was one solution. Not surprisingly, therefore, a 1767 conference attended by an Okfuskee headman saw an Upper Creek refer to occasions "when . . . our people for the benefit of Planting settle at a distance from their Towns." In fact, one of Okfuskee's oldest villages bore a name—Sugatspoges ("place for getting hogs")—suggestive of its people's connection to livestock raising, a connection that may have encouraged their desire to settle at a distance. Other Okfuskee villages were also home to "poultry, hogs," and "cattle," and the possibilities offered by these settlements tempted even Okfuskee's leading headmen. White Lieutenant, for example, was involved with the Chattahoochee villages from the 1770s on; at some point, he assumed "direction" of "a small Indian town on the Chatahoochee, called the Little Oakfuskees." By 1795, he had moved to the Okfuskee village of Nuyaka, where he died owning at least twenty-six cattle. These travels suggest that he was part of a larger Okfuskee (and Creek) trend that saw "both the Indians and traders chuse to settle at a very convenient distance, for the sake of their live stock." By the time of White Lieutenant's death, Okfuskees had known for thirty years that a dependence on un-fenced crops did not mix with a reliance on domesticated animals. Dis-persed villages helped patch over this problem. And, at least within the village of Okfuskenena, households were themselves "widely dispersed," a practice that further facilitated the conjunction of agriculture, herding, and social peace.[34]

Settlement Patterns

As this suggests, the physical and social geography of Okfuskee had changed noticeably, a change linked to the Okfuskees' growing familiarity with the problems and possibilities livestock presented. By the early 1770s, as domesticated animals became a community-wide concern, the Okfus-kees were in the midst of a remarkable period of sociospatial restructuring. Thus, Taitt noted in 1772 that Okfuskee's people had "scattered about the hunting grounds on account of plantations."[35] Modifications of this sort, if not on a par with the disruption and reformation following the sixteenth-century Spanish invasion, at least dwarfed all subsequent developments. The Okfuskees were embracing a new settlement pattern. The magnitude of the shifts are suggested by the journal Taitt kept during his 1772 trip through Upper Creek country.

Upon arriving in Okfuskee on March 22, Taitt noted that "This town some years ago was the largest in the Upper Creeks containing three hun-dred gun-men, but now not above thirty," a decline he attributed to the aforementioned quest for scattered "plantations." The next day, he visited "a small village called Elkhatchie about four miles NNW from Oakfuskee," and then "Sugatspoga, another village of the Oakfuskie Indians about five miles NNE from Elkhatchie." Had Taitt crossed the Tallapoosa and fol-lowed a creek three miles east, he would have come to another Okfuskee village, Epesaugee. He found that Sugatspoges had "about forty-five gun-men in it," but Elkhatchie consisted of only "four or five houses." On the other side of Sugatspoges, he encountered "several little villages or plan-tations scattered about the branch of this creek." Throughout Upper Creek country, in fact, Taitt encountered "small villages" and "scattered planta-tions." Several years later, Bartram "passed through continued plantations and Indian towns on my way up the Tallapoose river"; he listed fifty-five Creek towns, "besides many villages not enumerated."[36]

It is tempting to take Taitt's statements as evidence that Okfuskee broke apart in the late 1760s and early 1770s, splitting into a hodgepodge of closely spaced small villages. In fact, Taitt could even be accused of understating the degree of Okfuskee's disintegration. He knew (but failed to mention) that the town's five Chattahoochee settlements were home to a significant number of Okfuskees by 1772. Moreover, Taitt neglected to report on the extent of recent village formation in the area immediately around Okfuskee. The two Okfuskee villages he mentions, Elkhatchie and Sugatspoges, were familiar parts of the Creek landscape by 1772, and his report of "several little villages or plantations" concerned an area more than ten miles away from Okfuskee. Yet a 1773 map shows that Taitt undoubtedly passed through three other Okfuskee villages in the immediate neighborhood of the main town. The map, to which Taitt contributed written "Remarks," depicts two small villages between Okfuskee and Elkhatchie, and another between Elkhatchie and Sugatspoges.[37] Taitt's failure to mention these three villages suggests that they were either smaller than Elkhatchie ("four or five houses") or newer, or both.

Taitt thus neglected to list nine Okfuskee villages, a fact that lends weight to his assertion that the Okfuskees had scattered. Other evidence suggests, however, that the situation was more complex. The picture of Okfuskee as a town which had recently split into a number of villages must be qualified in two ways. In the first place, such a portrait does not accord well with Creek social theory. The Creeks defined a town in terms of a shared relationship to a sacred fire, not in terms of spatial proximity; the name of one Okfuskee village—Tukpafka: "Punk," material for starting a fire—may invoke just such a relationship. Villages were, in fact, an accepted part of the Creek social landscape in 1772, and had been for years. Thus, Sugatspoges, an Okfuskee village Taitt mentioned, was more than twenty years old. Another, Elkhatchie, had been inhabited since at least 1757. Others that Taitt did not mention were as old or older. Epesaugee was founded no later than 1760 and possibly as early as 1725; in addition, a 1761 census mentions Wichagoes, and Okfuskee's Chattahoochee village dates from the early years of the eighteenth century.[38] The existence of Okfuskee villages in the early 1770s, then, does not necessarily point to the recent disintegration of Okfuskee.

The second point requiring qualification concerns Taitt's report that Okfuskee's contingent of gunmen dropped from 300 to 30. Two 1764 censuses show that Okfuskee and its villages contained 300 men, but a 1799 report states that "Ocfuskee with its villages is the largest town in the nation," with "the number of gunmen of the old town at 180 and 270 in its villages or small towns." The population decline Taitt described in 1772 had, then, occurred quite recently—after 1764—and was followed by a significant rebound. In fact, the dip in population was likely related not to scattering but to another phenomenon Taitt mentioned: a 1770 flood that "did considerable damage to several villages and plantations on the sides of this river." Okfuskee's people moved their town from the Tallapoosa River's east bank to the west bank sometime between March 1772 and May 1774,[39] and the flood may have provided them with the impetus to relocate, either across the river or to more distant (and more temporary) villages.

Taitt's journal, then, misrepresents Okfuskee's population loss and misinterprets the presence of Okfuskee's villages. Still, it is difficult to read the journal and not conclude that Okfuskee in the early 1770s was a very different place than it had once been. In the dozen years between the May 1760 attack and Taitt's March 1772 visit, most Okfuskees moved away from the main townsite, opting for either the Chattahoochee villages or small settlements closer to home. Some moved back during the next quarter-century, but not enough to prevent a fundamental change in the relationship between Okfuskee and its villages. By 1799, even after the inhabitants of three of the five Chattahoochee villages had returned to Okfuskee proper, only 40 percent of Okfuskees lived in the main town. And the community itself—which, in 1799, "[spread] out on both sides of the river"—was almost certainly less compact than it had been in 1760; Okfuskee was, in fact, "coming fast to an old field." Spatially at least, "the town" had given way to "the settlement."[40] For all of its shortcomings, then, Taitt's journal suggests that a fundamental change had taken place in Okfuskee's settlement pattern. Its people may not have scattered, at least not for good; but they had drawn apart.

Their reasons for doing so were, of course, complex and multifaceted, but the intersection of European livestock and Creek agricultural traditions surely played a part. Simply put, in Okfuskee, domesticated animals that imperiled crops also undermined community. Unfenced corn, beans, and squash—and the physical well-being and social harmony they made possible—were stationary targets for unrestrained horses, cattle, and pigs. By themselves, livestock did not necessarily disrupt Okfuskee's agricultural norms and social networks. When combined, however, with the Okfuskees' own traditions regarding socioeconomic resources and sociospiritual re-

generation, the presence of European animals called into question the understandings and practices at the root of Okfuskee life. As a result, when
they dealt with the problems and possibilities presented by domesticated
animals, the Okfuskees—with their tradition of a town-centered agriculture that produced material, social, and spiritual fulfillment—simultaneously faced disquieting questions about the future of community-based
production and the dynamics of social reproduction. In a very real way,
the form and meaning of Okfuskee were at stake.

The similarities, therefore, between David Taitt's 1772 visit to Okfuskee—when the headman Will's Friend "caused some fowls to be prepared
for breakfast"—and Tobias Fitch's 1726 trip to the town—when Okfuskees
presented him with "Some Fowls"—were more apparent than real.[41] The
passage of almost a half-century had not changed the Okfuskees' tradition
of hospitality, but their relationship to the animals served up as a part of
this tradition had changed dramatically, as had the townspeople's ties to
each other. Not only were there more domesticated animals in the Okfuskees' daily lives, but those animals had begun to affect the ways the townspeople used space and interacted with fellow Okfuskees and visiting Euro-
Americans. Fences and feuds, villages and plantations, townspeople who
lived at a distance and animals who lived nearby—these things were suddenly part of what it meant to be Okfuskee. As the next two chapters make
clear, a variety of factors contributed to the changes in town life; livestock
did not, by themselves, revolutionize Okfuskee. When evaluating the role
European animals played in Okfuskee, however, we must remember—as
the Okfuskees surely did—the link between communal field, town square,
and sacred fire. Agricultural practice, social life, and other-than-human
power were bound together. To the extent that livestock severed those
bonds—to the extent that the physical, social, and spiritual were no longer
intertwined—domesticated animals required the townspeople to create a
new way of being Okfuskees.

Colonial British America—like Okfuskee—was an agricultural place, a
place where 75 to 85 percent of the people depended on agriculture for
their livelihood, a place where farm and plantation practices, social patterns, and individual identities were intimately connected. As J. Hector St.
John de Crevecoeur wrote at the end of the colonial era, "some few towns
excepted, we are all tillers of the earth, from Nova Scotia to West Florida."
Paeans to "the American, this new man" aside,[42] to argue for agriculture's

centrality is not to insist on uniformity. Rural life in New England looked nothing like its counterpart in the South Carolina lowcountry, and neither could be confused with backcountry or middle colonies lifeways. Distinctive regional patterns notwithstanding, however, agriculture's ubiquity and centrality meant that farming, planting, and herding were never simply economic activities. As with the Okfuskees, social networks, cultural values, and personal roles were implicated in the process of extracting a living from the land. Colonists found that changes in or problems with agricultural practices called into question aspects of life that had appeared unassailable; even fine-tuning one's methods had far-reaching implications. As such, colonists who confronted questions regarding the declining fertility and availability of land, fluctuating commodity prices, and shifting labor pools inevitably found themselves face-to-face with more fundamental questions. Okfuskees chasing livestock out of their gardens or clearing a new village's fields might have been comforted to know that their Euro-American contemporaries faced comparable problems.

In eighteenth-century New England, for example, the colonists' commitment to extensive agriculture, large families, and partible inheritance collided with the area's limited supply of fertile soil. Historians disagree about the state of the region's economy—characterizations range from "increasing scarcity in an environment of spreading blight" to "flourishing"—but even the rosiest analytical spectacles discern rising rates of landlessness and declining quality of soil. Gradually, New Englanders responded by embracing out-migration and novel relations between family members. Farmers in the middle colonies enjoyed better agricultural conditions, but they too experienced a shortage of land and its attendant socioeconomic fallout. Even Pennsylvania's Quakers—the poster-children for colonial-era stability—found that inadequate supplies of land meant that the children of poorer Friends often left the meeting. The situation in Virginia was, if anything, even more alarming. Fields planted with tobacco required frequent rotation and long fallow periods; a landowner had to have a great deal of land in reserve. Faced with Tidewater-area land shortages, poorer colonists both delayed starting families and moved to the colony's frontiers.[43]

Colonists who struggled with the implications of a limited supply of easily exhausted land often dealt simultaneously with unpredictable prices for agricultural commodities. Virginians experienced economic depressions "with appalling regularity" between 1700 and 1750 as tobacco prices re-

peatedly plummeted and rallied. Planters responded by pressing for government regulation of the tobacco trade and by adopting a more diversified
agricultural regime. Such changes "called into question the planters' self-
perceptions" and possibly laid the groundwork for the emergence of a
revolutionary political ideology. Their contemporaries in South Carolina's
low country also found that commercial emergencies led to "difficult times"
and spurred innovations ranging from requiring slaves to produce more of
their own food to adopting indigo, cotton, and tidal rice farming. As in
Virginia, South Carolinians "redefined themselves" as they dealt with these
"changes in agriculture."[44]

Shifts in the agricultural labor pool likewise called into question fundamental relationships, values, and identities. In the Chesapeake, land-
owners who purchased slave labor did not revolutionize the mechanical
aspects of tobacco agriculture, but it would nonetheless be difficult to over-
state the changes they produced in the lives of the region's inhabitants. In
South Carolina, by contrast, the shift toward an enslaved "black majority"
accompanied a commitment to novel sorts of productive enterprises, but
here too the emergence of a slave-based agricultural economy affected every
aspect of colonial life. Slavery's expansion beyond the southern low country
was likewise world-altering, creating not simply new slave societies but
also new political rivalries along lines of both region and status.[45] Northern
colonists who depended on freer—if not free—workers were not immune
to the disruptions that followed adjustments in the deployment of agricultural labor. In eighteenth-century New England, the declining productivity and availability of land meant that sons could no longer be fully
employed at home; as young men sought a competency away from their
families' farms, they contributed to "the gradual dissolution of the exaggerated interdependence" that had previously characterized the father–son
relationship. At the same time, in Pennsylvania, some Quaker families
began purchasing unfree laborers, thereby threatening the Friends' domestic holiness and contributing to economic inequality within Quaker
communities.[46]

Working a farm or a plantation, then, had implications for the workings
of colonial society more generally. Uncertainty regarding agricultural labor,
the land upon which it was employed, and the commodities produced
there required careful consideration. The answers colonists reached to the
interwoven questions of early American agriculture—Who should plant
what, where, and how?—helped to determine the shape of life in first

colonial British America and then the United States. Like the Okfuskees, Euro-Americans adjusted familiar agricultural relationships and, in the process, changed the form and meaning of their world. If the Okfuskees' experiences overlapped with those of the colonists, however, it is also true that Okfuskees, and Indians more generally, faced several unique challenges originating in their peculiar connections to colonial British America. Simply put, Euro-Americans could look to Native Americans for solutions to many of their land-use problems, but not vice versa. In this case, American challenges transcended political boundaries separating the colonies from Indian country; American solutions did not. Okfuskees and their Indian contemporaries confronted the American task of fundamentally reordering their relationship to land, animals, plants, and each other at the same time as they faced the Native dilemma of forging a working relationship with a geographically and demographically expansive people who were both hostile and covetous.

From a Euro-American perspective, there was not room—physically or intellectually—for Indian farmers and herders in early America. Physically, Indian agriculturalists were impediments, people whose land claims blocked colonial expansion, whose crops and animals depleted resources, and whose marketing efforts competed with Euro-American producers. Colonists responded both by rejecting Native traditions and by refusing to allow Indians a meaningful role in Euro-American developmental models. Thus, for example, the Euro-American "gaze of development" ignored the Creek belief in communal ownership of spiritually charged land, but colonists simultaneously refused to allow Native peoples "to play the great American game of western land speculation." Indians could neither sell parcels of land to individual colonists nor retain their holdings and wait for prices to increase. Indian land, in fact, became a marketable commodity only when it left Indian hands. In this way, expansion and intolerance coexisted, producing an increasingly prosperous and homogeneous society while shifting the burden of landlessness and impoverishment to others.[47]

Such a strategy could be justified because Euro-Americans of all stripes were certain that "Indian agriculturalist" was an oxymoron. Evidence to the contrary notwithstanding, Indians were known to be nomadic hunters, not farmers. Euro-American culture theory "traced cultural variations to different modes of subsistence," and the Indians' undoubted status as savages meant that their agricultural endeavors were no more than primitive dabblings unworthy of serious consideration. That Indian economic life began coming under serious scrutiny in the late eighteenth century—just as Euro-American pressures rendered traditional Native strategies increasingly ineffective—only enhanced Euro-American certainty that Indian agriculture was a contradiction in terms. Beliefs of this sort, of course, sanctioned the forcible incorporation of Indian land, but they also allowed Euro-Americans to fashion themselves as bearers of a virtuous civility that, once taught to Indians, would free them from their wandering profligacy. Moral justification and territorial expropriation, in other words, went hand in hand as long-standing connections between the experiences of Indians and Europeans were elided in favor of peculiarly blinkered notions of Native inferiority and American destiny.[48]

5

_____

Newcomers in the
"Old White Town": Traders
and Economic Life in Okfuskee

The attack of May 16, 1760, found Okfuskee's British traders engaged in
a variety of tasks. Moses Price "happened to be out horse-hunting," while
Robert French "was selling a Blanket to two young Indian Fellows" and
William Rae entertained a "leading warrior of the town . . . at his house."
John Ross, his slave Tom, and William Mitchell "were in the horsepen,
preparing that day to . . . set off with their returns to the English settlements." As the violence unfolded, Rae, Ross, Tom, and Mitchell were killed,
but Price managed to escape thanks to the warning provided by one townswoman and the "provisions" given him by another. French, too, survived
the attack. The men delegated to kill him declared they "would preserve
him" instead; eventually, a townswoman directed French to the Okfuskee
Captain, who "assisted him . . . with an Horse, sweet flour, a pair of moc-
cossons, and an old Blanket to get him safe off."[1]

The events of May 16, 1760, attest to the multifaceted nature of the
traders' presence in Okfuskee. Not surprisingly, the attack occurred while
most were involved in some aspect of the deerskin trade, from selling
blankets to preparing a pack train of skins. Other incidents from that day,
however, suggest that Okfuskee–trader relationships had moved well beyond the deerskin trade, well beyond formal ties linking merchant and
customer. After all, the traders who survived owed their lives to some
Okfuskees' willingness to brave their neighbors' disapproval and provide
the Euro-Americans not only with warnings and hiding places but also
with food and other necessities. Among the townspeople who did so were
Price's "wife" and French's "Friend."[2] In reality, of course, the deerskin trade
and the personal bonds of kinship and friendship were simply different

sides of the same coin, a currency forged by generations of traders and Okfuskees. By 1760, traders were very much part of Okfuskee, a development that had significant implications for the town.

This chapter focuses on the traders' place in, and effect on, Okfuskee's socioeconomic system. The various types of British–Okfuskee trade offered opportunities to the men and women of Okfuskee, and the town prospered, for a time, thanks to the Okfuskees' abilities as hunters, farmers, and traders. However, the importance of the goods acquired from the newcomers and the pervasiveness of economic relations with Euro-Americans endowed the new items and the unfamiliar relationships with the potential to disrupt even the most basic of Okfuskee's socioeconomic relationships. As Creek hunting and trading practices changed after midcentury, these latent possibilities surfaced with a vengeance. The Okfuskees' trade with the Euro-Americans in their midst increasingly worked to disrupt town and family life, contributing to social strife and community disaggregation. In ways both welcome and disturbing, the market revolution had come to Okfuskee. Townspeople struggling with the new settlement patterns and agricultural routines discussed in the previous chapter were thus grappling simultaneously with the implications of an increasingly unfamiliar exchange system. Changes in one sphere of life informed changes in the others. New patterns of trade encouraged new settlement patterns; novel relations of exchange-oriented production dovetailed with the novel associations encouraged by the reproduction of livestock. In the end, Okfuskee's newcomers—European and African, cow and horse, trade good and exchange system—contributed to the process by which the townspeople reshaped their community's physical form, social networks, and the understandings and meanings upon which both depended.

Traders and Headmen

During the 1760 attack, Creeks killed a trader at his store across the river from Okfuskee. According to James Adair, the man "might have been saved, if he had not been too desperate; for a strong-bodied leading warrior of the town was at his house when they [the attackers] came to it, who grasped him [the trader] from behind, with his face toward the wall, on purpose to save him from being shot; as they durst not kill himself [the warrior], under the certain pain of death. But very unluckily, the gentleman struggled, got hold of him, threw him to the ground, and so became too fair a mark." "Thus" died "the son of J. R. Esq., Indian trading merchant of Augusta." William Rae, son of John, was killed in the attack. A month later, the name "Will's Friend" first appeared in the historical record when Okfuskee messengers delivered a peace talk to the British from "Tamathly-Hago and Will's-Friend, headmen of their town." The attack, Will's Friend and his colleague asserted, occurred "without their knowledge," and they were currently gathering up "all the [traders'] effects" stolen by their people; in the meantime, "in token of their sincerity, they had sent that [silk cap full of] tobacco for the beloved white men to smoak, and prayed they would accept it." For the next quarter-century, Will's Friend worked closely with both the British and the Americans, all the while bearing a name commemorating his attempt to save a trader.[3]

Will's Friend was not the only Okfuskee headman to risk bodily harm to protect a trader. Indeed, except for the fact that his name first appeared immediately after the death of William Rae, Will's Friend could be mistaken for Okfuskee's One Handed King, who saved William Edwards from a whipping by Georgia's agent, Patrick McKay, in 1735: "the one-handed King came and cover'd him [Edwards], clasping him in his Arms, and said that if he [McKay] would whip the said William Edwards they should whip him too, for that he had never seen such doings by the white People before, and it was not their Method, and . . . ordered the said William Edwards to be discharged and so he escaped his punishment." For the most part, however, the protection Okfuskee's headmen afforded the town's traders depended on less dramatic gestures. For example, in the aftermath of the 1760 attack, Georgia's governor proposed that designated Creeks watch over the traders; Okfuskee's leaders responded enthusiastically. Tomathla-Hago stated that "when [the traders] return they must live in such Headmen's Houses as shall be thought proper and able to protect them for it will not do for the traders to live alone out of the Towns." Two Okfuskee headmen stayed in town "to protect the Traders" during the winter of 1760–1761. One was Handsome Fellow, who claimed that he took care "of the White People" again in 1763, "[a]s he has always made it his Business to stand firmly by them on Every Occasion."[4]

Whether Okfuskee's traders would have agreed with such a self-portrait from the leader of the 1760 attack remains an open question, but they could not deny that mutually beneficial relationships between traders and headmen were common. Creek history, in fact, is littered with headmen whose names—like that of Will's Friend—denoted their close ties to particular traders; to take only one example, a 1758 list of the most important Creek leaders mentions Cussing's Landlord, Duval's Landlord, Dalton's Friend, and Eycot's Brother-in-Law. The traders reciprocated by making sure that British officials knew of their hosts. Thus, John Stuart, when directing an officer to identify the leading headmen, cautioned that "you must of course avail yourself of the Intelligence of the Traders; I however recommend to you to take their information concerning the Leading men in the Town where they reside with Caution, as I have allways found them partial to the People with whom they happen to be particularly connected."[5] Okfuskee's traders and headmen found themselves "particularly connected" for reasons which had to do both with the goals of the people involved and with the dictates of Creek tradition.

In Creek society, a town's headman—the mico—provided for the townspeople's welfare and mediated between townspeople and outsiders. In dealing with traders, the mico combined both of these responsibilities. Traders, after all, were most definitely not townspeople, but their presence was, as the Okfuskees knew, crucial to a town's continued prosperity. As early as 1728, three Okfuskee headmen endorsed a talk in which Oboyhatchey told the British, "I am sensible of the benefit of your Trade, and I am not unacquainted with the want of the same"; he promised to "stand by you and your Traders, for it is not long since we dearly knew the want of them." A generation later, after the 1760 attack, an Okfuskee headman hoped that "the Traders will not be debarred from bringing a plentiful Supply of all Sorts of Goods, and . . . that the Traders will not be afraid to come for they can't live without them." In 1777, Handsome Fellow echoed this sentiment, acknowledging that in "my Town . . . We have been used so long to dress our Children up as soon as they are born in goods procured of the white people, that we cannot do with out."[6] A mico's obligation to secure the well-being of his town meant, therefore, seeing to the trader's welfare, a responsibility that entailed ensuring that the trader had food and shelter; that trade was conducted fairly; that daily relations between the trader and the townspeople remained amicable; that townspeople paid their debts to the trader; and that the trader was protected from harm.

Of course, an Okfuskee headman who integrated a trader into the town responded to more than a disinterested concern for the public good. Headmen benefitted from a trader's presence. In the first place, Creeks expected leaders to ensure a reliable trade; the failure to do so meant a loss of influence. As Handsome Fellow put it when asking for the resumption of trade, "if our people go back [from the conference] naked our Enimies will [get?] a handle of it and laugh at us." Later that year, White Lieutenant of Okfuskee underlined the point, saying that to return without trade goods "would open the Mouths of our Enemies against us." The Okfuskee leaders may have been thinking, at least in part, of the 1759 confrontation between Mortar of Okchai and a British agent, who wrote from Okfuskee of "destroying his [Mortar's] Credit & Influence . . . [by] taking away our Trader out of his Town . . . & raising at last such a Clamour against him from his own Warriours, & other People, even the Women of that Town, that he was forced to quit it."[7] A headman's authority, then, protected a trader's inventory, and vice versa.

Headmen could also shore up their influence by the prominent display of items that symbolized their British connections, items that traders procured for them. For example, the British gave medals, arm plates, and gorgets to headmen who "distinguished themselves in our cause." In January 1763, Macartan & Campbell's Okfuskee store purchased arm plates, gorgets, "hair Jewells," and broaches in Augusta. It was likely no coincidence that a Creek party—in which two of the three leaders were Okfuskees—was visiting Georgia at the time. Whether or not these particular Okfuskees received these particular gifts, the town's headmen knew that, as Georgia's governor told this party, the British ability to supply "a plentiful Trade" meant that "we can pour in Goods upon you like the Floods of a great River when it overflows; We bestow our Favours on our Friends heartily and without Reserve." Hyperbole regarding unreserved favors aside, the volume of prestige items that traders provided to Okfuskee's leaders is attested to by the grave goods that accompanied a headman buried at an Okfuskee village, a man who went to the afterlife with eighty-one "ornaments (dangles) of all kinds," fifty buttons, thirty brass hawks-bells, four buckles, four arm rings, two arm bands, a neck ring, and a folding knife "with an incised bone handle." Whether he acquired these goods through trade, as unsolicited gifts from "Friends," or as part of the "annual presents by the hands of the traders" that Creeks insisted these visitors provide to their Creek "protectors," the Okfuskee headman owed his impressive array of high-status items at least in part to his ties to British traders.[8]

Traders also provided Okfuskee's headmen with access to colonial officials and the gifts they bestowed. Alexander Wood's career demonstrates the range of perks a trader could bring to a headman's life. Wood escorted Okfuskee headmen to the colonies in 1739 and 1744, and he brought down other headmen (possibly Okfuskees) in 1741 and 1742. Each such trip offered the town's leaders the chance to solidify their ties to British officials and to receive gifts; on their 1739 visit to Charleston, for example, Okfuskee's "King" and "Head Warrior" each received a red coat with silver buttons, a ruffled shirt, a hat with lace trim, a pair of shoes, and red stockings. Wood also had a certain amount of influence with South Carolina officials, and could, for example, persuade them "that Commissions and Presents may be given to some Headmen in the Creek Nation." South Carolina, in fact, delegated him to distribute gifts to the Creeks, and at one point he opened his house to Tusk Keenie for thirty-eight days while the headman visited the colony. Irrespective of other issues, then, it is not surprising that an Okfuskee headman defended Wood's employee, William Edwards, from a beating. A later generation of traders expanded on Wood's legacy by offering Okfuskee's headmen credit and by employing at least one of them as a factor in his own town.[9]

Finally, ties to traders benefitted the mico's family, who gained access to supplies and services through the kinship networks that structured so much of Creek society. Headmen were eager to have traders marry into their families, and the appearance of children from these unions suggests that several Okfuskee traders did so. Alexander Wood likely fathered Dougald Wood, "a half Breed Indian," and possibly Dougald's brother as well.[10] We can be more certain about James Germany's ties. An employee of Alexander Wood, Germany came to Creek country in 1733; he lived in Okfuskee for much of the 1740s and 1750s. Alexander Germany traded in Okfuskee in the early 1760s, and in 1759, Edmond Atkin described James's 22-year-old son, Billy Germany, as "an half Breed, Head Warriour Creek of Ockfusky."[11] White Lieutenant of Okfuskee was also "a half breed," and may have been Billy Germany.[12] In any case, the fact that White Lieutenant had a Euro-American father suggests the eagerness with which Okfuskee's leaders welcomed traders into their families. After all, White Lieutenant was Handsome Fellow's nephew and successor, meaning most likely that he was the son of Handsome Fellow's sister. And Handsome Fellow's father—and thus the father of White Lieutenant's mother—was Red Coat King, Mico of Okfuskee.[13] White Lieutenant's Euro-American father had married into the most powerful family in town.

Trade in Okfuskee

The traders' connections to Okfuskee headmen and their families facilitated the inclusion of these men—and their employees and slaves—into Okfuskee society. Traders were not, however, simply kinsmen-by-marriage, and both the Okfuskees and the traders knew it; nor, though, were traders solely conduits for commodities. Instead, the traders' relations with Okfuskees represented something of a hybrid, combining instances of commercial exchange with moments of relatively unstructured reciprocity. Once settled in town, traders participated in two types of exchange with the Okfuskees: an informal, barter-driven, day-to-day exchange of goods and services; and a more formal and less quotidian exchange of manufactured goods for deerskins at prices set (in theory) during treaty negotiations. The latter provided the rationale for the traders' presence, but the former made the latter possible, providing the traders with the material and social resources necessary to sustain themselves. Neither type of exchange can be understood without reference to the other, and the structure of, and changes in, each exchange system can help us to understand Okfuskee's developmental trajectory.

Informal Exchange

In 1744, South Carolina's House of Commons refused to fund the garrisoning of "the Fort lately built by Mr. Wood" in Okfuskee, in part because "it is impracticable . . . to supply it with Provisions . . . the Distance being so great." Wood did not need the Commons to tell him that Euro-Americans in Okfuskee could not depend on provisions shipped from Augusta. Wood also knew, however, that traders and diplomats, in Adair's words, "lived in the greatest plenty" while in Creek country. They owed their standard of living, on the one hand, to Creek beliefs regarding the obligations inhering in the roles of kinsmen and hosts. On the other hand, though, Euro-Americans in Creek towns depended heavily on the Creeks' willingness to sell food. Because it served as both a means and an object of exchange, food offered Okfuskees the opportunity simultaneously to draw traders into the community and to profit from their presence.[14]

By all accounts, Creeks valued generosity, and sharing food stood at the center of their conception of what it meant to be generous. For example, upon Tobias Fitch's 1725 arrival in Okfuskee, the "King" had food brought to him, while apologizing that "I Cannot Entertain you With Such as I am Entertained When I go Down to your Great Town; But I hope you will Except of Such as I have and you are very Welcom to it." Creeks expected traders to live up to Creek standards, and chastised them for having "a slavish temper" if they did not: "they say we are covetous, because we do not give our poor relations such a share of our possessions, as would keep them from want. There are but few of themselves we can blame, on account of these crimes, for they are very kind and liberal to every one of their own tribe, even to the last morsel of food they enjoy." Thus, when three Cowetas killed the Okfuskee trader William Thompson in 1761, the first excuse offered by their headmen was that "they wanted some Victuals from him and he would not give them any." Thompson's killers, it turned out, acted for other reasons, but it is significant that the culprits' defense opened with an appeal to the importance of sharing "Victuals." For all of their emphasis on sharing food, however, Okfuskees were not always generous. In fact, two days after the Okfuskees welcomed Fitch in 1725, the town's headman felt it necessary to remind his people that Fitch was "a Beloved man Come from the great King of the English" and that they "must all provide for him that he may not Want any thing that our Town Can Supplye him with." Whether or not the headman's speech had any effect is impossible to know, but he appealed to a central tenet in Creek culture: food was shared with both kinsmen and guests. In doing so, new bonds were created and old ones strengthened.[15]

The value placed on feeding the Euro-Americans who lived among them did not mean, however, that Okfuskees and their fellow Creeks hesitated to sell food to the newcomers. An emblem of hospitality in one context, food served as a commodity in another. As early as the 1720s, the traders' dependence on purchased provisions had reached the point where Fitch believed that they should leave Creek country by May, "for here they lie all the Summer, Eating out the Proffitt of the Winter." Likewise, Georgia's soldiers who garrisoned Fort Okfuskee were expected "to find themselves food," a duty that led James Oglethorpe to issue Lieutenant Alexander Willey more than £12 to be used for one year's provisions; almost twenty years later, Edmond Atkin noted that he purchased "Beef, Corn, Pease, Potatoes & Pumpkins at sundry times" during his troop's stay in Okfuskee. In fact, so profound was the dependence of British visitors on Creek supplies that traders and diplomats took the food trade for granted, commenting on this central facet of their lives only when problems surfaced.

Thus, we read of the food trade when "Every Thing here continue[s] very scarce, so that Victuals can hardly be purchassed at the most extravagant Rates" and when Euro-Americans reminded distant British officials "that a Traffick for Provisions Poultry &c. is what no Person can subsist without in an Indian Nation." The food trade also was mentioned if traders sought price reductions—as when John Stuart told a Creek delegation, including an Okfuskee headman, that traders could not "afford provisions which your people sell at a double price"; and if traders hoped to be reimbursed for their expenses—as when John Buckles told South Carolina's governor that he remained in Okfuskee for a week to "provide Provisions for myself" and the seventeen Chickasaws accompanying him.[16]

Establishing the existence of the food trade within Okfuskee is easier than discerning its form. Again, few sources refer to such exchanges, and then only tangentially. Traders and their packhorsemen bartered for food from both men and women. Creek hunters brought "large heap[s] of fat barbecued brisketts, rumps, and tongues of buffalo and deer, as well as plenty of bear-ribs" to traders, who also valued Indian-produced bear oil, and "commonly supply themselves with plenty of this oil from winter to winter."[17] The introduction of horses facilitated exchanges of meat and oil by easing the task of hauling these bulky commodities out of the woods. Given the seasonal nature of Creek hunting practices, however, the involvement of Okfuskee's men in the food trade must have been episodic.

In contrast, agricultural produce served as a year-round staple, and Okfuskee's women controlled the products of the gardens and fields. Moreover, women were responsible for cooking, and "the white people was obliged to be satisfied with the same coarse food that we [Creeks] used." Not surprisingly, then, the few references to trading agricultural products mention women. For example, an Upper Creek noted in 1771 that "formerly our old Women and Motherless Children used, by exchanging a little Corn for Goods, to be able to cover their Nakedness." It was not just widows and orphans who traded agricultural products, however. Creek women of all sorts—married and "free single," old and young—dealt with traders. Thus, Creek men told a Loyalist in 1778 that "As corn is very scarce amongst us, the Women will expect that you will pay them for all that they provide"; and in 1764 an Okchai headman demanded that "If a woman brings any thing to the House of a white man, let him pay her, & let her go again."[18]

What the Okfuskees received for their food is difficult to document.

Certainly, some of it was bartered for services. For example, William Thompson was "a Blacksmith and Gunsmith" who "begged" a British agent to "let him settle in the Oakfushees that he might make what he could by mending Indian's Guns &c"; he lived in Okfuskee off and on from 1756 to 1761. The British frequently commented on the Indians' need for smiths, and Okfuskees must have availed themselves of the opportunity to have their kettles, guns, hoes, knives, and axes repaired.[19] However, given the gendered division of labor in both Creek and British society, and given the agricultural and household skills of Creek women, the balance of trade for services was most likely weighted in the Okfuskees' favor. Moreover, to the extent that Creeks perceived sex as a service, Okfuskee women again controlled the commodity in question.

Most likely, then, Okfuskee's traders purchased their daily bread with merchandise, not services. Again, though, what they traded or how much the Okfuskees would give for a particular item remains unclear. In 1723, Governor Francis Nicholson told a party of Creeks that "our Traders Shall have liberty to buy your fowls and other Provisions, for trifles," and much of what Creeks acquired in the food trade were indeed trifles by British standards. The trading system adopted by the Cherokees and the British in 1760 shows what the latter expected to offer to, and receive from, southeastern Natives. According to William Bull, "The Indians have been a considerable time without Goods, and their Women, like others, excessively fond of ribbons and paint, with these the Garrison can barter for Corn, Hogs and Fowls." He noted that "A Yard of Ribbon may subsist one Man for a Month." The French garrison in Upper Creek country also relied to some extent on Indian-produced food, and they too sought to use "ribbons in the English style" to trade for Creek produce.[20]

The personal goods Euro-American packhorsemen brought to Okfuskee suggest that a similar system emerged there. For example, James Lessely received a pack train's worth of Macartan & Campbell's merchandise to take to Okfuskee in 1764. Before leaving Augusta, he bought personal supplies and "1 Bunch Barley Corn Bead." These beads were popular with Creek women, and Lessely thought they warranted an outlay of sixty-five shillings. Over the next year, Macartan & Campbell's Okfuskee store sold Lessely a kettle and two installments of "Sundry articles." Lessely almost certainly intended to use some of these goods in the food trade, and other Okfuskee packhorsemen also purchased small quantities of trade goods. George Bell's transactions over the years included a 1763 purchase of three and a half pounds "common beads," a frock, twelve yards of ribbon, two kegs of rum, and two large knives; in 1764, he bought four yards of ribbon. In 1762, John Burroughs purchased both personal supplies and some trade goods, most notably four knives and two kegs of rum. Henry Dalton bought six "Trading Knives" in September 1762, three knives in December, and four knives, a bundle of barley corn beads, and two pounds "White Common beads" the following July. Packhorsemen such as David Owens, John Audrey, and Thomas Chavers had similar accounts, and no doubt similar relations with the Okfuskees. About other men—such as John Fyffe, who appears in the records only once, when buying an ivory comb in Okfuskee—we can only guess.[21]

One person's trifle could become another's cherished possession, and no evidence suggests that Creeks felt dissatisfied with the beads and ribbons they received for their corn. Moreover, even the British knew that the Okfuskees and their fellow Creeks received more "substantial" goods for their foodstuffs; Europeans, in fact, found themselves offering valuable manufactured goods in exchange for edible Native trifles. Thus, an officer in Georgia's Okfuskee garrison wrote that the commander at Fort Toulouse told a 1740 Creek conference, including Red Coat King, "how ready he was to let them have Arms Ammunition Strong Liquor &ct for Triffles as corn light Skins &ct." Almost two decades later, the French again offered "Necessaries" for "Oil, Meat, and other Trifles." The Okfuskee food trade also included nondecorative items, as the packhorsemen's purchases show. Along with beads and ribbons, these men brought knives and cloth, and packhorsemen had carried such items into Creek country for some time. Prior to a 1751 trip to the Upper Creeks, for example, a "pack Horse Man" received personal items and three "Spring Knives" from his supervisor. That same year, an official remarked that "it has long been a Custom by the Traders to allow their Packhorsemen . . . the Priviledge of carrying a Horse load or two of Goods into the Nation for their private Benefit."[22] Okfuskees who participated in the food trade both encouraged and profited from such traditions.

Although several generations of Okfuskees prospered from bartering food to traders, it would be a mistake to assume that the food trade was a static institution. Like other aspects of Creek life, the food trade evolved over time. The spotty nature of the evidence makes some guesswork necessary, but given Creek ideas about hospitality and their eagerness to tie traders to their towns and families, traders in the early eighteenth century likely received a significant portion of their food as gifts. As Creeks became more accustomed to traders, and as the deerskin trade became more regularized, the food trade moved toward a more balanced notion of reciprocity. From a Creek perspective, the emphasis shifted from food to trade. At least in certain contexts, food itself became a commodity. The influx of traders in the 1760s solidified the trend toward commodification as the Creeks felt less attached to, and more encumbered by, the newcomers. As a group of fifteen traders—including six who periodically did business in Okfuskee—noted in 1767, the Creeks "loudly complain . . . that their country does not afford a Sufficient quantity of provision for Support of themselves & family, with such an Additional number of white people as have lately come amongst them."[23]

As traders poured into Creek country and as food's economic (as opposed to social) character solidified, some traders began living in ways that gave them a measure of independence from the food trade. Increasingly, traders set up their houses outside of Creek towns, a trend that Okfuskee's traders eagerly embraced. One such establishment was described in 1759 as being "alone in the Woods, with other convenient Buildings." As traders became "especially" likely "to settle at a very convenient distance" from Creek towns, these complexes became the center of economic activities that went well beyond the purchase of deerskins. Most notably, traders used their "plantations" for herding livestock and for planting crops, projects on which, Stuart noted in 1767, "Negroes and Mulattoes are Employed." Okfuskee's traders, in fact, tended to be slaveowners; some of these slaves accompanied their masters to Okfuskee.[24]

The traders' increasing independence alarmed the Creeks. In 1759, Wolf "complained" about "[John] Spencer's so living in the Woods & not in his Town," and the 1760 statement by Tomathla-Hago of Okfuskee that traders "must live in . . . Headmen's Houses . . . for it will not do for the traders to live alone out of the Towns" may have been motivated as much by a desire to reintegrate the traders into Okfuskee as by the need to protect them. Headmen noted the hardships a decline in the food trade imposed on their people, as Emisteseguo did in 1771 when he stated that old women and orphans "formerly" could trade corn for clothes but "they now are deprived of this Resource, and often obliged on the Contrary to purchase Corn from the Traders." Less influential Creeks had their own methods of demonstrating their dissatisfaction. In 1772, the "young people" of an Upper Creek town, angry at a trader's prices, "broke [John] Bell's doors and destroyed his household utensils such as pots, bowls etc. and spoiled all his victuals." Bell was no doubt terrified, but the destruction of his cookware and provisions, coupled with the failure to harm his trade goods, suggests that the townspeople meant to remind him of the importance of the food trade. As late as 1790, an American agent reported that Creeks would not allow the traders "to cultivate much land, upon the supposition that if the traders raise produce themselves, they will not purchase the little they have to sell."[25]

Formal Exchange

For all of its importance to the Okfuskees and their fellow Creeks, however, the food trade remained a subsidiary to the deerskin trade. The townspeople's material and social aspirations depended on their abilities as hunters of deer, processors of skins, and traders for manufactured goods. Success in these areas permitted the Okfuskees to participate in a process which one scholar has labeled "develop-man": "a cultural self-realization on a material scale and in material forms never before known." Firearms allowed an elaboration of the male sphere, opening up new hunting horizons and permitting geographic expansion. Closer to home, clothing and personal decoration became more elaborate as European fabrics, mirrors, and ornaments became available. More efficient metal tools—hoes, axes, kettles, needles, scissors, knives—replaced their Native counterparts, while alcohol added a new dimension to social life. Through it all, the Okfuskees believed themselves to be, and were recognized by others as, Creeks. The townspeople found ways, in other words, to wring continuity out of innovation, security out of novelty. Even the surviving remnants of their material culture attest to their ability to domesticate the deerskin trade and its products. A bottle of wine, once emptied, was shattered to make a hide scraper; a gun barrel, once broken, was flattened to form a chisel; a silver cross, once etched with a new design, was buried with a dead child.[26] To be a "modern Creek," the Okfuskees' daily lives showed, was not an oxymoron. And to be modern, by the early eighteenth century, meant participating in the deerskin trade.

To acknowledge the central—and positive—role the deerskin trade played in the development of Creek culture is not, however, to dismiss the ways in which the same system of exchange exposed Creeks to tremendous strains. Most obviously, alcohol consumption contributed to social pathology and national indebtedness to such a degree that it became, in Peter Mancall's apt phrase, "Deadly Medicine." More insidiously, however, deerskins and the goods for which they were exchanged increasingly became the focus of Creek life. The deerskin trade reached into every corner of Okfuskee, exerting tremendous pressure on the interpersonal networks that held the community together. Adair suggests as much when, in his discussion of purification rituals, he notes that "Formerly, every hunter observed the very same religious economy; but now it is practiced only by those who are the most retentive of their old religious mysteries."[27] A declining religious economy meant broad-reaching changes in the relationships that linked Okfuskees, deer, manufactured goods, and Euro-American traders. Although a hunter committed to the old religious economy and a new-style hunter arrived home with the same goods (skins and meat), the end products of their hunts were different. A religious economy produced a set of connections between the hunter and both the nonhuman beings addressed in his rites and the human beings who shared in his ceremonies and consumed the products of his hunt. A nonreligious economy produced a different web of connections and relationships, a different society. The evolving deerskin trade, then, illuminates not only the Okfuskees' relations with the material world but also their connections to fellow townspeople and Euro-American traders. Changes in the Okfuskees' production and sale of deerskins—in the volume of skins traded, the ways those skins were processed, the seasonal nature of the work, the number and character of the town's traders—reveal profound shifts in community life.

The Okfuskees and their fellow Creeks devoted an ever-increasing amount of energy to the deerskin trade. Eighteenth-century export figures provide ample evidence of this trend. The approximately 90,000 pounds of deerskins exported from Charleston in 1721 pale in comparison with the 220,000 pounds of deerskins exported in 1738, a figure which, in turn, seems insignificant in the face of the 355,000 pounds of deerskins exported annually from Charleston in the late 1750s. By 1768, Savannah and Charleston each exported over 300,000 pounds of deerskins.[28] The Creeks achieved impressive production gains by committing to longer hunting seasons and an expansionist foreign policy that secured productive hunting grounds.

Export figures, however, can only begin to show the shifting nature of the deerskin trade in Creek communities. Not only did Okfuskees bring more skins back to town, but those skins arrived at different times of the year. Thus, during a July 20, 1726, Okfuskee meeting, Fitch demanded that the Upper Creeks reimburse a plundered trader. In response, the Okchai Captain, "by order of the Whole Body," stated, "this is not a Time of year To pay Debts in For there is not Skins in the Whole Nation To pay Half the Debt But by the Next Spring every on[e] of them Shall be paid." Fitch reiterated his demand on September 14, and the Creeks again responded, "we have not the Skin's among us." Fitch's difficulty in obtaining Creek deerskins during the summer was echoed by a Savannah merchant, who noted in 1739 that the traders seldom sent down many skins after the spring.[29]

The situation, however, began to change in the 1740s, and by the 1750s, statistics from South Carolina show that fall shipments from Creek country were second only to spring shipments in terms of skins produced for export, and that their importance was rising. By the 1760s, traders brought down significant numbers of deerskins in the fall, skins that had been processed in Creek towns during the summer. In 1763, for example, 1,767 pounds of deerskins from Macartan & Campbell's Okfuskee store reached Augusta on April 14; on June 13, the same store was credited with 2,674 pounds; and on October 27, a shipment of 1,156 pounds arrived from Okfuskee. A year later, two June shipments from Okfuskee brought in over 3,000 pounds of deerskins; a November shipment of over 1,700 pounds followed.[30] The fall cargoes represent the summer labor of many Okfuskees, labor previously confined to the winter and early spring.

Not only were Okfuskees producing deerskins at different times after midcentury, but they were also processing those skins in different ways. The Creeks traded deerskins classified as either "dressed"—indicating that the flesh and hair was removed, and the skin smoked—or "raw"—defleshed, but unsmoked and still "in the Hair." A raw skin was worth 50 to 70 percent of a dressed one. Prior to the 1760s, the Creeks dressed the vast majority of their skins, and merchants found it "surprising" when deerskins required "a second dressing . . . Indians commonly do them well enough." Creeks did trade some raw skins, but the practice tended to be confined to traders and customers intent on flouting accepted standards— trading for rum, doing business outside of towns, offering and receiving excessive credit. At other times, Creeks traded raw skins knowing that, as one British agent put it, the traders "cannot dress them themselves but must give one in ten to have drest & very often does not get half of what he give to be Dressed; but you say the Doggs eat them when they were in soak." Whether before or after the initial exchange, then, most Creeks dressed their deerskins. As late as 1752, less than 5 percent of the skins exported from Georgia were unprocessed.[31]

By the early 1760s, though, the Okfuskees and their fellow Creeks were dressing fewer and fewer of their deerskins. Part of the change stemmed from the rising number of illegal traders in Creek country, traders who, like their outlaw predecessors, eagerly accepted raw skins. Macartan & Campbell's accounts show, however, that illegal traders were not the only ones buying raw skins. Macartan & Campbell's reputation was sound, and yet, between 1762 and 1766, 22.9 percent of the deerskins that passed through their Augusta store were raw. Their Okfuskee store was even more likely to ship raw skins: 28.7 percent of the skins that left Okfuskee were raw. Overall, Okfuskee contributed 22 percent of the deerskins sent to Macartan & Campbell's Augusta store, but 27 percent of the raw skins. The trend toward trading raw skins, visible in the early 1760s, accelerated as the decade went on. In 1768, an agent stated that the Creeks "were for some Time Past accustom'd to deliver the Skins in the Hair"; by 1771, "the principal traders," including an Okfuskee firm, noted "that the Creek Indians could not be prevailed on, for several years past, to dress their Skins." By the mid-1770s, one merchant's accounts showed that only 12.5 percent of his deerskins were dressed.[32]

The early to mid-1760s, then, represent something of a transitional period in the Creek deerskin trade. As Creek production of deerskins continued its century-long rise, raw deerskins, once traded rarely and clandestinely, became a staple trade good and were increasingly accepted by even established traders. The transitional nature of these years is attested to by more than simple shifts in the raw versus dressed ratio, however. At the same time that more raw skins were changing hands, the Okfuskees modified their seasonal work patterns. Creeks in the early eighteenth century had traded their skins in the late winter and early spring. In the 1760s, the deerskin trade continued to exhibit seasonal patterns, but now the time of year influenced not whether the Creeks traded skins but whether those skins were dressed. In fact, the striking aspect of Macartan & Campbell's accounts is not the rising number of raw deerskins in circulation but the tendency for shipments of Creek deerskins to consist of either raw or dressed skins, but rarely both. Spring remained the busiest time for the deerskin trade, but now spring exchanges netted only raw skins; traders who wanted dressed skins had to wait until late summer or fall.

The shipments from Macartan & Campbell's Okfuskee store demonstrate the seasonal nature of deerskin processing. In November 1762, 3,528 pounds of dressed skins, and no raw ones, arrived in Augusta from Okfuskee, while in April 1763, the Okfuskee shipment consisted of 91 pounds of dressed skins and 1,676 pounds of raw ones. Mid-June 1763 brought 2,674 pounds of dressed Okfuskee leather to Augusta, and a late October shipment of 1,108 pounds of dressed and 48 pounds of raw skins followed. In early June 1764, an Okfuskee shipment (by way of Okfuskee's Chattahoochee villages) netted Macartan & Cambell 1,052 pounds of raw leather and 150 pounds of dressed skins,[33] while a late June shipment brought in 2,350 pounds of dressed skins. The November shipment from Okfuskee contributed 1,740 pounds of dressed and 8 pounds of raw leather, and the town's May 1765 shipment essentially reversed this ratio, bringing in 200 pounds of dressed and 1,640 pounds of raw leather. All told, between November 1762 and May 1765, 88.5 percent of the company's raw skins and 3.5 percent of its dressed leather arrived in spring shipments; the summer and fall, by contrast, netted 91.9 percent of the dressed leather and 1.1 percent of the raw skins.[34] Dressed skins had become synonymous with summer and fall, raw ones with spring. Not surprisingly, then, the few references to Macartan & Campbell paying Augusta residents to process skins appear in April, May, and June. Even goods sold on credit reflected the seasonal nature of deerskin processing, and trader account books from the late 1760s and early to mid-1770s suggest that seasonal variation in processing skins continued into the Revolutionary era.[35]

Of course, documenting an activity's existence is easier than determining its meaning. In terms of the growing trade in raw deerskins and the changes in seasonal processing habits, it seems that the Okfuskees responded, at least initially, to shifts in hunting practices. By the early 1760s, not only did Creek hunting parties return from their winter hunts later and later in the year, but these groups arrived home with more and more deerskins. Once in Okfuskee, the hunters and their families confronted the task of processing the skins before the onset of their spring agricultural responsibilities. Perhaps Okfuskees lacked the time to dress every deerskin; perhaps their need for goods after a long winter in the woods outweighed the lower prices raw skins brought; perhaps they simply wanted to enjoy their new wealth. For whatever reason, Okfuskees traded roughly a third of their raw skins immediately, while dressing the remaining two-thirds, which they traded a month or two later. The summer hunt produced fewer skins, which—the traders' fall shipments of dressed deerskins suggest—Okfuskees processed between the Busk and the harvest.[36] The Okfuskees thus showed an increased willingness to sacrifice purchasing power at certain times of the year. Despite the growing magnitude of the raw skin trade, however, the townspeople retained a tried-and-true approach to undressed skins. As in the past—when Okfuskees had periodically used these items to acquire alcohol or excess credit from unlicensed traders—such skins could be either sold or processed, depending on the people's needs.

Continuity of this sort notwithstanding, however, when approximately a third of the Okfuskees' deerskins were traded raw,[37] it had the potential to disrupt the town's web of social relations. Creeks believed that a deer's skin belonged to the hunter, but that his female relatives should dress the skin; the hunter then traded it and used the goods he received to provide for his family. If raw skins could be traded openly and in large quantities, then men (especially unmarried men) could trade without relying to such a large degree on women. Moreover, skins that did not require much processing could be disposed of, frequently to illegal traders, without bringing them back to town. Of course, such transactions meant that the town's traders could not collect the deerskins that Okfuskees owed them, a situation that made it difficult for the traders to pay their own creditors. One Okfuskee trader, "having lately been arrested [in Augusta] for debt," committed suicide in 1767. In addition, exchange in the woods or backcountry meant that, given the goods illegal traders carried, Okfuskees were more likely to receive rum for their leather. The trade in raw skins, then, exposed Okfuskee to the risks associated with diminished returns for skins, increased spending on alcohol, impoverished families, and dissatisfied traders. Not surprisingly, then, "all the Chiefs of the upper Creek Nation" told Stuart in 1769 that "they wished to see the practice of purchasing Raw Skins in the Hair . . . prevented, as thereby an opening is left for great Frauds, the Value of their Skins greatly diminished, & Trading in the Woods encouraged and Rendered Easy, for dressing the deer Skins is the work of their Women in their Towns after returning from Hunting."[38]

For the Okfuskees, high trader turnover enhanced the risks associated with the raw skin trade. The "principal traders" noted that, after "the year 1760 when several of His Majesty's Subjects were plundered & Murdered" and others "declined business," the chance for "Fortunes" attracted "many others to become" traders. Because the traders killed in 1760 had close ties to Okfuskee, the town's trading situation was especially unsettled. It remained so for years. In January 1761, men from Okfuskee helped loot stores in their own town and in Hillibee. The Okfuskee Captain put a stop to the robberies, promised to have the goods returned, and made the offenders release the Sugatspoges trader, Henry Dalton, "whom they detain[ed] as a slave." Dalton remained in the Okfuskee area as an employee of Macartan & Campbell until 1765, but John Highrider, whose Okfuskee store was also looted, soon abandoned the town, most likely after his employee, the blacksmith William Thompson, was killed by Cowetas later that year. Macartan & Campbell themselves abandoned Okfuskee by the summer of 1765, selling out to Paine, Scott & Munro. The Rae family and their associates continued to deal with Okfuskee despite William Rae's death, but long-term relationships between traders and Okfuskees were increasingly rare in the 1760s. When even Handsome Fellow thought it necessary to seek out Cherokee traders, as he did in 1766, it is clear that many Okfuskees were dealing with traders they did not know.[39]

Instability among established traders was, however, only part of the problem. The actions of the traders who remained added to Okfuskee's chaotic situation. Many operated on the edge of socially accepted behavior. For example, Robert French, gainfully employed as a packhorseman in 1760, resurfaced as an illegal trader in 1762; by 1772, however, he lived and traded in a respectable fashion at an Okfuskee village. Likewise, by 1768, Stephen Smith (licensed as an Okfuskee trader in 1761) and George Munro (a partner in the firm which bought Macartan & Campbell's Okfuskee store in 1765) had opened illegal stores on the Georgia frontier; their "Illicit" operations led a British official to authorize a Creek party to seize "a great amount of [their] leather and goods." Another Okfuskee trader, Robert Rae, employed men who violated trading regulations, while he himself ignored British embargoes and was accused of trading in the woods. Rae may, in fact, have traded in a small Okfuskee village, rather than in the woods, but he attracted the ire of some Okfuskee headmen, who felt that traders should base their operations in the central town.[40] Like Rae, Michael Myers and William Oates both faced accusations of trading in the woods and of setting up shop in Okfuskee villages. Other traders allowed their packhorsemen to operate small-scale trading operations in town, supplying them with goods and purchasing the deerskins they bought.[41]

Finally, in a development that further muddied the trading waters, some

Okfuskees became traders themselves, either as factors for Euro-Americans or as free agents. As early as 1761, two Okfuskees purchased "so much cloth"—one man bought eleven blankets—in Augusta that it "occasion[ed] some suspicions"; most likely, however, they simply planned to retrade the cloth in Creek country. By 1774, White Lieutenant was a factor for Robert Rae, who, Taitt reported, traveled to Creek country "to get Skins from Stochlita [White Lieutenant], he says that he left goods with him"; four years later, the headman's reputation was such that, as he put it, two traders "plagued me for my skins and wanted me to take a Cargo." By century's end, his brother was an "Indian factor" in Okfuskee.[42]

By the late 1760s and early 1770s, then, Okfuskees confronted a deerskin trade that bore little resemblance to the trading system of the 1750s. Raw deerskins had become the commodity of choice, and traders competed with each other both inside and outside of town to acquire deerskins. Rival traders flooded Creek country with trade goods and, after remaining stable for years, official and unofficial prices for European goods fell.[43] More competition for deerskins and lower prices for foreign merchandise should have been good news, but the effect of these developments on the Okfuskees' standard of living was offset by the shrinking deer herds, the increasing Euro-American pressure on hunting grounds, the ongoing Creek–Choctaw war, the growing trade in raw skins, and the rising consumption of non-durable goods, especially alcohol. The effect on Okfuskee society, on the other hand, was noticeable. By the late 1760s, the relationships that the deerskin trade had formerly encouraged and the town-focused life that resulted from those ties were under assault by the modes of interaction promoted by the new-style exchange system. Trade, which had helped to bind Okfuskee together, now threatened to tear it apart.

The challenges presented by the new trading patterns are best shown by the Creek headmen's complaints against trading in the woods and back-country. From their perspective, trade of this sort combined the worst aspects of the new system: unprocessed skins; year-round trade; itinerant traders; large purchases of alcohol. The headmen's complaints reflected both concerns that their traders were being harmed and fears that rum-drinking impoverished families. The headmen, however, obviously feared something else as well: the breakup of their towns. Again and again, Creek headmen linked the new deerskin trade to community disaggregation. Thus, during a 1767 conference attended by an Okfuskee headman, an Upper Creek stated, "I am to desire that a stop may be put to trading in the Woods"; he noted that "when any of our people for the benefit of Planting settle at a distance from their Towns, Traders immediately settle there." Stuart, in summarizing this conference, wrote that "the Chiefs desired that none of the detached Villages should be allowed Trade which would force them to rejoin their Nation." After a meeting two years later, Stuart reported on Upper Creek complaints that trading "in the Indians Hunting Ground & detached Villages" led to "very great Inconveniences," and that the backcountry trade "induce[d] the Indians to leave their Towns, & to form Settlements near the Frontiers." Four years later, two Okfuskee headmen told Taitt that a recent disturbance in their town was "the Fault" of "the White People for allowing Traders in the Woods which encourages their Young People to Committ such Things as they do." The next spring, an Upper Creek said "That formerly the Trade was Carried on by a few People, and in their principal Towns, but now Great Numbers of Traders Came among them from all Parts, and Trade in the Woods & Hunting Grounds & in the Villages, and wherever they can find a Single House, and that many unruly bad white Men are amongst them, & Carry great Quantitys of Rum, and that by this their Young People have become unruly also."[44] Traders like Robert Rae, William Oates, and Michael Myers followed the Okfuskees wherever they went, thereby contributing to the disintegration of Okfuskee.

As with livestock and agriculture's influence on settlement patterns, Taitt's 1772 trip can help us understand the Okfuskees' experiences with British traders. In less than three months in Upper Creek country, Taitt heard complaints about traders' livestock and reported on horses that wandered off or were stolen. He met a trader who owned a "plantation" and "Negroes," and traveled with a trader who hunted for his own meat. Taitt encountered packhorsemen who brought up rum and traders who exchanged rum for deerskins; again and again, he witnessed alcohol-induced problems. He visited towns that had several traders, and others with Creek factors. Headmen complained to him about trading in the woods and villages. The desire for trade goods, the fear of indebtedness, and the threat of violence pervade his journal and letters.[45] Taitt, in other words, visited the Creeks as they struggled with an economic system that threatened to undermine social order. Had he arrived a dozen years earlier, he would have witnessed a very different scene.

In the decades prior to 1760, the structure of the deerskin and food trades helped to focus both Okfuskees and traders on the town. In Okfuskee, traders found headmen who looked after them, women who provided them with food and services, and men who offered processed skins for manufactured goods. At the same time, Okfuskee's headmen found in their town the material and social support for their authority; the townswomen found both townsmen who needed their deerskins processed and British men who purchased food and services; and the townsmen found not only townswomen to process their deerskins but also traders to buy them. For several generations, Okfuskee's headmen, women, and hunters formed long-lasting relationships with their traders, relationships which both centered on their town and reinforced the town's place in their lives.

During the 1760s, however, Okfuskee became, in a sense, superfluous to the deerskin and food trades. The rising importance of raw skins meant that Okfuskee's men no longer needed to return home to trade their deer-skins; the production of marketable deerskins became a much more indi-vidualistic enterprise. The death of some traders, the departure of others, and the arrival of a host of replacements severed long-standing relation-ships between townspeople and traders, while simultaneously offering Okfuskees an expanded array of trading options, many of which were found outside of town. Headmen no longer functioned as facilitators and overseers of Okfuskee–British exchange relations, and some became traders in their own right, furthering the decentralization of the exchange system. Traders themselves set up plantations outside of Okfuskee, depriving townswomen of steady customers for their produce and becoming com-petitors for the business of itinerant traders and diplomats. The deerskin and food trades, in other words, ceased to function as arguments for the town's centrality. By the 1770s, the Okfuskees knew that manufactured goods, so important economically and socially, were often acquired in ways that called into question the forms and structures at the heart of Creek town life. To the extent that Okfuskees remained focused on their town, they did so despite their economic relations, not because of them.

Community life did not, in fact, fall apart, but Okfuskee's evolving eco-nomic situation led to significant changes. As livestock became a more important presence in the town; as good fences increasingly made good neighbors; as traders ceased to depend on townswomen for food; as hunting seasons lengthened; as raw skins moved to the fore; as trade shifted from the town to the woods; as traders flooded into the area—as each

development unfolded, the patterns of interaction knitting Okfuskee together began to unravel. That the end result was not the dissolution of the
town was due, at least in part, to the fact that Okfuskees were united by
aspects of Creek life that were reasonably independent of their way of
making a living: kinship and friendship; dances and black drink; histories
and legends; the Busk and the town fire. While the Okfuskees of the 1760s
and 1770s gained an ever-greater appreciation for the implications of the
new animals, people, and goods that made up their lives, they knew that
Okfuskee remained, in White Lieutenant's words, "an old white Town."[46]
As such, it retained a place in their lives, and its people continued to have
a call on their affections.

From trading deerskins and furs to peddling foodstuffs and crafts, from
serving as guides and teachers to laboring as servants and slaves, from
unintentionally clearing fields for the first generation of colonists to un-
willingly clearing the title to land desired by those colonists' descendants—
historians have long acknowledged that, in these ways and more, Indians
participated in early America's economic development. In fact, in a recent
effort to redefine the parameters of colonial-era economic growth, two
scholars refer to "the difficulty of disentangling some economic activity of
Native Americans from that of colonists"; they argue that "Native Americans
need to be taken into account . . . [E]conomic history's neglect of them
may have led to a misunderstanding of the forces that shaped the early
American economy."[47] Weighing Indian influence and charting their activities is both worthwhile and insufficient. To stop here is to leave ourselves
with sophisticated versions of the "Indian contribution" lists—corn and
tobacco, the tomahawk and the moccasin—memorized by generations of
elementary school students. We can look beyond measurable contributions
and particular encounters to the broad patterns of experience that crossed
cultural and political frontiers. All across early America, living standards
rose but so did dependence; new avenues for personal expression and self-
fulfillment emerged, but so did new ways for strangers to make their influence felt; markets revolutionized the material world but also reshaped
social life. As anyone familiar with early American economic history would
expect, Okfuskee's traders and the townspeople's market-oriented trade
brought trade-offs—compromises and choices that were at once specific
to Okfuskee and characteristic of early America more generally.

It is certainly far from surprising to witness the Okfuskees' efforts to purchase a wide array of consumer goods. The free inhabitants of colonial British America spent much of the eighteenth century in an unprecedented spasm of acquisition. Whether they label this process "the invention of comfort" or "the refinement of America," historians have recognized colonial America's "consuming interest" in consumption.[48] Rich and poor, planter and farmer, urban resident and backcountry pioneer—Euro-Americans from all walks of life and every colonial region reshaped their sociomaterial world. And, as in Okfuskee, the colonial effort at refashioning necessitated a prolonged engagement with markets. Whether or not British America was born capitalist, whether or not it became capitalist by the end of the colonial era, it is clear that most colonists were willing participants in market-based production and exchange. Commerce facilitated agendas ranging from the personal to the communal and from the material to the spiritual; it was "not only necessary but patently attractive." By the eve of the American Revolution, 30.5 percent of the average colonist's budget was devoted to imports from outside of his or her colony of residence. Okfuskees could hardly have been more dependent on market forces than their Euro-American neighbors.[49]

None of which is to say that colonists found markets to be entirely unproblematic. The early American goal of "competence" was itself predicated on keeping market forces at arm's length, on ensuring that one's family was both comfortable and independent. To the extent that the former depended on goods and services acquired in the market, it implicitly called the latter into question. Beyond fears of dependence—which appear to have worsened after 1740 as consumption of foreign goods rose— market-based consumption led colonial Americans to express concern regarding issues ranging from the leveling of social distinction and the pernicious effects of rampant entrepreneurship to the hollow and corrupt nature of a gentility that depended on material refinement.[50] Colonists also could not help but notice that market relations had the potential to call into question the form and content of social relationships. Individuals learned "to develop new stories about themselves," a process that implicated not just self-perception but also relations at all levels of society, from the familial and communal to the imperial. Southern slave owners—with their simultaneous reliance on modern commodity markets and premodern labor practices—were especially wary of the market's implications.[51]

The trade-offs that Okfuskees confronted would, then, have been familiar to their contemporaries in British North America. All free Americans sought to balance the demands and benefits of the market economy; all purchased a wide range of goods; all sought some form of competency; all went into debt at one time or another; all felt the pinch of dependence on seemingly uncaring distant suppliers; all found that the market called into question key relationships and understandings. Like their British neighbors, then, Okfuskees had many reasons to worry. And, like those neighbors, Okfuskees could be forgiven for believing that they could adjust to the challenges ahead, that they would harness the disturbing and unfamiliar in the service of the welcome and traditional. They had, after all, done so before. For Okfuskees, however, these market-centered experiences produced a profoundly different trajectory than they did for the inhabitants of the British colonies. There were two reasons why this was so, the first centering on the British Empire and the second on Okfuskee itself.

In terms of the latter, the values and beliefs at the center of Creek culture and society meant that communities like Okfuskee were, in the end, less tolerant of, and more endangered by, commercial markets than were Euro-American towns. Given the right conjunction of ideologies and institutions, community life and commercial transactions can reinforce each other, but the Okfuskees' family lives and community relations were centered on intellectual and social constructs that did not mesh easily with market-oriented behaviors. European-style commerce thus undermined the Creeks' central integrative units. The contrast between the Okfuskees' experiences and those of New England's Puritans—another town-centered people—is instructive. Puritans created a metaphysically grounded culture of development in which market-oriented behavior could produce social consolidation. Okfuskees exhibited similar acquisitive impulses but their desires lacked both an explicit moral justification and an implicit social function. The Puritan system of mobilizing social capital—political, social, and religious norms and networks—counterbalanced, humanized, and ultimately fed off commercial development, while in Okfuskee, interpersonal networks and traditional values were threatened by the activities encouraged by the emerging market economy. Similarly, although Puritans and Okfuskees shared ambivalent feelings about markets, the Okfuskees lacked the Puritans' deep-seated belief in both a redemptive, improvement-oriented individualism and a sacralized yet commercially focused community. In the end, then, Okfuskee could survive in a world dominated by commercial markets, but it lacked the civil structures and intellectual constructs that allowed some of its Euro-American neighbors to thrive in the same milieu.[52]

Cultural differences alone cannot, however, explain the Okfuskees' experiences with a commercial economy. Market relations were more destructive to Native communities than to Euro-American ones not simply because Indians failed to adjust to the new system (although some did) and not only because that system violated Indian traditions and norms (although it sometimes did), but because the racially charged political economy of the British Empire (and later, the United States) denied Native Americans room to maneuver. The Okfuskees' experiences remind us, in other words, of "the role of politics in political economy." The unwillingness, for example, to allow Indians to profit from land speculation or to market their agricultural surpluses represented a politically based constriction of Native economic opportunity. Markets were open to Indians only under certain circumstances. They could produce and purchase only a set range of goods, a range whose boundaries were increasingly set not by market forces or Indian cultures but by the political requirements of colonial and imperial life.[53]

In fact, however, the role of politics in setting Okfuskees and their Native contemporaries apart from the economic mainstream went beyond differential access to markets. Take, for example, the intertwined issues of indebtedness and credit. Creek debts were accumulated by individuals but Euro-American politics transformed personal debt into a political problem, one that entangled all Creeks when British officials insisted that communal land be ceded to discharge individual obligations. For British subjects, by contrast, personal and national debt were separate and distinct categories, a political arrangement that allowed the British government to wallow in red ink—"Borrowing reached such heights that if eighteenth-century Britain had gone to the International Monetary Fund for a loan it would have been shown the door"—without endangering personal fortunes or individual access to productive resources. In fact, the British government's ability to go into debt was a critical component in the "sinews of power" undergirding the personal prosperity that accompanied military victory and imperial expansion. The personal politics of credit were similarly weighted against the Creeks. Because "[c]redit was a matter of confidence, and confidence was a matter of opinion," Creeks were sharply limited in their ability to gain access to either large or long-lasting lines of credit. They lacked the literacy and English-language skills to participate fully in the transatlantic communication networks that mobilized economic resources, and they lacked the cultural standing necessary to deploy the "language of honorable service" and "the ties of instrumental friendship and connection that still structured eighteenth-century commerce."[54] The British would allow Creeks to fall into debt but they would never receive "credit"—the conjunction of economic resources and personal confidence—because they were not seen as creditable. Thus, Creeks already disadvantaged by an empire committed to converting individual Creek debt into a national Creek liability found themselves squeezed by a credit system predicated on a degree of social legitimacy that they could never attain.

Unlike greatness, then, peculiarity was something that some people in colonial America were both born to and had thrust upon them. Okfuskee children born in the 1770s grew up in a town with a generations-long tradition of close—if peculiar—connections to a European-style market economy; this tradition did not always harmonize well with other Creek customs but it nevertheless contributed to community-wide prosperity. And, of course, some of these children lived into the 1830s, long enough to witness the dispossession and pauperization that accompanied the thousand-mile forced migration from Okfuskee to Okfuskee, from Creek country in Alabama and Georgia to Oklahoma. They lived long enough, in other words, for real connections to atrophy and peculiar differences to come to the fore.

6

Big Women and Mad Men: Okfuskee Experiences with Gender and Generational Relations

There were many variations on the basic formula for the Creek Busk, a ceremony that could last for eight days in a town of Okfuskee's size. According to one version, at the end of the ceremony's third day—after the townspeople rekindled their sacred fire and cleansed their domestic hearths—the townswomen gathered outside the square ground, while the townsmen remained seated within. With the whole community assembled, the town's religious leader and fire-maker stood to address his people. He spoke first to "the warriors" in the square, explaining to "them all the particular positive injunctions, and negative precepts they yet retain of the ancient law, relating to their own manly station." The fire-maker then turned to the women grouped around the square. "[Changing] his note, and [using] a much sharper language," he enjoined them to respect the traditions regarding the town fire, the sanctification of the harvest, and the "marriage-law." Finishing this "sharp and prolix" speech, the fire-maker "[addressed] himself to the whole body," enumerating the crimes they had committed and the requirements "of the ancient law," the trials awaiting them if they transgressed, and the "health and prosperity" in store if they maintained "a strict observance of their old rites and customs." At the end of his speech, an assistant took "a sufficient quantity of the . . . holy fire, and lay it down on the outside of the holy ground," where the women "speedily take it up, gladly take it home, and lay it down on their unpolluted hearths."[1]

The fire-maker's speech and the spatial arrangement of his audience highlight several tenets of Creek social organization. Most fundamentally, Creek townspeople prospered or suffered together. Individuals who vio-

162

lated Creek traditions brought "dangerous evils both upon themselves, and all the beloved, or holy people," while proper behavior "[procured] them plentiful harvests, and [gave] their war-leaders victory over their enemies." At the same time, however, the Creek world encompassed several important fissures. Most notably, women and men were viewed as "separate people," a condition reflected in the women's exclusion from the square and in the fire-maker's sex-specific instructions and tone. The male–female opposition, in fact, characterized much of Creek life; in the words of one anthropologist, "an aesthetic of gender permeates Creek social interaction."[2] From the layout of domestic space to the structure of "the most common" dance, from the makeup of agricultural work-parties to the seating arrangements in the town square and rotunda, the Creeks testified to their belief that men and women lived in distinct, albeit related, spheres.[3]

Although more subtly than in the case of the male–female divide, townsmen were themselves split along lines of age and social role.[4] During the Busk, men enacted these divisions when an older member of the religious and civil leadership cadre instructed the younger "warriors." The Creeks had very specific ideas about the characteristics and responsibilities that men in each category were to embody. Young men were assumed to be impetuous warriors and hunters, eager for honors, difficult to control, "Mad," "hot headed," and "foolish." As one observer noted, "they measure mens understanding and judgement according to their years." Curbing and guiding the warriors was the responsibility of the older men, whom the Creeks divided into civil and military specialists. The "former are called head or beloved men, the latter head warriors; when any mischief is in view, the latter generally take over." If peace was the goal, a head warrior worked to "[keep] my Warriours at Home," as the Okfuskee Captain claimed he did in 1753. Once war was decided upon, however, war leaders believed that they must "talk of Nothing but Blood . . . not talk of any Thing that was good"; thus, less than two months after keeping his town's warriors in check, the Okfuskee Captain warned South Carolina's governor that "[i]f you cannot make a Peace immediately, let us know that we may go to war, and not detain us any longer in makeing a Peace."[5] For their part, the civil headmen—including a town's mico, second man, and council of beloved men—knew, as one headman put it, that "Its true my head Warriors may get in a Passion, but its my business to stop them; which I constantly strive to do." Lacking formal coercive mechanisms, "an old Man" like Okfuskee's Red Coat King "could do Nothing but talk which should always be for keeping of Peace"; such men could only, in the Okfuskee King's words, "admonish my people to behave well," much as the fire-maker did during the Busk. In doing so, however, they embodied the role claimed for them by an Upper Creek headman: "Guiders & Leaders to the Different Towns."[6]

The oppositions—male–female; old men–young men—enacted during the fire-maker's speech were, then, at the heart of eighteenth-century Creek life.[7] Okfuskee's history was shaped by these social facts, by the mixing of unity and dichotomy, cooperation and contradiction. Okfuskees approached challenges and opportunities not just as members of a particular town, clan, or moiety, but also as individuals with well-defined gender and generational identities. Gender and generation, in fact, provided lenses through which Okfuskees evaluated their world. Their understandings of the actions expected of, and the possibilities open to, them as gendered individuals of a certain age structured their initiatives and responses. These actions, in turn, helped determine how Okfuskee itself evolved.

The centrality of gender and generational oppositions was, however, a double-edged sword. In a perfect Creek world, social production and re-production flowed from the interaction of female generative power and the male capacity to order and define,[8] a capacity dependent, in turn, on male leaders' sociospiritual authority. Ideally, opposed but complementary spheres—male and female, old and young—came together in a way that was at once socially sustainable and distinctively Creek. Of course, the eighteenth-century Southeast was a difficult place to maintain ideal systems of social interaction, and the Okfuskees' engagement with the region's un-settled diplomatic, economic, and cultural milieu had serious implications for the relationship between their men and women, on the one hand, and their young men and older men, on the other. Over time, the system of interrelated gender and generational identities that had once allowed for difference while producing unity came to encourage disruptive levels of competition and an unsettling number of disputes. Processes of interaction that had once functioned to acknowledge and overcome social divisions increasingly worked to reify distinctions and undermine cooperation. More and more, Okfuskee's men and women found that performing basic social functions—from dealing with outsiders to consuming the necessities of life—called into question their ability to live as something other than "sep-arate peoples." Likewise, young men and old men discovered that the common ground provided by foundational concepts of Creek social or-ganization—the distinction between civil and military headmen; the respect youth owed to age—was vulnerable to erosion and contraction. Eventually, systems of intergenerational authority, like patterns of cross-gender relations, could no longer be counted upon to knit the townspeople together.

Such developments in Okfuskee's systems of gender and generational relations are at the center of this chapter. I argue that the breakdown of complementarity in these areas was due not to the townspeople consciously abandoning their traditions but rather to the initiatives of individual Okfuskees who sought to develop the implications of Creek culture within a rapidly changing colonial world. As Okfuskees confronted challenges ranging from European imperial realignment to Euro-American backcountry hostility, from market-oriented exchange to livestock-endangered crops, from intensively hunted forests to extensively organized communities, they simultaneously reevaluated their most basic relationships. The ties that linked the sexes and generations within Okfuskee remained broadly and recognizably Creek, but the specifics of these connections—the contours and the borders, the content of daily interaction and the boundaries dividing social groups—owed as much to recent choices as to inherited traditions. Okfuskees who came of age after Fanni Mico returned from Charleston in 1749 reconfigured old networks, redefined the meanings that animated those networks, and, in the process, reshaped Okfuskee. The problems and possibilities Okfuskees faced in their gender and generational relations attest both to the fundamental changes underway within the community and to the role the townspeople played in reworking their world.

Gender Relations

Because of their primacy in diplomacy and warfare, Okfuskee's men were responsible for dealing with outsiders. The mechanisms by which men welcomed visitors to town, however, were intimately connected to female productivity. To begin with, when Okfuskees greeted foreigners "in the Oakfuskey King's House," they used a space that belonged to the headman's wife and her family. Moreoever, the food provided to newcomers was prepared and served by women. The phrases Okfuskee's visitors typically used to record these occasions—"there was Some Fowls Brought in and Set Before me"; "Will's Friend had caused some fowls to be prepared for breakfast"—obscured the townswomen's actions.[9] Men talked and ate with men to indicate goodwill and hospitality, a necessary prelude to the conducting of any "substantive" business; but Okfuskee's women provided the venues, goods, and services that permitted the creation and reenactment of affective bonds. And, obscurant sentence construction notwithstanding, the act of incorporating outsiders into their community did not force townswomen to become invisible pawns whose services men could invoke and dispose of at will. Rather, through their participation in hospitality rituals, Okfuskee's women placed themselves at the heart of their town's effort to domesticate outsiders. They understood that their actions both ensured the community's continued prosperity and allowed them to benefit from the conjunction between their own and their visitors' power.

Creek women's ability to bring outsiders into Creek society appears most clearly in the realm of sexual relations. Creek leaders frequently offered visitors female sexual partners, either on a temporary basis or as a part of a long-lasting relationship. Reports from the early eighteenth century onward stress the willingness of Creek women to form sexual relationships with Euro-Americans.[10] In doing so, Okfuskee's women solidified and reinforced the alliances that men acted out in the square or rotunda. Creeks viewed the knowledge and power acquired through women's sexual alliances as important enough to merit mention in their origin story. In a 1735 version, Chigilli of Coweta told his audience that at one time his ancestors were daily being harassed and killed by a large bird. In response, "They made an image in the shape of a woman, and placed it in the way of this bird. The bird carried it off, and kept it a long time, and then brought it back. They left it alone, hoping it would bring something forth. After a long time, a red rat came forth from it, and they believed the bird was the father of the rat. They took council with the rat how to destroy its father. Now the bird had a bow and arrows; the rat gnawed the bowstring, so that the bird could not defend itself, and the people killed it." Creeks, then, were accustomed to women forming relationships with powerful and dangerous beings. In return, Creeks might receive peace—as when the bird apparently ceased its attacks—but they would most certainly learn how to deal with the outsider. Although Chigilli made no mention of it, such knowledge might come from the woman herself. If not, her offspring would know their father's secrets, and Okfuskees (in keeping with their matrilineal orientation) had no doubt that children—like the rat—would side with their mother's people. In fact, Billy Germany—an Okfuskee war leader who most likely became known as White Lieutenant—could not even speak to his father's people without "Linguists" being present. It was entirely appropriate, therefore, that White Lieutenant became an Okfuskee headman. The townspeople knew that his Okfuskee mother and Creek upbringing anchored him in the community, while her liaison with his Euro-American father allowed them all access to outside sources of power embodied by her son.[11]

Broader social benefits aside, individual Creek women saw their relationships with outsiders as personally rewarding. Creek women, for example, frequently opposed communal or national initiatives that threatened to undermine their ties to British traders. William Bartram noted that, "if their love and esteem for each other is sincere, and upon principles of reciprocity," women rarely betrayed "the interests and views of their temporary husbands," the traders. Okfuskee women, in fact, actively defended certain traders. Two days before the May 1760 attack, Robert French of Okfuskee was "warned by an Indian Woman to take Care of himself"; as the attack unfolded, "an Indian Wench, a Friend of his," directed him to her uncle, the Okfuskee Captain, who helped him escape. Moses Price of Sugatspoges, returning to town in the midst of the violence, "was called to by a wench to fly for his life"; later that night, "his wife fearing she might be watched, took a considerable sweep round, through the thickets, and by searching the place . . . where she expected he lay concealed, fortunately found him, and gave him provisions to enable him to get to our settlements." Likewise, in 1761, "an Indian woman" told a British trader that Henry Dalton had been taken prisoner at Sugatspoges. Seventeen years later, Richard Henderson, an American diplomat with strong Okfuskee ties, was freed from British hands when his "woman" alerted an Okfuskee headman. Almost a quarter-century earlier, Henderson, then an Okfuskee packhorseman, was "forewarned" of a potential Creek plot "by a particular friend Indian."[12]

The motivations that led Okfuskee women to help French, Price, Dalton, and Henderson are not recorded, but the traders' benefactors most likely responded to a number of factors. In the first place, as Bartram points out, some relationships between traders and Creek women were characterized by sincere bonds of affection, bonds most likely familiar to Okfuskee women now known only as French's "Friend" and Price's "wife." James Adair, in fact, reports that the latter "returned home in tears" after helping her trader husband to escape; another Okfuskee trader's wife of many years was "very amiable and . . . affectionate." Second, the presence of children fathered by traders may have encouraged Okfuskee women to protect their partners, both to safeguard the children's feelings and to preserve the advantages that a child with a living Euro-American father enjoyed. No evidence suggests that the four traders listed above fathered children in Okfuskee, but James Germany—who lived for years in Okfuskee, married the aforementioned "affectionate" Creek woman, and had several Creek children, including Billy, the Okfuskee war leader—survived the 1760 attack, despite being in Upper Creek country at the time and despite the fact that three of his partners were killed.[13]

Okfuskee women were not, however, motivated only by concerns for their trader husbands. After all, both French and Price apparently received warnings from two women, and in each case only one of the women was identified as the trader's wife or friend. Although the unidentified women's motives went unrecorded, all Okfuskee women benefited from the goods the traders brought to town. Fully stocked storehouses meant that Okfuskee men could trade the deerskins the women processed for metal tools, cloth, and decorative items, all of which enhanced the women's economic and social roles. Moreover, townswomen acquired goods directly from traders, either as gifts or in exchange for products and services; the cloth, beads, and metal goods carried up to Okfuskee by Macartan & Campbell's packhorsemen suggest the possibilities available to their female trading partners, friends, and lovers. In addition, those women with the closest ties to the traders had direct access to the stores as part of their role as wives and helpmates. In any case, women with a consistent supply of goods at their disposal could better fulfill their responsibilities, while at the same time being able to indulge in displays of generosity and personal adornment.[14]

Relationships between Okfuskee women and Euro-American traders, though, presented the town with a perplexing problem. On the one hand, the integrative function women performed by feeding, marrying, and trading with outsiders played a central role in the townspeople's efforts to harness the visitors' social, material, and spiritual powers. On the other hand, while performing these tasks, the townswomen's own access to power increased. To some extent, of course, such gains were foreseen: women were spiritually powerful and socially significant; their contributions were essential if Okfuskee was to thrive; the townswomen's prosperity would rise or fall along with that of the community. Relationships with Euro-American traders, however, offered Okfuskee's women revolutionary possibilities. They not only had access to goods and services of unprecedented importance, but that access was not mediated by Okfuskee's men. Goods that traditionally flowed into town through channels dominated by hunters, warriors, and headmen were now carried into the community by Euro-American traders, and only then distributed. The presence of these "intimate strangers," the importance of their goods, and the ability of women to acquire items directly from newcomers had profound implications for Okfuskee's gender relations.[15]

Unfortunately, given the nature of the historical records, direct references to Creek women—much less to their changing position in Creek society—are few and far between. By the 1750s, however, several pieces of evidence suggest that Creek men were increasingly uncomfortable with female conduct. Some headmen turned to British officials for help in controlling relations between Euro-American men and Creek women. In 1752, for example, a British agent wrote that two headmen "complained very heavily of the white People in general for debauching their Wifes." Their statement reads like a straightforward accusation of sexual assault, and it may well have been. But these headmen also suggested that the relations in question were characterized by more than coercion, noting that "strowling white People . . . go out a hunting with the Indians and catching of Beaver, carrying Indian Wives out with them, decoying them from their Husbands." Five years later, another agent in Upper Creek country passed along "Complaints" against "A Sett of idle Vagrants" who told "romancing Stories to ingratiate themselves among the Indians to procure a Livelyhood and gett an Indian Wife which is all their Desire and frequently they take the better of them." Women's consensual sexuality, therefore, worried Creek leaders, who looked to the British to remedy the situation.[16]

At the same time, other headmen, concerned about the disruptive potential of relationships between Creek women and traders, warned British officials that Creeks would enforce proper behavior if British offenders went unpunished. In a 1764 talk, for example, the "Oakchoys King" asserted that "Many . . . disturbances is owing to white men, who are very guilty with Women that have husbands. If a woman brings any thing to the House of a white man, let him pay her, & let her go again, or if a free single woman chooses to live with a white man, we have nothing to say against it, but many white men . . . are very Impudent & occasions uneasines." "Red people," the headman noted, "are subject to our Laws, & [traders] must be the same provided they are guilty of the same Errors."[17] Again, a headman's hints of coercion ("let her go") are undermined by suggestions of female agency ("free single"; "chooses") and by the indeterminancy of the "we" who experienced "uneasiness." It is difficult not to conclude, in fact, that "we" refers primarily to "husbands," not to the suddenly unpredictable "Women."

As the 1764 statement demonstrates, relations between traders and Creek women arising from seemingly innocuous economic transactions disturbed Creek men. In fact, some Creek men began to question the connection between trader–townswomen relations and their own economic interests. The Okchai King's talk contains hints of such tensions, most notably in the odd juxtaposition of women–trader economic relations— "let him pay her"—and the assertion, made earlier in his speech, that "hunting is our only dependence." More explicit, however, were the words and actions of a large Creek party, including seventeen Okfuskees, who attended a 1753 Charleston meeting. The issues on the table in South Carolina's capital—prices charged to men and gifts given to women; female access and male mediation—demonstrate that Creek men believed that male and female economic interests were diverging.

The breakdown in Creek gender relations entered the proceedings when Handsome Fellow stood and, speaking without the consent of the delegation's civil leaders, demanded "that the Trade [prices] should be lower." He listed the prices he would pay for sixteen items, the overwhelming majority of which were for male consumption. Three days later, after a Lower Creek civil headman and Governor James Glen agreed that only bullets would be reduced in price, Handsome Fellow again reasserted his position: "We hope that the Abatement of all the Artickles requested will be agreed to." Glen flatly refused, at which point the Okfuskee Captain stood up, stated that he had always tried to serve the British well, and resigned his British commission. When Glen asked him to "keep your Commission," the Okfuskee Captain "immediately went out of the Room leaving the Commission upon the Table and laying down the Present of Cloaths, &c. that had been delivered to him." The clamor that ensued was interrupted by Wolf, who stated, "No wonder that the Traders can not afford to sell their Goods at the Prices we desire when they give away such quantities to their Wives and Women which they keep. This is the true Reason, but we hope they shall not make Use of Goods for such Purposes any more." The problem, according to Wolf, lay not in the demands of the Creek men but rather in the relationship between Creek women and the traders. A combination of profligate traders and greedy women threatened the men's ability to purchase the trappings of manhood on Handsome Fellow's list. The Okfuskees believed that lower prices might remedy this situation, but the headmen were willing to explore other options. Thus, they asked Glen—who had already given the leaders gifts for "their wives"—for cloth, jewelry, metalware, "and some other Trifles" in the name of "their Women and Children." Red Coat King, Handsome Fellow, and the other Creek men may have hoped, in this way, to reassert control over their townswomen's access to European goods.[18]

The shifts in Okfuskee's economic life during the 1760s further strained the economic ties binding townswomen and men. The young men's increasing involvement in trade networks that emphasized raw skins, illegal traders, and rum meant that hunting was less and less likely to produce manufactured goods of use to Okfuskee's women. For their part, townswomen found that—as traders set up plantations and as livestock encroached on gardens and fields—familiar strategies of production and exchange were no longer reliable. Some Creek women responded by participating in the rum trade themselves. For example, Bartram's description of a ten-day drinking binge focused on the way the party allowed "the wenches to make their market." By pretending to swallow liquor offered by drunken men and then spitting it into concealed bottles, Creek women gathered a "secret store" of full bottles that each "retails" back to the men "at her own price."[19]

Other women assisted the traders in using rum to separate Creek men from their possessions. In 1772, David Taitt reported that Francis Lewis "makes a common practice to give rum to his wench for to purchase back the goods from the Indians which he has sold or trusted them with." Likewise, Richard Baillie and "several [other] hirelings" provided "their" woman with rum, which she used to purchase goods and horses "as her own property, thereby . . . preventing any recovery of stolen horses except by paying her a very good price for them." Similar behavior may have motivated an Upper Creek headman to tell the British "that as the Women in My Nation are apt to Steal Horses as well as the Young men, it will be necessary to give them some presents, in hopes to remedy that Evil." The headman feared, however, that if the gifts did "not produce the desired Effect" the problem was "incurable." As he must have suspected, women stealing horses was merely one manifestation of a more pervasive problem, one that would not be resolved by the occasional British willingness to offer women "a few of such articles as you have asked for."[20]

For women—certainly the large majority of female Okfuskees—who did not traffick in horses, retail rum, or marry a trader, the 1760s and 1770s offered a confusing array of problems and possibilities. Even the silver linings, it seemed, had clouds. So, for example, Adair complained that after 1763 there were "at least five times the number of trading houses," that European goods were "too cheap and plenty," and that Indian-produced food had reached "an exorbitant price." He immediately, however, undercut the benefits women could expect to reap in this situation, noting that the new traders, "by inebriating the Indians . . . purchase the necessaries of life, at four or five hundred per cent cheaper, than the orderly traders." In other words, rising competition for Creek goods and declining prices for European items were offset by the sale of alcohol. Such practices may explain the heavy investment Okfuskee packhorsemen made in rum. In July 1763 alone, Henry Dalton, Thomas Chavers, David Owens, and George Bell bought a total of eleven kegs of rum. That same month, John Audrey, another Okfuskee packhorseman, received credit for selling two kegs of rum—one to Macartan & Campbell's Okfuskee store—while in Creek country; seven months earlier, he had purchased a keg of brandy. Such transactions only hint at the volume of alcohol sold in Okfuskee. Even in the spring of 1774, as the British embargoed the Creeks' trade, a traveler reported that "Some of the Indians of that town had been drinking rum, and were pretty far gone."[21]

Okfuskee's women would thus have been familiar with trade-offs implied by Adair's comments. On the one hand, the growing number of deerskins brought in by hunting parties, the influx of traders, and the newcomers' need for food and domestic services all promised increased opportunities for townswomen to acquire European goods. On the other hand, the rise of the raw deerskin trade, the ever-increasing volume of liquor arriving in Creek country, and the Okfuskee traders' early embrace of detached plantations all suggest that Okfuskee's women faced a difficult situation. Moreover, the high turnover among Okfuskee traders after 1760 undermined the townswomen's personal connections with these outsiders, further eroding female access to gifts and informal exchange. Whether or not Adair's numbers—500 percent more traders; intoxicated Natives selling goods at 20 to 25 percent of their value—were correct, then, Okfuskee's women would have recognized the equation's outcome: unfamiliar trading patterns, diminished economic opportunity, and an ever-increasing sense of insecurity.

And numbers alone tell only part of the story. In the first place, while

Adair did not mention how traders purchased "the necessaries of life" or from whom, some traders likely dealt rum to Creek men for skins and trade goods, and then exchanged those goods with Creek women for food and services.[22] In the process, male and female spheres of consumption and production—traditionally separate but intertwined—became increasingly distinct. Second, even traders who adhered to more traditional exchange patterns accepted raw skins in increasing numbers, thereby contributing to the declining importance of women's labor. In both cases, exchange patterns that had united men and women now contributed to their separation, and a system that had once maximized relationships while producing an acceptable standard of living had reversed its priorities. Okfuskee's productive process had changed drastically, although both productive techniques and the resulting commodities were only minimally affected. However, the most important products of Okfuskee's system— men and women conditioned to live in separate but intertwined spheres— were in increasingly short supply.

Of course, the degree to which Okfuskee's men and women viewed their economic interests as adversarial should not be overstated. Many Creek men continued to accept responsibility for providing their families with clothing and related goods. Thus, Georgia's governor believed that familial concerns pushed Creek men to make significant concessions in the face of the 1774 trade embargo; reporting from a conference attended by Handsome Fellow, he noted that they "found themselves reduced to the greatest Necessity & Distress for having received no Supplies for ten months, their Stock was Exhausted, the Women & Children were begining to be Naked & Clamourous, and as Winter came on would have been outragious, these things they used to mention in their Talks and frequently Repeated now at the Congress." The governor was right: by the 1760s, Creek men did "frequently" link their ability to hunt and acquire ammunition through trade with their responsibility to clothe their wives and children. As an Upper Creek put it in 1760: "We are a people that take great Pains in hunting having no other Way to supply our Families with Clothing." A headman drew an even more straightforward connection between men's goods and women's economic condition in 1766: "My young Men are poor for Guns and Ammunition and our Women are very poor." Later that year, a "Warrior" asked "What are we to supply our Families with, we can neither Kill provisions to eat nor have Skins to purchase Cloathing with." Responsibilities of this sort, in fact, could be deployed by Creek men to request more favorable terms of exchange. Thus, Mortar told the British "that as Deer skins are become Scarce, the Trade [prices] may be reduced in proportion, so that we may be enabled to Clothe & maintain our Families." He then presented a list of goods with the prices he was willing to pay. Upon reaching the items intended for women, he mentioned the first one, callico, and then noted that "some of their Women are very big." Of course, Creek women were almost certainly not getting bigger—in the sense of heavier or larger. Rather, these women had always been big—in the sense of important or powerful—within their communities. Mortar thus used physiology as a shorthand for sociology: women's place in Creek society was secure; men would uphold their end of the Creek social contract.[23]

Just as many Creek men continued to provide cloth for their families, Creek women maintained labor practices that benefitted both men and women. Some women, for example, accompanied hunters on winter expeditions, as the presence of "young men and women belonging to the Oakfuske" in a 1777 party suggests. More centrally, though, women continued to produce the agricultural goods upon which families depended. In fact, the most comprehensive descriptions of Creek women's agricultural duties come from Adair and Bartram, the former writing in the 1760s and 1770s and the latter writing about his experiences in the 1770s. Beyond the obvious uses Okfuskee men had for the women's foodstuffs, some of it may have been traded for goods—especially gunpowder—required by men. The fact that White Lieutenant—a man with a Euro-American father and one of Okfuskee's most acculturated inhabitants—lived with his wife's family as late as the 1790s, and the fact that she welcomed a visitor with corn stew and peas, suggests that women and their agricultural produce retained their "big" profile in Okfuskee.[24]

Moreover, even when Okfuskee's women consumed manufactured goods, they frequently did so within the context of productive activities that benefitted their families. Like their Euro-American counterparts, Creek women often "consumed to produce," while Creek men frequently "produced to consume." For example, Creek women sewed clothes. Thus, when the Okfuskee packhorseman John Audry bought thirty yards of assorted fabrics, thirteen ounces of thread, and one "stick" of mohair, he was preparing to provide Okfuskee's women with the raw materials necessary to clothe and adorn their families; Henry Dalton's purchases—over 2 pounds of "White common beads," a bundle of barley corn beads, 4 types of fabric, and 100 needles—were destined to fulfill a similar purpose. Okfuskee men benefitted from the women's skills, but the men were also more likely to receive or buy finished attire. Thus, a 1759 invoice of "Annual Presents" for "the Indians" shows 800 "trade shirts for men," but none for women; an accompanying list of trade goods mentions 2,500 "men's trade shirts" and only 500 "women's shirts." As late as 1784, British plans for a visit by "600 Indian Gunmen and their families" called for the presentation of "600 shirts" and large amounts of cloth; a contemporary list estimated that "150 Indians with their families" required "150 Shirts" and, again, a great deal of cloth. Finished products—including shirts, guns, ammunition, and alcohol—were predominantly for Okfuskee men; finishing products was predominantly a job for Okfuskee women.[25]

Given the connections that continued to bind Okfuskee's women and men together, it is not surprising that Creek marriage ceremonies frequently emphasized the complementarity of gender roles. Men were called upon to demonstrate their ability to hunt for meat and skins; women were supposed to show their ability to provide, cook, and serve agricultural produce. Moreover, according to some observers, the ceremony involved women dressing game and men helping with the crops, thereby emphasizing the ways in which even gender-identified tasks required the couple to cooperate.[26] In a Creek marriage, then, gender-specific economic roles came together to assure the couple that they had the necessary skills to prosper. The continuation of similar rhetoric into the nineteenth century demonstrates that Creek men and women had not lost their appreciation for the importance of intertwining men's and women's spheres.

At the same time, however, the necessity of explicitly and publicly stating (as in a marriage ceremony) that gender spheres were intertwined may have assumed an increased importance by the 1760s or 1770s. As the Okfuskees' food and deerskin trades evolved, women and men experimented with traditional roles. Townswomen were producers and distributors of food, and the primary agents for integrating outsiders into the community; townsmen were hunters and traders, diplomats and warriors. Okfuskees understood that these roles could fit together, that they could reinforce each other, and that they could create a strong and vibrant community. But the same roles, played out on a different stage, could lead to scenarios that were distinctly unfamiliar. Throughout the eighteenth century, individual Okfuskees explored the implications of enacting aspects of traditional gender roles in contexts that were at once familiar and strangely altered. In the process, they called into question the mutuality upon which Creek gender roles, and thus Okfuskee society, were based.

Generational Relations

When he rose to speak at the 1753 Charleston conference, Handsome Fellow did so at a time when relationships between Creek men were undergoing an unsettling shift. His speech, and the reaction to it, reflected those changes. Speaking as a "Head Warriour," Handsome Fellow began by calling Glen's attention to "the Head Men of our Nation," Malatchi of Coweta and Red Coat King of Okfuskee. He went on to say that "The Kings and beloved Men are come down with one Heart and no Doubt you have the same Custome with you to have your beloved Men about you, and we, the Warriors, are come down to escort them." In other words, the Creek men present were acting out their accustomed roles: kings/leaders; beloved men/councilors; warriors/protectors.

As Handsome Fellow's speech went on, however, the boundaries between those roles became less clear-cut. He next commented on Glen's speech and agenda, and then turned to the matter of peace with the Cherokees, noting that "notwithstanding the King [Malatchi] has expressed himself fully on that Affair before, yet I shall speak a Word on it." After summarizing his own concerns as a warrior and hunter, he made it plain that a peaceful future depended as much upon "Matters . . . at Home" as upon the speeches of "Men of . . . Prudence" like Malatchi. Finally, Handsome Fellow came to trade. Noting that "what I am to speak is without the Derection of any Head Man," he stated that his talk "flows chiefly from myself, being a Head-warriour, and the Rest of the Head Warriours here present. That is, that the Trade [prices] should be lower," especially on a list of goods in which four of the first five items—guns, bullets, gunpowder, and flints—were essential for the male activities of war and hunting.

When the conference resumed, Malatchi was obviously out of sorts. He remarked on "our Young Men['s] . . . Faults and Follies," and ended by stating "All that has been said by the Warrior concerning the lowering of Goods was chiefly with a View to make our young People at Home easey; but as I perceive the Proposal will not take . . . I shall say no more upon that Head," except to request that traders lower the price of bullets. Handsome Fellow interrupted at this point to insist upon the full slate of "Abatements," the news of which "we would . . . tell our People . . . which would lighten their Hearts." When the smoke cleared from Glen's refusal, the Okfuskee Captain's resignation of his commission, and the departure of "many of the Warriors . . . seemingly displeased," Malatchi found himself reduced to apologies and recriminations: "I am very heartily sorry, that some of our People who call themselves Head Men and Warriours, should behave so like Children, but they are unacquainted with the Nature of public Business, and the true Interest of their own Nation. They ought therefore to be considered as Children, and no regard to be paid to any Thing they have said; they in a very rude and abrupt Manner broke in upon my Discourse without any Power or Commission from me or the Nation." Glen apparently accepted Malatchi's reasoning. Although he noted that "the Behaviour of some of your People upon this Occasion has been very extraordinary," Glen praised Malatchi's "good Conduct" and put him in charge of the gifts the warriors had left behind. And, in the end, the breach was glossed over. The Creeks asked for (and received) more presents, made their apologies to Glen, and, in the case of the Okfuskee Captain, reassumed the symbols of their attachment to the British.[27]

The diplomatic niceties that mended the rift could not, however, entirely disguise the divisions emerging within the male half of Creek society. Patterns and practices of authority that had tied common warriors, head warriors, and civil leaders together no longer produced consensus, and traditional hierarchies and spheres of influence were losing their relevance. Initially a dispute between civil and military leaders, the conflict eventually widened to include common warriors. Handsome Fellow's speech did not, then, appear out of nowhere. Rather, the warriors' actions at the 1753 conference were part of a long-running discussion between different interest groups within Creek society. When Handsome Fellow asserted the right of head warriors to speak without authorization, and when he demanded that the needs of his warrior constituency be looked after, he demonstrated the rising power of Creek head warriors. A decade after Handsome Fellow spoke, though, Creek military leaders were themselves scrambling to control their young warriors, who were increasingly eager to assert their independence from traditional structures of authority. By the late 1760s and early 1770s, then, debates that began in the early eighteenth century had resulted not only in the disruption of relations between civil and military headmen but also in the distancing of common warriors from their nominal leaders. By the 1780s, Okfuskees needed not only new leaders but also new patterns of leadership. The remainder of this chapter chronicles this transition.

Creek political science gave a town's civil and military headmen important roles in diplomatic affairs. Their responsibilities complemented each other, with the head warrior moving to the fore in times of danger and the mico—the leading civil headman—taking over in peacetime. In general, however, Creeks assumed the mico was the town's leader, and the diplomatic record attests to his importance in several ways. In the first place, Creek conference rhetoric emphasized the role civil leaders played in determining the town or nation's course. So, for example, in 1726, an Upper Creek head warrior told a British agent that "when I go home, I shall tell my King of" the situation "and he will know what to do"; given that the warrior had been appointed to speak for his Upper Creek division, his reliance on the wisdom of "my King" is especially significant. A generation later, another Upper Creek expressed surprise when Red Coat King refused to represent the Upper Creeks at the 1753 Charleston conference. Stepping into the void left by his father's silence, Handsome Fellow sought to communicate the old man's continued influence. He noted that "[here] are the Head Men of our Nation, here is the King [Malatchi], and here is the Red Coat King"; the Okfuskee "Head Warriour" then told Glen that "the Peace [with the Cherokees] was agreed to not as being your Desire only, but the Head Men all considered that the Thing was Good in itself." Handsome Fellow's relatively subtle point about the mico's power was made more directly six years later by another warrior: "This man (pointing to the Tookybahtchey Mico) is Master of the Town; without him nothing can be done."[28]

A second aspect of the diplomatic record attesting to the preeminence of micos concerns the order in which headmen signed treaties and talks. The most striking instances come from early in the century. For example, a 1705 treaty was signed by four micos and eight war leaders. Cossitee, "Great Captain" of Okfuskee, made his mark with the head warriors, all but one of whom signed after the micos. A similar pattern surfaces on a 1732 treaty, which lists ten Creek signatories; eight were micos, five of whom—including "Fannemiche King of the Oakfuskeys"—signed before any warrior. Micos also signed before their beloved men and councilors, and so the mark of "One Handed King of the Oakfuskeys" follows that of Fanni Mico on the 1732 treaty. Even when a warrior from one town signed before the mico from another town, the warrior in question generally signed after his town's mico. Thus, on a 1751 deed, the head warriors of Okchai and Okfuskee signed sixth and eighth, respectively, ahead of thirteen micos but behind the "head King[s]" of Okchai and Okfuskee, who signed first and second. Lists of headmen produced in less formal situations often continued to subordinate military specialists to civil leaders. So a 1735 list, "taken . . . from [the Creek headman] Tomochichis own Mouth," of invitees to Savannah mentions headmen from fourteen towns, but a warrior led a town's delegation in only two cases; and of the ten Lower Creek towns who sent representatives to a 1739 meeting, only one put a warrior at the head of its party. Handsome Fellow, therefore, followed a long-established tradition when he described the delegation at the 1753 Charleston conference as consisting of—in order—kings, beloved men, and warriors.[29]

Even during moments when micos appeared to dominate diplomatic efforts, however, the Creek system allowed head warriors to assert their importance. For example, Bartram's description of seating arrangements in the Creek rotunda notes that the head warrior both sat between the mico and any Euro-Americans and mediated between those visitors and the townspeople as the ceremonial pipes were passed around. Along the same lines, when an Upper Creek party greeted Edmond Atkin in 1759, ten of the twelve men whose ranks are known were war leaders, including the group's speaker, the Okfuskee Captain, and the Little Warrior from an Okfuskee village.[30] Treaties, even though nominally peaceful occasions, also offered head warriors opportunities. Thus, in the 1751 deed, the third and fourth headmen listed (before fourteen micos) were the "head Warrior[s]" of Puckatalahassee and Muccolossus. The head warriors' prestigious positions were due, in part, to the fact that no civil headmen from their towns signed the treaties. The two men were put forward, on these occasions, as their towns' representatives.

The head warriors, however, were also selected because of relationships between the Creek towns involved, relationships that further emphasized the war leaders' importance. Creek diplomatic norms allowed a head warrior to assert his importance not just in the face of enemies but also when his town confronted people who were structurally positioned as threats. The 1705 treaty signed by Okfuskee's head warrior, for example, was negotiated in Coweta, and the first headman to put his mark on the treaty was the "King of the Cowetas." Okfuskee was a white/peace town in the

Creeks' moiety system, while Coweta was a red/war town; people from one moiety referred to the other moiety's members as "my enemy or opponent." Okfuskees and Cowetas frequently opposed each other in matters of policy and diplomacy, a fact reflected by the Okfuskees' selection of a head warrior as their representative at the 1705 Coweta conference. It was, therefore, not surprising that, in a 1752 Coweta-led diplomatic initiative, the Okfuskee Captain represented his town, while Okfuskee's civil headman declined to participate and Coweta's civil headman avoided visiting Okfuskee.[31] The 1751 treaty mentioned above presented a similar opportunity for a head warrior. This document was drafted in Okchai, and the first two men to sign it were civil leaders from Okchai and Okfuskee, leading towns of the Upper Creeks' Abeika division. The Muccolossus head warrior who signed fourth represented a different Upper Creek division and, perhaps more importantly, his town often opposed Okfuskee's and Okchai's initiatives. Eight years later, when Creek warriors greeted Atkin outside Tuckabatchee, a Tallapoosa town, twelve of the fourteen men who can be identified were Abeikas.[32] The Okfuskee war leaders in this group were present because Okfuskees were, in a sense, on hostile ground when near Tuckabatchee. The Okfuskees' inter- and intranational relations thus provided numerous opportunities for their head warriors to come to the fore.

For Okfuskee's head warriors, gains in responsibility and status may, in fact, have occurred by the early eighteenth century. Their diplomatic and military roles offered them chances to acquire valuable contacts and desirable foreign goods. Thomas Nairne's 1708 letters even suggest that some civil headmen could be tempted by the options suddenly available to war leaders, tempted to the point that they sought to become head warriors in their own right. Thus, Nairne describes a Chickasaw "cheif," who, "finding that the warriors had the best time of it, that slave Catching was much more profitable than formall harranguing . . . turned Warrior too, and proved as good a man hunter as the best of them." Okfuskee's head warriors had similar opportunities for becoming "man hunter[s]." As early as 1707, a French letter mentions both Creek efforts "to take prisoners" and that Okfuskee was the staging ground for a large-scale assault on the Gulf Coast; at least one newly enslaved Gulf Coast Indian was brought to Okfuskee. A decade later, "the Oakfuskey Head Warrior" received "a Coat, a Pair Stockings and Shirt" from Carolina "for his taking up a Servant Man" who had fled the colony; by 1725, Okfuskee's "Dogg king" (a war leader's title) told a British agent, "I have heard that the Chocktawes makes as good slaves as Negros; if you think it will be good I will soon have some of them here." Okfuskee's civil officials, however, apparently resisted the lure of such expeditions—although "Ofoskee King" and another headman may have participated in a 1724 attack on the Yamasees—thereby avoiding the fate of Nairne's Chickasaw headman, whose military success came at a steep price. The Chickasaws, like the Creeks, believed that a civil leader's "Duty obliged him by all wayes and means to promote peace and quiet, and to be a Counterpoise to the fury of the Warriors." Thus, the headman, in seeking military preferment, had "[infringed] the Constitutions," and so "the people don't regard him as king."[33]

Even as they managed to sidestep such pitfalls and retain their credentials as men of peace, however, the Creeks' micos—including Okfuskee's civil leaders—faced significant pressure in the early decades of the eighteenth century. "Military Officers" were far from "carry[ing] all the sway," as Nairne claimed was true among the Chickasaws, but the Creek micos' authority was increasingly insecure. Thus, in 1725, a British agent reported that "I am told Privately by some of their Heads that they will not stay [in Creek country] unless their People will be more Governable for . . . they live in Geoperday every Day" because of the Creeks' habit of "Committ[ing] Trespasses on the English." Head warriors were part of the problem. In 1728, an Upper Creek mico—confronted with a British accusation that a "Man that belonged to your Towns gave out the talk and lead" an expedition that killed a trader—gave the rather plaintive response that "I have given the people a good talk till I am quite weary[.] Now I will give them a bad talk and see what that will do." A different solution to a similar problem emerged from the report of a trader who, while eavesdropping in Okfuskee's square, heard "a head man" say that "If You have a mind to be easey [about relations with the British,] you must Tye the Warriours; for they would not be quiet else." When presented with this account, Okfuskee's "King" confirmed that "we [were] Speaking pretty angre in the Square," but claimed that they were worried the warriors would attack the Chickasaws, not the British.[34]

Wherever the truth lay, tying head warriors clearly became difficult for Okfuskee's civil leaders to accomplish, a development due, at least in part, to British sponsorship of Creeks who promised them military support. As a Lower Creek mico put it in 1725, "any young Fellow" could get "a Commission and then . . . they are head Men and at the Same Time no more

[fit] for it then Doges." Notwithstanding such complaints, the British continued handing out commissions, including one to a trader of Creek-British descent who promised to lead a war party against the Yamasees in 1728; this man received his certificate in Okfuskee, and some Okfuskee warriors joined the expedition.[35] By the late 1730s, Okfuskees had received six British commissions. The bearers certainly did not feel obligated "to observe all Orders which shall be given you from me or any succeeding Governor," as Handsome Fellow's 1756 commission from Georgia's John Reynolds enjoined. British support, though, made it easier for them to disregard their mico's suggestions.[36]

The erosion of the micos' authority worsened with time. As a 1749 British list of Creek headmen—including six Okfuskee head warriors—noted, "all Head Warriors are Men that bear great sway in their Towns even more than their beloved Men." Boys born to Okfuskee families in the 1720s and 1730s came of age knowing that warfare, diplomacy, and trade were intimately linked, that European imperial agendas and economic ambitions offered Native military specialists avenues for personal advancement unforeseen by their parents' generation. Young men's activities—hunting and warfare—became ever more important; everything from family well-being to international relations depended on these men and, of course, their leaders. As a result, head warriors found that their public roles were enhanced. By the 1750s and 1760s, in fact, individual head warriors often asserted their ability to act and speak, if not independently of micos, then at least on reasonably equal footing. At times, as Okfuskee's head warriors demonstrated at the 1753 Charleston conference, their actions were explicitly confrontational. Thus, four years after Handsome Fellow interrupted Malatchi, Okfuskee's Mad Warrior met with Georgia's governor. The Okfuskee stated that "he had long entertained thoughts of coming down from the Nation to Visit the white People, but whenever he proposed it, the Indians always endeavoured to divert him from it, and that he now came against the Will of the Heads of his Town." His promise to deliver the governor's talks and his "Desire of having his Share of the Presents now" were designed to obtain tokens of British esteem, tokens that could be used upon returning to Okfuskee to claim a status to which he was not entitled. It was entirely appropriate, therefore, that this Okfuskee head warrior chose to visit Savannah rather than Charleston, where other Okfuskee headmen were already well connected.[37]

For the most part, however, the challenges offered by head warriors were more subtle. They did not seek to supplant the micos. So, only two years after he supported Handsome Fellow in Charleston, the Okfuskee Captain spoke "in great wrath" against the idea that "the few [micos] that is left" would risk falling ill in the British colonies. A year later, Handsome Fellow, while mediating a backcountry crisis, told Governor Henry Ellis, "I have no authority to talk about the removal of the Ogechee Settlement and will not talk about what I have not in Charge." The following year, "a Head Warriour of the Oakfushees called the Beau" bowed to the wishes of "some Head Men of his Town" and refused to serve as a messenger for a British agent. These were not the actions of men contemplating a power grab, and thus it is not surprising that Okfuskee's entry on a 1758 list of "principal [Creek] headmen" begins with "Old red Coat King," before coming to the Okfuskee Captain, Handsome Fellow, "Fogg a great Warriour," and "Great beloved Man, owner of all the Lands."[38]

At the same time, though, the 1758 list also suggests that traditional verities were crumbling. If Red Coat King's pride of place was a nod to the old, then the fact that three warriors were ranked above the "Great beloved Man" represented a bow toward a new set of expectations. Rather than a mutiny or a whole-scale overturning of Okfuskee's social structure, however, the town's head warriors intended experimentation, a testing of the limits of traditional roles. Therefore, when a party of head warriors reached Savannah in 1760 and found that "their Kings" had not arrived, they stated that they were not empowered to speak for the nation. However, the fact that, as the Okfuskee Captain put it, "all those who were present were Head Warriors," did not stop this war leader from expressing satisfaction at Governor James Wright's speech, nor from explaining the causes of the May 1760 attack, nor from promising that the Creeks "were determined to hold [the British] fast by the hand." The speaker who followed the Okfuskee, another Upper Creek head warrior, demonstrated the tension between traditional roles and new opportunities even more explicitly when he stated that "they were not impowered to speak nationally, but that the Nation in general was in very good Humour." In other words, in one breath, he first expressed the limits of his position, and then transcended them. And, like the Okfuskee Captain, he went on to review the importance the Creeks assigned to their relationship with the British, promising "that from this Day forward nothing, in their Power to prevent, should be done to the Prejudice of the English." Earlier that year, at another meeting of "head-warriors," the Okfuskee Captain again spoke for his colleagues: "The talk was sent to the king of this town [Okchai], and we know not the reason why he is not come; but as I am one of the White Towns, I am pitched upon to give an answer."[39]

Over the years, head warriors continued to seek ways to express their growing influence in forms acceptable to Creeks. The Okfuskee Captain, for example, could "give an answer" in 1760 because he called on tradition—"I am one of the White Towns"—to overcome the discomfort his people felt when a head warrior spoke for them. Seven years earlier, Handsome Fellow acknowledged that his request for price reductions represented an innovation—"what I am to speak is without the Derection of any Head Man"—but he invoked the weight of "the Head Warriours here present" to offset his indiscretion. British actions also provided cover for novelty. A commission, the Okfuskee Captain noted, was "of the same Nature" as a war title, something which "should continue" to provide its bearer with the status that Creeks attached to honorifics.[40] The head warrior could thus reconcile new opportunities with his people's customs.

And yet the freedom exhibited by the head warriors as they experimented with Creek norms left each community, and the confederacy as a whole, vulnerable to a host of problems. At the most basic level, there were too many leaders with too many agendas. Thus, the participants—including two Okfuskee headmen—at a 1764 Upper Creek conference warned the British against taking "any Notice of any Talks that may be sent by every particular Head Man that takes it into his Head to Sent Talks, and Look upon no Talks but what are sent by a Number of Headmen together." Not only did head warriors and micos find themselves working at cross-purposes, but head warriors also discovered that their plans clashed with those of their fellow war leaders. During the 1760 attack, for example, Handsome Fellow led the warriors who killed eleven traders. The Okfuskee Captain, by contrast, told Governor Ellis that "he happened not to be in the Way when the People were murdered; if he had he would have dropt with them, or saved their Lives, but he says that it gave him a great deal of Pleasure that he saved the Life of one Man and sent him to his own Countrey." A second "leading warrior of the town" attempted to shield William Rae with his body, and Okfuskee's "War-King," who was in Augusta when news of the attack arrived, found his life endangered by Handsome Fellow's efforts. Almost a decade and a half later, "one of our [Okfuskee's] Great Warriours" and a man "of Consequence in his Village" was executed by his relatives when his own attack on colonists was repudiated by his kinsmen and Okfuskee's leaders.[41]

As unsettling as such incidents were, however, more alarming to Okfuskee's civil and military headmen was the fact that competing leadership agendas and the region's fluid diplomatic and military situation offered common warriors unprecedented opportunities for innovations of their own. Complaints about young men's "madness" had, of course, surfaced prior to midcentury. In fact, the phrase Long Warrior used while visiting Okfuskee in 1728—"I have told them to be good so long till I am weary"—became something of a refrain in Creek country. Colonial officials often sang a similar tune. Thus, a Georgia minister, advised in 1741 to ask the local headman to discipline the "young men" bothering his parishioners, made it plain that the proposal was risible since "[t]hey pay no attention to their chiefs."[42] For all of the kvetching, however, intergenerational disputes were more of an undercurrent than a dominant theme in Creek society at midcentury.

By the late 1750s, however, the young men's willingness to flout the advice of their leaders was beginning to become business as usual. Thus, Atkin reported in 1755 that, among South Carolina's Indian neighbors, "a licentiousness hath crept in among the young men, beyond the power of the Head Men to Remedy." That same year, an Okfuskee headman fretted that "some of their hot headed young Warriours . . . might do Mischief without considering what they were about"; a year later, Handsome Fellow fulminated against "Stragling runagates" who threatened to trigger a Creek–British war.[43] By 1759, Atkin himself acted to reinforce the authority of Upper Creek head warriors, telling Tuckabatchee's mico, "I have some Ammunition which I design to give the chief Leading Warriour in a Town, & leave it to him to dispose of it as he thinks fit. I think this will be the best way, because it will cause the Young Warriours to pay the more Regard to him." The outcome of such ploys can perhaps best be measured by the ease with which Okfuskee's headmen shifted the blame for the 1760 attack onto "the madness of a few of their young People." An incident shot through with historical and cultural meaning could plausibly be reduced to the actions of "a few giddy-headed young fellows" because young men were, by all accounts, increasingly out of control.[44]

As a result, the 1760s and 1770s saw a dramatic rise in the number of complaints leveled against disobedient and unruly young Creek men. Thus, in 1761, a newspaper editor wrote that "it seems too plain, that if ever the Creek headmen had influence enough to keep things quiet in their nation, they can no longer preserve it over the young men, who of late years are becoming very numerous." As with "big" women, no evidence suggests that young Creek men were significantly more numerous than before, but their actions increasingly brought them to the authorities' attention. Five years later, an Upper Creek, commenting on a treaty he had negotiated, noted that "the Head Warriors of this Nation thought every thing was Settled to the satisfaction of both Parties at the meeting . . . but we find our young People are still bad"; while Wolf lamented the impossibility of "Curbing and Humbling the Rebellious Set in our Nation" since "any Thing the Head Men advance is entirely disregarded." The following year a British agent asked "what . . . are the promises of these Creeks to be depended upon[?] There are some old Men among them that would willingly Support our Interest if they had it in their power, but their Young men are become so Boisterous & Wanton." In 1768, John Stuart wrote even more emphatically that "there is very little subordination amongst them, and their young men pay little or no Regard to the Authority of their Seniors." Four years later, a Lower Creek headman lamented that "formerly the Old People had more sense than we have and Could manage their young men better than we Can."[45]

Okfuskee fared as badly in this regard as any Creek town. The 1761 editorial regarding the headmen's inability to control the younger men, for example, was provoked by the news that some Okfuskees had raided the traders' stores in Okfuskee and Sugatspoges. The raids, in fact, suggest that the situation in Okfuskee was worse than the editor knew: headmen from eight Upper Creek communities "staid at Home last Winter [1760–1761] to protect the Traders," but only Okfuskee kept two headmen in town, neither of whom apparently could prevent the community's young men from robbing the traders. And, as time wore on, Okfuskee's young men became, if anything, more troublesome. Thus, 1763 began with Handsome Fellow and the Okfuskee Captain helping to lead a party whose spokesman mentioned "rash young Men" before inveighing against people who sought to "avoid Controul"; the year ended with an outburst of frontier violence triggered by "a Parcell of young Fellows," including an Okfuskee. By 1767, the "Oakfuskie King" felt it necessary to tell Stuart, "I am determined that no Mad young fellow shall break and Interrupt the peace & Harmony which ought to Subsist between us."[46] And yet that is exactly what happened. The next decade saw Okfuskee's young men referred to as "Murtherers" whose kinsmen "had Consented" to their execution, as "rash Men" prone to "Mischief," as "Murderers" yet again, as wanting "to fall on the white people," as "Renegadoes" who "[beat] one of their own Headmen for speaking against what they had done," and as the "wors[t] Sett of Villains in the Nation." The nine-man Okfuskee party that earned this last appellation included two men who killed colonists in the past, a third who attempted to kill a trader, and a fourth who "often threatened" violence; "the rest," Taitt wrote, "are no better than these." By 1778, then, it made perfect sense that two Okfuskee headmen expressed reluctance to leave town because they were "afraid to trust the People alone."[47] Okfuskee's leaders had apparently lost control.

In June 1773, Stuart informed the Earl of Dartmouth of reports that the Creeks "meditated some thing hostile against us." Although Stuart did "not apprehend that it is the Intention of the Nation in general to break with us," he decided to limit the amount of ammunition sent to Creek country. The policy soon had an impact. In August, Taitt wrote from Upper Creek country to warn of "a good deal of Murmuring for want of the Ammunition," and reports of Creek anger over ammunition shortages continued to pour in throughout the fall. By January 1774, Taitt cautioned Stuart, "I have a great Deal of Trouble with the Indians on this Account and when they all Come in [from hunting], I expect they will Pay themselves," that is, take what they needed from the traders.[48] Some Creeks, in fact, had already begun. In September, warriors from three Upper Creek towns stole "Cloaths," horses, saddles, provisions, and guns from a party of Euro-Americans traveling past the village of Fish Ponds. Headmen from two of the towns saw to it that their people returned their share of the booty, but offenders from the third town refused to follow suit. Two of their headmen reported that the robbers "say that they will give Ear to no Talks from [Stuart] or any Governor," and that "the worse they use the White People the better they will be supplied with goods." The two headmen further stated that "they can do nothing with their People now, for they will hear nothing from them"; Tomahajo, they explained, "is the Leader of the Young People to a Mischief." His influence, together with that of the traders in the woods, rendered "their Young People . . . regardless of their Head men." As a partial remedy, they asked Taitt to prevent three traders from purchasing deerskins illegally.[49]

On its face, the 1773 incident seems a fairly straightforward example of uncontrollable young men and hapless headmen, just the sort of thing that decades of generational conflict should produce. A closer examination, however, reveals a more complicated picture. In the first place, it is worth noting that headmen from two of the towns succeeded in gathering up the stolen goods, and that they did so quickly.[50] Second, and more centrally, the actions of both the young men and the headmen from the third town—which was, of course, Okfuskee—are not as transparent as they seem. To begin with, the young men involved were not disaffected renegades rebelling against all authority and structure. True, they did state that "they were once of the Same Fire with Charleston but now they will be by themselves," but, in doing so, they simultaneously rejected the town's past alliances and reaffirmed their connection to that town, whose policies they were trying to shape. Moreover, "the Young People" were not without a leader. In fact, the two headmen who visited Taitt described Tomahajo as "King of the Town." Thirteen years before, in the aftermath of the May 1760 attack, this man stated that "he himself thinks he is come to the Years of Knowledge, and says that he takes great Pains to rule his young People, and thinks he can do it as he looks upon himself to be the Head Man of that Town."[51] The "Leader of the Young People to a Mischief," then, was a headman of long standing, a man confident of his ability to control the townspeople, a mico in the fullest sense of the term.

Finally, the identity and role of one of the headmen—Handsome Fellow—who spoke to Taitt raises some interesting questions. Handsome Fellow bore the title of head warrior in the 1750s, and he continued to be referred to as such until at least 1766; no evidence suggests that he ever became Okfuskee's mico. A man with his background might have been expected to have a better rapport with young warriors than did the town's civil headman. He had, after all, led them in the May 1760 attack, and he had labored for a decade to preserve their hunting grounds. Moreover, head warriors, not civil leaders, were traditionally the ones to propose and carry out "bloody" acts. If long-standing beliefs about a mico's responsibilities still held, then Tomahajo risked his position by encouraging the young warriors to behave as they did.[52]

Several significant points emerge from a close analysis of the 1773 incident. Most obviously, Okfuskee was in flux. Young warriors asserted their ability to challenge the status quo, while civil and military headmen vied for control and traditional spheres of influence fell by the wayside. It is, moreover, difficult to ignore the role Euro-Americans played in the disruption of town life. As instigators of embargoes, targets for robbery, objects of complaint, and ameliorators of worrisome conditions, Euro-Americans appear at every step of the narrative. Finally, it is important to acknowledge that, although Okfuskee was in flux, it had not ceased to be a community. The 1773 incident shows Okfuskees arguing about the terms of their relationship and strategies for their town's future. Whatever else they were, the men involved remained Okfuskees. Less than a year later, nine of Okfuskee's most troublesome young men arrived in Augusta bearing the symbols and talks that Okfuskees had long used to shape their world and to claim a prominent place in it. These envoys sought to reopen the trade that was so central to young men's lives, but they did so by returning to geographical constructions—"the Path . . . from Oakfuskie to this white House"—and historical relationships—"formerly the Oakfuskies & Charlestown were one Fire"—rooted in their community. That they could be both young and envoys suggests the extent to which life in Okfuskee had changed; but that they would march through hostile territory to speak of "white" paths and shared fires attests to the fact that Okfuskee continued to have meaning for them. The nine Okfuskees, like their fellow townspeople, experienced new opportunities and novel problems within the context of the town, and they continued to make reference to a shared past while they planned for a common future.[53]

Throughout the eighteenth century, to call a Creek man "woman" was a terrible insult. So, in 1725, when Okfuskee's mico told the town's leaders that "We act like Women more than Head Men" in "Slight[ing]" their British visitor, he spoke in a way calculated to get the men's attention. If the Okfuskee mico had delivered this talk in the 1790s rather than the 1720s, he might very well have used the same rhetoric. Given the tremendous changes Creek society underwent during these seventy years, the continuity in male reactions to "woman" is striking. At the very least, the insult's staying power suggests the enduring relevance of gender roles in Creek life, and it is tempting to argue that Creek men could not use "woman" as an epithet so consistently without feeling deep-seated hostility toward women in general. In fact, though, the reaction Creek men exhibited when called "woman" had less to do with feelings for women than with beliefs about their own role in society. Or, to put it another way, "woman" served as a stinging insult when directed at a Creek man not because women were not respected but because men who assumed women's roles were not respectable.[54]

A 1772 incident involving the Upper Creek headman Emisteseguo allows us to witness the nuanced nature of Creek gender relations. At the time, Emisteseguo was greatly concerned about British demands for Creek land. During what must have been a particularly low moment, he asked a trader, William Gregory, "how [Gregory] would like it if [Emisteseguo] Should Come to fetch him Wood & Water." Gregory, taken aback, stated "that he did not believe it would ever be the Case for it might Come to Emisteseguo's turn to fetch im Wood & Water." The headman, obviously in a fatalistic mood, replied "I do not think so."[55] Emisteseguo had not picked the services he expected to perform at random: in Creek households, women hauled firewood and carried drinking water. A headman who performed such tasks assumed characteristics antithetical to his masculine identity. When Emisteseguo spoke of performing women's tasks, then, he foretold the end of Creek society as he knew it. The tasks, however, were not dishonorable, nor were the people who performed them on a daily basis. Women procured wood and water without stain or reproach. Gendered spheres of behavior, in other words, were both separate and sacrosanct. To trespass was dangerous, but to inhabit the appropriate sphere was commendable.

The Creeks' continued emphasis on men's and women's spheres did not mean, of course, that relations between men and women remained unchanged during the eighteenth century. As Creek men and Creek women recognized the problems and possibilities offered by their Euro-American neighbors, complementary gender roles lost their allure and mutuality became increasingly difficult to achieve. Intercultural exchange undermined long-standing patterns of reciprocity, and gender-based patterns of consumption and production encouraged competition rather than cooperation. In fact, changes in gender relations may have encouraged Emisteseguo to speak as he did. In a world where Creek men and women no longer depended on each other, in a society where familiar customs were being questioned, the headman may have suspected that men might take on women's roles.

For all of his gender-based imagery, however, Emisteseguo spoke in a context demonstrating that his concerns focused at least as much on relations between men as on ties binding women and men. In 1772, Augusta merchants were pushing the Creeks to cede a large part of "their most valuable hunting Grounds" to pay debts run up by their "Young men." Emisteseguo knew that headmen could no longer control the warriors' buying patterns, and he believed that they would never accept the cession proposed by the merchants. War, he suspected, was both inevitable and unwinnable.[56] The inability of headmen to control their young men, then, threatened the Creeks with the short-term loss of their hunting grounds and the long-term loss of their independence. The pessimism evinced by Emisteseguo attests to the shifting nature of intergenerational relations among Creek men.

Emisteseguo's encounter with Gregory, then, brings together Creek experiences with changing systems of gender and generational relations. According to the headman, unruly young men threatened to destroy not only the bonds that linked young and old men but also the boundaries that separated men from women. Other Creeks no doubt placed responsibility for these changes on different shoulders, but, by the 1770s, few Creeks would have denied the legitimacy of Emisteseguo's fears. The inhabitants of Okfuskee certainly experienced similar moments of uncertainty and anxiety. Their headmen, after all, were intimately involved in resisting British pressure for land cessions, while their young men exhibited both an eagerness for European goods and an unwillingness to accept the territorial agreements their leaders negotiated. At the same time, Okfuskee's headmen were increasingly powerless and divided; familiar patterns of influence and authority could no longer be counted upon to weave together white and red, old and young. Moreover, Okfuskees found that women and men were drawing apart. The Creek conception of the sexes as "separate people" was taking on a concreteness that had never been intended; spheres of production and consumption no longer functioned as an argument for bridging the differences that divided Okfuskee's two sorts of "people." Okfuskees knew that big women and mad men could coexist; they had done so for generations. Okfuskees must, however, have wondered if they could continue to do so. After three generations of intense contact with Euro-Americans, Okfuskees were confronted with the task of reevaluating the systems of rights and responsibilities that bound together women and men, young and old.

As Okfuskees restructured their most basic relations, the peculiar connections binding Native and newcomer forced them to take into account their Euro-American neighbors, a people with their own strongly held ideas about gender roles and generational authority. Okfuskees on the receiving end of a colonist's lecture—about their headmen's powerlessness or their young warriors' waywardness, their inappropriate gender roles or their unnatural reliance on matrilineal and matrilocal households—most likely responded in kind. The former Okfuskee trader who was "affect[ed] very sensibly" when he could not "prevail on his [Creek] wife to consent to" schooling their children in Charleston or Savannah was not alone in feeling frustrated by foreign customs. Early America's frontiers, in fact, drew much of their staying power from arguments of this sort, from the construction and maintenance of contrasting systems for organizing gender and generational relations. And yet, having acknowledged that fact, we have only begun to scratch the surface of these arguments' explanatory power. Watching colonists and Okfuskees define themselves against each other helps us to understand how the latter became Native; it does little, however, to advance our understanding of the ways in which both peoples confronted American dilemmas. The problems—gender anxieties and authority crises, intergenerational tensions and unstable sex roles—that plagued the Okfuskees were, in the second half of the eighteenth century, concerns characteristic of America more generally.[57]

Thus, historians writing about eighteenth-century Euro-American women emphasize the "convoluted and sometimes tangled embroidery of loss and gain, accommodation and resistance" that characterized their lives. Economically, many women found that a more mature market economy meant increased material comfort, improved opportunities for wage labor, and enhanced autonomy from husbands and fathers. At the same time, however, those women found that much of their economic life continued to be phrased in terms of the family, that gendered divisions of labor could become more rigid, that they were increasingly unable to participate in the large-scale credit and debt transactions at the heart of the market economy, and that they failed to gain either a greater share of the society's productive capital or a significant alteration of the coverture laws. Politically, too, Euro-American women experienced "ambiguous" developments. The Revolution and its aftermath enhanced women's status and broadened their sphere of action, while laying the foundation for a domestic ideology that emphasized woman's role as consumer rather than producer, as homebody rather than active community member, as sentimentalized molder of citizens rather than pragmatic citizen in her own right. And, to further women's marginalization, men's authority came to be perceived as flowing from natural and immutable differences between the sexes, not from the contingent political authority of king over subject. As in Okfuskee, then, Americans struggled with what Susan Juster calls "the broader crisis in gender norms."[58]

As with gender relations, the colonists' traditions and practices of authority were increasingly embattled. Lockean philosophy encouraged both a tightening of family bonds and a loosening of patriarchal authority. Economic changes furthered these developments. In New England, for example, agricultural problems led to a decline in sons' dependence on fathers, who could no longer be counted on to provide an adequate inheritance; by the time of the early republic, throughout the United States, filial autonomy often outweighed paternal dictates. Daughters too became more independent, often working outside the household to earn money. Such shifts were reflected in social changes ranging from an increased reliance on wage labor to a rise in "consumer sovereignty" and a decline in the age at which men achieved personal independence. At the same time, in a development that "began naturally enough with the family," traditional social bonds predicated on hierarchy and deference eroded. Although historians have noted preexisting chinks in the deference that armored colonial America's elites, it is clear that, from midcentury onward, Americans became significantly less committed to long-standing habits of marking, exercising, and obeying authority.[59] Insecurity became the order of the day for those men accustomed to thinking of themselves as society's natural leaders. As in Okfuskee, then, political, economic, and cultural factors combined to undermine the authority of superiors, to encourage individualistic and assertive behavior among subordinate groups, and to call into question the prevailing social order.

Okfuskees thus took part in what Mechal Sobel has called Revolutionary America's "category crisis": "boundaries, which had been widely accepted as ideals before, were being altered, both by design and by happenstance."[60] When it came to even the most fundamental of social facts, early Americans were suddenly unsure of how to reconcile the proper and the possible. That the Okfuskees' place in this process was primarily invisible to those— both Okfuskees and Euro-Americans—participating in it does not make the townspeople's involvement any less real. Early America's connections enmeshed people whom neither Natives nor newcomers were accustomed to regarding as part of their world. As in early America's other crises, however, Native people found themselves peculiarly disadvantaged when confronting challenges to their traditional systems. Gender and generational change exposed Okfuskee's increasingly precarious place in early America.

To begin with, while shifts in gender and generational relations characterized early America more generally, changes of this sort were especially problematic for Okfuskee and other Native towns. The difficulty stemmed less from cultural content than social scale. Okfuskee was, finally, a small-scale, locally oriented place. Like their Euro-American neighbors, Okfuskees found that their traditional gender and generational models often conflicted with the demands of new behavioral and intellectual systems; unlike those neighbors, however, Okfuskees confronted these challenges within a social system whose methods for producing order and validating identities depended almost exclusively upon face-to-face interaction and intimate personal ties. Faced with comparable problems at the communal or familial level, their Euro-American contemporaries could fall back upon more expansive mechanisms and more extensive venues for social integration. The increasing centralization and rationalization of colonial and imperial government could, for example, counterbalance local disorder, while transatlantic communication facilitated efforts to maintain political equilibrium and personal power. At the same time, intracolony correspondence networks linked educated professionals and newspapers expanded public access to—and investment in—political debate. Developments of these sorts "served to homogenize English-speaking culture and to consolidate membership in it," a process which could not reverse the changes that accompanied shifting gender and generational relations but which did allow them to be contained to a degree unimaginable in Native towns. Okfuskee's modest social scale—its dependence on the intersection of intimate personal connections and formal political integration—meant that its people were especially vulnerable to disrupted gender and generational relations. Compared to their Euro-American contemporaries, Okfuskees were working without a net.[61]

The dangers inherent in such a situation were exacerbated by the fact that those same contemporaries often treated Indian affairs as an avenue to redress their own gender- or generationally based insecurities. Euro-American men, for example, sought validation for their masculinity and confirmation of their maturity in Indian country. Colonists—and later, United States citizens—used diplomatic and military dealings with Indians to present themselves as manly father figures worthy of not just ruling over feminized, childlike Natives but also of achieving recognition as virtuous leaders from their fellow Euro-Americans.[62] Indians were, of course, free to play the same game, and many did. Okfuskee's young men were far from alone in using assaults on colonists and livestock to highlight their masculinity, and its women were not the only ones seeking the enhanced status that came from marriage to a British trader. As Native power waned in the late eighteenth and early nineteenth centuries, however, Indian actions of these sorts were often peculiarly counterproductive. Far from ameliorating the Indians' gender- and generational-related problems, connections to Euro-Americans only brought renewed challenges. A young man's raids exposed his people to military invasion and compensatory land cessions; a woman's marriage earned her and her family only suspicion and hostility from Euro-Americans increasingly attuned to racial identity.[63] Native Americans confronting their own peculiarly altered personal relations, in other words, simultaneously encountered neighbors intent on asserting and maintaining the Indians' status as inferiors.

Conclusion: "The Fiends of the Tallapoosie"—Nuyaka, Tohopeka, and the Rise of Andrew Jackson

On December 17, 1813, a troop of Georgia militia commanded by General David Adams attacked the Okfuskee village of Nuyaka, twenty miles up the Tallapoosa River from Okfuskee itself. "[T]o our mortification," Adams reported, "we found . . . not a single Indian, though there were abundant signs of a very recent evacuation, and repeated yells within our hearing on the opposite side of the river"; after exchanging "a few shots with the enemy" across the river—and possibly killing one Creek—the soldiers burned "the town." Adams's men were in Nuyaka because a violent Creek civil war caused by debates over social order and religious belief had become enmeshed in the United States' ongoing war with Great Britain. For the first time since De Soto's invasion, a foreign army—now supported by a Creek faction—marched through Upper Creek country. Nuyaka was not, then, the only Okfuskee settlement in danger. On March 27, 1814, less than a mile downstream from Nuyaka, an army composed primarily of Tennessee militia commanded by General Andrew Jackson attacked the fortified Creek town of Tohopeka. Among the people at Tohopeka were refugees from Nuyaka, as well as Okfuskees from the main town, its village of Elkhatchie, and, most likely, Little Okfuskee, which had itself been burned in November 1813. The Battle of Horseshoe Bend utterly destroyed Tohopeka and killed between 800 and 900 of the 1,000 Creek warriors involved. Two Okfuskees reported later that "not more than twenty warriors belonging to the Ocfushee Towns" survived, and that, of the Nuyaka warriors, "but three escaped"; one of the survivors was Menawa of Okfuskee, reputed to have been Tohopeka's head warrior. So closely affiliated with Tohopeka were the Okfuskees, in fact, that Jackson, in writing about the site, noted that the Creeks were "forting in at Oakfuskey."[1]

Okfuskee's story, of course, continues into the present day. Now located in northeastern Oklahoma, the town's survival attests to the resilience of Native American communities and to their centrality in Indian life. This continuity notwithstanding, however, the destruction of Nuyaka and Tohopeka provides a logical end point for this book. The histories of these two places vividly illustrate the end results of the century's worth of peculiar connections that followed the 1708 day when Thomas Nairne witnessed Cossitee's "Coronation" in Okfuskee's town square.

On the one hand, the differences between Nuyaka and Tohopeka encapsulate the Okfuskees' struggles over how best to adapt to the realities of life in the early republic. Nuyaka, for its part, was a typical Okfuskee village, a village that clearly fit within the town's colonial-era developmental trajectory, a village whose social, economic, and political life attested to the Okfuskees' long-standing ties to their Euro-American neighbors. Tohopeka, by contrast, was a distinctly atypical Creek town, a town whose shape and purpose reflected the exigencies of civil war and religious fervor, a town whose history attested to the degree to which Okfuskees and their fellow Creeks were questioning the peculiarly destructive nature of their connections to the United States.

On the other hand, the real differences between Nuyaka and Tohopeka fade in the face of one striking similarity, one shared truth: by the nineteenth century, any option visualized by the Okfuskees was intimately connected to, and peculiarly ineffective against, their Euro-American neighbors. The demolition of Nuyaka and Tohopeka underscores the degree to which all Okfuskees confronted an impossible situation. They could no longer fend off—via diplomatic skill or military force, socioeconomic engagement or socioreligious estrangement—Euro-American neighbors who believed that an Indian presence in the area was unnecessary, unappealing, or unacceptable.

Consider, for example, Andrew Jackson's celebration of the deaths of the Okfuskees and their allies at Tohopeka. "The fiends of the Tallapoosie," he told his soldiers after the battle, "will no longer murder our women and children, or disturb the quiet of our borders." In Jackson's rhetoric, even the town-square fire took on devilish overtones, becoming a "midnight flambeaux" that shone "upon the victim of their infernal orgies." Instead of sheltering diabolic savages and their demonic blazes, the victory meant that "the wilderness, which now withers in sterility, and mourns the desolation which overspreads her, will blossom as the rose, and become the nursery of the arts." And then, of course, there was the land itself, now apparently free for the taking. As Jackson put it to his troops prior to marching against the Creeks: "The country to the South is inviting. Let us consolidate it as part of our Union."[2]

Over fifty years earlier, in the aftermath of another violent incident—the May 16, 1760, attack—the Okfuskee Captain had articulated a very different vision for his townspeople, their neighbors, and Okfuskee's fire: "the Oakfuskee People were always reckoned one People and one Fire with the English, but this mad Affair had like to have put the Fire out, but it was again kindled and got to its former State, and I hope will continue so as long as the Sun shines and the Rivers empty themselves into the Sea." The destruction of communities as different as Nuyaka and Tohopeka suggested that this was not to be. In the nineteenth-century United States, as Jackson's and Adams's armies showed, Nuyakas could not share a fire with Americans, and Tohopekas could not have their own fire. Euro-Americans no longer welcomed Native connections or tolerated the peculiarities of people they did not see as American. The possibilities—the promise of a world at once Native and American—offered by the eighteenth century's peculiar connections were lost to memory in the dislocation and violence of the nineteenth century.[3]

The townspeople who, in 1777, settled at what became Nuyaka migrated from the Okfuskee village of Tukpafka, and the new site likely remained "Tukpafka" for almost fifteen years. Both names reflected the Okfuskees' sustained engagement with their Euro-American neighbors. "Tukpafka" means "punk" or "material for starting a fire," a name that may have referred to the fire that united Tukpafka with Okfuskee and Okfuskee with Charleston. The original Tukpafka was one of the five Okfuskee villages founded on the Chattahoochee River in the early 1760s; its inhabitants were thus among the Okfuskees who elected to move closer to the British colonies and to engage more fully with the backcountry's frontier exchange economy. In 1777, they had second thoughts: "They would not take part in the war between the United States and Great Britain and determined to retire from their settlements, which through the rage of war might feel the effects of the resentment of the people of the United States." The new village that they built upstream from Okfuskee was not, however, a bastion of anti-American sentiment. It became the home of White Lieutenant, Fanni Mico's grandson and a man who threw himself into facilitating peaceful relations with the United States. Of course, as his grandfather discovered before him, ties to Euro-Americans inevitably disrupted intracommunity bonds. By 1793, White Lieutenant was complaining that Euro-American outlaws "have learned our young men their bad ways," making his people "miserable." Still, the inhabitants of Tukpafka recognized the value of their relationship with the United States, and, in the early 1790s, these Okfuskees renamed their village Nuyaka to further solidify that connection. This name, adopted in honor of a 1790 treaty which the Creeks signed in New York City, served as a powerful symbol of the Okfuskees' continued faith in town-based links to their Euro-American neighbors. "Nuyaka" signified that the Okfuskees would, as White Lieutenant put it, "stand by" the understandings solemnized in the United States capital. Previous generations of Okfuskees had made similar commitments.[4]

As with their diplomatic relations, the Nuyakas' land-use strategies show them building on the experiences of earlier generations of Okfuskees. Nuyaka became a large village. General Adams's militia burned "85 houses" which were laid out "in a linear fashion along a terrace" above the river. Today, "material remains . . . are scattered over a very large area." Nuyaka was not, then, a nucleated community, and even in this loosely organized settlement, "[a] few . . . people . . . settled out from the town"; White Lieutenant, in fact, lived across the river from the main site by 1796. Nuyaka's inhabitants thus took part in the movement away from not only Okfuskee proper but also from their nearest neighbors. As in Okfuskee, these developments were likely related, in part, to livestock herding by men. White Lieutenant owned a herd of cattle, and Benjamin Hawkins, the United States' Creek agent, mentioned seeing "poultry, hogs," and "cattle" during a 1796 visit; cow and pig bones and chicken eggshells dot Nuyaka's archaeological record. Moreover, Okfuskee's young men were among those Creeks who continued to view "stealing horses" as a "reputable martial employment," and so Nuyakas certainly owned horses, as well. The presence of these animals may explain why one of the village's agricultural fields—the locus of much of the women's work—was situated across the river and another was two miles downstream; by 1813, Nuyakas had abandoned the first field, perhaps because the river—with its "fine ford at the upper end of the town"—offered insufficient protection from hungry livestock. These Okfuskee women did not, however, forsake Native agricultural traditions. Their fields remained productive enough to allow Adams's men to burn "a considerable quantity of corn," and the only non-Native plants found by archaeologists were peaches. The agricultural routines and settlement patterns adopted by Nuyakas in the late eighteenth and early nineteenth centuries were, then, in keeping with those followed by Okfuskees of the 1770s.[5]

Other aspects of the Nuyakas' economic lives are also recognizable, most notably their willingness to exploit wild resources. The village's men, for example, continued hunting. Thus, when Hawkins visited in December 1796, "few Indian men [were] at home" and White Lieutenant himself "was out hunting"; when White Lieutenant died in 1799, his brother brought a trader almost 100 of the dead man's skins. That deer bones outnumber cow bones in the village's waste pits suggests that other Nuyakas were also successful hunters. One Okfuskee headman, in fact, "was the owner of a store" at which he traded Euro-American goods to "his own people for the products of the chase," no doubt primarily deerskins; "[h]e carried on a brisk trade with Pensacola, and was known to load, at one time, a hundred horses with furs and peltries." Likewise, Nuyaka's women had not forsaken their role as gatherers of plants. The same pits that contained deer bones also showed that Nuyakas utilized eight different wild food plants, plus others that were converted into medicines, dyes, cosmetics, and poisons.[6]

The Nuyakas' material culture likewise reflected their connection to Okfuskee traditions, Native and American alike. Nuyaka's ceramicists, for example, were "highly skilled and meticulous craftswomen" whose products demonstrated a distinct "conservatism" in style; the village's men, for their part, manufactured chipped-stone projectile points and ground-stone pipes. Nuyakas also continued another old Okfuskee tradition: purchasing goods from Euro-Americans. A bottle of "Invented Balsam of Life" and a chatelaine—a gold-washed piece of brass jewelry—were simply the most eye-catching items on a shopping list that included beads, metalware, ammunition, and—although none survived for archaeologists to uncover—cloth. The villagers purchased at least some of these goods from their resident trader, James Sullivan, who was prosperous enough to employ an assistant. And, as in Okfuskee, these apparently American goods were, by this time, quintessentially Native, a point underlined by the Nuyakas' willingness to convert a broken bottle into a hide scraper and a worn-out kettle into copper beads. Nuyakas who purchased, used, and then modified these manufactured items enacted—on a personal level—the peculiar connections between Native and American worlds that were now an inescapable part of village life.[7]

Their names alone suggest the very different orientations of Nuyaka and Tohopeka. "Nuyaka" illustrated the villagers' efforts to incorporate and profit from outsiders. "Tohopeka"—"wooden fence," fortification—testified to a desire for isolation. Tohopeka was located in the base of a horseshoe-shaped bend in the Tallapoosa River, and the inhabitants built a breastwork—"a sophisticated structure consisting of a trench, stacked log wall, and fraising"—across the top of the bend. The community they constructed behind this barricade was a Nativist town, a place founded in 1813 by those Okfuskees and their fellow Creeks intent on establishing a sacred way of life, a place where prophets preaching a message of pan-Indian alliance and Native-based spirituality held sway. Its leaders selected the site in part for defensive reasons and in part because they believed it had never been occupied before; "it was," as one historian puts it, "a good place to make a new beginning." The town they built seems to have been a fairly ordered place. The breastwork itself reflected a great deal of planning and organized effort, and the arrangement of houses was likewise orderly. Thus, two maps made by soldiers in Jackson's army—one by the officer with the best view of the town during the battle and the other by an engineer—show five rows of houses; the officer also depicts what might be a square ground near the center of the houses.[8]

   Although intended primarily to fend off armies, the breastwork at Tohopeka was aimed more generally at unbelievers, a category that included Euro-Americans, of course, but also the Creeks who rejected the teachings of Nativist prophets and allied themselves with the United States. In Hawkins's words, "[t]he declaration of the prophets is to destroy . . . all the Chiefs and their adherents who are friendly to the customs and ways of the white people," by whom the prophets meant "the Americans," not "their friends the British"; the latter, the prophets hoped, would help them crush the United States. Okfuskees were heavily involved in the Creek-on-Creek violence that ensued. Most shockingly, the townspeople put to death five "of the principle chiefs of Ockfuskee" who "Took [Hawkins's] talks"; no doubt in response, the faction opposed to the prophets "went to [Little] Ockfuskee a small village where they had taken the prophets talk . . . and put them [the inhabitants] to death." By the fall of 1813, Okfuskee warriors were setting out to attack other Creek towns, and the prophets' supporters "had a meeting at the fuckias"—a contemporary footnote identifies this as "O, fuck, shee"—to set a date "to come against" their Creek enemies. Again, developments of this sort were something new in Creek country. Whatever else it may have accomplished, then, Tohopeka's fortification signaled the degree to which old loyalties and understandings had come undone.[9]

Tohopeka's archaeological record attests to the seriousness with which the inhabitants sought to remake their world. The list of typical Creek goods not found at Tohopeka is a long one. Gone were the silver and brass jewelry; gone were the glass beads; gone were clay pipes and iron tools. Gone, in other words, were the goods which generations of Okfuskees had sought from Euro-American traders and British officials. Gone, too, were European livestock: when the Okfuskees killed their own headmen, they also "destroyed almost all the cattle in town." Okfuskees also destroyed the "loom and bolt of cloth" owned by a woman "invited there by the Chiefs of the town to teach the women to spin and weave." As impressive as this list is, however, the Tohopekas did not completely purge non-Native items. Just as they could seek ties to "their friends the British," they could make room for certain European goods. For example, they refashioned "thin scrap iron" into arrowheads—archaeologists found three at Tohopeka but none at Nuyaka—and they cached glass fragments for use as scrapers. European guns and ammunition were even more central to the Tohopekas' fate. Between a quarter and a third of Tohopeka warriors at the Battle of Horseshoe Bend possessed guns; the rest tried desperately to acquire them from British traders in Florida, only to be turned away as bad credit risks. Their lack of guns helped doom the town; Jackson's heavily armed soldiers could not be held off with bows and arrows. In the end, then, the Tohopekas' inability to acquire European military implements or to gain access to European fiscal instruments undermined their ability to defend their Nativist community. A superb breastwork, a deeply held faith, and a cohort of committed warriors were not enough. Peculiarly enough, by the nineteenth century, even Nativists needed connections.[10]

The commonalities linking Nuyaka and Tohopeka, then, went further than simply their ties to Okfuskee or their destruction at Euro-American hands. Both communities, after all, sought connections to Europeans; both depended upon foreign goods. Moreover, of course, the two communities shared personnel. Again and again, Jackson referred to Nuyakas who "had gathered in," "concentrated in," or "returned to" Tohopeka. Nuyakas eventually fought and died at Tohopeka in large numbers. The American soldier whose map referred to "New Yauca or Horse Shoe Town" was not entirely wrong, therefore, to conflate the two. In fact, the deeper one looks into the histories of Nuyaka and Tohopeka, the more their stories run together.[11]

Take, for example, the personal histories of the Okfuskee headmen most clearly associated with the two settlements: Menawa of Tohopeka and White Lieutenant of Nuyaka. On the surface, these men—like their respective communities—seem to have little in common beyond being Okfuskees, an identity that hardly seems enough to overcome the divide between the leader of the largest Nativist military force in Creek history, on the one hand, and the man who spent much of his life building ties to Euro-Americans, on the other. And yet their biographies are surprisingly similar. Both Menawa and White Lieutenant were, most obviously, noted war leaders; the former held the title "Great Warrior" and the latter was "Great War Mico." Menawa and White Lieutenant were also heavily involved in the commerce that linked their townspeople to Euro-Americans, the latter as a factor and trader and the former as the aforementioned store owner who sent 100-horse packtrains to Pensacola. Both men were, moreover, dedicated livestock raisers, although White Lieutenant's cattle herd likely paled beside Menawa's "thousand head of cattle, an equal number of hogs, and several hundred horses." They even shared a biological heritage: both were "half blooded Creek[s]."[12]

And if the comparative lens is widened to encompass White Lieutenant's uncle—Handsome Fellow—the parallels continue. Like Handsome Fellow, Menawa came slowly to the notion that he should lead warriors against the Euro-Americans; Menawa "agreed to his towns painting for war and painted himself likewise" only after considering the issue "at length." Neither man, therefore, fits the profile of a lifelong or enthusiastic Nativist. Like Handsome Fellow, Menawa emerged from a violent episode with his reputation among the Creeks intact. After Horseshoe Bend, he "resumed his authority over the remnants of the Oakfuskee band"; he became an important enough figure to serve on the Creek National Council, to take the lead in executing a Coweta headman who illegally ceded Creek land, and to sign the 1827 treaty between the Creeks and the United States. And, like Handsome Fellow, Menawa used his later years to rebuild relations with Euro-Americans. The 1827 treaty included a provision granting him $10,000, and by 1836 he was wearing an American uniform—recalling, perhaps,

Handsome Fellow's father, the British-affiliated and -clothed Red Coat King—and fighting for the United States against the Seminoles. Except for the evident differences in age between White Lieutenant and Menawa—the former died in 1799 at the age of 62; the latter was still active militarily thirty-seven years later—the two men could have been brothers.[13]

The difference, then, between Nuyaka and Tohopeka—like the difference between White Lieutenant and Menawa—was not that the former embraced Okfuskee's peculiar connections to Euro-Americans while the latter rejected them. Each was a creation of those connections; each represented an effort by Okfuskees to adjust to generations' worth of experience with Euro-Americans. And each was ultimately unsuccessful. In a tragic—and peculiar—irony, the legacy Tohopeka and Nuyaka left to the United States was neither a religious community controlled by Indians nor a more secular Native village connected to Americans, but rather the political ascendancy of Andrew Jackson. The most powerful Euro-American of his day, the man who did more than any other to promote Indian removal, began his rise to national prominence by killing the descendants of Fanni Mico of Okfuskee.

Notes

Abbreviations

ADAIR   Samuel C. Williams, ed., *Adair's History of the American Indians* (New York: Promontory Press, 1974 [1775]).

BPRO, CO 5   British Public Records Office, Colonial Office: America and West Indies, Plantations General, 1760–1784.

BPRO-SC   W. Noel Sainsbury, ed., *Records in the British Public Records Office Relating to South Carolina, 1663–1782,* 11 reels, Georgia Historical Society, Savannah.

CGAHS   Collections of the Georgia Historical Society, Savannah.

CLEM   Papers of the Clements Library, University of Michigan, Ann Arbor.

CRSGA   *The Colonial Records of the State of Georgia.* Volumes 1–28, edited by Allen D. Candler, Kenneth Coleman, and Milton Ready (Atlanta and Athens, 1904–1916, 1974–1976). Volumes 29–38, in the microfilm collection of the Georgia Department of Archives and History, Atlanta.

DRIA   William L. McDowell Jr., ed., *The Colonial Records of South Carolina: Documents Relating to Indian Affairs, 1750–1765,* 2 vols. (Columbia: South Carolina Department of Archives and History, 1958, 1970).

GA-GAZ   Georgia *Gazette,* Savannah.

GAGE   Thomas Gage Papers, Clements Library, University of Michigan.

HAWKINS   C. L. Grant, ed., *Letters, Journals and Writings of Benjamin Hawkins* (Savannah, Ga.: Beehive Press, 1980).

HUNT   Collections of the Huntington Library, San Marino, California.

JCIT   William L. McDowell Jr., ed., *The Colonial Records of South Carolina: Journals of the Commissioners of the Indian Trade, September 20, 1710– August 29, 1718* (Columbia: South Carolina Department of Archives and History, 1955).

LAURENS   Henry Laurens Papers, Roll 17: Papers Concerning Indian Affairs, South Carolina Historical Society, Charleston.

LYTTEL   William Lyttelton Papers, Clements Library, University of Michigan.

MC&CAMP   Account Book, Macartan & Campbell, Augusta Store, August 1762– June 1766, South Caroliniana Library, University of South Carolina,

Columbia; microfilm copy of the original housed at the Clemson University Library.

MPA-ED   Dunbar Rowland, ed., *Mississippi Provincial Archives, 1763–1766, English Dominion: Letters and Enclosures to the Secretary of State from Major Robert Farmer and Governor George Johnstone* (Nashville, Tenn.: Press of Brandon Printing Co., 1911).

MPA-FD   *Mississippi Provincial Archives: French Dominion,* 5 vols., edited by Dunbar Rowland, A. G. Sanders, and Patricia K. Galloway (Jackson and Baton Rouge: Mississippi Department of Archives and History and Louisiana State University Press, 1927–1932, 1984).

PA-GAZ   Pennsylvania *Gazette,* Philadelphia.

SALZ   *Detailed Reports on the Salzburger Emigrants Who Settled in America,* 17 vols., edited by George F. Jones et al. (Athens: University of Georgia Press, 1978–1993).

SC-CJ   Journals of South Carolina's Council. Bound copies in South Carolina Department of Archives and History, Columbia; microfilm in "Early State Records. E-1p," *Records of the States of the United States of America* (Washington, D.C.: Library of Congress, 1949–1951).

SC-GAZ   South Carolina *Gazette,* Charleston.

SC-JCHA   Journals of South Carolina's Commons House of Assembly. For sessions prior to 1736, see miscellaneous sessions edited by Alexander S. Salley and published by the General Assembly of South Carolina; see also microfilm versions in "Early State Records. A-1b," reels 1–5, *Records of the States of the United States of America* (Washington, D.C.: Library of Congress, 1949–1951). For sessions from 1736 to 1757, see J. H. Easterby et al., eds., *The Colonial Records of South Carolina: The Journals of the Commons House of Assembly,* 12 vols. (Columbia: Historical Commission of South Carolina, 1951–1983).

SC-UH   Journals of South Carolina's Upper House of Assembly in "Early State Records. A.1a," reels 1–6, *Records of the States of the United States of America* (Washington, D.C.: Library of Congress, 1949–1951).

UGA   Collections of the Hargrett Rare Book and Manuscript Library, University of Georgia, Athens.

Introduction

1. CRSGA, vol. 28 (1), p. 88.
2. Henry Glassie, *Passing the Time in Ballymenone: Culture and History of an Ulster Community* (Philadelphia: University of Pennsylvania Press, 1982), p. 621.
3. For a map with symbols for "Native people," "British town," and "Spanish town," see Alan Taylor, *American Colonies* (New York: Penguin Putnam, 2001), p. 227.

4. For the assertion that "[d]efining tribe is a little like trying to nail jelly to the wall," see Raymond D. Fogelson, "The Context of American Indian Political History: An Overview and Critique," in Frederick E. Hoxie, ed., *The Struggle for Political Autonomy: Papers and Comments from the Second Newberry Library Conference on Themes in American Indian History* (Chicago: The Newberry Library, 1989), pp. 5–21, quotation from p. 15. For earlier bows in a similar direction, see Jack Campisi, "The Iroquois and the Euro-American Concept of Tribe," *New York History* 63 (1982): 165–182; James A. Clifton, "The Tribal History—An Obsolete Paradigm," *American Indian Culture and Research Journal* 3 (1979): 81–100. William Fenton has long advocated a localized, community-centered approach to Native history; see especially "The Concept of Locality and the Program of Iroquois Research," in Fenton, ed., *Symposium on Local Diversity in Iroquois Culture,* Bureau of American Ethnology Bulletin 149 (Washington, D.C.: U.S. Government Printing Office, 1951), pp. 35–54. See also Morton H. Fried, *The Notion of Tribe* (Menlo Park, Calif.: Cummings Publishing, 1975).

5. For the disjuncture between Euro-American models and Native reality, see Patricia Galloway, " 'So Many Little Republics': British Negotiations with the Choctaw Confederacy, 1765," *Ethnohistory* 41 (1994): 513–537, especially pp. 513–514; Gerald Sider, *Lumbee Indian Histories: Race, Ethnicity, and Indian Identity in the Southern United States* (New York: Cambridge University Press, 1993), p. 233.

6. James H. Merrell, "Some Thoughts on Colonial Historians and American Indians," *William and Mary Quarterly* 46 (1989): 94–119, quotation from p. 117; Richard White, *The Middle Ground: Indians, Empires, and Republics in the Great Lakes Region, 1650–1815* (New York: Cambridge University Press, 1991), p. xiv; Sider, *Lumbee Indian Histories,* p. 233; Colin G. Calloway, *The American Revolution in Indian Country: Crisis and Diversity in Native American Communities* (New York: Cambridge University Press, 1995), p. xiii; Frederick E. Hoxie, "Ethnohistory for a Tribal World," *Ethnohistory* 44 (1997): 595–615, quotations from pp. 605–606; Daniel H. Usner Jr., *American Indians in the Lower Mississippi Valley: Social and Economic Histories* (Lincoln: University of Nebraska Press, 1998), p. 12.

7. James P. Ronda, "The Sillery Experiment: A Jesuit–Indian Village in New France, 1637–1668," *American Indian Culture and Research Journal* 3 (1979): 1–18; Patrick Frazier, *The Mohicans of Stockbridge* (Lincoln: University of Nebraska Press, 1992); John Demos, *The Unredeemed Captive: A Family Story from Early America* (New York: Vintage Books, 1994), pp. 120–166; Jean O'Brien, *Dispossession By Degrees: Indian Land and Identity in Natick, Massachusetts, 1650–1790* (New York: Cambridge University Press, 1997); John H. Hann and Bonnie G. McEwan, *The Apalachee Indians and Mission San Luis* (Gainesville: University Press of Florida, 1998); Amy

C. Schutt, "Tribal Identity in the Moravian Missions on the Susquehanna," *Pennsylvania History* 66 (1999): 378–398.

8. Daniel K. Richter, "Iroquois vs. Iroquois: Jesuit Missions and Christianity in Village Politics, 1642–1686," *Ethnohistory* 32 (1985): 1–16; White, *The Middle Ground;* Robert E. Bieder, *Native American Communities in Wisconsin, 1600–1960: A Study of Tradition and Change* (Madison: University of Wisconsin Press, 1995); Jane T. Merritt, "Kinship, Community, and Practicing Culture: Indians and the Colonial Encounter in Pennsylvania, 1700–1763" (Ph.D. diss., University of Washington, 1995); Jennifer L. Baszile, "Communities at the Crossroads: Chiefdoms, Colonies, and Empires in Colonial Florida, 1670–1741" (Ph.D. diss., Princeton University, 1999); Lucy Eldersveld Murphy, *A Gathering of Rivers: Indians, Metis, and Mining in the Western Great Lakes, 1737–1832* (Lincoln: University of Nebraska Press, 2000).

9. For such communities, scholars have to rely on a handful of articles, book chapters, and essays, the best of which are M. Thomas Hatley, "The Three Lives of Keowee: Loss and Recovery in Eighteenth-Century Cherokee Villages," in Peter H. Wood, Gregory A. Waselkov, and Hatley, eds., *Powhatan's Mantle: Indians in the Colonial Southeast* (Lincoln: University of Nebraska Press, 1989), pp. 223–248; James H. Merrell, "Shamokin, 'the very seat of the Prince of darkness': Unsettling the Early American Frontier," in Andrew A. L. Cayton and Fredrika J. Teute, eds., *Contact Points: North American Frontiers, 1750–1830* (Chapel Hill: University of North Carolina Press, 1998), pp. 16–59.

10. Darrett Rutman, "Assessing the Little Communities of Early America," *William and Mary Quarterly* 43 (1986): 163–178. Merrell, "Some Thoughts," p. 118, argues that "Rutman, by uncovering the similarities among the many species of community in Anglo-America, implicitly invites us to continue widening the search by venturing into Indian country."

11. Edward Countryman refers to "our professional grail: an account of American society through time and across issues that shows shared experiences and an ultimate common identity without homogenizing the diverse American people"; "Indians, the Social Order, and the Social Significance of the American Revolution," *William and Mary Quarterly* 53 (1996): 342–362, quotation from pp. 343–344. See also Philip Morgan's call for "a single analytical field" revealing "not merely a catalogue of similarities and differences" but "one vast interconnected world"; "Encounters Between British and 'Indigenous' Peoples, c. 1500–c. 1800," in Martin Daunton and Rick Halpern, eds., *Empire and Others: British Encounters with Indigenous Peoples, 1600–1850* (Philadelphia: University of Pennsylvania Press, 1999), pp. 42–78, quotation from p. 68.

12. For Okfuskee as an Abeika town, see MPA-FD, vol. 4, map opposite p. 143; SC-CJ, 9/6/1749; Jerome Courtonne, "List of the Headmen of the Creeks," in Courtonne to Lyttelton, 10/17/1758, LYTTEL; "Speeches 3rd, 4th, & 7th of July 1759," pp. 4 and 7, and Edmond Atkin to Creek Headmen, 9/28–9/29/1759, pp. 1–2, both in Atkin to Lyttelton, 11/30/1759, LYTTEL; SC-GAZ, 3/29/1760, 4/7/1760; MPA-ED, p. 95; BPRO, CO 5/79, ff33–34.

13. References to eighteenth-century Creek towns' autonomy abound in recent scholarship. See Michael D. Green, *The Politics of Indian Removal: Creek Government and Society in Crisis* (Lincoln: University of Nebraska Press, 1982), p. 12; J. Leitch Wright Jr., *Creeks and Seminoles: The Destruction and Regeneration of the Muscogulge People* (Lincoln: University of Nebraska Press, 1986), p. 30; Joel Martin, *Sacred Revolt: The Muskogees' Struggle for a New World* (Boston: Beacon Press, 1991), p. 11; Duane Champagne, *Social Order and Political Change: Constitutional Governments among the Cherokee, the Choctaw, the Chickasaw, and the Creek* (Stanford, Calif.: Stanford University Press, 1992), pp. 27–28; Kathryn E. Holland Braund, *Deerskins & Duffels: Creek Indian Trade with Anglo-America, 1685–1815* (Lincoln: University of Nebraska Press, 1993), p. 22; George E. Lankford, "Red and White: Some Reflections on Southeastern Symbolism," *Southern Folklore* 50 (1993): 53–80, especially pp. 56–57; Vernon J. Knight Jr., "The Formation of the Creeks," in Charles Hudson and Carmen Chaves Tesser, eds., *The Forgotten Centuries: Indians and Europeans in the American South, 1521–1704* (Athens: University of Georgia Press, 1994), pp. 372–392, especially pp. 386–387; Claudio Saunt, *A New Order of Things: Property, Power, and the Transformation of the Creek Indians, 1733–1816* (New York: Cambridge University Press, 1999), p. 19; Marvin T. Smith, *Coosa: The Rise and Fall of a Southeastern Mississippian Chiefdom* (Gainesville: University Press of Florida, 2000), pp. 58–63; Jean Chaudhuri and Joyotpaul Chaudhuri, *A Sacred Path: The Way of the Muscogee Creeks* (Los Angeles: UCLA American Indian Studies Center, 2001), pp. 59, 69, 85, 89–90. For individual Creek communities, see the entries in John R. Swanton, *Early History of the Creek Indians and Their Neighbors,* Bureau of American Ethnology Bulletin 73 (Gainesville: University Press of Florida, 1998 [1922]).

14. For twentieth-century Creek towns, see Morris E. Opler, "The Creek 'Town' and the Problems of Creek Indian Political Reorganization," in Edward Spicer, ed., *Human Problems in Technological Change: A Casebook* (New York: Russell Sage Foundation, 1952), pp. 165–180; J. Anthony Paredes, "Back from Disappearance: The Alabama Creek Indian Community," in Walter L. Williams, ed., *Southeastern Indians Since the Removal Era* (Athens: University of Georgia Press, 1979), pp. 123–141; Alexander Spoehr,

"Changing Kinship Systems: A Study in the Acculturation of the Creeks, Cherokee, and Choctaw," *Anthropological Series, Field Museum of Natural History* 33 (1947): 153–235, especially pp. 160, 210. Craig S. Womack refers to town-centered government as a tradition—"old as dirt in Creek country"—retained by his Creek kinsmen; see his *Red on Red: Native American Literary Separatism* (Minneapolis: University of Minnesota Press, 1999), pp. 35, 42–43, quotation from p. 35.

15. "Speeches 3rd, 4th, & 7th of July 1759," p. 5, in Edmond Atkin to William Lyttelton, 11/30/1759, LYTTEL; CRSGA, vol. 9, p. 72 (Handsome Fellow); SC-JCHA, 5/26/1722; SC-CJ, 7/8/1721; CRSGA, vol. 25, p. 421 (1749). The French and Spanish also invited representatives from each Creek town on occasion. See SC-JCHA, 12/15/1736; DRIA, vol. 1, p. 216; BPRO, CO 5/70, f94. "Talk," as used by Nicolson and throughout this book, refers to an official communication or decision. The Creeks placed a premium on the spoken word; they referred to important messages as "talks." Euro-American diplomats adopted the expression.

16. SC-GAZ, 6/2/1733; BPRO, CO 5/70, f263 ("Keggs"); CRSGA, vol. 9, p. 75 (Lower Creeks); CRSGA, vol. 20, p. 78 (1734).

17. For the Okfuskee–Charleston relationship, see Chapters 1 and 2, this volume. SC-CJ, 12/22/1769; DRIA, vol. 1, p. 404 ("neighbouring"). For a talk linking governors to colonial capitals, see BPRO, CO 5/77, ff56–57. MPA-ED, p. 530 ("King"). William Bartram wrote that "the governors of Carolina, Georgia, &c. are called micos" by the Creeks, with mico signifying "the first and greatest man in the town or tribe." Interpreters likely rendered "mico" as "governor," while retaining the Creek phrasing linking micos with particular towns. Mark Van Doren, ed., *Travels of William Bartram* (Dover, Del.: Dover Publications, 1928), p. 388.

18. In fact, the stones were not inconsequential, as their place in town life demonstrates. See ADAIR, p. 402; Gregory A. Waselkov and Kathryn E. Holland Braund, eds., *William Bartram on the Southeastern Indians* (Lincoln: University of Nebraska Press, 1995), p. 154. J. Leitch Wright Jr., *The Only Land They Knew: The Tragic Story of the American Indians in the Old South* (New York: Free Press, 1981), p. 192 ("Father"). See also William Sturtevant, "Creek into Seminole," in Eleanor Burke Leacock and Nancy Oestreich Lurie, eds., *North American Indians in Historical Perspective* (New York: Random House, 1971), pp. 92–128.

19. The most frequently cited version of the origin story was narrated by Chigelley of Coweta in 1735; see John R. Swanton, "Social Organization and Social Usages of the Indians of the Creek Confederacy," *Forty-second Annual Report of the Bureau of American Ethnology, 1924–1925* (Washington, D.C.: U.S. Government Printing Office, 1928), pp. 23–472, especially

pp. 34–38. Swanton, "Social Organization," p. 40, argues that the town names in Chigelley's narrative refer to multicommunity branches of the Muskogees. I disagree. Chigelley phrased his story in terms of the most important Lower Creek towns. To say that he meant something else is beside the point. Towns, whether real or metaphorical, structure the narrative. Champagne, *Social Order and Political Change,* p. 266, n. 53. For an explicitly town-centered origin story, see HAWKINS, pp. 326–327.

20. Opler, "The Creek 'Town,' " pp. 170–171; Swanton, "Social Organization," p. 242. For Okfuskee villages, see Chapter 4, this volume. Throughout this book, I use "village" for *talofa* and "town" or "community" for *talwa.* Green, *The Politics of Indian Removal,* p. 4 ("institutionally"); Alexander Moore, ed., *Nairne's Muskhogean Journals: The 1708 Expedition to the Mississippi River* (Jackson: University of Mississippi Press, 1988), p. 32 ("town"). For the relationship between town fire and town membership, see Chapter 2, this volume.

21. David Corkran, *The Creek Frontier, 1540–1783* (Norman: University of Oklahoma Press, 1967), p. 26 ("appears"); see also Wright, *Creek and Seminoles,* p. 19. Swanton, "Social Organization," pp. 35, 36.

22. In subordinating clan to town, I rely on Greg Urban's distinction between Creek clans ("segmentary" units) and Cherokee clans ("structural" units). The Cherokees had a fixed number of clans, which could not change "without radically affecting" society. In Creek society, by contrast, the number of clans fluctuated, and each clan was both smaller and more localized. Urban, "The Social Organization of the Southeast," in Raymond J. DeMallie and Alfonso Ortiz, eds., *North American Indian Anthropology: Essays on Society and Culture* (Norman: University of Oklahoma Press, 1994), pp. 172–193, especially pp. 174–178. Vernon Knight's socially based analysis supports Urban's conclusions, as does John Moore's discussion of Creek origin stories. See Vernon J. Knight Jr., "Social Organization and the Evolution of Hierarchy in Southeastern Chiefdoms," *Journal of Anthropological Research* 46 (1990): 1–23; John H. Moore, "Truth and Tolerance in Native American Epistemology," in Russell Thornton, ed., *Studying Native America: Problems and Prospects* (Madison: University of Wisconsin Press, 1998), pp. 271–305, especially pp. 278–284.

23. For a discussion of the Busk—the Green Corn Dance at the center of the Creeks' ritual cycle—demonstrating that it resolved tensions between clan and communal identities in favor of the latter, see Martin, *Sacred Revolt,* pp. 34–42. For the *talwa*'s cosmological centrality, see Patricia Riles Wickman, *The Tree That Bends: Discourse, Power, and the Survival of the Maskoki People* (Tuscaloosa: University of Alabama Press, 1999), p. 48. For an analysis of Creek color symbolism that argues for the importance of

towns, see Lankford, "Red and White." See also Morris E. Opler, "Report on the History and Contemporary State of Aspects of Creek Social Organization and Government," *Papers in Anthropology* 13 (1972): 30–75, especially pp. 39–40; Opler, "The Creek 'Town,' " pp. 172–174.

24. SC-CJ, 6/13/1746, 5/3/1749. See also James Glen, "A Description of South Carolina" (1761), in Chapman J. Milling, ed., *Colonial South Carolina: Two Contemporary Descriptions* (Columbia: University of South Carolina Press, 1951), p. 67.

1. Okfuskee and the British, 1708–1745

1. For the suggestion that historians focused on Indian communities pay "[c]areful attention to . . . outward linkages," see James H. Merrell, "Some Thoughts on Colonial Historians and American Indians," *William and Mary Quarterly* 46 (1989): 94–119, quotation from p. 118.

2. Alexander Moore, ed., *Nairne's Muskhogean Journals: The 1708 Expedition to the Mississippi River* (Jackson: University of Mississippi Press, 1988), pp. 35–36.

3. British Records Collection, Sloane Manuscripts, SL 3331, folio 413, North Carolina Division of Archives and History, Raleigh; Eric Hinderaker, "The 'Four Indian Kings' and the Imaginative Construction of the First British Empire," *William and Mary Quarterly* 53 (1996): 487–526.

4. Verner W. Crane, *The Southern Frontier, 1670–1732* (Ann Arbor: University of Michigan Press, 1956 [1929]), pp. 75–81; J. Leitch Wright Jr., *The Only Land They Knew: The Tragic Story of the American Indians in the Old South* (New York: The Free Press, 1981), pp. 113–115; John H. Hann, *Apalachee: The Land Between the Rivers* (Gainesville: University Press of Florida, 1988), pp. 264–282; Jennifer L. Baszile, "Communities at the Crossroads: Chiefdoms, Colonies, and Empires in Colonial Florida, 1670–1741" (Ph.D. diss., Princeton University, 1999), chap. 7.

5. For European activities in the Southeast, see Paul E. Hoffman, *A New Andalucia and a Way to the Orient: The American Southeast During the Sixteenth Century* (Baton Rouge: Louisiana State University Press, 1990), chaps. 4 and 7; David J. Weber, *The Spanish Frontier in North America* (New Haven, Conn.: Yale University Press, 1992), pp. 30–91. Marvin T. Smith provides both an overview of this period of Creek history and an in-depth study of one branch of the emerging Creek Confederacy. See *Archaeology and Aboriginal Culture Change in the Interior Southeast: Depopulation During the Early Historic Period* (Gainesville: University Press of Florida, 1987) and *Coosa: The Rise and Fall of a Southeastern Mississippian Chiefdom* (Gainesville: University Press of Florida, 2000).

6. Gregory A. Waselkov, "Seventeenth-Century Trade in the Colonial Southeast," *Southeastern Archaeology* 8 (1989): 117–133; Waselkov, "The Macon Trading House and Early European–Indian Contact in the Colonial Southeast," in David J. Halley, ed., *Ocmulgee Archaeology, 1936–1986* (Athens: University of Georgia Press, 1994), pp. 190–196; Joel W. Martin, "Southeastern Indians and the English Trade in Skins and Slaves," in Charles Hudson and Carmen Chaves Tesser, eds., *The Forgotten Centuries: Indians and Europeans in the American South, 1521–1704* (Athens: University of Georgia Press, 1994), pp. 304–324.

7. W. Stitt Robinson, *The Southern Colonial Frontier, 1607–1763* (Albuquerque: University of New Mexico Press, 1979), chaps. 4, 5; Crane, *The Southern Frontier,* pp. 22–108; David H. Corkran, *The Creek Frontier* (Norman: University of Oklahoma Press, 1967), pp. 53–59.

8. For Creek population movements, see Steven Hahn, "The Invention of the Creek Nation: A Political History of the Creek Indians in the South's Imperial Era" (Ph.D. diss., Emory University, 2000), chaps. 2–4. Vernon J. Knight Jr. and Sheree L. Adams, "A Voyage to the Mobile and Tomeh in 1700, with Notes on the Interior of Alabama," *Ethnohistory* 28 (1981): 179–194, especially pp. 181, 189–191; Gregory Waselkov, "Indian Maps of the Colonial Southeast," in Peter H. Wood, Waselkov, and M. Thomas Hatley, eds., *Powhatan's Mantle: Indians in the Colonial Southeast* (Lincoln: University of Nebraska Press, 1989), pp. 292–343, especially pp. 313–320 (Towasa). For Chattahoochee, see Thomas Nairne, "A Map of South Carolina Shewing the Settlements of the English, French, & Indian Nation from Charles Town to the River Missisipi," 1711, HUNT; Anonymous, [Indian Villages] ca. 1715, in William P. Cumming, ed., *The Southeast in Early Maps,* 3rd ed., revised and enlarged by Louis De Vorsey Jr. (Chapel Hill: University of North Carolina Press, 1998), pp. 205–206 and plate 46A.

9. For the trail, see Cumming, ed., *Early Maps,* pp. 205, 218–219, plates 48 and 48A-D. BPRO-SC, vol. 5, p. 208 ("trade"); JCIT, p. 57 ("Girl"); MPA-FD, vol. 3, pp. 113–115 ("allies").

10. Historians have assumed that these undated "Articles" were signed in 1717. The document does not surface in South Carolina's records until 1736; SC-JCHA, 12/15/1736. The only evidence that might date the "Articles" to 1717 is the signature of Robert Johnson, South Carolina's governor at the time. However, Johnson—deposed in 1719—returned for a second tour of duty in 1730. He was still in office when "The Head Men of several Indian Towns in the Creek Nation" arrived in June 1732; SC-GAZ, 6/3/1732. These Creeks negotiated the "Articles," which were printed in Pennsylvania a month later; PA-GAZ, 7/17/1732, 7/24/1732.

11. Crane, *The Southern Frontier,* pp. 162–186; Corkran, *The Creek Frontier,* pp. 61–65; John Philip Reid, *A Better Kind of Hatchet: Law, Trade, and Diplomacy in the Cherokee Nation During the Early Years of European Contact* (University Park: Pennsylvania State University Press, 1976), chaps. 6, 7; Steven J. Oatis, "A Colonial Complex: South Carolina's Changing Frontiers in the Era of the Yamasee War" (Ph.D. diss., Emory University, 1999), chaps. 4, 6; "Journal of Captain Tobias Fitch's Mission from Charleston to the Creeks, 1725," in Newton Mereness, ed., *Travels in the American Colonies* (New York: Macmillan Company, 1916), pp. 176–212, quotation from pp. 189–190 ("Difference"); see also DRIA, vol. 2, p. 61.

12. Tom Hatley, *The Dividing Paths: Cherokees and South Carolinians through the Era of Revolution* (New York: Oxford University Press, 1993), pp. 77–78, 193; Daniel H. Thomas, *Fort Toulouse: The French Outpost at the Alabamas on the Coosa* (Tuscaloosa: University of Alabama Press, 1989 [1960]), pp. 6–14; Gregory A. Waselkov, Brian M. Wood, and Joseph M. Herbert, *Colonization and Conquest: The 1980 Archaeological Excavations at Fort Toulouse and Fort Jackson, Alabama,* Auburn University Archaeological Monograph 4 (Montgomery, 1982), chap. 3. For Creek–Spanish diplomacy, see Corkran, *The Creek Frontier,* pp. 61–64; Baszile, "Communities at the Crossroads," pp. 276–281; Oatis, "A Colonial Complex," pp. 299–303.

13. For references to the Chattahoochee village from 1729 and 1733, see Cumming, ed., *Early Maps,* plate 50 and p. 206; John R. Swanton, *Early History of the Creek Indians and Their Neighbors,* Bureau of American Ethnology Bulletin 73 (Gainesville: University Press of Florida, 1998 [1922]), plate 4. For more on Cherokee–Okfuskee violence, see Chapter 2, this volume and "Journal of Colonel George Chicken's Mission from Charleston, S.C., to the Cherokees, 1726," in Mereness, ed., *Travels,* pp. 97–172, especially pp. 156–157.

14. "Fanni" is the Chickasaw word for squirrel; "Mico" was the Creek honorific for their towns' most important headmen. Michael Green, personal communication, suggests that, since "Fanni" had no meaning in the language most Creeks (including the Okfuskees) spoke, they most likely borrowed the title from the Chickasaws or Choctaws, who called such men Fanni Mingo.

15. John R. Swanton, "Social Organization and Social Usages of the Indians of the Creek Confederacy," *Forty-second Annual Report of the Bureau of American Ethnology, 1924–1925* (Washington, D.C.: U.S. Government Printing Office, 1928), pp. 23–472, quotation ("common") from p. 31; Moore, ed., *Nairne's Muskhogean Journals,* p. 40; Patricia Galloway, " 'The Chief Who Is Your Father': Choctaw and French Views of the Diplomatic Relation," in Wood et al., eds., *Powhatan's Mantle,* pp. 254–278, quotations from

pp. 271, 256. See also Vernon J. Knight Jr., "The Formation of the Creeks," in Charles Hudson and Carmen Chaves Tesser, eds., *The Forgotten Centuries: Indians and Europeans in the American South, 1521–1704* (Athens: University of Georgia Press, 1994), pp. 372–392, especially 390.

16. Moore, *Nairne's Muskhogean Journals,* pp. 40–41; Galloway, " 'The Chief Who Is Your Father,' " p. 270. The calumet was the sacred pipestem at the center of a multiday ritual of greeting and peace. George Sabo III, "Rituals of Encounter: Interpreting Native American Views of European Explorers," in Jeannie Whayne, ed., *Cultural Encounters in the Early South: Indians and Europeans in Arkansas* (Fayetteville: University of Arkansas Press, 1995), pp. 76–87; Tanis C. Thorne, *The Many Hands of My Relations: French and Indians on the Lower Missouri* (Columbia: University of Missouri Press, 1996), chap. 1; Robert L. Hall, *An Archaeology of the Soul: North American Indian Belief and Ritual* (Champaign: University of Illinois Press, 1997).

17. For the ceremonies, see Moore, *Nairne's Muskhogean Journals,* pp. 35–36, 40–41.

18. Ibid., p. 36. Nairne may have misunderstood the headmen's fears. Robert Hall suggests that the calumet ceremony originated "in mourning ritual," and served initially to welcome newcomers in place of departed kinsmen. The Okfuskee headmen, then, may have feared offending the dead by misperforming the ceremony that provided their replacements. The headmen's ordeal was similar to the punishment meted out in 1929 for breaking a ceremonial rule in an Upper Creek town: "they made him stay in the square ground all night without eating." Hall, "Calumet Ceremonialism, Mourning Ritual, and Mechanisms of Inter-Tribal Trade," in Daniel W. Ingersoll Jr. and Gordon Bronitsky, eds., *Mirror and Metaphor: Material and Social Construction of Reality* (Lanham, Md.: University Press of America, 1987), pp. 30–43, especially pp. 32–33; John R. Swanton, "Modern Square Grounds of the Creek Indians," *Smithsonian Miscellaneous Collections* 85, no. 8 (1931): 27.

19. CRSGA, vol. 26, p. 391 (1751); SC-CJ, 9/4/1749, 9/6/1749.

20. Moore, *Nairne's Muskhogean Journals,* 40. For coat color and status, see Wilbur R. Jacobs, ed., *The Appalachian Indian Frontier: The Edmond Atkin Report and Plan of 1755* (Lincoln: University of Nebraska Press, 1954), pp. 85–86; SC-CJ, 7/28/1744, 11/22/1746, 7/24/1747, 9/7/1749; CRSGA, vol. 28 (1), pp. 81, 83. Bevan Papers, folder 5A, item 30, CGAHS ("Colours").

21. A 1721 map places "an English Factory" where the trading path crossed the Tallapoosa River, that is, at Okfuskee; Cumming, ed., *Early Maps,* plate 48. In 1718, Daniel Dicks was appointed assistant factor to Okfuskee's Upper Creek division; Dicks was based in Okfuskee by the mid-1720s, so

he may have set up the factory there in 1718. JCIT, p. 304; SC-CJ, 9/1/1726; BPRO-SC, vol. 13, p. 148.

22. An influential Okfuskee trader was referred to as "a trader to the Choctaw Nation"; SC-JCHA, 7/21/1731. For Okfuskee and the Choctaw trade, see Crane, *The Southern Frontier,* p. 258, n. 10; MPA-FD, vol. 4, p. 120. A. S. Salley, ed., *Journal of Colonel John Herbert, Commissioner of Indian Affairs for the Province of South Carolina, October 17, 1727–March 19, 1727/8* (Columbia: Historical Commission of South Carolina, 1936), p. 7; SC-JCHA, 5/13/1725.

23. Mereness, ed., "Journal of Captain Fitch," pp. 195, 207 (1725); BPRO-SC, vol. 13, pp. 113, 121–122 (1728).

24. SC-CJ, 4/29/1726 ("dispatch"), 8/24/1725 ("Flagg"). Fitch also requested a commission for an Okfuskee.

25. BPRO-SC, vol. 10, pp. 176, 179, 158.

26. Ibid., vol. 13, pp. 72–73, emphasis added.

27. Mereness, ed., "Journal of Captain Fitch," pp. 197–198 (1725); BPRO-SC, vol. 13, p. 102 ("acquainting").

28. Phinizy Spalding, *Oglethorpe in America* (Chicago: University of Chicago Press, 1977); Peter H. Wood, "Circles in the Sand: Perspectives on the Southern Frontier at the Arrival of James Oglethorpe," in Phinizy Spalding and Harvey H. Jackson, eds., *Oglethorpe in Perspective: Georgia's Founder after Two Hundred Years* (Tuscaloosa: University of Alabama Press, 1989), pp. 5–21; Gregory A. Waselkov, "Introduction: Recent Archaeological and Historical Research," in Thomas, *Fort Toulouse,* pp. vii–xlii, especially p. xii; Michael J. Foret, "On the Marchlands of Empire: Trade, Diplomacy, and War on the Southeastern Frontier, 1733–1763" (Ph.D. diss., College of William and Mary, 1990), chap. 4.

29. SC-CJ, 9/22/1727; Larry E. Ivers, *British Drums on the Southern Frontier: The Military Colonization of Georgia, 1733–1749* (Chapel Hill: University of North Carolina Press, 1974); Robinson, *Southern Colonial Frontier,* chap. 9.

30. I have, for example, found no direct evidence that Okfuskees participated in the British–Spanish hostilities. However, Anthony Willey, who commanded Fort Okfuskee from 1736 to 1742, received six months' pay for serving as captain "on ye Expedition" in 1739. Georgia's Indian allies raided Florida that year; Willey may have accompanied an Upper Creek party. If so, it most likely included Okfuskees. Keith Read Collection, MS 921, box 19, folder 53, UGA.

31. Phinizy Spalding, "South Carolina and Georgia: The Early Days," *South Carolina Historical and Genealogical Magazine* 69 (1968): 83–96; Brian M. Wood, "Fort Okfuskee: A British Challenge to Fort Toulouse aux Aliba-

mons," in Gregory A. Waselkov, ed., *Fort Toulouse Studies,* Auburn University Archaeological Monographs 9 (Montgomery, Ala., 1984), pp. 41–51; PA-GAZ, 10/21/1736.

32. No firm date for either the conference or the Edwards–McKay dispute survives, but see SC-JCHA, 12/15/1736, pp. 113–114, 116, 117, 120–121.

33. For McKay's views on Indian trade, see CRSGA, vol. 20, pp. 109, 291; CRSGA, vol. 21, pp. 10–11; SC-JCHA, 12/15/1736, pp. 121–122. The cause of the dispute remains unclear, with one witness noting that "there happened some Difference" between Edwards and one of McKay's escorts; SC-JCHA, 12/15/1736, pp. 113–114, 120–121, quotation from p. 114. Edwards's employer was Alexander Wood, a South Carolina–based Okfuskee trader. The Georgia agent may have used the "Difference" to demonstrate his power over South Carolina's traders. For Wood's early ties to Okfuskee, see SC-CJ, 9/1/1726; BPRO-SC, vol. 13, p. 148. For the attempted whipping, see SC-JCHA, 12/15/1736, pp. 120–121, 113–114.

34. SC-JCHA, 12/15/1736; BPRO-SC, vol. 13, p. 83. Given that the "little Lieutenant" acted in Okfuskee's square in conjunction with an Okfuskee headman, he most likely was an Okfuskee. Okfuskees with similar names appear in the documents. SC-CJ, 9/6/1749; CRSGA, vol. 28 (1), pp. 42, 81; Edmond Atkin to the Upper Creeks, 7/3–7/9/1759, p. 4, in Atkin to William Lyttelton, 11/30/1759, LYTTEL.

35. For the conference, see SC-JCHA, 12/15/1736, p. 114; SC-CJ, 7/6/1736; CRSGA, vol. 20, p. 422 ("Officer"). As of summer 1736, the fort remained unbuilt; SC-CJ, 7/6/1736. It was likely built between July and December 1736. The project may have gone forward when Creeks returned from Charleston with the news that South Carolina, too, supported it. Waselkov, "Introduction," pp. xii–xiii; SC-GAZ, 7/10/1736, 7/17/1736; PA-GAZ, 10/21/1736; SC-JCHA, 12/15/1736; CRSGA, vol. 4, p. 241; CRSGA, vol. 20, pp. 492–493; CRSGA, vol. 21, p. 289; Benjamin Martyn, "An Impartial Inquiry into the State and Utility of the Province of Georgia," *Collections of the Georgia Historical Society,* vol. 1 (Savannah, Ga., 1840 [1741]), pp. 154–201, especially p. 182.

36. Corkran, *The Creek Frontier,* p. 94; Wood, "Fort Okfuskee," p. 44. SC-JCHA, 12/15/1736, pp. 114, 122.

37. For Wolf, see SC-CJ, 11/1/1746, 11/3/1746; SC-JCHA, 2/17/1747, 4/16/1747, 5/16/1747; CRSGA, vol. 26, p. 64; DRIA, vol. 2, pp. 298–299, 372. South Carolina's governor noted, "Several Years ago some of the Creeks gave a small spot of Land to the French and liberty to build a Fort upon it, and tho' the rest of the Nation disapproved of it yet they still keep possession"; SC-JCHA, 9/16/1755.

38. SC-JCHA, 12/15/1736, p. 132 (regulations); CRSGA, vol. 4, p. 241 ("ob-

serve"); "Oglethorpe Account Book," box 19, Folder 53, Keith Read Collection, MS 921, UGA; BPRO-SC, vol. 20, p. 257 (1740).

39. In 1740, South Carolina's Committee on Indian Affairs recommended appointing Wood as the colony's Creek agent; SC-JCHA, 5/1/1740. By 1741, Wood and his partner employed more men and horses than any South Carolina–based trader; Thomas Stephens and Richard Everhard, "A Brief Account of the Causes that Have Retarded the Progress of the Colony of Georgia in America," *Collections of the Georgia Historical Society,* vol. 2 (Savannah, Ga., 1843), pp. 88–161, especially p. 123. CRSGA, vol. 21, p. 303 (discipline). For Wood's activities, see SC-JCHA for 1740: 1/31, 4/29, 4/30, 5/1, 7/25, 9/11; ADAIR, p. 325.

40. SC-CJ, 8/15/1739, 8/18/1739. Georgia's records often mention "Indian" or "Creek" visitors; it is thus impossible to be certain that Okfuskees absented themselves from Savannah in the 1730s and 1740s. The comments of the few Okfuskees who came there during the 1750s, however, suggest that their townspeople did not habitually make such visits; CRSGA, vol. 7, pp. 419–425, 613–617. SC-JCHA, 5/22/1742 ("Distinctions"); SC-UH, 5/21/1742 (Red Coat King).

41. For Creek debates, see SC-CJ, 10/7/1743, 10/10/1743, 10/12/1743, 12/10/1743; Marquis de Vaudreuil to "My Lord," 2/12/1744 and 5/10/1744, in Pierre De Rigaud, Marquis de Vaudreuil-Cavagnal, Letterbook, Loudoun Collection, box 9, vol. 1, folder 2, HUNT. For British mediation, see SC-CJ, 10/6–10/7/1743. For Bull, see SC-CJ, 10/12/1743, 12/10/1743. For Okfuskee–Cherokee relations, see Chapter 2, this volume. Jacobs, ed., *The Edmond Atkin Report,* 64.

42. South Carolina's effort bogged down in fiscal squabbles. SC-JCHA 12/14/1743, 12/16/1743, 6/30/1744, 7/3/1744, 7/4/1744; SC-CJ 10/7/1743, 10/10/1743, 10/12/1743, 3/21/1744, 4/20/1744, 6/27/1744; SC-UH, 7/4/1744. MPA-FD, vol. 4, pp. 246 ("Akfaske"), 256.

43. Waselkov, "Indian Maps of the Colonial Southeast," pp. 297–298, 324–332.

44. For governmental layers and "effective," see Ian K. Steele, "The Annointed, the Appointed, and the Elected: Governance of the British Empire, 1689–1784," in P. J. Marshall, ed., *The Oxford History of the British Empire,* vol. 2, *The Eighteenth Century* (New York: Oxford University Press, 1998), pp. 105–127, quotation from p. 105. For composite monarchy, see David Armitage, *The Ideological Origins of the British Empire* (New York: Cambridge University Press, 2000), chap. 2. See also Jeremy Black, *A System of Ambition: British Foreign Policy, 1660–1793,* 2nd ed. (Phoenix Mill, U.K.: Sutton Publishing, 2000), p. 6.

45. For local power and negotiated authority, see Jack P. Greene, "Transat-

lantic Colonization and the Redefinition of Empire in the Early Modern Era," in Christine Daniels and Michael V. Kennedy, eds., *Negotiated Empires: Centers and Peripheries in the Americas, 1500–1820* (New York: Routledge, 2002), pp. 267–282, especially p. 269. For increased royal power, see Richard P. Johnson, "Growth and Maturity: British North America, 1690–1748," in Marshall, ed., *Oxford History,* vol. 2, pp. 276–299, quotation ("most") from p. 295. For "towns," see Kathleen Wilson, *The Sense of the People: Politics, Culture, and Imperialism in England, 1715–1785* (New York: Cambridge University Press, 1995), p. 6. For the assertion that "[s]tate power declined at the periphery," see John B. Brewer, *The Sinews of Power: War, Money, and the English State, 1688–1783* (New York: Knopf, 1989), p. 176. For the political centrality of local units, see Jack P. Greene, "The Growth of Political Stability: An Interpretation of Political Development in the Anglo-American Colonies, 1660–1760," in Greene, ed., *Negotiated Authorities: Essays in Colonial Political and Constitutional History* (Charlottesville: University Press of Virginia, 1994), pp. 131–162, especially p. 134. For consent and "not insignificant," see Greene, "The Glorious Revolution and the British Empire, 1688–1763," in Greene, *Negotiated Authorities,* pp. 78–92, quotation from p. 86.

46. For relations with colonies, see James H. Merrell, *The Indians' New World: Catawbas and Their Neighbors from European Contact through the Era of Removal* (New York: W. W. Norton, 1989); Richard Aquila, *The Iroquois Restoration: Iroquois Diplomacy on the Colonial Frontier, 1701–1754* (Detroit, Mich.: Wayne State University Press, 1983); Francis Jennings, *The Ambiguous Iroquois Empire: The Covenant Chain Confederation of Indian Tribes with English Colonies from Its Beginning to the Lancaster Treaty of 1744* (New York: W. W. Norton, 1984); Richard L. Haan, "Covenant and Consensus: Iroquois and English, 1676–1760," in Daniel K. Richter and James H. Merrell, eds., *Beyond the Covenant Chain: The Iroquois and Their Neighbors in Indian North America, 1600–1800* (Syracuse, N.Y.: Syracuse University Press, 1987), pp. 41–57. For Iroquoian efforts to address local problems by manipulating relations with various levels of colonial officials, see Timothy J. Shannon, *Indians and Colonists at the Crossroads of Empire: The Albany Congress of 1754* (Ithaca, N.Y.: Cornell University Press, 2000).

47. For negative reactions to Albany's tradition of illicit fur trade, see John Demos, *The Unredeemed Captive: A Family Story from Early America* (New York: Vintage Books, 1994), pp. 131–137. Jane Landers, "Gracia Real de Santa Teresa de Mose: A Free Black Town in Spanish Colonial Florida," *American Historical Review* 95 (1990): 9–30, especially pp. 21–23, 29.

48. Greene, "Transatlantic Colonization," p. 278 ("substitute"); Shannon, *Indians and Colonists,* p. 13 ("decidedly"). For the superintendency, see J.

Russell Snapp, *John Stuart and the Struggle for Empire on the Southern Frontier* (Baton Rouge: Louisiana State University Press, 1996).

49. For political centralization at the colony level, see Jon Butler, *Becoming America: The Revolution before 1776* (Cambridge, Mass.: Harvard University Press, 2000), p. 90; Steele, "The Annointed," pp. 114, 118. For compatible loyalties, see Steele, "The Annointed," p. 126. For the trend "towards a greater uniformity," see Johnson, "Growth and Mastery," p. 295.

50. Brewer, *Sinews of Power,* pp. xviii–xix; Eliga H. Gould, *The Persistence of Empire: British Political Culture in the Age of the American Revolution* (Chapel Hill: University of North Carolina Press, 2000), pp. 59–60 (ocean, "zone," "acknowledged").

2. Okfuskee and the British, 1749–1774

1. South Carolina and American *General Gazette,* 11/20/1767; DRIA, vol. 1, p. 380 ("Satisfaction," "Blood"); SC-GAZ, 6/12/1753 ("shot"); PA-GAZ, 7/26/1753 (witness).

2. The reverse was also true: an Okfuskee attack badly damaged Creek–Cherokee relations. Thus, in 1758, Okfuskees killed two Cherokees; "[t]his unexpected Blow threw the latter into such a consternation that it gave an immediate turn to all their plans." Lachlan McGillivray to Henry Ellis, 8/24/1758, in Ellis to William Lyttelton, 11/5/1758, LYTTEL.

3. DRIA, vol. 1, pp. 257, 258, 289, 216 (1751–1753). For Okfuskee "Suspicions" that a war party lurked in the area "to prevent the Peace," see DRIA, vol. 1, p. 464. DRIA, vol. 1, pp. 407, 398 ("since," "Hopes"); SC-CJ, 6/6/1753 (son); PA-GAZ, 7/26/1753 ("Northern"); DRIA, vol. 1, pp. 380, 379 (slaves). Creeks were angered by both "Northerns" (who attacked Creek towns) and Cherokees (who provisioned war parties and allowed them passage through Cherokee country); SC-JCHA, 5/31/1750. For a Northern assault on Okfuskee, see SC-CJ, 6/21/1744. For a 1745 Okfuskee talk cautioning the Cherokees not to supply the "French Indians," see SC-UH, 6/21/1748.

4. SC-JCHA, 4/29/1752 (Glen). For the Upper Creeks, see BPRO-SC, vol. 23, p. 450; SC-CJ, 9/4/1749 ("value"), 9/5/1749, 9/6/1749, 9/7/1749, 9/11/1749; PA-GAZ, 10/12/1749.

5. David Corkran, *The Creek Frontier, 1540–1783* (Lincoln: University of Nebraska Press, 1967), pp. 131–144 (Savannah), 129–130 (Charleston). Neither of the headmen Corkran names appear on a contemporary list of participants. For the list and Fanni Mico, see SC-CJ, 9/6/1749.

6. Corkran, *The Creek Frontier,* pp. 103–130; W. Stitt Robinson, *The Southern Colonial Frontier, 1607–1763* (Albuquerque: University of New Mexico Press, 1979), pp. 200–201; M. Eugene Sirmans, *Colonial South Carolina: A*

Political History, 1663–1763 (Chapel Hill: University of North Carolina Press, 1966), pp. 266–275; Larry E. Ivers, *British Drums on the Southern Frontier: The Military Colonization of Georgia, 1733–1749* (Chapel Hill: University of North Carolina Press, 1974), pp. 204–214; J. Leitch Wright Jr., *Anglo-Spanish Rivalry in North America* (Athens: University of Georgia Press, 1971), pp. 97–105.

7. For a Lower Creek's perspective on Fanni Mico's mission, see Chigelley's talk in SC-CJ, 9/4/1749.

8. For the war, see Corkran, *The Creek Frontier,* pp. 127–130; Tom Hatley, *The Dividing Paths: Cherokees and South Carolinians through the Era of Revolution* (New York: Oxford University Press, 1993), pp. 70–71; Kathryn E. Holland Braund, *Deerskins & Duffels: Creek Indian Trade with Anglo-America, 1685–1815* (Lincoln: University of Nebraska Press, 1993), p. 133. For 1745, see SC-CJ, 5/4/1745; SC-JCHA, 6/20/1748. DRIA, vol. 2, p. 236 ("War").

9. SC-JCHA, 5/25/1749; SC-CJ, 5/22/1749, 6/2/1749, 9/4/1749.

10. SC-CJ, 9/4/1749.

11. Ibid., 9/5/1749, 9/11/1749.

12. For the Creeks thanking Glen, see note 9 above; for the Cherokees, see DRIA, vol. 1, p. 64. See also Glen's statements in DRIA, vol. 1, pp. 207, 209. For Glen praising Red Coat King's role in the peace effort, see DRIA, vol. 1, p. 207. DRIA, vol. 1, pp. 380 ("Son"), 465 ("Goodness"), 397, 412.

13. CRSGA, vol. 26, pp. 389–395 (deed); Bevan Papers, folder 5A, item 30, CGAHS (flag). For other Upper Creek towns asking for—but not receiving—flags in 1751, see "Conference with Tookybatchy Mico," 7/24/1759, in Edmond Atkin to William Lyttelton, 11/30/1759, LYTTEL. In 1757, South Carolina's agent noted that Okfuskee was one of the Upper Creek towns "who are in our Interest [that] have been complaining to me, that they have no English Colours to hoist to show that they are our Friends"; DRIA, vol. 2, p. 355. For Savannah's diminished importance to the Okfuskees see note 25 below and CRSGA, vol. 7, pp. 419–425; SC-CJ, 7/12/1757.

14. For Sugatspoges as an Okfuskee village, see CRSGA, vol. 8, p. 523; MPA-ED, p. 95. For the attack, see CRSGA, vol. 8, pp. 314–316; SC-GAZ, 6/21/1760; ADAIR, pp. 278–283; CRSGA, vol. 28 (1), pp. 250–251, 280–283, 286–287; SC-GAZ, 5/31/1760; BPRO-SC, vol. 28, p. 348; PA-GAZ, 6/19/1760; SC-CJ, 6/20/1760. CRSGA, vol. 8, pp. 419–421 ("Mischief," "Affair"); see also SC-GAZ, 7/19/1760.

15. Hatley, *The Dividing Paths,* pp. 125–132; John Oliphant, *Peace and War on the Anglo-Cherokee Frontier, 1756–1763* (Baton Rouge: Louisiana State University Press, 2001); SC-GAZ, 6/14/1760.

16. Corkran, *The Creek Frontier,* pp. 215–219; John R. Alden, *John Stuart and*

the Southern Colonial Frontier: A Study of Indian Relations, War, Trade, and Land Problems in the Southern Wilderness, 1754–1775 (New York: Gordian, 1966 [1944]), pp. 109–110; Braund, *Deerskins & Duffels,* pp. 108, 241, n. 38; Edward J. Cashin, *Lachlan McGillivray, Indian Trader: The Shaping of the Southern Colonial Frontier* (Athens: University of Georgia Press, 1992), pp. 203–204; Cashin, *Governor Henry Ellis and the Transformation of British North America* (Athens: University of Georgia Press, 1994), p. 142. The only work devoted to the attack is an early-twentieth-century manuscript emphasizing Mortar's role and Superintendent Edmond Atkin's incompetence; H. S. Halbert, "The Killing of the English Traders in the Creek Nation in 1760," n.d., Collections of the Alabama Department of Archives and History, Montgomery.

17. SC-GAZ, 6/21/1760.
18. SC-GAZ, 5/24/1760, 7/19/1760 (Mortar). For Okfuskee's responsibility, see note 14 above and SC-GAZ, 2/7/1761; SC-CJ, 6/23/1760, 7/24/1760, 2/11/1761.
19. SC-CJ, 6/20/1760 ("white"). Five traders died in the attack. William Rae (killed at Okfuskee) and John Ross (killed at Sugatspoges) had long ties, either personal or familial, to Okfuskee. The partners George Johnson and Lachlan McIntosh were killed at Calilgies. Red Coat King referred to Johnston as "Trader for my Town" in 1753; he held a license to trade there in 1754. Johnson connected McIntosh to Okfuskee, although men named McKintosh dealt with Okfuskees in 1728 and 1761. Richard Hughes (killed at Fushatchie) was Johnson and McIntosh's partner. For locations, see SC-GAZ, 6/21/1760. For Ross, see DRIA, vol. 1, p. 336; CRSGA, vol. 6, p. 149. For the Raes, see Braund, *Deerskins & Duffels,* pp. 44–46; CRSGA, vol. 8, p. 523; BPRO, CO 5/73, f261; "A Treaty of Peace and Commerce," 11/6/1777, LAURENS. For Johnson and McIntosh, see Telamon Cuyler Collection, box 38, folder 53, UGA; DRIA, vol. 1, p. 380; DRIA, vol. 2, p. 10; SC-GAZ, 9/1/1759, 9/22/1759; PA-GAZ, 1/24/1760; BPRO-SC, vol. 13, pp. 146–148; CRSGA, vol. 8, p. 523. For Hughes, see Edmond Atkin to Lyttelton, 11/30/1759, pp. 22–23, LYTTEL.
20. Corkran, *The Creek Frontier,* pp. 215–216; Alden, *John Stuart,* p. 109.
21. CRSGA, vol. 8, p. 419 ("reckoned"); SC-JCHA, 9/16/1755 ("Affections"); SC-JCHA, 9/20/1755 ("Circumstance"); CRSGA, vol. 7, p. 421 ("King"); SC-CJ, 7/12/1757 ("Friendship"); SC-CJ, 9/6/1749 ("Old"). Greg O'Brien argues that, "by the mid to late eighteenth century," the Choctaws abandoned the institution of fanni mingo because Europeans failed "to live up to the standards of behavior" that accompanied the title; *Choctaws in a Revolutionary Age, 1750–1830* (Lincoln: University of Nebraska Press, 2002), p. 63.

22. CRSGA, vol. 8, pp. 420–421 (Captain); SC-GAZ, 3/21/1760 (visiting); BPRO, CO 5/75, f17, and 5/72, f102 ("friends," "Promise").

23. Joel Martin, *Sacred Revolt: The Muskogees' Struggle for a New World* (Boston: Beacon Press, 1991), pp. 36–42, quotation ("represented") from p. 36; Morris E. Opler, "The Creek 'Town' and the Problems of Creek Indian Political Reorganization," in Edward Spicer, *Human Problems in Technological Change: A Casebook* (New York: Russell Sage Foundation, 1952), pp. 165–180, especially pp. 171–173 ("Mother Towns"); "A Treaty of Peace and Commerce," 11/6/1777, LAURENS ("Friendship").

24. Hatley, *The Dividing Paths*, pp. 92–115; SC-CJ, 2/11/1761.

25. For invitations, see Ellis to Lyttelton, 7/21/1757, LYTTEL; Lyttelton to Ellis, 11/4/1757, LYTTEL ("promises"); CRSGA, vol. 28 (1), pp. 85–86. For Creeks present in Savannah, see Ellis to Lyttelton, 10/31/1757, LYTTEL; CRSGA, vol. 7, pp. 657, 667; Ellis to Lyttelton, 11/11/1757, LYTTEL; CRSGA, vol. 7, p. 668 ("Proceedings"). DRIA, vol. 2, p. 3 ("mad").

26. After over three months among the Upper Creeks, Atkin finally spent a month and a half in Okfuskee. For Atkin's initial actions, see "Speeches 3rd . . . of July 1759," pp. 4–6; "Conferences with Tookybahtchy Mico," pp. 2, 5 (emphasis added); "Atkin to Tallapoosas Headmen," 9/15/1759 ("rely"); Atkin to Creek Headmen, 9/28–9/29/1759 (Tuckabatchee). The above are enclosed in Atkin to Lyttelton, 11/30/1759, LYTTEL. Atkin to John Cleland, 12/23/1759 ("Store"), in Atkin to Lyttelton, 1/9/1760, LYTTEL; CRSGA, vol. 8, pp. 165 ("Regard"), 321 ("Abuse"). For a 1758 Georgia-sponsored Muccolossus conference which the Okfuskees did not attend, see John T. Juricek, ed., *Early American Indian Documents: Treaties and Laws, 1607–1789,* vol. 11, *Georgia Treaties, 1733–1763* (Frederick, Md.: University Publications of America, 1989), pp. 277–278.

27. CRSGA, vol. 28 (1), p. 246 ("embroil"). See also SC-GAZ, 4/7/1760; BPRO-SC, vol. 28, pp. 340–341. Atkin believed that Ellis's policy led to Creek "dissatisfaction" and "most probably gave encouragement" for the Okfuskee attack; Edith Mays, ed., *Amherst Papers, 1756–1763: The Southern Sector* (Bowie, Md.: Heritage Books, 1999), p. 147. For the Okfuskees' 1750s peace efforts, see DRIA, vol. 2, pp. 3, 10–12, 153, 156, 236; SC-CJ, 8/31/1756; Raymond Demere to William Lyttelton, 6/26/1757, LYTTEL. SC-CJ, 2/11/1761 (Wolf); SC-GAZ, 2/7/1761 ("amongst"), 3/7/1761, 3/14/1761 (looting).

28. For 1753, see Chapter 6, this volume; for 1755, see DRIA, vol. 2, pp. 56, 62–65, quotations from p. 65. For rumors, see CRSGA, vol. 7, p. 41; DRIA, vol. 2, pp. 56, 60–61. *Abstracts of Colonial Wills of the State of Georgia, 1733–1777,* index by Willard E. Wright (Spartanburg, S.C.: Re-

print Company, 1981 [1962]), p. 120; "Lachlan Mcintosh: Secret Information," 8/22/1759, in Atkin to Lyttelton, 11/30/1759, LYTTEL. ADAIR, 278 (Ross); CRSGA, vol. 8, p. 315.

29. John R. Swanton, "Social Organization and Social Usages of the Indians of the Creek Confederacy," *Forty-second Annual Report of the Bureau of American Ethnology, 1924–1925* (Washington, D.C.: U.S. Government Printing Office, 1928), pp. 23–472, especially pp. 338–345, 363–365; Michael D. Green, *The Politics of Indian Removal: Creek Government and Society in Crisis* (Lincoln: University of Nebraska Press, 1982), pp. 5–6. See also John Philip Reid, *A Law of Blood: The Primitive Law of the Cherokee Nation* (New York: New York University Press, 1970), chaps. 5, 9–10; Rennard Strickland, *Fire and the Spirits: Cherokee Law from Clan to Court* (Norman: University of Oklahoma Press, 1975), chap. 2.

30. DRIA, vol. 1, pp. 279, 291, 292. For a similar incident involving an Okfuskee, see BPRO-SC, vol. 13, p. 95. In the letter describing Cossitee's "Coronation," Thomas Nairne noted that "If a man kills his Brother (tho that is Extraordinarily seldom) their is no punishment inflicted, all that they'le say, what can be done it was his own flesh, he was mad when he did it, and will be sory enough when he comes to his right sences"; Alexander Moore, ed., *Nairne's Muskhogean Journals: The 1708 Expedition to the Mississippi River* (Jackson: University of Mississippi Press, 1988), p. 34.

31. SC-GAZ, 3/21/1760 ("Coal"); "Atkin and Billy Germany Conference," 8/20/1759 (Father), and "Lachlan McIntosh: Secret Information" (warning), both enclosed in Atkin to Lyttelton, 11/30/1759, LYTTEL; SC-GAZ, 3/29/1760 ("hold"). For the Captain's actions, see CRSGA, vol. 8, pp. 315, 420–421; CRSGA, vol. 8, p. 314 ("fellows"). In another sign that some Okfuskees did not favor the attack, or even know of it, eleven townspeople were in Augusta on May 16; SC-GAZ, 5/31/1760. For townswomen saving two traders, see Chapter 6, this volume.

32. BPRO-SC, vol. 28, p. 340 ("confusion"); "Atkin and Billy Germany Conference," 8/20/1759 ("Patience"), in Atkin to Lyttelton, 11/30/1759, LYTTEL. Handsome Fellow's speech comes to us third-hand; it contains some incorrect information and may not be reliable.

33. Corkran, *The Creek Frontier*, p. 216 ("conspiracy"); CRSGA, vol. 28 (1), p. 287 ("Rupture"); SC-GAZ, 7/19/1760 (tobacco). For the talk delivered in Okfuskee, see PA-GAZ, 9/4/1760; CRSGA, vol. 28 (1), pp. 348–349. SC-GAZ, 9/13/1760 ("stick"); SC-GAZ, 9/27/1760 ("met").

34. CRSGA, vol. 28 (1), p. 287 (scalp, "vindicate"); SC-GAZ, 9/13/1760; SC-GAZ, 9/27/1760 ("maintain").

35. "A Talk from the head men of the Upper and Lower Creeks," 10/13/1777, and "A Treaty of Peace and Commerce," 11/6/1777, both in LAURENS

(Handsome Fellow). "A Short Description of the Province of South-Carolina (By George Milligen-Johnson)," in Chapman J. Milling, ed., *Colonial South Carolina: Two Contemporary Descriptions* (Columbia: University of South Carolina Press, 1951), pp. 111–206, quotation from p. 185 ("Nations").

36. SC-GAZ, 4/4/1761 ("clear up"; "professions"); CRSGA, vol. 8, p. 777, and vol. 9, pp. 15–16; "A Talk Given at the King's Fort in Augusta," 3/26/1764, in John Stuart to Thomas Gage, 4/11/1764, GAGE ("Power"; "fast"); CRSGA, vol. 28 (2), pp. 52–53.

37. BPRO, CO 5/75, ff212–216; CRSGA, vol. 12, p. 407 ("material").

38. BPRO, CO 5/75, ff212, 214.

39. Corkran, *The Creek Frontier,* p. 252; Joel Martin, "Southeastern Indians and the English Trade in Skins and Slaves," in Charles Hudson and Carmen Chaves Tesser, eds., *The Forgotten Centuries: Indians and Europeans in the American South, 1521–1704* (Athens: University of Georgia Press, 1994), pp. 304–324, especially pp. 316–320.

40. Braund, *Deerskins & Duffels,* pp. 158–159; J. Leitch Wright Jr., *Creeks and Seminoles: The Destruction and Regeneration of the Muscogulge People* (Lincoln: University of Nebraska Press, 1986), pp. 101–110; Joshua Piker, " 'White & Clean' & Contested: Creek Towns, Trading Paths, and Diplomatic Networks in the Aftermath of the Seven Years' War," *Ethnohistory* 50 (2003): 315–347.

41. GA-GAZ, 2/2/1774 ("Chattahugee"). For Mad Turkey's town, see GA-GAZ, 5/25/1774; Chapter 4, this volume. GA-GAZ, 2/2/1774 ("safe"). For Mad Turkey's travels, see GA-GAZ, 3/16/1774. GA-GAZ, 4/13/1774 ("invited"). See also GA-GAZ, 3/30/1774; K. G. Davies, *Documents of the American Revolution, 1770–1783,* vol. 8 (Dublin: Irish University Press, 1975), pp. 90–95, 109; CRSGA, vol. 38 (1-A), pp. 237, 240.

42. John Stuart to Gage, 5/12/1774, GAGE; GA-GAZ, 5/11/1774 (Myers), 3/16/1774 ("disposed"), 5/25/1774 ("uncle"). For Graham and Rae, see Andrew McLean to William Ogilvy, 5/13/1774, GAGE; BPRO, CO 5/77, f133; GA-GAZ, 5/25/1774. McLean to Stuart, 5/29/1774, GAGE ("Right"). Augusta's role requires comment. By 1763, Creek–British diplomacy centered on this Georgia town built where the trail linking Okfuskee and Charleston crossed the Savannah River. The trail predated Augusta, as did the South Carolina town located on the opposite bank. In his 1774 talk, Cujesse Mico mentioned, "formerly there was a House on Savannah Bluff." The Okfuskees associated Augusta with Charleston. From their perspective, Augusta was to Charleston as the Chattahoochee village was to Okfuskee: an outpost along the trail which further established the town's identification with the "old white path."

43. Taitt wrote that the "Leaders" in "the Murders at Ogueechie" included

"Ochtalky an Okfuske Indian." He was "one of" the Creeks' "Great War-riours" and "of Consequence in his Village." BPRO, CO 5/75, ff52, 180, 190; Stuart to Gage, 7/5/1774, GAGE.

44. Of the nine Okfuskees, Taitt singled out five as dangerous: three of Mad Turkey's nephews (one of whom had threatened Graham), each of whom the Creeks would expect to avenge his uncle, and two men who had killed several colonists three years before. BPRO, CO 5/75, ff212–215.

45. During the crisis, Robert Rae, an Okfuskee trader, traded illegally with Okfuskees. Ibid., ff190, 216; CRSGA, vol. 12, p. 407; Taitt to Stuart, 8/29/1774, GAGE. BPRO, CO 5/75, f213 ("poor").

46. BPRO, CO 5/75, ff67–68 ("Hillabie"); Piker, " 'White & Clean' & Con-tested." BPRO, CO 5/75, ff16–17 ("Young").

47. A Treaty of Peace and Commerce," LAURENS (Rae). For the Okfuskees' role in deterring war parties, see BPRO, CO 5/78, f209; BPRO, CO 5/79, ff30–31, 33–34, 160; Richard Henderson to [George Galphin?], 6/12/1778, LAURENS; John Rutledge to "Gentlemen," 8/30/1777, John Rut-ledge Collection, South Caroliniana Library, University of South Carolina, Columbia; Henderson to [Galphin?], 6/12/1778, LAURENS ("while). Corkran, *The Creek Frontier,* pp. 307–308 (1777). For Cujesse Mico, see BPRO, CO 5/78, ff210–211; Patrick Carr to [], 6/10/1778, LAURENS.

48. "Creek Indians: Letters, Talks, and Treaties, 1705–1839," vol. 1, compiled by Mrs. J. E. Hays (Works Progress Administration, 1939–1940), pp. 30, 129–131, quotations from pp. 30, 131, bound manuscripts in UGA. For White Lieutenant's family, see Chapter 5, this volume.

49. Thomas Bender, "Wholes and Parts: The Need for Synthesis in American History," *Journal of American History* 73 (1986): 120–136, especially pp. 125, 126.

50. Richard White, *The Middle Ground: Indians, Empires, and Republics in the Great Lakes Region, 1650–1815* (New York: Cambridge University Press, 1991).

51. For the significance of empire and expansion, see P. J. Marshall, "Intro-duction," in Marshall, ed., *The Oxford History of the British Empire,* vol. 2, *The Eighteenth Century* (New York: Oxford University Press, 1998), pp. 1–27, especially pp. 1 ("new"), 7–9. For forces encouraging expansion, see Bernard Bailyn, *Voyagers to the West: A Passage in the Peopling of America on the Eve of the Revolution* (New York: Knopf, 1986), pp. 355–359. For civilization, see Michael Warner, "What's Colonial about Colonial America?" in Robert Blair St. George, ed., *Possible Pasts: Becoming Colonial in Early America* (Ithaca, N.Y.: Cornell University Press, 2000), pp. 49–70, especially pp. 67–70, quotation from p. 69. For subjects, see Gregory Evans Dowd, *War under Heaven: Pontiac, the Indian Nations, and the British*

Empire (Baltimore, Md.: Johns Hopkins University Press, 2002), pp. 70, 174 ("conviction"), 175.

52. Greg O'Brien, "The Conqueror Meets the Unconquered: Negotiating Cultural Boundaries on the Post-Revolution Southern Frontier," *Journal of Southern History* 67 (2002): 39–72. For sociopolitical reform among the Creeks, see Green, *The Politics of Indian Removal;* Claudio Saunt, *A New Order of Things: Property, Power, and the Transformation of the Creek Indians, 1733–1816* (New York: Cambridge University Press, 1999). For the Native Southeast, see Duane Champagne, *Social Order and Political Change: Constitutional Governments among the Cherokee, the Choctaw, the Chickasaw, and the Creek* (Stanford, Calif.: Stanford University Press, 1992). For Creek supernatural solutions, see Martin, *Sacred Revolt.*

3. Leaving Okfuskee

1. Handsome Fellow spoke in Charleston about Cherokee peace negotiations and British trade relations; DRIA, vol. 1, pp. 398, 406. "A Talk from the Creeks to the Chactaws," in John Stuart to Thomas Gage, 12/13/1770, GAGE; Joshua Piker, " 'White & Clean' & Contested: Creek Towns and Trading Paths in the Aftermath of the Seven Years' War," *Ethnohistory* 50 (2003): 315–347.

2. James Axtell, *Beyond 1492: Encounters in Colonial America* (New York: Oxford University Press, 1992), chap. 5.

3. Daniel H. Usner Jr., *Indians, Settlers, and Slaves in a Frontier Exchange Economy: The Lower Mississippi Valley Before 1783* (Chapel Hill: University of North Carolina Press, 1992).

4. DRIA, vol. 1, p. 504 (1754). For 1771, see CRSGA, vol. 12, pp. 80–87, 148–150; CRSGA, vol. 38 (2), pp. 569–575.

5. Kathryn E. Holland Braund, *Deerskins & Duffels: Creek Indian Trade with Anglo-America, 1685–1815* (Lincoln: University of Nebraska Press, 1993), pp. 63–69; CRSGA, vol. 12, p. 149 (three).

6. BPRO, CO 5/78, f158 ("young"); Kristian Hvidt, ed., *Von Reck's Voyage: Drawings and Journal of Philip Georg Friedrich von Reck* (Savannah, Ga.: Beehive Press, 1990), p. 117; CRSGA, vol. 12, pp. 81–82 ("Skins").

7. For Creek hunting proficiency, see Braund, *Deerskins & Duffels,* pp. 69–71. Estate Inventory of John Ross, 12/1/1760, the Telamon Cuyler Collection, MS 1170, box 38A, folder 1, UGA (village); MC&CAMP.

8. SC-GAZ, 6/26/1736; SC-CJ, 9/4/1749, p. 581. For the 1750s, see DRIA, vol. 1, pp. 304, 311, 321 (1752); DRIA, vol. 2, p. 24 (1754); CRSGA, vol. 7, p. 268 (1755); DRIA, vol. 2, p. 252 (1756); "Treaty with the Albhama Indians," 10/10/1759, in Edmond Atkin to William Lyttelton, 11/30/1759,

LYTTEL; Jean-Bernard Bossu, *Travels in the Interior of North America, 1751–1762*, ed. and trans. Seymour Feiler (Norman: University of Oklahoma Press, 1962), p. 146. CRSGA, vol. 6, p. 296 (1749); DRIA, vol. 2, p. 236 (1756); "Some Remarks on the Creek Nation," in Daniel Pepper to Lyttelton, 1756, LYTTEL ("gone"); CRSGA, vol. 8, pp. 420–421 (1760); BPRO, CO 5/75, f212 (1774).

9. For Glover, see BPRO-SC, vol. 13, pp. 83, 97, 98, 107. Fluctuations in return dates seem related to two factors: the hunter's age and the diplomatic situation. Young men generally hunted longer than their elders; crises brought hunters home quickly. "Some Remarks," in Pepper to Lyttelton, 1756, LYTTEL (February 25). DRIA, vol. 2, p. 57 ("few"); CRSGA, vol. 9, p. 169 (1764); MPA-ED, p. 513 (1766).

10. After returning to Savannah, Ellis wrote on May 1, "I have lately had many partys of the Creek hunters with me"; CRSGA, vol. 28 (1), p. 17; Ellis to Lyttelton, 5/1/1757, LYTTEL. SC-GAZ, 5/24/1760 ("young"); CRSGA, vol. 9, p. 72 (1763).

11. For agriculture, see Chapter 4, this volume; ADAIR, 276 ("helped"). "David Taitt's Journal to and through the Upper Creek," in K. G. Davies, ed., *Documents of the American Revolution 1770–1783*, vol. 5 (Dublin: Irish University Press, 1974), pp. 251–272, quotation from p. 279.

12. Atkin and Billy Germany, Conference, 8/20/1759, p. 1, in Atkin to Lyttelton, 11/30/1759, LYTTEL; "A Talk by an Oakfusky Fellow," 7/19/1778, LAURENS. For 1770, see BPRO, CO 5/72, f85; John Stuart to Thomas Gage, 12/13/1770, GAGE; CRSGA, 28 (2), p. 351; CRSGA, vol. 38 (2), pp. 474, 483–487, 489–498, 490 ("March").

13. Braund, *Deerskins & Duffels*, pp. 69–71, quotation from p. 70 ("conservative"). For deer scarcity, see DRIA, vol. 2, p. 192; Atkin to Creek Headmen, 9/28–9/29/1759, p. 8, in Atkin to Lyttelton, 11/30/1759, LYTTEL; MPA-ED, p. 204; "At a Congress held at the Fort of Picolata," in Stuart to Gage, 1/21/1766, GAGE. For the argument that deer were not becoming scarce, see Gregory A. Waselkov, "The Eighteenth-Century Anglo–Indian Trade in Southeastern North America," in Jo-Anne Fiske, Susan Sleeper-Smith, and William Wicken, eds., *New Faces of the Fur Trade: Selected Papers of the Seventh North American Fur Trade Conference, Halifax, Nova Scotia, 1995* (East Lansing: Michigan State University Press, 1998), pp. 193–222, especially pp. 203–205. For Creek expansion into Florida, see Brent Richard Weisman, "Archaeological Perspectives on Florida Seminole Ethnogenesis," in Bonnie G. McEwan, ed., *Indians of the Greater Southeast: Historical Archaeology and Ethnohistory* (Gainesville: University Press of Florida, 2000), pp. 299–317.

14. DRIA, vol. 2, p. 10 (mission). For northern hunting grounds, see Braund,

Deerskins & Duffels, p. 62; Claudio Saunt, *A New Order of Things: Property, Power, and the Transformation of the Creek Indians, 1733–1816* (New York: Cambridge University Press, 1999), p. 4; HAWKINS, pp. 302–303 (corn house), 12 (path).

15. SC-CJ, 9/4/1749. For 1751–1752, see DRIA, vol. 1, pp. 215, 216, 255. DRIA, vol. 1, p. 398 ("frontier"). For diplomacy, see DRIA, vol. 1, pp. 379–381, 464–465, 501–502 ("met"); DRIA, vol. 2, pp. 3, 10–11.

16. For 1754, see DRIA, vol. 1, p. 504; DRIA, vol. 2, pp. 28, 29, 57. For Okfuskees, see SC-GAZ, 2/17/1761; BPRO, CO 5/78, f158. For the villages, see HAWKINS, p. 303; "A Treaty of Peace and Commerce," 11/6/1777, LAURENS.

17. DRIA, vol. 2, p. 44 ("influx"); BPRO, CO 5/73, f165 (1772); MPA-ED, pp. 204 (Mortar), 517 ("Hunts").

18. Lachlan McGillivary to Henry Ellis, 8/24/1758, in Ellis to William Lyttelton, 11/5/1758, LYTTEL; Braund, *Deerskins & Duffels,* p. 133 (treaty).

19. CRSGA, vol. 9, p. 148 (1763); DRIA, vol. 1, p. 380 (1753). An Okfuskee village, Chattahoochee, was located seventy miles east of town. Okfuskees certainly hunted nearby. These hunters most likely headed north, to the Chattahoochee River's headwaters, rather than east.

20. James Germany to Rae & Barksdale, 6/10/1756, LYTTEL ("Indians"); DRIA, vol. 2, p. 153 ("Hunting"). In his conversation with Georgia's governor, Handsome Fellow said that his people looked favorably on Savannah River settlements, especially Augusta, and that he was not authorized to discuss the Ogeechee area; CRSGA, vol. 7, pp. 420–425, quotation ("time") from p. 425. The following summer, Handsome Fellow and the Little Warrior of Okfuskee both suggested that the "Nation will not embroil themselves further about" the violence; according to Handsome Fellow, "all things relating to that matter were . . . made streight." CRSGA, vol. 28 (1), p. 42; SC-CJ, 7/12/1757.

21. Atkin to Lyttelton, 12/16/1759, LYTTEL ("Captain"); SALZ, vol. 17, p. 121 ("Creek"); SC-GAZ, 3/21/1760 ("Leader"); Atkin to Lyttelton, 2/21/1760, LYTTEL ("Party"); SC-GAZ, 1/31/1761, 4/15/1761 (Okfuskees). For 1762, see CRSGA, vol. 8, p. 777; CRSGA, vol. 9, pp. 12–16; CRSGA, vol. 28 (1), p. 405. CRSGA, vol. 9, pp. 114–116 (1763). For 1770, see CRSGA, vol. 38 (2), p. 474; BPRO, CO 5/72, f85; Stuart to Gage, 12/13/1770, GAGE.

22. ADAIR, p. 275. By 1773, two of these villages contained "about Sixty Gunmen belonging to the Oakfuskee Indians"; David Taitt, "Remarks," in Bernard Romans, "A Map of West Florida, part of E. Florida, Georgia, part of South Carolina" (1773), CLEM. For more on Okfuskee–Chattahoochee connections, see GA-GAZ, 5/25/1774; Carolyn Thomas Foreman, "The White Lieutenant and Some of His Contemporaries," *Chronicles of*

Oklahoma 38 (1960): 425–440, especially p. 435; Mark Van Doren, ed., *The Travels of William Bartram* (Dover, Del.: Dover Publications, 1928), p. 366; John R. Swanton, *Early History of the Creek Indians & Their Neighbors,* Bureau of American Ethnology Bulletin 73 (Tuscaloosa: University of Alabama Press, 1998 [1922]), pp. 248–249; CRSGA, vol. 38 (2), p. 486 (1770); "Journal of the Superintendant's Proceedings," p. 26, enclosed in John Stuart to Thomas Gage, 7/21/1767, GAGE. For the 1770s, see Chapter 5, this volume.

23. CRSGA, vol. 9, p. 72 (1763). The Creeks referred to the colonists flooding into the backcountry from the north as "Virginia People" or "Virginians." "A Talk from the Mortar to John Stuart," 7/22/1764, in Stuart to Gage, 11/30/1764, GAGE; "Journal of the Superintendent's Proceedings," in Stuart to Gage, 8/27/1767, GAGE.

24. Unrecorded visits by Okfuskees may have occurred. For example, the 1769 Augusta meeting involving "all the Chiefs of the Upper Creek Nation" most likely included Okfuskees; BPRO, CO 5/70, ff9–13.

25. Taitt to Stuart, 10/19/1772, in Stuart to Gage, 11/24/1772, GAGE; Davies, "Taitt's Journal," p. 262. See also BPRO, CO 5/74, ff30–31, 64.

26. BPRO, CO 5/74, f29 (letter); Stuart to Gage, 9/7/1772, GAGE ("claim"); Braund, *Deerskins & Duffels,* pp. 150–152 (cession); BPRO, CO 5/75, f190 ("Virginians"); "A Treaty of Peace and Commerce," 11/6/1777, LAURENS (Stochlitca).

27. Betty Wood, *Slavery in Colonial Georgia, 1730–1775* (Athens: University of Georgia Press, 1984), chap. 6; Joyce C. Chaplin, *An Anxious Pursuit: Agricultural Innovation and Modernity in the Lower South, 1730–1815* (Chapel Hill: University of North Carolina Press, 1993); Alan Gallay, *The Formation of a Planter Elite: Jonathan Bryan and the Southern Colonial Frontier* (Athens: University of Georgia Press, 1989); Braund, *Deerskins & Duffels,* p. 160.

28. Usner, *Indians, Settlers, and Slaves,* pp. 6–7.

29. For Usner's discussion of the differences between Louisiana and other colonial societies, see ibid., pp. 79–80.

30. Okfuskee headmen visited Charleston in 1739, 1744, and 1749, and attended a 1746 New Windsor meeting. Moreover, Okfuskees probably joined a 1743 Upper Creek party that permitted construction of Ft. Okfuskee, and an Okfuskee trader brought down a headman named Tusk Keenie in 1742; he may have been Ifa Tuskenia of Okfuskee. For the confirmed visits, see SC-CJ, 8/15/1739, 8/18/1739, 6/21/1744, 7/25/1744, 7/28/1744, 10/29/1746, 9/5–9/11/1749. For 1743, see SC-CJ, 10/6–10/7/1743; SC-JCHA, 10/8/1743. For 1742, see SC-CJ, 2/16/1742, 2/4/1742. For 1731 to 1753, see SC-CJ, 7/20/1731, 9/6/1749; DRIA, vol. 1, p. 410; PA-GAZ, 7/10/1732.

31. Usner, *Indians, Settlers, & Slaves,* p. 45; Brownfield to Tuckwell and Pytt, 4/6/1736, in John Brownfield's Copy Book, 1735–1740, CGAHS; original in the Archives of the Moravian Church, Bethlehem, Pa.

32. For the evolving Creek–Yuchi relationship, see BPRO-SC, vol. 13, p. 150; SC-CJ, 8/16/1732; DRIA, vol. 1, pp. 85, 170. SC-CJ, 9/1/1726 ("Stragling"). For Indians in the colonies, see James Merrell, *The Indians' New World: Catawbas and Their Neighbors from European Contact through the Era of Removal* (New York: W. W. Norton, 1989); Gene Waddell, *Indians of the South Carolina Lowcountry, 1562–1751* (Spartanburg, S.C.: The Reprint Company, 1980). For Indian slavery, see J. Leitch Wright Jr., *The Only Land They Knew: The Tragic Story of the American Indians in the Old South* (New York: The Free Press, 1981), pp. 126–150; Alan Gallay, *The Indian Slave Trade: The Rise of the English Empire in the American South, 1670–1717* (New Haven, Conn.: Yale University Press, 2002). James Glen, *A Description of South Carolina* (London: R. and J. Dodsley, 1761), pp. 79, 60–61.

33. SALZ, vol. 8, p. 378 ("friendly"). British officials made periodic efforts to persuade Creeks to move closer to the colonies. SC-JCHA, 2/3/1702–3, 12/14/1737, 3/1/1743, 5/21/1747; SC-CJ, 8/24/1725, 4/14/1743; BPRO-SC, vol. 13, pp. 105, 150, 167. In addition, governors generally insisted that Creek delegations visit colonial capitals, thereby ensuring that Creeks traveled through the colonies. SC-JCHA, 5/26/1749.

34. Unless otherwise noted, the material in the preceding three paragraphs is drawn from Joshua Piker, "Creeks and Colonists: Re-thinking the Southern Backcountry," *Journal of Southern History* (forthcoming).

35. BPRO, CO 5/75, f214 (Taitt). Cujesse Mico referred to clearing the path "from Oakfuskie to this white House," which was owned by Lachlan Mc-Gillivray and occupied by his employee, Robert Mackay. McGillivray had once employed William Trevin to oversee his Augusta-based trading interests; the Okfuskees traded with Trevin by 1761. BPRO, CO 5/75, f212 ("House"); SC-GAZ, 4/25/1761 (Trevin). For McGillivray's house, see Edward J. Cashin, *William Bartram and the American Revolution on the Southern Frontier* (Columbia: University of South Carolina Press, 2000), p. 48. For Trevin in 1761, see Cashin, *Lachlan McGillivray, Indian Trader: The Shaping of the Southern Colonial Frontier* (Athens: University of Georgia Press, 1992), pp. 208–209.

36. CRSGA, vol. 7, p. 703 (1758); DRIA, vol. 2, p. 371 ("Stores"); DRIA, vol. 1, p. 258 ("People"); SC-GAZ, 4/25/1761; Atkin to Lyttelton, 2/21/1760, LYTTEL ("trade"). In 1767, two Upper Creek diplomatic parties arrived in Augusta. Each included an Okfuskee headman, but the first asked that Creeks not be allowed to trade "at this place," while the second expressed "Surprize" that "some of our people desired that we Shou'd not be per-

mitted to Trade in the Settlements." "Journal of the Superintendent's Proceedings," in Stuart to Gage, 7/21/1767, GAGE, pp. 23–29, quotations from pp. 26, 28.

37. CRSGA, vol. 38 (2), pp. 573–574 ("Means"); CRSGA, vol. 7, p. 424 ("Objection"); Samuel Savery, "Sketch of the Boundary Line Between the Province of Georgia and the Creek Nation," CLEM ("Sanders"). For Whitefield's dealings in Okfuskee, see MC&CAMP, pp. 179, 249, 251, 252. CRSGA, vol. 10, p. 827 (Rae).

38. "Journal of the Superintendent's Proceedings," p. 28, in Stuart to Gage, 7/21/1767, GAGE ("Terms"). For Creeks favoring a backcountry system of weighing deerskins that "often makes a difference of 50 percent," see Ellis to Lyttelton, 4/13/1758, LYTTEL. MC&CAMP, p. 125; CRSGA, vol. 28 (1), p. 88 (re-supply). For Creeks avoiding debts, see Atkin to Ellis, 1/25/1760, p. 14, Ellis Papers, CGAHS; CRSGA, vol. 9, p. 75; BPRO, CO 5/71, ff12–13.

39. SC-GAZ, 5/31/1760; Stuart to Gage, 5/12/1774, GAGE ("Escorted"); CRSGA, vol. 8, p. 544 ("Guards"); GA-GAZ, 5/11/1774 ("even"). I argue in Chapter 2 that the "presents" were meant not for the escorts but for Mad Turkey's grieving relatives. The fact, however, that the colonists interpreted the Okfuskees' demands as a call for payment for services rendered suggests how common such arrangements were. The Okfuskees received "these presents, with others added."

40. For Okfuskees carrying messages see note 41 below and SC-CJ, 9/4/1749 (for this messenger's Okfuskee identity, see SC-CJ, 9/5/1749); SC-GAZ, 5/15/1762; Richard Henderson to [George Galphin?], 6/12/1778, LAURENS.

41. SC-JCHA, 9/20/1755; White Outerbridge to William Lyttelton, 9/14/1756, LYTTEL; David Douglass et al., "To Our Good Friends," 9/13/1756, in Outerbridge to Lyttelton, 9/14/1756, LYTTEL; CRSGA, vol. 7, p. 422; DRIA, vol. 2, pp. 155–156, 211–212, 238, 297, 300; CRSGA, vol. 7, pp. 419–425; CRSGA, vol. 28 (1), pp. 80–84; John Reynolds to Lyttelton, 11/26/1756, LYTTEL.

42. For gifts' meanings and ambiguities, see David Murray, *Indian Giving: Economies of Power in Indian–White Exchanges* (Amherst: University of Massachusetts Press, 2000). For the relationship between gifts and trade, see Richard White, *The Middle Ground: Indians, Empires, and Republics in the Great Lakes Region, 1650–1815* (New York: Cambridge University Press, 1991), chap. 3. For gifts in a southeastern context, see Usner, *Indians, Settlers, & Slaves,* pp. 26–27; Gregory Evans Dowd, " 'Insidious Friends': Gift-Giving and the Cherokee–British Alliance in the Seven Years' War," in Andrew R. L. Cayton and Fredrika J. Teute, eds., *Contact Points: North American Frontiers, 1750–1830* (Chapel Hill: University of North Carolina Press, 1998), pp. 114–150.

43. John Stuart to Thomas Gage, 4/11/1764, GAGE; "A Talk Given at the King's Fort in Augusta," 3/24/1764, enclosed in Stuart to Gage, 4/11/1764, GAGE; SC-GAZ, 3/31/1764; MC&CAMP, p. 220.

44. John Reynolds to William Lyttelton, 11/26/1756, LYTTEL ("demand," "Rum," "Suit"); CRSGA, vol. 7, p. 425 ("Sundry"); CRSGA, vol. 28 (1), pp. 81–84 (goods received). To convert the gifts into pounds of deerskins, I rely on three price lists from the mid-1760s. See CRSGA, vol. 28 (2), pp. 118, 121–122; BPRO, CO 5/68, f145. SC-CJ, 9/3/1756 (earlier party).

45. SC-CJ, 5/28/1753; DRIA, vol. 1, p. 410 (Okfuskees); BPRO, CO 5/79, f154 (1778); CRSGA, vol. 8, p. 416 ("Supply"); DRIA, vol. 2, p. 89 ("Presents"). For Okfuskees in this party, see DRIA, vol. 2, p. 83, and SC-CJ, 1/23/1756. For the 1753 party's presents, see SC-JCHA, 4/18/1753, and DRIA, vol. 1, p. 410 ("Addition"). Daniel McMurphy to John Martin, 9/22/1782, in "Georgia Creek Indian Letters, Talks, and Treaties," vol. 1, compiled by Mrs. J. E. Hays (Works Progress Administration, 1939–1940), pp. 30 ("expect"), 31, bound manuscript in UGA.

46. For St. Jago's land, see CRSGA, vol. 10, pp. 579–580 ("middle"); CRSGA, vol. 28 (2), p. 370. For Aleck's land, see CRSGA, vol. 8, pp. 467–468; BPRO-SC, vol. 30, pp. 75, 96–97; "At a Congress," in Stuart to Gage, 1/21/1766, GAGE. Account Book, 1765–1782, Telfair Family Papers, box 13, folder 106, item 433, CGAHS; SC-GAZ, 9/20/1760. "[G]reat numbers" of Creeks traded at Indian Land; Henry Ellis to Lyttelton, 4/13/1758, LYTTEL.

47. Lachlan McGillivray et al., "Talks re Cherokee disturbances," 2/11/1760 ("rewarded," "preserving"), in White Outerbridge to Lyttelton, 2/12/1760, LYTTEL. For looting, see Outerbridge to Lyttelton, 2/6/1760, LYTTEL; Atkin to Lyttelton, 2/13/1760, LYTTEL. SC-GAZ, 4/25/1761 ("early"); CRSGA, vol. 12, p. 81 ("bad"). For Mad Turkey, see GA-GAZ, 4/13/1774 ("invited"); John Stuart to Thomas Gage, 5/12/1774, GAGE; Stuart to Frederick Haldimand, 6/25/1774, in Haldimand to Gage, 7/14/1774, GAGE. "A Talk Delivered at Ogeechee," 6/18/1777, LAURENS.

48. Harold E. Davis, *The Fledgling Province: Social and Cultural Life in Colonial Georgia, 1733–1776* (Chapel Hill: University of North Carolina Press, 1976), pp. 29, 31–32; Peter H. Wood, "The Changing Population of the Colonial South: An Overview by Race and Region, 1685–1790," in Wood, Gregory A. Waselkov, and M. Thomas Hatley, eds., *Powhatan's Mantle: Indians in the Colonial Southeast* (Lincoln: University of Nebraska Press, 1989), pp. 35–103, especially pp. 38, 56–61; J. Anthony Paredes and Kenneth J. Plante, "A Reexamination of Creek Indian Population Trends: 1738–1832," *American Indian Culture and Research Journal* 6 (1982): 3–28; "An Account taken by Captn [Charlesworth] Glover & his Traders," in Christian F. Feest, "Creek Towns in 1725," *Ethnologische Zeitschrift Zurich*

1 (1974): 161–175, especially pp. 162–163. For 1764, see MPA-ED, pp. 94–97; "A List of the Towns & Number of Gun Men in the Creek Nation," in Francis Ogilvie to Thomas Gage, 7/8/1764, GAGE.

49. CRSGA, vol. 28 (1), p. 334 ("Vagrants"). See also DRIA, vol. 1, p. 12; CRSGA, vol. 28 (2), p. 235; BPRO-SC, vol. 32, pp. 108–109; CRSGA, vol. 8, p. 167 (1759). For a 1765 example of Creeks killing hunters, see BPRO, CO 5/67, f50; CRSGA, vol. 9, p. 437; CRSGA, vol. 28 (2), p. 129; GA-GAZ, 10/24/1765. For the colonists' use of forest products, see Rachel N. Klein, *Unification of a Slave State: The Rise of the Planter Class in the South Carolina Backcountry* (Chapel Hill: University of North Carolina Press, 1990), pp. 24, 54; CRSGA, vol. 26, p. 236 ("Deer"); Ralph Wilson to Mr. Freutler, 2/1/1768, Keith Read Collection, box 29, folder 5, UGA ("Beaver").

50. For Handsome Fellow, see DRIA, vol. 2, pp. 103, 104; CRSGA, vol. 28 (1), pp. 80–84; White Outerbridge to William Lyttelton, 9/14/1756, LYTTEL. Timothy Silver, *A New Face on the Countryside: Indians, Colonists, and Slaves in the South Atlantic Forests, 1500–1800* (New York: Cambridge University Press, 1990), pp. 72–74; Terry G. Jordan, *North American Cattle-Ranching Frontiers: Origins, Diffusion, and Differentiation* (Albuquerque: University of New Mexico Press, 1993), pp. 109–120, 170–178, 189–194. "A Talk from Homahta," in John Stuart to Gage, 8/27/1767, GAGE ("Living"); CRSGA, vol. 8, p. 544 (1762); CRSGA, vol. 12, p. 84 ("other").

51. CRSGA, vol. 9, p. 71 (provisions); CRSGA, vol. 10, p. 272 (dissatisfaction). For boundaries, see CRSGA, vol. 28 (2), p. 40; "A Talk from the head men of the Covetaws," 6/18/1766, in Stuart to Gage, 1/7/1767, GAGE. CRSGA, vol. 9, p. 73 (Mortar); CRSGA, vol. 28 (2), pp. 367–368 ("Green"); SC-CJ, 8/31/1756 ("Earth"). For the trader's livestock, see the description of Alexander Wood's Augusta-area plantation; SC-GAZ, 4/28/1757. John Rae, another Okfuskee trader, was also a cattle rancher. See CRSGA, vol. 7, pp. 697–698, 922; CRSGA, vol. 10, pp. 194–195, 516; George Fenwick Jones, "Portrait of an Irish Entrepreneur in Colonial Augusta: John Rae, 1708–1772," *Georgia Historical Quarterly* 83 (1999): 427–447.

52. J. Russell Snapp, *John Stuart and the Struggle for Empire on the Southern Frontier* (Baton Rouge: Louisiana State University Press, 1996); Edward J. Cashin, "Sowing the Wind: Governor Wright and the Georgia Backcountry on the Eve of the Revolution," in Harvey H. Jackson and Phinizy Spalding, eds., *Forty Years of Diversity: Essays on Colonial Georgia* (Athens: University of Georgia Press, 1984), pp. 233–250; Harvey H. Jackson, "The Rise of the Western Members: Revolutionary Politics and the Georgia Backcountry," in Ronald Hoffman, Thad W. Tate, and Peter J. Albert, eds., *An Uncivil*

War: The Southern Backcountry during the American Revolution (Charlottesville: University Press of Virginia, 1985), pp. 276–320; Chaplin, *An Anxious Pursuit*, chaps. 5, 8. Gregory Nobles warned against ignoring the bonds linking the two regions; "Breaking into the Backcountry: New Approaches to the Early American Frontier," *William and Mary Quarterly* 49 (1989): 641–670. Albert H. Tillson Jr., "The Southern Backcountry: A Survey of Current Research," *Virginia Magazine of History and Biography* 98 (1990): 387–422; Klein, *Unification of a Slave State*.

53. At the same time, many Indians began to question the place of Euro-Americans and their goods in Native life; these beginnings of a Nativist movement complicated relations between the generations. Gregory Evans Dowd, *A Spirited Resistance: The North American Indian Struggle for Unity, 1745–1815* (Baltimore Md.: Johns Hopkins University Press, 1992), especially pp. 23–46. For these developments in Okfuskee, see Conclusion, this volume.

54. CRSGA, vol. 9, p. 15 (1763). For the headmen, see CRSGA, vol. 8, p. 777. BPRO, CO 5/75, ff17 ("Woods"), 180 (1774).

55. For 1770, see note 21 above; for 1771, see note 4 above. December 1773 and January 1774 saw a series of Creek attacks on the British backcountry; one of the leaders was an Okfuskee, who was executed in June 1774. BPRO, CO 5/75, ff42–44, 52, 180, 190; GA-GAZ, 2/2/1774, 2/16/1774, 3/16/1774, 4/13/1774, 4/27/1774; John Stuart to Thomas Gage, 7/3/1774 and 7/5/1774, GAGE. Elk, another headman involved in the attacks, was killed by Euro-Americans in March 1774; a statement regarding "the Murder of the two Indians of Oakfuskees" almost certainly refers to Elk and Mad Turkey. GA-GAZ, 3/16/1774, 3/23/1774, 4/20/1774; Alexander Cameron to John Stuart, 4/12/1774, and David Taitt to John Stuart, 4/8/1774 ("Murder"), both in the British Library, Haldimand Collection, MG 21, Add. Ms. 21673, (B13).

56. CRSGA, vol. 12, p. 149 ("Uncle"). For the trader, see GA-GAZ, 5/25/1774; Andrew McLean to William Ogilvy, 5/13/1774, in Ogilvy to Frederick Haldimand, 6/8/1774, GAGE. BPRO, CO 5/70, f90 (Aleck, Escotchaby); George Galphin to Stuart, 6/2/1768, in Stuart to Gage, 7/2/1768, GAGE (Ogeechee); Stuart to Gage, 8/6/1770, GAGE ("thefts"); Andrew McLean to William Ogilvy, 5/13/1774, in Oglivy to Frederick Haldimand, 6/8/1774, GAGE ("Crackers"); BPRO, CO 5/75, f190 ("Virginians").

57. BPRO, CO 5/75, ff212–215 (Okfuskees); Grierson traded in Creek country, although not in Okfuskee. For Carter, see Galphin to Stuart, 6/2/1768, GAGE; CRSGA, vol. 10, p. 491. A 1769 map places "Carter's" ten miles south of the main trading path and twenty-five miles east of Creek country; Savery, "Sketch of the Boundary Line," CLEM.

58. Timothy Barnard to [], 7/12/1790, Cuyler Collection, box 1, folder 11,

UGA ("eating," "meanly"); Harold A. Huscher, *Archaeological Investigations in the West Point Dam Area: A Preliminary Report* (Athens: Laboratory of Archaeology, University of Georgia, 1972), pp. 21 ("Wont"), 19 ("friendly"), 20 (note); White, *The Middle Ground.* Hawkins notes that one village moved west in 1777; he names three others that returned by 1799; the fifth village, Okfuskenena, was the one burned in 1793. At least some Okfuskenenas returned to the Tallapoosa Valley. HAWKINS, pp. 302, 306.

59. Usner, *Indians, Settlers, & Slaves,* p. 106.

60. For fishermen, see Daniel Vickers, *Farmers and Fishermen: Two Centuries of Work in Essex County, Massachusetts, 1630–1850* (Chapel Hill: University of North Carolina Press, 1994). For frontier livestock raising, see Jordan, *North American Cattle-Ranching Frontiers;* for the content and diffusion of a backcountry culture, see Terry G. Jordan and Matti Kaups, *The American Backwoods Culture: An Ethnic and Ecological Interpretation* (Baltimore, Md.: Johns Hopkins University Press, 1989). For the efforts land speculation called forth, see Charles Royster, *The Fabulous History of the Dismal Swamp Company: A Story of George Washington's Times* (New York: Borzoi Books, 1999).

61. For young men using the military to achieve personal independence, see Fred Anderson, *A People's Army: Massachusetts Soldiers and Society in the Seven Years' War* (New York: W. W. Norton, 1984), chap. 2. For the over-representation of "economically marginal men" among Virginia recruits, see Jean B. Lee, *The Price of Nationhood: The American Revolution in Charles County* (New York: W. W. Norton, 1994), pp. 161–169, quotation from p. 166. See also John Shy, *A People Numerous and Armed: Reflections on the Military Struggle for American Independence,* rev. ed. (Ann Arbor: University of Michigan Press, 1990), chaps. 2, 5, 7.

62. For farmers' marketing efforts, see Richard L. Bushman, "Markets and Composite Farms in Early America," *William and Mary Quarterly* 55 (1998): 351–374; Allan Kulikoff, *From British Peasants to Colonial American Farmers* (Chapel Hill: University of North Carolina Press, 2000), pp. 210–211. For women's wage labor, see Gloria Main, "Gender, Work, and Wages in Colonial New England," *William and Mary Quarterly* 51 (1994): 39–66; Laurel Thatcher Ulrich, "Martha Ballard and Her Girls: Women's Work in Eighteenth-Century Maine," in Stephen Innes, ed., *Work and Labor in Early America* (Chapel Hill: University of North Carolina Press, 1988), pp. 70–105; Cynthia A. Kierner, *Beyond the Household: Women's Place in the Early South, 1700–1835* (Ithaca, N.Y.: Cornell University Press, 1998), chap. 1. For men, see Vickers, *Farmers and Fishermen,* chaps. 5–6. For New England's transient laborers, see Ruth Wallis Herndon, *Unwelcome Americans:*

Living on the Margins in Early New England (Philadelphia: University of Pennsylvania Press, 2001), pp. 85–120. For agricultural wage labor and craft work, see Paul G. E. Clemens and Lucy Simler, "Rural Labor and the Farm Household in Chester County, Pennsylvania, 1750–1820," in Innes, *Work and Labor,* pp. 106–143.

63. Anderson, *A People's Army,* pp. 23, 25; Charles Royster, *A Revolutionary People at War: The Continental Army and American Character, 1775–1783* (Chapel Hill: University of North Carolina Press, 1979), chap. 7. For "metropolitan" and "frontier" views of Indians, see Michael L. Oberg, *Dominion and Civility: English Imperialism and Native America, 1585–1685* (Ithaca, N.Y.: Cornell University Press, 1999). T. H. Breen and Timothy Hall, "Structuring Provincial Imagination: The Rhetoric and Experience of Social Change in Eighteenth-Century New England," *American Historical Review* 103 (1998): 1411–1438, quotations from pp. 1414, 1415.

64. For a comparison of Euro-American and Native American "nomads," see Colin G. Calloway, *New Worlds for All: Indians, Europeans, and the Remaking of Early America* (Baltimore, Md.: Johns Hopkins University Press, 1997), chap. 7. For merchants, see David Hancock, *Citizens of the World: London Merchants and the Integration of the British Atlantic Community, 1735–1785* (New York: Cambridge University Press, 1995), chap. 4. For farmers, see Kenneth E. Lewis, "The Metropolis and the Backcountry: The Making of a Colonial Landscape on the South Carolina Frontier," *Historical Archaeology* 33 (1999): 3–13. Alison Games, *Migration and the Origin of the English Atlantic World* (Cambridge, Mass.: Harvard University Press, 1999), p. 189 ("normative"); Bernard Bailyn, *The Peopling of British North America: An Introduction* (New York: Vintage Books, 1986), p. 60 ("movement").

65. For "serial town settlement" in the eighteenth century, see David Jaffee, *People of the Wachusett: Greater New England in History and Memory, 1630–1860* (Ithaca, N.Y.: Cornell University Press, 1999), chaps. 3, 4, quotation from p. 137.

66. For migration and emigration, see James Horn, "British Diaspora: Emigration from Britain 1680–1815," in P. J. Marshall, ed., *The Oxford History of the British Empire,* vol. 2, *The Eighteenth Century* (New York: Oxford University Press, 1998), pp. 28–52, especially p. 29. For the growing focus on territory and exclusion, see Chapter 2, this volume, and Elizabeth Mancke, "Negotiating an Empire: Britain and Its Overseas Peripheries, c. 1550–1780," in Christine Daniels and Michael V. Kennedy, eds., *Negotiated Empires: Centers and Peripheries in the Americas, 1500–1820* (New York: Routledge, 2002), pp. 235–265, especially p. 235.

4. Agriculture and Livestock

1. HAWKINS, 302 ("derived," "flat"); GA-GAZ, 5/25/1774 ("houses"); "Captain Musgrave's . . . Intelligence," 1771, GAGE (river); John H. Goff, "The Path to Oakfuskee: Upper Trading Route in Georgia to the Creek Indians," *Georgia Historical Quarterly* 39 (1955): 1–36; Goff, "The Path to Oakfuskee: Upper Trading Route in Alabama to the Creek Indians," *Georgia Historical Quarterly* 39 (1955): 152–171.

2. E. L. Pennington, "Thomas Campbell to Lord Deane Gordon: An Account of the Creek Indian Nation, 1764," *The Florida Historical Quarterly* 30 (1930): 156–163, quotation ("always") from p. 159; Mark Van Doren, ed., *The Travels of William Bartram* (Dover, Del.: Dover Publications, 1928), p. 400 ("isthmus"); Gregory A. Waselkov and Kathryn E. Holland Braund, eds., *William Bartram on the Southeastern Indians* (Lincoln: University of Nebraska Press, 1995), p. 174 ("common").

3. Charles Hudson, *The Southeastern Indians* (Knoxville: University of Tennessee Press, 1976), pp. 218–222; "David Taitt's Journal to and through the Upper Creek Nation," in K. G. Davies, *Documents of the American Revolution, 1770–1783,* vol. 5 (Dublin: Irish University Press, 1974), pp. 251–272, especially p. 264 ("square"); HAWKINS, p. 302 ("town house"). The Oakfuskenena rotundas were used sequentially. Harold A. Huscher, *Archaeological Investigations in the West Point Dam Area: A Preliminary Report* (Athens: Laboratory of Anthropology, University of Georgia, 1972), pp. 9–46; Marvin T. Smith, *Historic Period Indian Archaeology of Northern Georgia* (Athens: Laboratory of Anthropology, University of Georgia, 1992), p. 72. For another Okfuskee village's rotunda, see HAWKINS, p. 12. DRIA, vol. 1, pp. 379 ("Slave"), 380.

4. Bartram's original map was drawn sometime after his trip and based on "the best of my remembrance." Taitt, "Remarks," in Bernard Romans, "A Map of West Florida, part of E. Florida, Georgia, part of South Carolina" (1773), CLEM; Van Doren, ed., *Travels,* 318 ("habitation"); Waselkov and Braund, eds., *Bartram,* pp. 137, 167 ("best"), 180 ("family," "situated"), 181–183, 279, n. 80. For the family–lineage spatial relationship, see Vernon J. Knight Jr., *Tukabatchee: Archaeological Investigations at an Historic Creek Town, Elmore County, Alabama, 1984,* Report of Investigations 45 (Tuscaloosa: Office of Archaeological Research, Alabama State Museum of Natural History, 1985), pp. 118–120; Allan D. Meyers, "Household Organization and Refuse Disposal at a Cultivated Creek Site," *Southeastern Archaeology* 15 (1996): 132–144; Cameron B. Wesson, *Households and Hegemony: An Analysis of Historic Creek Culture Change* (Ph.D. diss., University of Illinois at Urbana–Champaign, 1997).

5. For gardens and town fields, see Taitt, "Remarks"; ADAIR, pp. 435–436,

438; Van Doren, ed., *Travels,* pp. 168–169, 400; Romans, "A Map of West Florida"; Waselkov and Braund, eds., *Bartram,* pp. 155, 158, 160. See also Gregory A. Waselkov, "Changing Strategies of Indian Field Location in the Early Historic Southeast," in Kristen Gremillion, ed., *People, Plants, and Landscape: Case Studies in Paleoethnobotany* (Tuscaloosa: University of Alabama Press, 1997), pp. 179–194. Van Doren, ed., *Travels,* p. 354 ("mode"); ADAIR, p. 443 ("towers); William Bonar, "A Draught of the Upper Creek Nation, taken in May 1757," CLEM. George Johnson's store "near" Calilgies appears on the map; Edmond Atkin to William Lyttelton, 11/30/1759, p. 23, LYTTEL. For Johnson's Okfuskee ties, see Chapter 2, this volume. ADAIR, p. 279 (1760).

6. For Okfuskee, see Jerome Courtonne, "List of Headmen of the Creeks," in Courtonne to Lyttelton, 10/17/1758, LYTTEL; "A Talk Given at the King's Fort in Augusta," in John Stuart to Gage, 4/11/1764, GAGE. Atkin to Tallapoosas Headmen, 9/15/1759, Atkin to Creek Headmen, 9/28–9/29/1759, and Great Britain & Alabamas, Treaty, 10/10/1759, all enclosed in Atkin to Lyttelton, 11/30/1759, LYTTEL. Thomas Nairne's list of clan names includes "Ogilisa"; John R. Swanton gives "Okilisa" as a war name and "Okilisalgi" as a clan name meaning "Weevil (?) (or English?)." Neither links the name to "Master of the Ground." Alexander Moore, ed., *Nairne's Muskhogean Journals: The 1708 Expedition to the Mississippi River* (Jackson: University of Mississippi Press, 1988), pp. 60, 64; Swanton, "Social Organization and Social Usages of the Indians of the Creek Confederacy," *Forty-second Annual Report of the Bureau of American Ethnology, 1924–1925* (Washington, D.C.: U.S. Government Printing Office, 1928), pp. 23–472, especially pp. 106, 116.

7. CRSGA, vol. 9, p. 73 ("Masters"); Atkin to Henry Ellis, 1/25/1760 ("Owners"), Ellis Papers, folder 942, item 3, p. 11, CGAHS. For "Okeelysa" as Mortar's nephew, see "Conference with Billy Germany," 8/20/1759, in Atkin to Lyttleton, 11/30/1759, LYTTEL. Bartram linked "overseer" with a family, but he "suppose[d]" the post rotated "throughout the Families of the Town"; Waselkov and Braund, eds., *Bartram,* p. 159. Moore, ed., *Nairne's Muskhogean Journal,* p. 64.

8. For Creek officials, see John R. Swanton, "Modern Square Grounds of the Creek Indians," *Smithsonian Miscellaneous Collections* 85, no. 8 (1931): 9, 11–12. In the above examples, "Okeelysa" twice referred to a "Head Beloved Man," which could signify Second Man; but on several occasions the Master of the Ground was a "Chief Warrior" or "Mico." For dividing land, see Van Doren, ed., *Travels,* pp. 170, 400; Michael D. Green, *The Politics of Indian Removal: Creek Government and Society in Crisis* (Lincoln: University of Nebraska Press, 1982), p. 5.

9. James Germany to Messrs. Rae & Barksdale, 6/10/1756, LYTTEL ("in-

gross"); DRIA, vol. 2, p. 188 ("get"); BPRO-SC, vol. 13, p. 93 ("French"); Kathryn E. Holland Braund, "The Creek Indians, Blacks, and Slavery," *Journal of Southern History* 57 (1991): 601–636; Claudio Saunt, "'The English has Now a Mind to Make Slaves of them all': Creeks, Seminoles, and the Problems of Slavery," *American Indian Quarterly* 22 (1998): 157–180.

10. ADAIR, pp. 436–437; see also p. 462. Van Doren, ed., *Travels,* pp. 169–170, 400–401.

11. For gardens, see Waselkov and Braund, eds., *Bartram,* pp. 155, 160. Creek society was matrilocal. Houses were women's property, and the household garden—as an offshoot of the house—belonged to the woman and her clan. Kathryn E. Holland Braund, "Guardians of Tradition and Handmaidens to Change: Women's Roles in Creek Economic and Social Life During the Eighteenth Century," *American Indian Quarterly* 14 (1990): 239–258, especially pp. 241–242. For Okfuskee matrilocality, see HAWKINS, p. 13. For planting dates, see ADAIR, pp. 436, 437.

12. Pennington, "Thomas Campbell," 159 ("beginning"); ADAIR, pp. 435, 437 (corn types); Waselkov and Braund, eds., *Bartram,* 160 ("earlier"); "Taitt's Journal," 264. For March–June food shortages in 1728, 1731, 1748, 1759, 1761, 1766, 1777, 1778, and 1785, see BPRO-SC, vol. 13, p. 161; SC-CJ, 3/3/1731, 4/27/1748; "Buffalo Skin to Demere," in Paul Demere to Lyttelton, 8/28/1759, LYTTEL; SC-GAZ, 5/30/1761; MPA-ED, p. 522; BPRO, CO 5/78, ff145–146, 157; BPRO, CO 5/79, f84; John Pigg to George Galphin, 6/13/1778, LAURENS; "Indian Treaties: Cessions of Land in Georgia, 1705–1837," compiled by Mrs. J. E. Hays (Works Progress Administration, 1941), p. 169, bound manuscript in UGA.

13. ADAIR, pp. 106, 107; BPRO, CO 5/79, f185; SALZ, vol. 15, p. 88; Kristian Hvidt, ed., *Von Reck's Voyage: Drawings and Journal of Philip Georg Freidrich von Reck* (Savannah, Ga.: Beehive Press, 1980), p. 49; Louis Leclerc Milfort, *Memoirs or A Quick Glance at My Various Travels and My Sojourn in the Creek Nation,* ed. and trans. Ben C. McCary (Kennesaw, Ga.: Continental Book Co., 1972 [1802]), p. 98.

14. Van Doren, ed., *Travels,* 399. For "burn[ing] all of the new corn," see Pennington, "Thomas Campbell," p. 162.

15. My interpretation of the Busk owes a great deal to Joel W. Martin, *Sacred Revolt: The Muskogees' Struggle for a New World* (Boston: Beacon Press, 1991), pp. 34–42. For the Busk, see John R. Swanton, "Religious Beliefs and Medical Practices of the Creek Indians," *Forty-Second Annual Report of the Bureau of American Ethnology, 1924–1925* (Washington, D.C.: U.S. Government Printing Office, 1928), pp. 473–672, especially pp. 546–614; Hudson, *The Southeastern Indians,* pp. 366–375.

16. For European crops, see J. Leitch Wright Jr., *Creeks and Seminoles: The*

Destruction and Regeneration of the Muscogulge People (Lincoln: University of Nebraska Press, 1986), p. 22. For agricultural continuity, see Kristen J. Gremillion, "Comparative Paleoethnobotany of the Three Native Southeastern Communities of the Historic Period," *Southeastern Archaeology* 14 (1995): 1–16. For pits, see Claire C. B. Vaught, "Archaeobotanical Remains," in Roy S. Dickens Jr., *Archaeological Investigations at Horseshoe Bend National Military Park, Alabama,* Special Publication 3 (University: Alabama Archaeological Society, 1979), pp. 171–187, especially p. 187. For peaches, see HAWKINS, p. 302. For Chattahoochee, see Marion R. Hemperley, "Benjamin Hawkins' Trip Across Western and Northern Georgia, 1798," *Georgia Historical Quarterly* 56 (1972): 415–431, especially pp. 421–422.

17. ADAIR, pp. 435, 438–439 ("laziness," "commonly," "crops"); Bernard Romans, *A Concise Natural History of East and West Florida,* ed. Kathryn E. Holland Braund (Tuscaloosa: University of Alabama Press, 1999 [1775]), p. 145 ("greatest"). For responses to European-style agriculture, see Braund, "Guardians of Tradition," pp. 251–253.

18. For mission horses, see John H. Hann, *Apalachee: The Land Between the Rivers* (Gainesville: University Press of Florida, 1988), pp. 240–241; J. Leitch Wright Jr., *The Only Land They Knew: The Tragic Story of the American Indians in the Old South* (New York: Free Press, 1981), p. 115. For the Yamasee War, see JCIT, pp. 257, 298, 301, 309; "Law to Reclaim Slaves and Horses from Western Indians," 12/11/1717, in Alden T. Vaughan and Deborah A. Rosen, eds., *Early American Indian Documents: Treaties and Laws, 1607–1789,* vol. 16, *Carolina and Georgia Laws* (Bethesda, Md.: University Publications of America, 1998), pp. 203–204. For other methods of acquiring horses, see Chapter 3, this volume and DRIA, vol. 1, pp. 301, 323–324; CRSGA, vol. 27, pp. 7–8; SALZ, vol. 7, p. 224. For theft, see SC-CJ, 9/5/1749; DRIA, vol. 1, pp. 290, 294 (1752); BPRO-SC, vol. 30, p. 95 (1763).

19. SC-JCHA, 12/15/1736; ADAIR, p. 231; box 68, folder: "Georgia; Revolution; Indian Transport," Telamon Cuyler Collection, UGA (1776); Joseph V. Bevan Papers, folder 5A, item 31A, CGAHS (1740); DRIA, vol. 2, p. 89 (1755); "An Inventory of Goods," 6/17/1736, John Brownfield's Copy Book, 1735–1740, CGAHS, original in the Archives of the Moravian Church, Bethlehem, Pa.; "A Return for Provisions," in John Stuart to Thomas Gage, 12/31/1763, GAGE; BPRO, CO 5/65, f74 (1763); BPRO, CO 5/73, f386 (1771).

20. SC-JCHA, 12/15/1736 (1732). For 1755, see DRIA, vol. 2, p. 83; SC-CJ, 1/23/1756. For 1756, see CRSGA, vol. 28 (1), pp. 81–82; White Outerbridge to Lyttelton, 9/14/1756, LYTTEL. CRSGA, vol. 8, p. 315 (1760).

For 1728, see BPRO-SC, vol. 13, pp. 112, 116 ("several"). SC-CJ, 8/15/1739, 8/18/1739 (lecture). John Rae, John Ross, and Isaac Barksdale signed the 1749 complaint. For Ross and Rae's Okfuskee connections, see Chapter 2, this volume; for Barksdale, see DRIA, vol. 1, pp. 128, 289, 326. DRIA, vol. 1, pp. 290–291 (1752).

21. For accusations, see SC-GAZ, 7/19/1760; BPRO, CO 5/72, f85; John Stuart to Gage, 12/13/1770, GAGE; CRSGA, vol. 12, pp. 81–86; BPRO, CO 5/75, ff16–17; Tallisey King to George Galphin, 10/10/1778, LAURENS; Patrick Carr to Galphin, 11/4/1778, LAURENS. For 1771, see CRSGA, vol. 12, p. 82; CRSGA, vol. 38 (2), p. 592. For White Lieutenant promising to have the stolen horses "in his town gathered," see Timothy Bernard to [ ], 5/1/1787, Telamon Cuyler Collection, box 1, folder 11, UGA.

22. For the map, see Chapter 1, this volume. For the French, see Verner W. Crane, *The Southern Frontier, 1670–1732* (Ann Arbor: University of Michigan Press, 1956 [1929]), p. 258, n. 10; MPA-FD, vol. 4, p. 120.

23. David Corkran, *The Creek Frontier, 1540–1783* (Norman: University of Oklahoma Press, 1967), p. 200 (Atkin's troop); Atkin to Upper Creeks, 7/3–7/9/1759, p. 3, in Atkin to Lyttelton, 11/30/1759, LYTTEL (horses); Edith Mays, ed., *Amherst Papers, 1756–1763: The Southern Sector* (Bowie, Md.: Heritage Books, 1999), p. 117 ("Light," "Provisions"). For conferences in Okfuskee, see Atkin to Lyttelton, 11/30/1759, LYTTEL, pp. 14–16, 23, 29, 34, and two enclosures: Atkin & Choctaws Headman, 10/25–11/1/1759; Speech of the Wolf King, 11/16/1759. SC-JCHA, 12/15/1736 ("general," traders, headmen, "Week"). For McKay's party and its horses, see SC-JCHA, 12/15/1736; CRSGA, vol. 20, pp. 281, 422.

24. For Pettycrew, see DRIA, vol. 1, pp. 351 ("Horses"), 383–384. For Buckles, see DRIA, vol. 1, pp. 384–385, 508–514, quotations from p. 509. MC&CAMP, pp. 141–142, 159, 170, 182. For Brown, see SC-GAZ, 9/24/1763, 10/15/1763. Goff, "Path to Oakfuskee," p. 3 ("Chelucconene").

25. Thomas Stephens and Richard Everhard, "A Brief Account of the Causes that Have Retarded the Progress of the Colony of Georgia in America," *Collections of the Georgia Historical Society,* vol. 2 (Savannah, Ga., 1843), pp. 88–161, especially p. 123 (1741). At his death, Wood owned "about 200" horses; SC-GAZ, 4/28/1757. MC&CAMP, pp. 92, 163, 248, 289; E. R. R. Greene, "Queensborough Township: Scotch-Irish Emigration and the Expansion of Georgia, 1763–1776," *William and Mary Quarterly* 17 (1960): 183–191, quotation ("furnish") from p. 186. Okfuskee traders William Rae and Richard Henderson stocked saddles, bridles, and "Housings"; Mays, *Amherst Papers,* pp. 110–111.

26. For cattle, see Kathryn E. Holland Braund, *Deerskins & Duffels: The Creek Indian Trade with Anglo-America, 1685–1815* (Lincoln: University of Ne-

braska Press, 1993), pp. 75–76. CRSGA, vol. 8, p. 333 ("killed"). For complaints, see "At a Congress held at the Fort of Picolata," p. 25, in John Stuart to Gage, 1/21/1766, GAGE; CRSGA, vol. 28 (1), p. 457; Atkin to Creek Headmen, 9/28–9/29/1759, p. 11, in Atkin to Lyttelton, 11/30/1759, LYTTEL; MPA-ED, pp. 193, 196, 212; CRSGA, vol. 38 (2), pp. 494–495. For Okfuskee, see CRSGA, vol. 38 (2), pp. 570, 573.

27. "At a Congress held at Savannah," in Stuart to Gage, 11/19/1774, GAGE ("drive"); Davies, ed., "Taitt's Journal," p. 280 ("would"). For Creeks stealing horses and cattle, see CRSGA, vol. 28 (2), p. 351; Lilla M. Hawes, "The Papers of Lachlan McIntosh, 1774–1779," *Collections of the Georgia Historical Society,* vol. 12 (Savannah, Ga., 1957), pp. 59–60; John Houstoun to Richard Caswell, 9/20/1778, box 2, folder 7, Colonial Dames of America, Georgia Society, CGAHS, originals in the Historical Society of Pennsylvania, Philadelphia. For the Revolution, see Claudio Saunt, *A New Order of Things: Property, Power, and the Transformation of the Creek Indians, 1733–1816* (New York: Cambridge University Press, 1999), pp. 46–50.

28. CRSGA, vol. 21, p. 303 ("frequently"). For Gun Merchant, see SC-CJ, 9/4/1749; DRIA, vol. 1, p. 312; DRIA, vol. 2, p. 104; SC-CJ, 1/25/1756; BPRO-SC, vol. 30, p. 60.

29. Pennington, "Thomas Campbell," p. 160; ADAIR, p. 242. MPA-FD, vol. 4, p. 256 ("diminished"); Paula F. Edmiston, "Zooarchaeological Remains," in Dickens, *Archaeological Excavations,* pp. 171–187, especially p. 193 (bones); HAWKINS, p. 302 ("range"). For distances, see Romans, "A Map of West Florida," CLEM.

30. For horses, see Braund, *Deerskins & Duffels,* pp. 76–77. "Journal of Captain Tobias Fitch's Mission from Charleston to the Creeks, 1726," in Newton Mereness, ed., *Travels in the American Colonies* (New York: Macmillan Company, 1916), pp. 176–212, quotations from pp. 190, 176; BPRO-SC, vol. 13, p. 100 ("three"); SALZ, vol. 10, p. 208 ("fowls"); ADAIR, pp. 139–140 (beliefs); DRIA, vol. 2, p. 255 (scarcity). For Creeks hunting cattle when hungry, see Chapter 3, this volume.

31. DRIA, vol. 2, p. 372 (Beau); Lachlan McIntosh, Secret Information, in Atkin to Lyttelton, 11/30/1759, LYTTEL (Rae). For Sugatspoges, see ADAIR, p. 278; SC-GAZ, 5/31/1760; SC-CJ, 6/20/1760. SC-CJ, 8/24/1725 ("Corn"); DRIA, vol. 2, pp. 153–154 ("much"). For complaints, see folder 6, item 36, Bevan Papers, CGAHS; CRSGA, vol. 28 (2), p. 119; BPRO, CO 5/73, f263; Taitt, "Journal," pp. 257, 269; ADAIR, pp. 138, 242, 436.

32. Taitt, "Remarks"; ADAIR, p. 436.

33. DRIA, vol. 2, p. 154 ("chop"). For traders' cattle, see BPRO, CO 5/73, ff268–269; SC-CJ, 9/1/1726. HAWKINS, p. 302 ("fences," "range").

34. "Journal of the Superintendent's Proceedings," in John Stuart to Gage, 7/

21/1767, GAGE, p. 26; John R. Swanton, *Early History of the Creek Indians & Their Neighbors,* Bureau of American Ethnology Bulletin 73 (Gainesville: University Press of Florida, 1998 [1922]), p. 248 (Sugatspoges). For Okfuskee villages, see HAWKINS, pp. 12, 13, 303, quotation from p. 13. For White Lieutenant, see Carolyn Thomas Foreman, "The White Lieutenant and Some of His Contemporaries," *Chronicles of Oklahoma* 38 (1960): 425–440, quotation ("direction") from p. 435; Saunt, *New Order,* p. 99 (Nuyaka); Daniel McGillivray to William Panton, 6/5/1799, Greenslade Papers, P. K. Yonge Library of Florida History, University of Florida, Gainesville (twenty-six); I am endebted to Claudio Saunt for this reference. ADAIR, p. 443 ("convenient"); Smith, *Historic Indian Archaeology,* p. 79 ("dispersed"). Okfuskee's Chatahoochee villages had "good quality" land; Hemperley, "Benjamin Hawkins' Trip," p. 421.

35. Davies, ed., "Taitt's Journal," p. 264.
36. Ibid., pp. 264–265. For Epesaugee, see CRSGA, vol. 8, p. 315; HAWKINS, pp. 303–304. Van Doren, ed., *Travels,* pp. 356, 366–367.
37. Romans, "A Map of West Florida," CLEM; Taitt, "Remarks."
38. Swanton, *Early History,* p. 248 ("Punk"). Creek social theory explains why Adair, in a book published soon after Taitt visited, listed Okfuskee first among the "principal" Creek towns; Alexander McGillivray wrote in 1786 that "the okfuskee Town is among the largest & most respectable & of great influence among the rest." ADAIR, p. 274; John W. Caughy, *McGillivray of the Creeks* (Norman: University of Oklahoma Press, 1936), p. 132. DRIA, vol. 1, p. 128 (Sugatspoges); Bonar, "A Draught of the Upper Creek Nation," CLEM (1757); CRSGA, vol. 8, pp. 315 (1760), 523 (1761); Christian F. Feest, "Creek Towns in 1725," *Ethnologische Zeitschrift Zurich* 1 (1974): 161–175, especially pp. 162–163, 171.
39. For the censuses, see MPA-ED, pp. 94–97; "A List of the Towns & Number of Gun Men in the Creek Nation," in Francis Ogilvie to Gage, 7/8/1764, GAGE; HAWKINS, p. 302 (1799). For the flood, see Taitt, "Remarks"; Davies, "Taitt's Journal," p. 253. For Okfuskee's move, see Davies, ed., "Taitt's Journal," p. 263; GA-GAZ, 5/27/1774.
40. HAWKINS, p. 302 (1799). For town to settlement, see Gerald M. Sider, *Lumbee Indian Histories: Race and Ethnicity in the Southeastern United States* (New York: Cambridge University Press, 1993), p. 241.
41. Davies, ed., "Taitt's Journal," p. 264; Mereness, ed., "Fitch's Journal," p. 176.
42. For 75 to 85 percent and an overview of colonial agriculture, see Jon Butler, *Becoming America: The Revolution before 1776* (Cambridge, Mass.: Harvard University Press, 2000), pp. 7 (Crevecoeur), 51–65. Allan Kulikoff's work provides a sustained argument for the centrality of agriculture

in colonial America; see most recently *From British Peasants to Colonial American Farmers* (Chapel Hill: University of North Carolina Press, 2000).

43. Robert A. Gross, *The Minutemen and Their World* (New York: Hill and Wang, 1976), p. 88 ("scarcity"); Gloria L. Main and Jackson T. Main, "The Red Queen in New England?" *William and Mary Quarterly* 56 (1998): 121–147, quotation ("flourishing") from p. 121; Barry Levy, *Quakers and the American Family: British Settlement in the Delaware Valley* (New York: Oxford University Press, 1988), pp. 134–137, 144, 179–182, 236–248; Allan Kulikoff, *Tobacco and Slaves: The Development of Southern Cultures in the Chesapeake, 1680–1800* (Chapel Hill: University of North Carolina Press, 1986), chap. 2.

44. For prices and regulation, see Kulikoff, *Tobacco and Slaves,* pp. 79–85, quotation from p. 79, chap. 3. For diversification, see Lorena S. Walsh, "Summing the Parts: Implications for Estimating Chesapeake Output and Input Subregionally," *William and Mary Quarterly* 56 (1999): 53–94. For self-perception, see T. H. Breen, *Tobacco Culture: The Mentality of the Great Tidewater Planters on the Eve of Rebellion* (Princeton, N.J.: Princeton University Press, 1985), pp. 178–182, 185–186, 204–206, quotation from p. 182. Russell R. Menard, "Slavery, Economic Growth, and Revolutionary Ideology in the South Carolina Lowcountry," in Ronald Hoffman, John J. McCusker, Russell R. Menard, and Peter J. Albert, eds., *The Economy of Early America: The Revolutionary Period, 1763–1790* (Charlottesville: University Press of Virginia, 1988), pp. 244–274, especially pp. 248 ("difficult"), 253–255 (slaves, indigo); Joyce E. Chaplin, *An Anxious Pursuit: Agricultural Innovation and Modernity in the Lower South, 1730–1815* (Chapel Hill: University of North Carolina Press, 1993), p. 3 ("redefined"), chap. 6 (indigo, cotton), chap. 7 (tidal).

45. Ira Berlin, *Many Thousands Gone: The First Two Centuries of Slavery in North America* (Cambridge, Mass.: Harvard University Press, 1998); Philip D. Morgan, *Slave Counterpoint: Black Culture in the Eighteenth-Century Chesapeake & Lowcountry* (Chapel Hill: University of North Carolina Press, 1998); Peter H. Wood, *Black Majority: Negroes in Colonial South Carolina from 1670 through the Stono Rebellion* (New York: W. W. Norton, 1974); Robert Olwell, *Masters, Subjects, and Slaves: The Culture of Power in the South Carolina Low Country, 1740–1790* (Ithaca, N.Y.: Cornell University Press, 1998). For slavery's spread, see Chaplin, *An Anxious Pursuit,* chaps. 5, 6, 8; Rachel N. Klein, *Unification of a Slave State: The Rise of the Planter Class in the South Carolina Backcountry, 1760–1808* (Chapel Hill: University of North Carolina Press, 1990); Jon F. Sensbach, *A Separate Canaan: The Making of an Afro-Moravian World in North Carolina, 1763–1840* (Chapel Hill: University of North Carolina Press, 1998).

46. For a comparison of unfree labor in the North and South, see Kulikoff, *From British Peasants to Colonial American Farmers,* pp. 248–250. For changes in New England's labor system, see Daniel Vickers, *Farmers and Fishermen: Two Centuries of Work in Essex County, Massachusetts, 1630–1850* (Chapel Hill: University of North Carolina Press, 1994), chap. 5, quotation from p. 227. Levy, *Quakers and the American Family,* pp. 138–140.

47. William G. McLoughlin, *Cherokee Renascence in the New Republic* (Princeton, N.J.: Princeton University Press, 1986), p. 98 ("game"); Martin, *Sacred Revolt,* chap. 4 ("gaze").

48. For Euro-American views, see Daniel H. Usner Jr., "Iroquois Livelihood and Jeffersonian Agrarianism: Reading behind the Models and Metaphors," in Frederick E. Hoxie, Ronald Hoffman, and Peter J. Albert, eds., *Native Americans and the Early Republic* (Charlottesville: University Press of Virginia, 1999), pp. 200–225, quotation from p. 206; Daniel K. Richter, " 'Believing That Many of the Red People Suffer Much for the Want of Food': Hunting, Agriculture, and a Quaker Construction of Indianness in the Early Republic," *Journal of the Early Republic* 19 (1999): 601–628.

5. Newcomers in the "Old White Town"

1. SC-GAZ, 5/31/1760 (Price), 6/21/1760; CRSGA, vol. 8, pp. 314–315 (French); ADAIR, pp. 278–279 (Rae, Ross, "provisions").

2. ADAIR, p. 279 (Price); CRSGA, vol. 8, p. 315 (French).

3. ADAIR, p. 279; SC-GAZ, 7/19/1760 (Will's Friend).

4. SC-JCHA, 12/15/1736 (Edwards); CRSGA, vol. 8, pp. 333, 420 ("Houses"), 544 ("protect"); "A Talk Given at the King's Fort," in John Stuart to Gage, 4/11/1764, GAGE ("White").

5. Jerome Courtonne, "List of the Headmen of the Creeks," in Courtonne to Lyttelton, 10/17/1758, LYTTEL; Stuart to James Pampellonne, 7/16/1764, in Stuart to Gage, 7/19/1764, GAGE.

6. BPRO-SC, vol. 13, pp. 72–73 (1728); CRSGA, vol. 8, p. 420 (1760); "A Talk from the Handsome Fellow," 6/18/1777, LAURENS.

7. "A Talk from the Handsome Fellow," 6/18/1777, LAURENS; "A Treaty of Peace and Commerce," 11/6/1777, LAURENS; Edmond Atkin to William Lyttelton, 11/30/1759, p. 3, LYTTEL.

8. SC-GAZ, 7/16/1760 ("distinguished"). For 1763, see MC&CAMP, p. 121; CRSGA, vol. 8, p. 777; CRSGA, vol. 9, pp. 12–17; CRSGA, vol. 28 (1), p. 376. CRSGA, vol. 9, p. 14 ("plentiful"). For the burial, see Harold A. Huscher, *Archaeological Investigations in the West Point Dam Area: A Preliminary Report* (Athens: Laboratory of Anthropology, University of Georgia,

1972), pp. 33, 94–95, 99, quotations from pp. 94, 99. SC-GAZ, 7/26/1760 ("annual").

9. For trips, see SC-CJ, 8/15–8/18/1739, 6/21/1744; SC-JCHA, 2/25/1741, 2/24/1742. SC-JCHA, 3/18/1741 ("Commissions"). For presents, see BPRO-SC, vol. 20, pp. 282–283; SC-JCHA, 4/30/1740, 1/19/1742, 2/24/1742, 1/13/1744; SC-CJ, 6/27/1744. For Tusk Keenie, see SC-JCHA, 2/16/1742, 2/24/1742. MC&CAMP, p. 220 (credit). The Raes employed White Lieutenant and other Native factors. BPRO, CO 5/75, ff190, 216; Roderick McIntosh to John Stuart, 5/29/1768, in Stuart to Gage, 7/2/1768, GAGE.

10. Alexander Wood traded in Okfuskee from the 1720s through the mid-1740s. The other Creek trader named Wood—William Wood—appears only in 1726; he too traded in Okfuskee. CRSGA, vol. 12, pp. 337–339 (Dougald); "Journal of Captain Tobias Fitch's Mission from Charleston to the Creeks, 1726," in Newton Mereness, ed., *Travels in the American Colonies* (New York: Macmillan Company, 1916), pp. 176–212, especially pp. 195, 197 (William).

11. John Cleland, 12/23/1759, in Atkin to Lyttelton, 1/9/1760, LYTTEL (1733); SC-CJ, 6/27/1744 (employee); DRIA, vol. 1, pp. 289, 326, 336 (1740s–1750s); Atkin and Billy Germany, Conference, 8/20/1759, in Atkin to Lyttelton, 11/30/1759, LYTTEL; SC-CJ, 2/26/1761 (Alexander Germany).

12. In 1790, White Lieutenant was "about fifty years of age" and "the great *War Mico* of the whole district of the Oakfuskies." Billy Germany, a war leader in 1759, would have been 53 in 1790. The names Billy Germany and the White Lieutenant do not overlap in time, the former last appearing in 1759 and the latter first appearing in 1765. Bartram noted that James Germany married a Creek, who would not send their "several children" to school in the colonies. Caleb Swan, "Position and State of Manners and Arts in the Creek, or Muscogee Nation in 1791," in Henry R. Schoolcraft, ed., *Information Respecting the History, Condition, and Prospects of the Indian Tribes of the United States,* vol. 5 (Philadelphia: Lippincott, 1855), pp. 251–283, quotations ("breed," "fifty," "great") from p. 255. For 1765, see CRSGA, vol. 28 (2), p. 114; MPA-ED, p. 210. Mark Van Doren, ed., *The Travels of William Bartram* (Dover, Del.: Dover Publications, 1928), pp. 356–357.

13. BPRO, CO 5/78, f198 (nephew); "A Treaty of Peace and Commerce," LAURENS; DRIA, vol. 2, p. 10 (father).

14. SC-JCHA, 7/3/1744; ADAIR, p. 444. For food as a means and object of exchange, see Daniel H. Usner Jr., *Indians, Settlers, & Slaves in a Frontier*

Exchange Economy: The Lower Mississippi Valley Before 1783 (Chapel Hill: University of North Carolina Press, 1992), pp. 191–218, especially p. 192.

15. Mereness, ed., "Fitch's Journal," p. 176; ADAIR, pp. 462–463 ("slavish"). For Thompson, see CRSGA, vol. 8, pp. 553–556, quotation ("victuals) from p. 553; SC-GAZ, 6/20/1761, 7/11/1761; SC-CJ, 6/16/1761.

16. SC-CJ, 9/1/1726 ("Summer"); CRSGA, vol. 5, p. 242 ("find"). For Oglethorpe, see box 19, folder 53, Keith Read Collection, UGA, especially 12/27/1739; "Letters from General Oglethorpe to the Trustees of the Colony and Others, from October 1735 to August 1744," *Collections of the Georgia Historical Society*, vol. 3 (Savannah, Ga., 1873), pp. 1–156, especially p. 91. Edith Mays, ed., *Amherst Papers, 1756–1763: The Southern Sector* (Bowie, Md.: Heritage Books, 1999), pp. 116–117 (Atkin); DRIA, vol. 2, p. 296 ("scarce"); BPRO, CO 5/73, f178 ("Traffick"); "Journal of the Superintendent's Proceedings," in Stuart to Gage, 7/21/1767, GAGE; DRIA, vol. 1, p. 509 (Buckles).

17. ADAIR, pp. 447, 446, 115.

18. For contrasting views on female control of agricultural produce, see Richard Sattler, "Women's Status Among the Muskogee and Cherokee," in Laura F. Klein and Lillian A. Ackerman, eds., *Women and Power in Native North America* (Norman: University of Oklahoma Press, 1995), pp. 214–229; Theda Perdue, "Native Women in the Early Republic: Old World Perceptions, New World Realities," in Frederick E. Hoxie, Ronald Hoffman, and Peter J. Albert, eds., *Native Americans and the Early Republic* (Charlottesville: University Press of Virginia, 1999), pp. 85–122. Creek women were strongly enough identified with cooking that, during the Busk, men referred to women as "food preparer"; Charles Hudson, *The Southeastern Indians* (Knoxville: University of Tennessee Press, 1976), pp. 368–369. CRSGA, vol. 28 (2), pp. 42 ("House"), 368 ("obliged"); BPRO, CO 5/73, f34 ("formerly"); BPRO, CO 5/80, f37 ("corn"); CRSGA, vol. 28 (2), p. 42.

19. DRIA, vol. 2, p. 372 ("Blacksmith"); Daniel Pepper, "Some Remarks on the Creek Nation," 1756, LYTTEL. For smiths, see DRIA, vol. 2, p. 372; Wilbur R. Jacobs, ed., *The Appalachian Indian Frontier: The Edmond Atkin Report and Plan of 1755* (Lincoln: University of Nebraska Press, 1954), pp. 9–10; CRSGA, vol. 7, p. 662.

20. BPRO-SC, vol. 10, p. 182 (1723); BPRO-SC, vol. 28, pp. 332–333 (1760); MPA-FD, vol. 3, p. 780; Gregory A. Waselkov, Brian M. Wood, and Joseph M. Herbert, *Colonization and Conquest: The 1980 Archaeological Excavations at Fort Toulouse and Fort Jackson, Alabama*, Auburn University Archaeological Monograph 4 (Montgomery, Ala., 1982), chap. 6.

21. A 1753 Creek party that included Okfuskees requested beads "for their

Women and Children"; DRIA, vol. 1, p. 409. For packhorsemen, see MC&CAMP. Lessely: pp. 209, 218, 242, 251, 278, 287; Bell: pp. 153, 174, 180, 240, 289; Burroughs: pp. 114, 197, 198; Dalton: pp. 92, 115, 150; Owens: pp. 141, 178, 182, 251, 288, 289; Audrey: pp. 142, 149, 152, 160; Chavers: pp. 142, 152, 158; Fyffe: p. 141.

22. BPRO-SC, vol. 20, p. 258 (1740); DRIA, vol. 2, p. 410 ("Necessaries"). For 1751, see Bevan Papers, folder 5A, item 25, CGAHS; CRSGA, vol. 26, p. 169.

23. BPRO, CO 5/68, f143.

24. For Okfuskee traders settling outside of town, see Chapter 4, this volume. Deposition of Thomas Perriman, 11/23/1759, in Atkin to Lyttelton, 1/9/1760, LYTTEL. ADAIR, p. 443 ("especially"); Kathryn E. Holland Braund, *Deerskins & Duffels: Creek Indian Trade with Anglo-America, 1685–1815* (Lincoln: University of Nebraska Press, 1993), p. 192 (Stuart). The Rae family, Isaac Barksdale, James Germany, Alexander Wood, and John Ross owned slaves. CRSGA, vol. 10, pp. 437, 827 (Raes). *Abstracts of Colonial Wills of the State of Georgia, 1733–1777,* index by Willard E. Wright (Spartanburg, S.C.: Reprint Company, 1981 [1962]), p. 10 (Barksdale). For Germany, see DRIA, vol. 2, p. 357; CRSGA, vol. 7, p. 432. For Wood, see SC-GAZ, 4/28/1757; Eirlys Mair Barker, " 'Much Blood and Treasure': South Carolina's Indian Traders, 1670–1755" (Ph.D. diss., College of William and Mary, 1993), pp. 181–182. For Ross, see note 1 above.

25. Atkin to James Germany, 9/18/1759, in Atkin to Lyttelton, 1/9/1760, LYTTEL; CRSGA, vol. 8, p. 420 (1760); BPRO, CO 5/73, ff33–34 (1771); Davies, ed., "Taitt's Journal," p. 266 (1772); Swan, "Position and State of Manners," p. 282 (1790). See also Claudio Saunt, *A New Order of Things: Property, Power, and the Transformation of the Creek Indians, 1733–1816* (New York: Cambridge University Press, 1999), pp. 150–151, 153–161.

26. Marshall Sahlins, "Cosmologies of Capitalism: The Trans-Pacific Sector of 'The World System,' " *Proceedings of the British Academy* 74 (1988): 1–51, quotation from p. 7. Braund, *Deerskins & Duffels,* pp. 121–126. For the modified items in an Okfuskee village, see Huscher, *Archaeological Investigations,* pp. 95, 96, 103.

27. Peter C. Mancall, *Deadly Medicine: Indians and Alcohol in Early America* (Ithaca, N.Y.: Cornell University Press, 1995); ADAIR, p. 124.

28. Braund, *Deerskins & Duffels,* pp. 88–89, 97–98; PA-GAZ, 12/14/1738.

29. Mereness, ed., "Fitch's Journal," pp. 180, 191; John Brownfield to Rowland Pytt and Thomas Tuckwell, 1/16/1739, Copy Book, CGAHS.

30. SC-GAZ, 9/8/1759; MC&CAMP, pp. 135, 145–146, 175, 212, 241.

31. For processing, see Braund, *Deerskins & Duffels.* For prices, see MC&CAMP. John Brownfield to Thomas Tuckwell, 10/9/1739, Copy

Book, CGAHS ("surprizing"). Creeks and traders occasionally disagreed about what constituted a dressed skin; for a conflict involving an Okfuskee-led party, see SC-CJ, 9/5/1749. For raw skins, see BPRO-SC, vol. 13, p. 146; Jacobs, ed., *Atkin Report,* pp. 35–36; DRIA, vol. 2, pp. 42, 105; SC-CJ, 10/8/1726 ("Doggs"). CRSGA, vol. 26, pp. 447–448 (1752).

32. MC&CAMP; Roderick McIntosh to John Stuart, 5/29/1768, in Stuart to Gage, 7/2/1768, GAGE; CRSGA, vol. 28 (2), p. 375 (1771); Andrew Mc-Lean Ledger, collection #1561, CGAHS (mid-1770s).

33. These raw skins arrived relatively late for a spring shipment; the delay was caused both by the Chattahoochee stopover and by backcountry problems that hampered trade relations. "A Talk Given at the King's Fort in Augusta," in Stuart to Gage, 4/11/1764, GAGE; David H. Corkran, *The Creek Frontier* (Norman: University of Oklahoma Press, 1967), pp. 241–243.

34. The December 1762 Okfuskee shipment—553 pounds of dressed skins and 508 pounds of raw skins—does not fit the pattern. Shipments with a significant percentage of both raw and dressed skins appear in the early winter, possibly reflecting a transitional period in the Creeks' seasonal cycle. For the Okfuskee shipments mentioned here, see MC&CAMP, pp. 111, 117, 135, 145, 175, 212, 241, 278. The percentages of raw and dressed skins do not add up to 100 because I include the December 1762 shipment in Macartan & Campbell's totals but not in the seasonal totals.

35. Ibid., pp. 202, 215, 247, 274, 333; George Galphin Account Books, 1767–1772, CGAHS; McLean Ledger, CGAHS.

36. For discussions of the rise of a raw-skin trade that emphasize European demands, see Braund, *Deerskins & Duffels,* pp. 68–69, 225, n. 53; Charles M. Hudson Jr., "Why the Southeastern Indians Slaughtered Deer," in Shepard Krech III, ed., *Indians, Animals, and the Fur Trade: A Critique of "Keepers of the Game"* (Athens: University of Georgia Press, 1981), pp. 155–176.

37. Raw skins accounted for 28.7 percent of the skins shipped from Macartan & Campbell's Okfuskee store, but some dressed skins may have been processed only after Okfuskees traded them; moreover, Okfuskees traded raw skins in the backcountry.

38. Braund, *Deerskins & Duffels,* p. 69, argues that Creek women favored the raw skin trade; Saunt, *New Order,* p. 144, believes it was driven by young Creek men. See also "A Talk from the Lower Creeks," 8/19/1772, in John Stuart to Thomas Gage, 11/24/1772, GAGE. South Carolina and American *General Gazette,* 6/12/1767; BPRO, CO 5/71, ff9, 13 (1769).

39. CRSGA, vol. 28 (2), p. 374 ("principal"); SC-GAZ, 3/7/1761 ("slave"), 3/14/1761. For Dalton as an employee, see MC&CAMP, pp. 92, 141–142, 249, 288, 289, 332. For Thompson, see note 15 above. For Highrider, see

DRIA, vol. 1, pp. 38–40, 383, 510; Atkin to Chicasaws Indian Traders, 9/20/1759, in Atkin to Lyttelton, 11/30/1759, LYTTEL; SC-GAZ, 3/14/1761; BPRO-SC, vol. 30, p. 73; John McIntosh to John Stuart, 8/30/1767, in Stuart to Gage, 11/27/1767, GAGE. For selling out, see MC&CAMP, pp. 289, 312, 318. MPA-ED, p. 516 (1766).

40. CRSGA, vol. 8, pp. 314–315, 708 (1760); Davies, ed., "Taitt's Journal," p. 264 (1772); SC-CJ, 2/26/1761. For illegal stores, see three enclosures in Stuart to Gage, 7/2/1768, GAGE: "Deposition of William Frazier, Indian Trader," 3/16/1768; Roderick McIntosh to Stuart, 4/18/1768 and 5/29/1768. For Rae, see McIntosh to Stuart, 5/29/1768, in Stuart to Gage, 7/2/1768, GAGE; BPRO, CO 5/73, f261; BPRO, CO 5/75, ff17–18, 190, 216; CRSGA, vol. 12, p. 407; Taitt to Stuart, 8/29/1774, GAGE.

41. For Myers, see "Journal of the Superintendent's Proceedings," in John Stuart to Gage, 7/21/1767, pp. 21, 26, GAGE; Roderick McIntosh to John Stuart, 5/29/1768, in Stuart to Gage, 7/2/1768, GAGE; GA-GAZ, 5/11/1774, 5/25/1774; BPRO, CO 5/75, ff17–18. For Oates, see BPRO, CO 5/73, ff31–32; 5/75, ff17–18; 5/78, ff158–159. For small-scale trading, see MC&CAMP, pp. 275, 278.

42. SC-GAZ, 4/25/1761; BPRO, CO 5/75, f216 (1774); "A Talk from the Half Breed to George Galphin," 6/9/1778, LAURENS ("Cargo"); HAWKINS, pp. 16–17 (brother).

43. For long-term prices, see Braund, *Deerskins & Duffels,* p. 127. For the 1760s and early 1770s, see MPA-ED, p. 517; James Wright to Gage, 7/18/1766, GAGE; Roderick McIntosh to John Stuart, 2/18/1768, in Stuart to Gage, 3/30/1768; CRSGA, vol. 28 (2), pp. 157, 353; BPRO, CO 5/67, f53; 5/68, ff140–142; 5/71, ff12–13; 5/73, ff103, 261; 5/75, ff124–125; ADAIR, pp. 395, 444.

44. "Journal of the Superintendent's Proceedings," in Stuart to Gage, 7/21/1767, pp. 25–26, GAGE; BPRO, CO 5/68, f163 ("detached"); 5/71, ff12–13 ("Inconveniences"); 5/75, ff17 ("Fault"), 124–125 ("formerly").

45. Davies, ed., "Taitt's Journal," 251–272; BPRO, CO 5/73, ff259–264, 268–269.

46. "A Treaty of Peace and Commerce," 11/7/1777, LAURENS. For the manner in which "narrative shapes communal consciousness" and allows Creeks to "reexperience history," see Craig S. Womack, *Red on Red: Native American Literary Separatism* (Minneapolis: University of Minnesota Press, 1999), p. 26.

47. Peter C. Mancall and Thomas Weiss, "Was Economic Growth Likely in Colonial British North America?" *The Journal of Economic History* 59 (1999): 17–40, quotations from pp. 21, 19.

48. John E. Crowley, *The Invention of Comfort: Sensibilities & Design in Early*

Modern Britain & Early America (Baltimore, Md.: Johns Hopkins University Press, 2001); Richard L. Bushman, *The Refinement of America: Persons, Houses, Cities* (New York: Vintage Books, 1992); Cary Carson, Ronald Hoffman, and Peter J. Albert, eds., *Of Consuming Interests: The Style of Life in the Eighteenth Century* (Charlottesville: University Press of Virginia, 1994).

49. Daniel Vickers, "Competency and Competition: Economic Culture in Early America," *William and Mary Quarterly* 47 (1990): 3–29, quotation from p. 7 ("attractive"); Carole Shammas, *The Pre-industrial Consumer in England and America* (Oxford, U.K.: Clarendon Press, 1990), p. 68 (30.5 percent). James Axtell argues that Indians "were no more—or less—imprisoned by the capitalist world-system than were their European partners or rivals"; *The Indians' New South: Cultural Change in the Colonial Southeast* (Baton Rouge: Louisiana State University Press, 1997), p. 71.

50. For competency as "propertied independence," see Vickers, "Competency and Competition," p. 7. For post-1740 fears, see T. H. Breen, " 'Baubles of Britain': The American and Consumer Revolutions of the Eighteenth-Century," in Carson et al., eds., *Of Consuming Interests*, pp. 444–482, especially pp. 461–462. For leveling and entrepreneurship, see Thomas N. Ingersoll, " 'Riches and Honour Were Rejected By Them As Loathsome Vomit': The Fear of Leveling in New England," in Carla G. Pestana and Sharon V. Salinger, eds., *Inequality in Early America* (Hanover, N.H.: University Press of New England, 1999), pp. 46–66; T. H. Breen and Timothy Hall, "Structuring Provincial Imagination: The Rhetoric and Experience of Social Change in Eighteenth-Century New England," *American Historical Review* 103 (1999): 1411–1438, especially pp. 1420–1423; Margaret E. Newell, *From Dependency to Independence: Economic Revolutions in Colonial New England* (Ithaca, N.Y.: Cornell University Press, 1998), especially part 2. For critiques of gentility, see Bushman, *The Refinement of America*, chap. 6; Kevin M. Sweeney, "High-Style Vernacular: Lifestyles of the Colonial Elite," in Carson et al., eds., *Of Consuming Interests*, pp. 1–58.

51. Breen and Hall, "Structuring Provincial Imagination," p. 1432 ("stories"); Joyce C. Chaplin, *An Anxious Pursuit: Agricultural Innovation and Modernity in the Lower South, 1730–1815* (Chapel Hill: University of North Carolina Press, 1993).

52. This paragraph relies heavily on Stephen Innes, *Creating the Commonwealth: The Economic Culture of Puritan New England* (New York: W. W. Norton, 1995), pp. 7, 25–28, 101–106, 308–310. See also Christine Leigh Heyrman, *Commerce and Culture: The Maritime Communities of Colonial Massachusetts, 1690–1750* (New York: W. W. Norton, 1984); Mark A. Peterson, *The Price of Redemption: The Spiritual Economy of Puritan New England* (Stanford, Calif.: Stanford University Press, 1997).

53. Michael Merrill, "Putting 'Capitalism' in Its Place: A Review of Recent Literature," *William and Mary Quarterly* 52 (1995): 315–326, quotation from p. 322.

54. John B. Brewer, *The Sinews of Empire: War, Money, and the English State, 1688–1783* (New York: Knopf, 1989), pp. xvii ("Borrowing"), 187 ("confidence"); Toby L. Ditz, "Secret Selves, Credible Persons: The Problematics of Trust and Public Display in the Writing of Eighteenth-Century Philadelphia Merchants," in Robert Blair St. George, ed., *Possible Pasts: Becoming Colonial in Early America* (Ithaca, N.Y.: Cornell University Press, 2000), pp. 219–242, quotation from p. 228. For nonliterate, see Ian K. Steele, *The English Atlantic, 1675–1740: An Exploration of Communication and Community* (New York: Oxford University Press, 1986), p. 251.

6. Big Women and Mad Men

1. HAWKINS, p. 322 (eight days). For the Busk described here, see ADAIR, pp. 112–114. See also John R. Swanton, "Religious Beliefs and Medical Practices of the Creek Indians," *Forty-Second Annual Report of the Bureau of American Ethnology, 1924–1925* (Washington, D.C.: U.S. Government Printing Office, 1928), pp. 473–672, especially pp. 546–614.

2. ADAIR, p. 113 ("dangerous"); Amelia Rector Bell, "Separate People: Speaking of Creek Men and Women," *American Anthropologist* 92 (1990): 332–345, quotations from pp. 333, 341. My conclusions regarding the Busk's community-centered and gendered nature have been influenced by Joel W. Martin, *Sacred Revolt: The Muskogees' Struggle for a New World* (Boston: Beacon Press, 1991), pp. 38–41.

3. For domestic space, see Vernon J. Knight Jr., *Tukabatchee: Archaeological Investigations at an Historic Creek Town, Elmore County, Alabama, 1984,* Report of Investigations 45 (Tuscaloosa: Office of Archaeological Research, Alabama State Museum of Natural History, 1985), pp. 118–119. For the dance, see Mark Van Doren, ed., *Travels of William Bartram* (Dover, Del.: Dover Publications, 1928), p. 396. For the square, see Van Doren, ed., *Travels,* pp. 357, 361; ADAIR, pp. 49, 127. For work-parties, see Chapter 4, this volume.

4. Women had their own age- and achievement-graded status divisions, but we know little about them. Our inability to discuss the variety in eighteenth-century Creek women's experiences suggests how tentative our conclusions about Creek society must be.

5. E. Merton Coulter, ed., *The Journal of Peter Gordon, 1732–1735,* Wormsloe Foundation Publications 6 (Athens: University of Georgia Press, 1963), p. 36 ("measure"). Fred Gearing notes that for Cherokees, "the phrase young man comes . . . to mean not-yet-man, and the roles of young men

come to be conduct expected of the morally immature"; *Priests and War-riors: Social Structures for Cherokee Politics in the 18th Century,* American Anthropological Association, Memoir 93, vol. 64 (1962), p. 46. For Creeks, see George E. Lankford, "Red and White: Some Reflections on Southeastern Symbolism," *Southern Folklore* 50 (1993): 53–80, especially pp. 54–56. SC-GAZ, 7/11/1760 ("former"); DRIA, vol. 1, pp. 407 ("Home"), 379 ("Blood"), 381 ("Peace").

6. CRSGA, vol. 28 (2), p. 42 ("Passion"); DRIA, vol. 1, p. 318 ("Nothing"); "Journal of the Superintendent's Proceedings," p. 29 ("admonish"), in John Stuart to Gage, 7/21/1767, GAGE; BPRO, CO 5/68, f90 ("Guiders").

7. For Creek efforts "to maintain rather than dissolve" tensions "that leant strength to their peoples," see Claudio Saunt, *A New Order of Things: Property, Power, and the Transformation of the Creek Indians, 1733–1816* (New York: Cambridge University Press, 1999), pp. 22–25, quotations from p. 24.

8. Bell, "Separate Peoples," p. 337.

9. BPRO-SC, vol. 13, p. 73 ("House"); "Journal of Captain Tobias Fitch's Mission from Charleston to the Creeks, 1726," in Newton Mereness, ed., *Travels in the American Colonies* (New York: Macmillan Company, 1916), pp. 175–212, quotation ("Brought") from p. 176; "David Taitt's Journal to and through the Upper Creek Nation," in K. G. Davies, *Documents of the American Revolution, 1770–1783,* vol. 5 (Dublin: Irish University Press, 1974), pp. 251–272, quotation ("breakfast") from p. 264.

10. Alexander Moore, ed., *Nairne's Muskhogean Journal: The 1708 Expedition to the Mississippi River* (Jackson: University of Mississippi Press, 1988), pp. 44–45, 60–61; Mark F. Boyd, ed., "Documents Describing the Second and Third Expeditions of Lieutenant Diego Pena to Apalachee and Apalachicolo in 1717 and 1718," *Florida Historical Quarterly* 31 (1952): 109–138, especially p. 118; Jean-Bernard Bossu, *Travels in the Interior of North America, 1751–1762,* ed. Seymour Feiler (Norman: University of Oklahoma Press, 1962), p. 131.

11. For the origin story, see John R. Swanton, "Social Organization and Social Usages of the Indians of the Creek Confederacy," *Forty-Second Annual Report of the Bureau of American Ethnology* (Washington, D.C.: U.S. Government Printing Office, 1928), pp. 25–472, especially pp. 34–38, quotation from p. 36; "Atkin and Billy Germany Conference," 8/20/1759, in Atkin to Lyttelton, 11/30/1759, LYTTEL ("Linguists").

12. Van Doren, ed., *Travels,* p. 170; CRSGA, vol. 8, pp. 314–315 ("Woman," "Friend"); SC-GAZ, 5/31/1760 ("fly"); ADAIR, p. 279 ("wife"). Tom, an African-American slave owned by a Sugatspoges trader, had "a wife" in that Okfuskee village. He was killed during the May 1760 attack; one

report blamed the violence on a beating Tom administered to a headman's son who "had a fancy" for his wife. SC-GAZ, 6/21/1760. SC-GAZ, 3/7/1761; Patrick Carr to [George Galphin?], 6/10/1778, LAURENS ("woman"); DRIA, vol. 2, pp. 60–61, quotation ("friend") from p. 60.

13. ADAIR, p. 279; Van Doren, ed., *Travels,* p. 357 ("amiable"). For Germany, see Chapter 5, this volume; SC-GAZ, 7/12/1760. For Germany's partners, see Edmond Atkin to Germany, 11/19/1759, in Atkin to William Lyttleton, 11/30/1759, LYTTEL; Atkin to John Cleland, 12/23/1759, in Atkin to Lyttelton, 1/9/1760, LYTTEL; Chapter 2, this volume.

14. For the packhorsemen, see Chapter 5, this volume. For trade goods and personal display, see Kristian Hvidt, ed., *Von Reck's Voyage: Drawings and Journal of Philip Georg Freidrich von Reck* (Savannah, Ga.: Beehive Press, 1980), p. 46; ADAIR, p. 179; Van Doren, ed., *Travels,* pp. 110–111, 393–395.

15. Martin, *Sacred Revolt,* pp. 76–79.

16. DRIA, vol. 1, p. 306 (1752); DRIA, vol. 2, p. 355 ("Sett").

17. CRSGA, vol. 28 (2), p. 42.

18. DRIA, vol. 1, pp. 397–398, 406–407 (speeches), 409 ("wives"), 410 ("Trifles"); SC-JCHA, 4/18/1753 ("wives").

19. Van Doren, ed., *Travels,* pp. 214–215.

20. Davies, ed., "Taitt's Journal," pp. 255, 258–259; MPA-ED, pp. 201–202 ("Steal," Effect"), 208 ("articles").

21. ADAIR, pp. 444–445; MC&CAMP, pp. 113, 150, 152, 153, 157, 160; GA-GAZ, 5/25/1774.

22. Gregory Waselkov, "Introduction: Recent Archaeological and Historical Research," in Daniel H. Thomas, *Fort Toulouse: The French Outpost at the Alabamas on the Coosa* (Tuscaloosa: University of Alabama Press, 1989 [1960]), pp. vii–xlii, especially p. xxvii.

23. CRSGA, vol. 38 (1-B), p. 347 (1774). For Handsome Fellow, see BPRO, CO 5/77, f44. CRSGA, vol. 8, p. 311 (1760); BPRO, CO 5/67, f237 (1766); BPRO, CO 5/68, f91; MPA-ED, pp. 204–205 (Mortar).

24. BPRO, CO 5/78, f158 (1777). For Bartram and Adair, see Chapter 4, this volume. For foodstuffs being traded for gunpowder, see Wilbur R. Jacobs, ed., *The Appalachian Indian Frontier: The Edmund Atkin Report and Plan of 1755* (Lincoln: University of Nebraska Press, 1967), pp. 63–64; "Conferences with Tookybahtchy Mico," 7/24–7/25/1759, p. 11, in Atkin to Lyttelton, 11/30/1759, LYTTEL. HAWKINS, p. 13 (White Lieutenant).

25. Elizabeth Mancke quoted in Laurel Thatcher Ulrich, "Wheels, Looms, and the Gender Division of Labor in Eighteenth-Century New England," *William and Mary Quarterly* 55 (1998): 3–38, especially pp. 14–15. MC&CAMP, pp. 113, 152 (Audry), 150 (Dalton). For women making

clothes, see ADAIR, p. 454; Van Doren, ed., *Travels,* p. 401. MPA-FD, vol. 5, pp. 228, 231 (1759); BPRO, CO 5/82, ff434 ("Gunmen"), 445 ("150 Indians"). For descriptions of Creek craft skills that emphasize women's dominant role but that also mention men's contributions, see Van Doren, ed., *Travels,* p. 401; ADAIR, pp. 454–457.

26. Charles Hudson, *The Southeastern Indians* (Knoxville: University of Tennessee Press, 1976), pp. 197–199; Swanton, "Social Organization," pp. 368–376.

27. These paragraphs rely on DRIA, vol. 1, pp. 388–414. For Handsome Fellow, see pp. 397–398, 406; for Malatchi, see pp. 403–406, 408; for the Okfuskee Captain, see pp. 407, 413; for the warriors' response, see pp. 407–408; for Glen, see p. 408; for gifts, see p. 409; for apologies, see pp. 411–413.

28. SC-CJ, 10/8/1726; DRIA, vol. 1, p. 397 (1753); Atkin & Upper Creeks, Conferences, 7/24–7/25/1759, p. 5, in Atkin to Lyttelton, 11/30/1759, LYTTEL.

29. British Records Collection, SL 3331, f413, North Carolina Division of Archives and History, Raleigh (1705); SC-JCHA, 12/15/1736 (1732); CRSGA, vol. 26, pp. 391–395 (1751); CRSGA, vol. 20, pp. 317–318 (1735); Joseph V. Bevan Papers, folder 6, item 33, CGAHS (1739).

30. For the rotunda, see Van Doren, ed., *Travels,* pp. 358–359; Gregory A. Waselkov and Kathryn E. Holland Braund, eds., *William Bartram on the Southeastern Indians* (Lincoln: University of Nebraska Press, 1995), p. 147. "Speeches, July 1759," p. 4, in Atkin to Lyttelton, 11/30/1759, LYTTEL.

31. Members of the same moiety referred to each other as "my friend"; Hudson, *Southeastern Indians,* pp. 234–237. DRIA, vol. 1, pp. 289–291 (1752).

32. For Muccolossus–Okchai relations, see Atkin to Lyttelton, 11/30/1759, p. 29, LYTTEL. For Muccolossus–Okfuskee relations, see Wolf's reaction to the 1760 attack in CRSGA, vol. 8, pp. 469–470; SC-GAZ, 2/7/1761; MPA-ED, p. 527; ADAIR, pp. 280–281. "Speeches, July 1759," pp. 4, 7, in Atkin to Lyttelton, 11/30/1759, LYTTEL. The only Tallapoosas present to greet Atkin were from Tuckabatchee.

33. Moore, ed., *Nairne's Muskhogean Journals,* pp. 38–39; MPA-FD, vol. 3, pp. 113–115 (1707); for the slave, see Chapter 1, this volume. JCIT, p. 303 ("Oakfuskey"); Mereness, ed., "Fitch's Journal," p. 207 ("Chocktawes"). SC-JCHA, 6/5/1724; SC-UH, 6/10/1724.

34. SC-CJ, 8/24/1725; BPRO-SC, vol. 13, pp. 102, 106 (1728); Mereness, ed., "Fitch's Journal," pp. 195–197 ("Tye").

35. For 1725, see Mereness, ed., "Fitch's Journal," p. 194. For 1728, see BPRO-SC, vol. 13, pp. 84, 150. See also SC-JCHA, 7/15/1731, p. 748. The British

also passed out war-related supplies, thereby making it easier for war leaders to attract a following. For a 1723 incident involving Okfuskee's Dog King, see SC-JCHA, 10/4/1723, p. 280; BPRO-SC, vol. 10, p. 158.

36. For the commissions, see Moore, ed., *Nairne's Muskhogean Journal,* p. 35; SC-UH, 5/25/1722; BPRO-SC, vol. 10, p. 176; SC-CJ, 8/24/1725, 8/15/1739, 10/29/1746. State of Georgia, Commissions: Volume B1: 1754–1778, p. 45, Georgia Department of Archives and History, Atlanta ("observe").

37. SC-CJ, 9/6/1749. For Mad Warrior, see CRSGA, vol. 7, pp. 613–617, quotations from p. 614.

38. DRIA, vol. 2, pp. 63–64 ("Wrath"), 372 (Beau); CRSGA, vol. 7, p. 424 ("authority"); Jerome Courtonne, "List of Headmen of the Creeks," in Courtonne to Lyttelton, 10/17/1758, LYTTEL.

39. For Savannah, see CRSGA, vol. 8, pp. 427–433, quotations from p. 432. SC-GAZ, 3/29/1760.

40. For "White Towns" and "Derection," see notes 39 and 27 above. DRIA, vol. 1, p. 413 ("Nature").

41. "A Talk from the Mortar to John Stuart," 7/22/1764, in Stuart to Gage, 11/30/1764, GAGE; CRSGA, vol. 8, p. 420 (Captain); ADAIR, p. 279 (Rae); SC-GAZ, 5/31/1760 ("War-King"); BPRO, CO 5/75, ff52, 180 ("Great"); Stuart to Gage, 7/5/1774, GAGE ("Village").

42. BPRO-SC, vol. 13, p. 89 ("weary"); SALZ, vol. 8, pp. 436–437 ("attention").

43. Atkin noted that such problems were most prevalent among the Cherokees; Jacobs, ed., *The Edmond Atkin Report,* pp. 35–36 ("licentiousness"), 62. DRIA, vol. 2, p. 61 ("Mischief"); CRSGA, vol. 7, p. 422 ("runagates"). See also Saunt, *New Order,* pp. 33–37.

44. "Conference with the Tookybahtchy Mico," 7/24–7/25/1759, pp. 11–12, in Atkin to Lyttelton, 11/30/1759, LYTTEL. For 1760, see CRSGA, vol. 8, p. 432; SC-GAZ, 7/19/1760.

45. SC-GAZ, 3/14/1761; BPRO, CO 5/67, ff17, 41–42 ("Settled"); Roderick MackIntosh to Stuart, 11/16/1767, in Stuart to Gage, 12/26/1767, GAGE ("promises"); BPRO, CO 5/69, ff194–195 (1768); 5/73, f271 ("formerly").

46. SC-GAZ, 3/7/1761, 3/14/1761; CRSGA, vol. 8, p. 544 ("protect"); see also SC-CJ, 2/11/1761. For 1763, see CRSGA, vol. 9, p. 16; CRSGA, vol. 8, p. 777. For "Parcell" and the Okfuskee, see CRSGA, vol. 9, pp. 148, 116. "Journal of the Superintendant's Proceedings," p. 29, in Stuart to Gage, 7/21/1767, GAGE ("King").

47. Stuart to Gage, 12/13/1770, GAGE ("Murtherers"); CRSGA, vol. 12, pp. 87, 86 ("rash Men"), 148 ("Murderers"), 149 ("fall"); BPRO, CO 5/75,

ff180 ("Renegadoes"), 65 ("beat"), 52 (Okfuskee involvement); Taitt to Stuart, 8/26/1774, in Stuart to Gage, 9/14/1774, GAGE ("Villians"); BPRO, CO 5/79, f195 (1778).

48. BPRO, CO 5/74, f148 ("meditated"); 5/75, ff17 (August), 52 (January). For shortages, see 5/75, ff15, 16, 21, 46, 51.

49. Unless otherwise noted, quotations in the following paragraphs come from Taitt's letters; BPRO, CO 5/75, ff16–18.

50. Taitt reported the robbery on 9/24/1773; the goods were returned by the time of his letter of 10/25/1773.

51. CRSGA, vol. 8, p. 419.

52. MPA-ED, pp. 516–517 (1766).

53. For the envoys, see Chapter 2, this volume.

54. Mereness, ed., "Fitch's Journal," p. 177 (1725); Caleb Swan, "Position and State of Manners and Arts in the Creek, or Muscogee Nation in 1791," in Henry R. Schoolcraft, ed., *Information Respecting the History, Condition, and Prospects of the Indians Tribes of the United States,* vol. 5 (Philadelphia: Lippincott, 1855), pp. 251–283, especially p. 280; Clara Sue Kidwell, "Choctaw Women and Cultural Persistence in Mississippi," in Nancy Shoemaker, ed., *Negotiators of Change: Historical Perspectives on Native American Women* (New York: Routledge, 1995), pp. 115–134, especially p. 117; ADAIR, p. 454; Raymond D. Fogelson, "On the 'Petticoat Government' of the Eighteenth-Century Cherokee," in David K. Jordan and Marc J. Swartz, eds., *Personality and the Cultural Construction of Society* (Tuscaloosa: University of Alabama Press, 1990), pp. 161–181, especially pp. 172–175.

55. Deposition of Joseph Dawes, 8/4/1772, in John Stuart to Gage, 9/7/1772, GAGE.

56. Ibid.

57. For the trader, see Van Doren, ed., *Travels,* p. 357. For recent treatments of perception and identity, see Joyce E. Chaplin, *Subject Matter: Technology, the Body, and Science on the Anglo-American Frontier, 1500–1676* (Cambridge, Mass.: Harvard University Press, 2001); Karen Ordahl Kupperman, *Indians & English: Facing Off in Early America* (Ithaca, N.Y.: Cornell University Press, 2000); Ann Marie Plane, *Colonial Intimacies: Indian Marriage in Early New England* (Ithaca, N.Y.: Cornell University Press, 2000); Theda Perdue, "Native Women in the Early Republic: Old World Perceptions, New World Realities," in Frederick E. Hoxie, Ronald Hoffman, and Peter J. Albert, eds., *Native Americans in the Early Republic* (Charlottesville: University Press of Virginia, 1999), pp. 85–122. Susan Juster, *Disorderly Women: Sexual Politics and Evangelicalism in Revolutionary New England* (Ithaca, N.Y.: Cornell University Press, 1994), p. 213 (gender anxieties).

58. Laurel Thatcher Ulrich, *Good Wives: Image and Reality in the Lives of Women*

in Northern New England, 1650–1750 (New York: Knopf, 1982), p. 241 ("convoluted"). For women seizing opportunities offered by expanding markets, see Allan Kulikoff, *The Agrarian Origins of American Capitalism* (Charlottesville: University Press of Virginia, 1992), p. 32. For wages and autonomy, see Gloria Main, "Gender, Work, and Wages in Colonial New England," *William and Mary Quarterly* 51 (1994): 39–66, especially pp. 42, 51, 65; Mary Beth Norton, *Liberty's Daughters: The Revolutionary Experience of American Women, 1750–1800* (Boston: Little, Brown and Company, 1980), chap. 5; Cynthia A. Kierner, *Beyond the Household: Women's Place in the Early South, 1700–1835* (Ithaca: N.Y.: Cornell University Press, 1998), chap. 1. For family, see Ulrich, *Good Wives*, p. 50. For market exchange and the division of labor, see Ulrich, "Wheels, Looms, and the Gender Division of Labor," pp. 6, 29. For women's inability to draw on new economic mechanisms, see Cornelia Hughes Dayton, *Women Before the Bar: Gender, Law, & Society in Connecticut, 1639–1789* (Chapel Hill: University of North Carolina Press, 1995), chaps. 1, 2. For capital, see Carole Shammas, "Early American Women and Control over Capital," in Ronald Hoffman and Peter J. Albert, eds., *Women in the Age of the American Revolution* (Charlottesville: University Press of Virginia, 1989), pp. 134–154, especially p. 140. For coverture, see Linda K. Kerber, *Women of the Republic: Intellect and Ideology in Revolutionary America* (New York: W. W. Norton, 1980), chap. 5. Norton, *Liberty's Daughters*, p. 299 ("ambiguous"). For the rise of essentialist theories, see Juster, *Disorderly Women*, pp. 138–139, 213 ("broader crisis"). For women's transition from subservience to difference, see Lisa Norling, *Captain Ahab Had a Wife: New England Women and the Whalefishery, 1720–1870* (Chapel Hill: University of North Carolina Press, 2000).

59. For elderly men's situation, see Lisa Wilson, *Ye Heart of a Man: The Domestic Life of Men in Colonial New England* (New Haven, Conn.: Yale University Press, 1999), pp. 171–185; Glenn Wallach, *Obedient Sons: The Discourse of Youth and Generations in American Culture, 1630–1860* (Amherst: University of Massachusetts Press, 1997); David Hackett Fischer, *Growing Old in America*, exp. ed. (New York: Oxford University Press, 1978). For changing family practices, see Helena M. Wall, *Fierce Communion: Family and Community in Early America* (Cambridge, Mass.: Harvard University Press, 1990), pp. 129–148. For New England, see Daniel Vickers, *Farmers and Fishermen: Two Centuries of Work in Essex County, Massachusetts, 1630–1850* (Chapel Hill: University of North Carolina Press, 1994), pp. 64–77, 205–206, 219–229. For the early republic, see Joyce Appleby, *Inheriting the Revolution: The First Generation of Americans* (Cambridge, Mass.: Harvard University Press, 2000), pp. 170–174. For daughters' labor and gen-

erational authority, see Laurel Thatcher Ulrich, *A Midwife's Tale: The Life of Martha Ballard, Based on Her Diary, 1785–1812* (New York: Vintage Books, 1990), chaps. 4, 8. Carole Shammas, *The Pre-Industrial Consumer in England and America* (Oxford, U.K.: Clarendon Press, 1990), chap. 7 ("sovereignty"). For deference, see Gordon S. Wood, *The Radicalism of the American Revolution* (New York: Knopf, 1991), quotation from p. 147 ("naturally"); "Deference or Defiance in Eighteenth-Century America? A Round Table," *Journal of American History* 85 (1998): 13–97.

60. Mechal Sobel, *Teach Me Dreams: The Search for Self in the Revolutionary Era* (Princeton, N.J.: Princeton University Press, 2000), p. 165.

61. For communication, see Ian K. Steele, *The English Atlantic, 1675–1740: An Exploration of Communication and Community* (New York: Oxford University Press, 1986), pp. 261–262, 270 ("homogenize"); Richard D. Brown, *Knowledge Is Power: The Diffusion of Information in Early America* (New York: Oxford University Press, 1989).

62. For an analysis of the ways colonists' anxieties about gender relations and authority influenced relations with Native neighbors, see Tom Hatley, *The Dividing Paths: Cherokees and South Carolinians through the Era of Revolution* (New York: Oxford University Press, 1993), pp. 141–154, 197–200. For post-Revolutionary experiences, see Andrew R. L. Cayton, " 'Noble Actors' upon 'the Theatre of Honour': Power and Civility in the Treaty of Greenville," in Cayton and Fredrika J. Teute, eds., *Contact Points: North American Frontiers, 1750–1830* (Chapel Hill: University of North Carolina Press, 1998), pp. 235–269; Richard White, "The Fictions of Patriarchy: Indians and Whites in the Early Republic," in Hoxie et al., eds., *Native Americans and the Early Republic*, pp. 62–84.

63. For another Native people's experiences with these issues, see Theda Perdue, *Cherokee Women: Gender and Culture Change, 1700–1835* (Lincoln: University of Nebraska Press, 1998), part 3; Nathaniel Sheidley, "Hunting and the Politics of Masculinity in Cherokee Treaty-Making, 1763–1775," in Martin Daunton and Rich Halpern, eds., *Empire and Others: British Encounters with Indigenous Peoples, 1600–1850* (Philadelphia: University of Pennsylvania Press, 1999), pp. 167–185; Perdue, *Mixed Blood Indians: Racial Construction in the Early South* (Athens: University of Georgia Press, 2003), chap. 3.

Conclusion

1. "Georgia Military Affairs," vol. 3, compiled by Mrs. J. E. Hays (Works Progress Administration, 1940), bound manuscript in the Georgia Department of Archives and History, Atlanta; Adams quotations from

pp. 318, 319; Roy S. Dickens Jr., *Archaeological Investigations at Horseshoe Bend National Military Park, Alabama,* Special Publications 3 (University: Alabama Archaeological Society, 1979), p. 1. For Nuyakas and Okfuskees at Tohopeka, see Harold D. Moser, David R. Hoth, Sharon Macpherson, and John H. Reinbold, eds., *The Papers of Andrew Jackson,* vol. 3 (Knoxville: University of Tennessee Press, 1991), p. 52. John Brannan, ed., *Official Letters of the Military and Naval Officers of the United States, During the War with Great Britain in the Years 1812, 13, 14, and 15* (New York: Arno Press, 1971 [1823]), p. 281 (Little Okfuskee). For Elkhatchie, see H. S. Halbert and T. H. Hall, *The Creek War of 1813 and 1814* (Chicago: Donohue and Henneberry, 1895), p. 100; Thomas L. McKenny and James Hall, *History of the Indian Tribes of North America,* vol. 2 (Philadelphia: D. Rice and J. Clark, 1842), p. 101. "Creek Indian Letters, Talks, and Treaties, 1705–1839," vol. 3, p. 859 ("twenty"), compiled by Mrs. J. E. Hays (Works Progress Administration, 1939–1940), bound manuscript in UGA. For Menawa, see McKenney and Hall, *History of the Indian Tribes,* vol. 2, pp. 97–105. Moser et al., eds., *Jackson Papers,* vol. 3, p. 10 ("forting"). For the dominant interpretations of the Creek civil war, see Joel Martin, *Sacred Revolt: The Muskogees' Struggle for a New World* (Boston: Beacon Press, 1991); Claudio Saunt, *A New Order of Things: Property, Power, and the Transformation of the Creek Indians, 1733–1816* (New York: Cambridge University Press, 1999).

2. Moser et al., eds., *Jackson Papers,* vol. 3, p. 58; Thomas Kanon, " 'A Slow Laborious Slaughter': The Battle of Horseshoe Bend," *Tennessee Historical Quarterly* 58 (1999): 2–15, quotation from p. 13, n. 4 ("inviting").
3. CRSGA, vol. 8, pp. 420–421.
4. HAWKINS, p. 302 (Tukpafka, 1777, "take part"); John R. Swanton, *Early History of the Creek Indians & Their Neighbors,* Bureau of American Ethnology Bulletin 73 (Gainesville: University Press of Florida, 1998 [1922]), p. 248 ("Punk"). For White Lieutenant, see Chapter 4, this volume; Hays, "Creek Indians," vol. 1, pp. 129–131, and vol. 1 (2), p. 242 ("stand"). Saunt, *New Order,* p. 109 ("miserable").
5. Hays, "Georgia Military Affairs," vol. 3, p. 319 ("houses," fields, "corn"); Dickens, *Archaeological Investigations,* pp. 78 ("linear"), 100 ("scattered"); HAWKINS, pp. 13 (White Lieutenant, "poultry," "ford"), 302 ("settled," two miles). For livestock, see Saunt, *New Order,* p. 99; Charles H. Fairbanks, "Excavations at Horseshoe Bend, Alabama," *Florida Anthropologist* 15 (1962): 41–56, especially p. 54. McKenney and Hall, *History of the Indian Tribes,* vol. 2, p. 97 ("horses"); Claire C. B. Vaught, "Archaeobotanical Remains," and Paula F. Edmiston, "Zooarchaeological Remains," in Dickens, *Archaeological Excavations,* pp. 171–187 and 187–194.

6. HAWKINS, p. 13; Daniel McGillivray to William Panton, 6/5/1799, Greenslade Papers, P. K. Yonge Library of Florida History, University of Florida, Gainesville (skins); Edmiston, "Zooarchaeological Remains," p. 193; McKenney and Hall, *History of the Indian Tribes,* vol. 2, p. 101 ("store"); Vaught, "Achaeobotanical Remains," pp. 185–186.

7. Fairbanks, "Excavations at Horseshoe Bend," p. 51 ("skilled," "conservatism"); Dickens, *Archaeological Investigations,* pp. 101–102 (chipped), 109 (ground); Linda Carnes, "European Artifacts," in Dickens, *Archaeological Investigations,* pp. 149–165, especially pp. 156–157 (chatelaine), 162 ("Balsam"); HAWKINS, p. 13 (Sullivan).

8. Dickens, *Archaeological Investigations,* pp. 13–14, 48 (maps); Albert S. Gatschet, "Towns and Villages of the Creek Confederacy in the XVIII and XIX Centuries," *Alabama Historical Society, Miscellaneous Collections* 1 (1892): 386–415, quotation ("fence") from p. 398; Gregory A. Waselkov and Marvin T. Smith, "Upper Creek Archaeology," in Bonnie McEwan, ed., *Indians of the Greater Southeast: Historical Archaeology and Ethnohistory* (Gainesville: University Press of Florida, 2000), pp. 242–264, quotation ("sophisticated") from p. 256; Martin, *Sacred Revolt,* p. 161 ("beginning").

9. HAWKINS, pp. 651–652 ("declaration," "village"); Hays, "Creek Indian," vol. 3, pp. 786 ("Talks"), 790–792 ("principal"), 825 ("meeting"), 833; Harold D. Moser and Sharon Macpherson, eds., *The Papers of Andrew Jackson,* vol. 2 (Knoxville: University of Tennessee Press, 1984), pp. 451–452.

10. Carnes, "European Artifacts," pp. 150–151; Fairbanks, "Excavations at Horseshoe Bend," p. 48; Waselkov and Smith, "Upper Creek Archaeology," p. 256; HAWKINS, p. 652 ("destroyed," "loom"); Martin, *Sacred Revolt,* p. 162 (25 percent to 33 percent, credit); John Buchanan, *Jackson's Way: Andrew Jackson and the People of the Western Waters* (New York: John Wiley and Sons, 2001), p. 286.

11. Moser et al., eds., *Jackson Papers,* vol. 3, p. 52 ("gathered"); John S. Bassett, ed., *Correspondence of Andrew Jackson,* vol. 1 (Washington, D.C.: Carnegie Institution, 1926), pp. 448 ("concentrated"), 462 ("returned"); Benjamin W. Griffith Jr., *McIntosh and Weatherford: Creek Indian Leaders* (Tuscaloosa: University of Alabama Press, 1988), p. 146 (map).

12. For White Lieutenant, see Chapters 4 and 5, this volume. For Menawa, see McKenney and Hall, *History of the Indian Tribes,* vol. 2, pp. 97–105, quotations from pp. 98 ("Great"), 101 ("Cattle"), and 97 ("half").

13. For Handsome Fellow, see Chapters 2, 4, and 5, this volume. For Menewa, see George Stiggins, *Creek Indian History: A Historical Narrative of the Genealogy, Traditions and Downfall of the Ispocoga or Creek Indian Tribe of Indians,* ed. Virginia P. Brown (Birmingham, Ala.: Birmingham Public Li-

brary Press, 1989), p. 133 ("length"); McKenny and Hall, *History of the Indian Tribes*, vol. 2, p. 102 ("resumed"); Michael D. Green, *The Politics of Indian Removal: Creek Government and Society in Crisis* (Lincoln: University of Nebraska Press, 1982), pp. 96 (Council, execute), 124 (1827); Kanon, " 'A Slow Laborious Slaughter,' " p. 15, n. 34 (uniform).

Index